DISCIPLINARY LITERACIES

DISCIPLINARY LITERACIES

Unpacking Research, Theory, and Practice

edited by
Evan Ortlieb
Britnie Delinger Kane
Earl H. Cheek, Jr.

THE GUILFORD PRESS
New York London

A Division of Guilford Publications, Inc.
370 Seventh Avenue, Suite 1200, New York, NY 10001
www.guilford.com

Printed in the United States of America

This book is printed on acid-free paper.

Last digit is print number: 9 8 7 6 5 4 3 2 1

Library of Congress Cataloging-in-Publication Data

Names: Ortlieb, Evan, editor. | Kane, Britnie Delinger, editor. | Cheek, Earl H., editor.
Title: Disciplinary literacies : unpacking research, theory, and practice / edited by Evan Ortlieb, Britnie Delinger Kane, Earl H. Cheek, Jr.
Description: New York : The Guilford Press, 2024. | Includes bibliographical references and index.
Identifiers: LCCN 2023027831 | ISBN 9781462552870 (paperback) |
ISBN 9781462552887 (hardcover)
Subjects: LCSH: Literacy—Study and teaching. | Reading comprehension. | Language arts—Correlation with content subjects. | BISAC: EDUCATION / Teaching / Subjects / Reading & Phonics | EDUCATION / Professional Development
Classification: LCC LC149 .D57 2024 | DDC 372.6/044—dc23/eng/20230717
LC record available at *https://lccn.loc.gov/2023027831*

About the Editors

Evan Ortlieb, PhD, is Dean and Zucker Endowed Chair in Entrepreneurial Education Leadership in the Zucker Family School of Education at The Citadel. His expertise centers on literacy teacher preparation, leveraging diversity as an asset in classrooms, and educational leadership. Dr. Ortlieb currently serves as coeditor of the journal *Literacy Research and Instruction*. He has served as an area chair of the Literacy Research Association and a board member of the Specialized Literacy Professionals Special Interest Group of the International Literacy Association. He is Founder and President of the Ortlieb Foundation, a nonprofit organization that provides college scholarships for cancer survivors.

Britnie Delinger Kane, PhD, is Associate Professor of Literacy Education and the department head for the Zucker Family School of Education at The Citadel. Her primary area of expertise is how teachers learn to teach in ways that are both conceptually rich and equitable. Dr. Kane is interested in teachers' development across their careers, especially in the design of preservice teacher education, how teachers' collaborative talk supports their professional learning, and how instructional coaching supports teachers' professional learning. She studies these supports for teachers' learning especially as they relate to disciplinary literacy, writing instruction, and the STEM fields, and has published in leading journals of research and practice.

Earl H. Cheek, Jr., PhD, is the Patrick and Edwidge Olinde Endowed Professor Emeritus in the School of Education at Louisiana State University. He is an expert in literacy education, with specific interests in assessment, diagnostic–prescriptive instruction, content reading, struggling readers, and dyslexia. Dr. Cheek is a former middle and high school teacher and elementary reading specialist. He has served on the editorial boards of several national and international journals; is author or coauthor of over 120 books, articles, and chapters; and has presented more than 100 papers at state, regional, national, and international conferences.

Contributors

Megin Charner-Laird, EdD, McKeown School of Education, Salem State University, Salem, Massachusetts

Earl H. Cheek, Jr., PhD, Department of Education (Emeritus), Louisiana State University, Baton Rouge, Louisiana

Natalie Colosimo, doctoral student, School of Teaching and Learning, University of Florida, Gainesville, Florida

Jamie Colwell, PhD, Darden College of Education, Old Dominion University, Norfolk, Virginia

Keri-Anne Croce, PhD, Department of Elementary Education, Towson University, Towson, Maryland

Christina L. Dobbs, EdD, Wheelock College of Education and Human Development, Boston University, Boston, Massachusetts

Zhihui Fang, PhD, School of Teaching and Learning, University of Florida, Gainesville, Florida

Rachael E. Gabriel, PhD, Neag School of Education, University of Connecticut, Storrs, Connecticut

Jodi Patrick Holschuh, PhD, College of Education, Texas State University, San Marcos, Texas

Corey A. Humphrey, MA, doctoral candidate, School of Education, University of Pittsburgh, Pittsburgh, Pennsylvania

Amy Hutchison, PhD, College of Education, University of Alabama, Tuscaloosa, Alabama

Jacy Ippolito, EdD, McKeown School of Education, Salem State University, Salem, Massachusetts

Britnie Delinger Kane, PhD, Zucker Family School of Education, The Citadel, Charleston, South Carolina

Shannon Kelley, PhD, Seidel School of Education, Salisbury University, Salisbury, Maryland

Jodi P. Lampi, PhD, College of Education, Northern Illinois University, DeKalb, Illinois

Alison E. Leonard, PhD, College of Education, Clemson University, Clemson, South Carolina

Michael Manderino, PhD, College of Education, Northern Illinois University, DeKalb, Illinois

Danny C. Martinez, PhD, School of Education, University of California, Davis, Davis, California

Kavin M. Ming, EdD, Richard W. Riley College of Education, Winthrop University, Rock Hill, South Carolina

Gianina Morales, MEd, College of Engineering, Universidad de Valparaíso, Valparaíso, Chile, and doctoral student, School of Education, University of Pittsburgh, Pittsburgh, Pennsylvania

Jennifer D. Morrison, PhD, Wardlaw College of Education, University of South Carolina, Columbia, South Carolina

Ian O'Byrne, PhD, Department of Teacher Education, College of Charleston, Charleston, South Carolina

Evan Ortlieb, PhD, Zucker Family School of Education, The Citadel, Charleston, South Carolina

Emily C. Rainey, PhD, School of Education, University of Pittsburgh, Pittsburgh, Pennsylvania

Todd Reynolds, PhD, School of Teacher Education, College of Education, University of Wyoming, Laramie, Wyoming

Leslie S. Rush, PhD, School of Teacher Education, College of Education, University of Wyoming, Laramie, Wyoming

Rachelle S. Savitz, PhD, College of Education, East Carolina University, Greenville, North Carolina

Tamara Shreiner, PhD, College of Liberal Arts and Sciences, Grand Valley State University, Allendale, Michigan

Philip Wilder, PhD, College of Education, Clemson University, Clemson, South Carolina

Alexis Patterson Williams, PhD, School of Education, University of California, Davis, Davis, California

Preface

Although research in disciplinary literacy has become increasingly prominent, how educators facilitate the acquisition of disciplinary literacies remains an underresearched area of study. Improving our understanding of the unique ways that reading, writing, and thinking interrelate in distinct academic disciplines is fundamental to the improvement of PreK–20 schooling. This edited collection delves into the latest research in disciplinary literacies, examines theories that underpin these inquiries, and embeds classroom-based practices for educators to apply in their own classrooms.

We use the term *disciplinary literacies*, as opposed to the singular *disciplinary literacy*, to highlight the idea that literacy is not a single set of predefined or codified technical skills, but is instead a set of social practices that are adapted by and to the needs of particular social groups in particular places and times. From this perspective, all literacy practices—including, but not limited to, disciplinary literacy practices—are always multiple because individuals must always improvise and hybridize the ways they use literacy, given that we all use literacy from a particular position within a social group and in response to the social conventions, tools, purposes, and uses of language that define those groups. In short, we use *disciplinary literacies* to highlight a sociocultural stance on literacy learning. Sociocultural theories of literacy are most conducive to an understanding of disciplinary literacies because they highlight the role of communities in the practice of literacy, and academic disciplines are exactly that: broad social groups characterized by specific sets of social conventions, tools, purposes, and uses of language. As scholars before us have pointed out, the social conventions, tools, purposes, and uses of language that characterize academic disciplines carry somewhat different meanings across PreK–12 contexts than they do within the academy. This, too, is a reason for adopting the term *disciplinary literacies,* because PreK–12 students necessarily engage in varied, improvised, and hybridized versions of the literacy practices that characterize disciplinary work in the academy or workforce.

In addition, our use of *disciplinary literacies* in the plural highlights that disciplinary literacy cannot long stand as a field unless it recognizes the multiple, varied ways that we must approach literacy given a broadened view of text. That is, the future of disciplinary literacies will necessitate that *text* is understood not only as monomodal, print-based, linear, and alphabetic, but also as multimodal and digital. We must take seriously that, in current and future disciplinary texts, the communicative load may be carried by non-alphabetic and/or non-linguistic semiotic structures. Such multimodal, non-alphabetic texts have long typified disciplinary work, and they are poised to do so all the more as the digital world becomes ever more entrenched in every aspect of our lives. We clarify our use of the term *disciplinary literacies* here as a means of stating a conceptual stance on literacy, but we also note that we have, as an editorial team, provided autonomy for authors to use whichever term they prefer based on the transitional nature of terminology in this field.

This text begins with a historical account of shifts of content reading instruction, disciplinary literacy, disciplinary literacies, and multidisciplinary literacies over the last 50 years. It serves to provide a clear understanding of where we have been, where we are today, and where the field is going in the future. It provides the depth of perspective necessary for understanding progressive efforts to bolster disciplinary literacy instruction. Introductory Chapter 1 also sets the stage for subsequent chapters organized into four sections on core content-area classrooms and other subject classrooms, as well as opportunities and challenges in disciplinary literacies, before discussing research and the professional development of teachers in regard to disciplinary literacies. Together, this edited collection provides an in-depth analysis of the various literacies required for success in all disciplines. The book also includes practical examples and case studies to illustrate the concepts discussed so that novice and experienced educators alike can implement these in their classrooms.

Within "Part I: Disciplinary Literacies in Core Content-Area Classrooms," four author teams describe disciplinary literacies in core content-area classrooms. In Chapter 2, Rainey, Humphrey, and Morales provide a nuanced definition of literary literacy, or the practice of generating critical knowledge from texts within interpretive communities. They focus on how to participate and facilitate interpretive critique within English education classrooms while honoring the knowledge and resources that students already possess. Literary sources include traditional written narratives as well as cultural and historical texts, artifacts, digital media, and visual art.

In Chapter 3, Croce describes how disciplinary literacies in the mathematics classroom have evolved to include interacting with and creating verbal and visual representations of text. Furthermore, this chapter showcases how teachers can scaffold students' understandings of languages to be used in mathematical engagements in classroom discussions. These engagements involve communication with not only classmates, but also other individuals outside and between communities across a wide range of mathematical texts. Croce explores how apprenticeships can foster the development of disciplinary literacies and mathematical knowledge simultaneously.

Fang and Colosimo's Chapter 4 provides a praxis-based account of how educators can promote science literacy through reading. The prioritization of reading and critical comprehension skills is central to the scientific method, yet the amount of time traditionally allocated to reading in science classrooms is only negligible. Examining and learning about phenomena also require the activation of interest and prior knowledge paired with using cognitive strategies like inferring, summarizing, questioning, verifying, and predicting. The authors further explore how these skills can be promoted toward text evaluation and meaning construction.

In Chapter 5, Shreiner examines how the field of social studies is a space for culturally responsive disciplinary literacy instruction. New standards demand that students have the capacity to know, analyze, and explain multifaceted challenges in a global context. Disciplinary literacies provide the means through which students might interact and thrive in increasingly complex civic and political environments for academic and career readiness.

"Part II: Disciplinary Literacies in Other Areas" includes four chapters on the following disciplines: physical education, visual arts, performing arts, and computer science. Distinct chapters in these areas are unique to the broad scope of this text; furthermore, disciplinary literacies are deemed equally important to learning in these disciplines as they are to fields like English and mathematics, which have been more frequently studied through a disciplinary literacies lens.

In Chapter 6, Ming presents a research base for and practical applications of students engaging in reading, writing, thinking, and communicating in the physical education classroom. She demonstrates how literacy in the physical education classroom positively impacts students' motor skill development and knowledge of language concepts. Strategies for developing thinking and reasoning skills in physical education are presented to leverage naturally imaginative and creative dispositions. The disciplinary literacy skills that students learn in physical education can also be applied in and beyond the classroom, allowing them to become lifelong learners and agents of movement.

In Chapter 7, on disciplinary literacies in the visual arts, Morrison highlights the need for academic vocabulary acquisition to effectively participate and communicate. Morrison also explains several key underpinnings to the visual arts, which shape how disciplinary literacies can be taught effectively in these disciplines. Specifically, disciplinary literacies in the visual arts are multimodal, social, multifaceted, and shaped by digital tool development. Recommendations are provided for teachers regarding integrating disciplinary literacies throughout variations of visual arts across the grade levels.

Savitz and Leonard explore disciplinary literacy in the performing arts in Chapter 8. Guided by a Universal Design for Learning framework, they describe how multiple means of representation, action, and engagement are required to provide access to a myriad of diverse learners with extensive ways to construct and demonstrate knowledge and learning in the performing arts. Specific approaches are suggested for classroom implementation via reading and interpreting, listening and critiquing, writing and composing, and performing and participating. These contexts for the development of disciplinary literacies are spotlighted to provide ideas for how to infuse literacy practices with and through the performing arts and to collaborate with arts practitioners in schools.

In Chapter 9, Hutchison and Colwell provide an in-depth account of integrating disciplinary literacies into computer science. They explain how disciplinary literacies are relevant for computer science instruction and challenge other educators to consider how computer science and computational thinking promote a dual-focus lens on disciplinary literacy. This chapter provides classroom applications for engaging students and enhancing their interest levels in computer science by embedding disciplinary literacies into the fabric of its curriculum and instruction.

"Part III: Opportunities and Challenges in Disciplinary Literacies" includes four chapters that illuminate the opportunities and challenges that disciplinary literacies present in education. In Chapter 10, Williams and Martinez discuss how we can provide students access to specialized literacy practices of disciplines while valuing the repertoires of practice and communication styles of marginalized communities. By aligning students' literacy practices with disciplinary modes of reasoning, we can promote and nurture pluralinguistic learning environments.

Gabriel and Kelley describe in Chapter 11 the need to determine the grade levels at which instruction in disciplinary literacies can and should be integrated. The authors investigate the extent to which texts commonly used in PreK–12 schools evince disciplinary specificity, and whether disciplinary differences are identifiable from an examination of disciplinary literacy practices. Robust discussion on how these disciplinary literacies develop and can be utilized across PreK–12 schooling is included, equipping students with multifarious language use opportunities to engage in an ever-changing social and literate world.

In Chapter 12, Wilder and Manderino provide insight into the processes involved in cultivating disciplinary literacy spaces for youth connection and agency. Their work is grounded in many years of research in both the United States and Tanzania. Questions about who has expertise, and who gets positioned as the authoritative owner of knowledge, challenge the very nature of disciplinary literacy. The authors examine the purpose of disciplinary literacy, highlighting its ability to encourage youth to produce, critique, and leverage disciplinary knowledge as a means of connecting and reconciling with communities.

In an effort to stretch the field's current take on disciplinary literacies, O'Byrne considers in Chapter 13 disciplinary literacies given the influence of the digital world. Specifically, he addresses how we might transcend a bounded view of specific disciplines by broadening our views of text construction and representation. This move toward transdisciplinarity defies disciplinary paradigms; instead, transdisciplinarity focuses on socially relevant issues and the common good, alongside an interrogation and transformation of knowledge itself. O'Byrne provides practical suggestions for the integration of digital literacy in disciplinary literacy instruction for students to collaboratively explore and make connections with the discipline, the community, and the world.

"Part IV: Research and Teaching Teachers in Disciplinary Literacies" includes two chapters that offer an overview of current research methodologies for investigating disciplinary literacies in the classroom as well as ways in which disciplinary literacies can be embedded purposefully in teacher education programs. In Chapter 14, Lampi, Holschuh, Rush, and Reynolds detail some instructional studies involving classroom observations and interventions as well as linguistic analyses and epistemological investigations as examples of frameworks in which disciplinary literacy can be studied. They provide tutorials on how novice and expert case studies can be conducted in an English language arts classroom through numerous means of qualitative data collection and analysis.

Finally, in Chapter 15, Dobbs, Ippolito, and Charner-Laird provide a novel account of how numerous pedagogical possibilities for disciplinary literacy instruction can become a cornerstone of ongoing efforts in a teacher's professional development journey. From preservice teacher programs to iterative professional development series, they argue that an inquiry-based approach, or one that promotes learning, experimentation, and iteration, best fits the adaptive work of developing disciplinary literacy practices. They highlight that, if widespread changes are to be achieved beyond individual classrooms, successful implementation must frame disciplinary literacy as collaborative work.

This edited volume aims to widely represent literacy practices throughout all disciplines. Chapters are founded on a wealth of research and written work from leading experts across these diverse domains. Yet, the connective tissue between these disciplines, sometimes perceived as disparate, is that language and literacy serve as the backbone to disciplinary learning and reasoning. The editors of this volume view literacy not as a distinct field, but as a means to investigate, interrogate, create, and synthesize information in and beyond other disciplines. Taken together, the chapters provide an overview of what the field has learned, to date, across eight specific subject areas, while also addressing opportunities and challenges with which the field might grapple. In short, our aim in bringing this work together has been to highlight the voices of those whose work will help to chart where the field might productively move forward.

This book is intended for educators, students, and professionals who are interested in understanding the role of disciplinary literacies in academic and professional success. We hope that it will serve as a valuable resource for anyone looking to improve their knowledge of disciplinary literacies and to succeed in implementing them within their respective classrooms.

ACKNOWLEDGMENTS

We would like to recognize all educators who constantly seek out professional development opportunities in support of lifelong learning and improving their pedagogical proficiencies, their families that work behind the scenes to avail these time commitments, and the administrators that create environments for discovery and advancement of praxis. We express our gratitude to the educators and experts who have contributed to this book, as well as others who have challenged us to expand our understanding of the importance of disciplinary literacies. Additionally, we would like to thank our students (former and current) for their invaluable input, which has helped us gain a deeper understanding of the challenges and opportunities related to disciplinary literacies.

Contents

Tracing the History of Disciplinary Literacies

Britnie Delinger Kane
Evan Ortlieb
Earl H. Cheek, Jr.

For the last 15 years, the United States has experienced a resurgence of interest in domain-specific literacy practices (e.g., Jacobs, 2008; Lee & Spratley, 2010; Moje, 2008, 2010; Shanahan & Shanahan, 2008). This resurgence arose in response to what was framed as an adolescent literacy "crisis" (Goldman et al., 2016; Jacobs, 2008). In the United States, the 1990s and aughts saw improvements in standardized reading scores in the primary grades, yet scores were flatlining for students in the third and fourth grade and beyond. Thus, stakeholders assumed that students were presumably not receiving support in "learn[ing] how to learn" from discipline-specific texts (Jacobs, 2008, p. 14), and disciplinary literacy was born—or, depending on one's perspective, reborn.

Yet, as we will detail in the rest of this chapter, exactly what disciplinary literacy is and how it differs from what many consider to be its forerunner, content-area literacy, is still very much in development. In this chapter, we provide a historical account of shifts in content reading instruction, disciplinary literacy, disciplinary literacies, and multidisciplinary literacies. Importantly, manifestations of what reading and literacy instruction looks like within or beyond subject areas have shifted over time and, as such, research connected to these overlapping eras should be viewed through these lenses if it is to be more fully understood (Spires et al., 2018). We do all of this in an effort to situate the work of the multiple, diverse voices represented in the current volume within the broader history in which reading and literacy research have attempted to understand the complex but undoubted relationships between literacy and content-area learning. In our final section, we describe how chapters in this volume are both unique and connected, each raising significant questions that, we hope, will support the field to better support teachers and students.

HISTORICAL OVERVIEW

Researchers and scholars have understood for over 100 years that literacy development and learning in the content areas are interwoven. In 1908, Edmund Huey, a psychologist, noted that students would need to learn to read widely in the "central subjects" if they were to read well (Anders & Guzzetti, 1996, p. 342). Like Huey, Thorndike (1917) highlighted that it might be the "study of geography, history, and the like" that supports children as they learn to read (Anders & Guzzetti, 1996, p. 282). Indeed, in these examples, both Huey and Thorndike presaged the now robust finding that greater knowledge of the wider world—learned not only in core academic subjects like social studies, science, and mathematics, but also in domains outside the so-called core, including music and physical education, and, indeed, outside of school—is a key support for reading comprehension (e.g., Wright & Cervetti, 2017; Hiebert, 2020; Kaefer, 2020).

Despite this recognition that reading and content-area learning are interrelated, no real effort to integrate reading into the content areas was pursued until the late 1940s, when basal readers began to incorporate stories using social studies and science content with suggestions on how reading could be integrated into these subject areas (Smith, 1965). Interest continued to build through the 1950s and into the early 1960s. In 1961, one of the most influential leaders in the area of reading, William S. Gray, stated the need for teaching reading in the content as being urgent and critical to ensure competent readers in the future (Gray, 1961). During the latter half of the 1960s, and to the present day, the emphasis on integrating reading into the content areas exploded exponentially, giving rise—first—to what has become known as content-area literacy.

Writing in what was arguably the heyday of the content-area literacy movement, McKenna and Robinson (1990) defined *content literacy* as the "ability to use reading and writing for the acquisition of new content in a given discipline" (p. 184). The idea was—and, importantly, continues to be—that, if educators across the content areas work to better support a set of content-neutral reading comprehension skills, such as making predictions or monitoring comprehension, students would be able to perform better and learn more in specific areas of study (e.g., Cheek & Cheek, 1983; McKenna & Robinson, 1990; Dobbs et al., 2017). For example, content-area literacy research lays out several reading comprehension strategies that typically fall into "one of seven categories of cognitive routines that good readers presumably use fluidly and automatically: making connections, generating questions, visualizing, making inferences, determining importance, synthesizing, and monitoring or fixing up comprehension" (Dobbs et al., 2017, p. 16). In short, content-area literacy is about supporting students' general reading comprehension and vocabulary needs by using domain-neutral strategies that may or may not be modified for use in various subject areas. This stance became especially predominant in the 1980s and 1990s: By 1986, 36 states had required all teachers—even those teaching subjects such as art and physical education and "other fields tending to involve little use of prose materials"—to take coursework in content-area reading (McKenna & Robinson, 1990, p. 185).

Yet, as was mentioned at the outset of this chapter, the turn of the most recent century led literacy researchers to "call for change," as is evident in the subtitle of Moje's (2008) seminal piece on the need to more intentionally "foreground the disciplines" in secondary literacy instruction. Specifically, researchers like Moje (2007, 2008, 2010), Shanahan and Shanahan (2008), and others began to attend more carefully to literacy as a set of domain-specific practices, a subfield that is now known as disciplinary literacy (Gabriel & Wenz, 2017). Disciplinary literacy rests on the idea that literacy, broadly defined, differs markedly across academic disciplines and other types of domains, and thus students must be taught discipline-specific ways of reading, writing, listening, speaking, and thinking if they are to participate in disciplinary work (Gabriel & Wenz, 2017; Moje, 2015; Shanahan & Shanahan, 2014). Importantly, students' participation in discipline-specific inquiry practices is central to an understanding of disciplinary literacy (Spires et al., 2020), as is the idea that to be literate in a discipline, students must understand how knowledge is constructed in that domain (Goldman et al., 2016; Moje, 2010). As Moje (2010) highlights, "Disciplinary literacy is about providing learners with the opportunity to engage in the kinds of knowledge production and representation, on a limited scale, of course, that members of the various disciplines enact on a regular basis" (p. 275).

Thus, disciplinary literacy, as a construct, rests on the assumption that its supposed precursor, content-area literacy, is invested in content-neutral literacy strategies. Yet, not all literacy researchers are willing to grant that assertion: Dunkerly-Bean and Bean (2016) argue that "the 'new' strategies of disciplinary literacy have their foundations in content-area literacy, and in fact utilize many similar approaches" (pp. 11–12). In their view, disciplinary literacy owes an historical debt to content-area literacy, since content-area reading approaches often did attend to discipline-specific ways of supporting adolescents' literacy. Thus, they argue persuasively that disciplinary literacy is, in fact, an outgrowth of content-area literacy. As they put it, "by positioning content reading approaches as 'passe' and removed from the needs of 21st century learners, proponents of disciplinary literacy somewhat conveniently dismiss the integrated approach to discipline and strategies that is a hallmark of content-area literacy instruction" (Dunkerly-Bean & Bean, 2016, p. 11).

The quote above highlights the ways in which the debate between proponents of content-area literacy and of disciplinary literacy have ranged from polite and collegial (e.g., Heller, 2010; Moje, 2010) to direct and dismissive, with some advocates of disciplinary literacy declaring that content-area literacy is "dead" (Shanahan, 2012a, 2012b). Yet, cooler heads have prevailed, and both conceptual and theoretical work continue to point to students' need for both content-neutral and domain-specific approaches to literacy. Brozo and his colleagues (2013), while arguing a case for the "radical center," worry that heated debates between content-area and disciplinary literacy advocates risk creating an "artificial *literacy–content dualism* . . . which hinders healthy discussion about how to effectively teach students in the content classroom" (p. 353; emphasis in original). They are supported by empirical work, which finds that students and teachers rely on a blend of domain-specific and content-neutral literacy strategies to support students' subject-specific inquiry (e.g., Dobbs et al., 2016), as well as by statements put out by the International Literacy Association (ILA, 2017), which contends that "literacy—including the interpretation and production of texts and representations—is vital to participation and learning in different academic disciplines. Content area literacy and disciplinary literacy are umbrella terms that describe two approaches to literacy instruction embedded within different subject areas or disciplines" (p. 2).

Others agree that debates between content-area and disciplinary literacy present a false dichotomy between the two, describing that both approaches to literacy are very much alive and well in intellectually rigorous and equitable classrooms. For example, Spires et al. (2020) note the need for both approaches, differentiating between the two elegantly: "Whereas content literacy is literacy *in* a domain, disciplinary literacy is considered the literacy *of* the domain" (p. 11). Even Dunkerly-Bean and Bean (2016), whose critiques of disciplinary literacy are—as mentioned above—at times fiery, finally conclude that if the field is to move forward, we must allow that content-area literacy approaches "underplay differences across content-areas," whereas disciplinary literacy has not attended well to differences between "disciplines," which present very differently in secondary schools than they do in university curricula (p. 19). They suggest, instead, that scholars turn their attention to interdisciplinary work. Thus, if anything has characterized work in content-area and disciplinary literacy, it has been ongoing controversy and critique. In the following sections, we outline some of the most pressing, describing how chapters in this volume contribute to ongoing questions in the field.

CONTROVERSIES

Epistemological Questions

What Is a Discipline?

As disciplinary literacy began to arise as an area of research interest, so, too, did the critique that disciplinary literacy, as a construct, lacked validity (e.g., Dunkerly-Bean & Bean, 2016; National Council of Teachers of English [NCTE], 2011; Heller, 2010). According to the NCTE position paper "Literacies of the Disciplines" (2011):

> Discipline is likewise a complicated term. One complication arises from *the fact that disciplines, as they are conceived in higher education, do not exist in secondary schools. Content areas or school subjects in secondary schools are organized differently—social studies, for example, does not exist as a discipline although it is a high school subject*—and school subjects often operate to constrain or control how knowledge is presented, while disciplines emphasize the creation of knowledge. (italics added for emphasis)

Critics noted that the subject areas in K–12 schools are not necessarily disciplines. Even so-called core subject areas, such as social studies, science, and the English language arts, are an amalgamation of multiple disciplinary traditions. Social studies, for example, draws on the very different fields of the social sciences (i.e., psychology, sociology, and political science); the liberal arts, including subjects like history, religion, and philosophy; and economics. In the same way, English language arts—as it is typically taught in middle and high schools in the United States—draws from multiple disciplines, including literary criticism, literary theory, linguistics, language arts, creative writing, composition, rhetoric, journalism, and communications" (Spires et al., 2020, p. 29). Middle and high school science classes, too, are typically informed by multiple disciplines, drawing predominantly from the natural sciences, especially the life and physical sciences, earth and space science, and sometimes engineering (Spires et al., 2020). Thus, the charge has been that disciplinary literacy ultimately lacks cogency because the disciplines, as taught in secondary schools, are not disciplinary at all.

If the charge that disciplinary literacy is not based in discipline-specific work shakes the foundations of this new subfield, then it seems that the whole thing would crumble and fall in the face of content taught outside of so-called core content areas. We must not forget that so-called core subject matter is not the only content taught in schools. Indeed, work on disciplinary literacy in the visual arts, the performing arts, world languages, and physical education is less well developed in the literature than is work on disciplinary literacy in core subject areas. Recent scholarship is working to rectify this, as scholars have been pushed to consider what it means for teachers of art, drama, music, or physical education to teach disciplinary literacy (see Chapters 6, 7, and 8, this volume). Many of the scholars now pushing those boundaries are represented in this book.

What Is a Text?

With the evolution of texts from traditional books to e-books to multimodal and interactive formats, what constitutes a text today can be multifarious. Some argue that the literacy landscape has morphed from one centered on passive consumption of information to one ripe for active engagement (Dalton, 2014). While the degree to which this manifests in K–12 classrooms varies widely, these formats offer new pedagogical possibilities that include narration, multiple representations, e-text features, online communities, and even technical assistance to support student learning. Along with these enhancements come challenges to their integration and productive usage in disciplinary literacy teaching and learning (Duhaylongsod et al., 2015). Frameworks like Universal Design for Learning (UDL) offer support for the development of word learning and reading comprehension across the disciplines (Coyne et al., 2012; Dalton et al., 2002, 2011; Dalton & Palincsar, 2013). Positioning students to read for meaning and read like writers enables them to construct more sophisticated disciplinary understandings (Gravel, 2018).

The specific role of a text in disciplinary literacy work has been discussed for more than 20 years (Moje et al., 2000), yet debates remain about its purpose(s). Simply put, if students are to read, there needs to be text available in all subject domains across a number of modalities for offline and online viewing (Kervin et al., 2017). Access to high-quality texts is a prerequisite to expanding on and integrating disciplinary literacies in the content areas (Berson & Berson, 2013). Hiebert (2017) reports that even from the early years (1) texts need to be meaningful, (2) reread, and (3) substantial enough to stretch reading capacities. Shifts in textual diets based on learner demands (e.g., using a digital resource to support vocabulary growth in complex texts) can support disciplinary learning and language development (Trainin et al., 2016). These opportunities are further explored in Chapter 13 (this volume), on transcending disciplinary literacy in a digital world.

Whether traditional texts or alternative forms, the role of text in disciplinary literacy (Colwell, 2018) serves as a springboard to dive deep or extend the reach of a lesson, the primary drawback of which is time constraints. Effective disciplinary literacy instruction requires balancing the coverage of content with hands-on investigations and making ongoing adjustments through progress monitoring (Howell et al., 2021).

For Whom Is Disciplinary Literacy Intended?

As Shanahan and Shanahan (2014) ask, "Does disciplinary literacy have a place in elementary school?" With the rise of Common Core State Standards (CCSS; National Governors Association Center for Best Practices & Council of Chief State School Officers, 2010), informational texts were deemed to be equally important to literature in the elementary grades. Differences between content-area reading in social studies and science, for instance, begin to emerge well before middle and high school. Schools are beginning to foster disciplinary literacy skills in an effort to bolster comprehension development in the elementary years (Shanahan, 2021). While wide reading of multiple texts related to a topic has been a mainstay in many elementary classrooms, the associated approaches to interrogate texts and deepen disciplinary knowledge in these grade levels remain underresearched. The CCSS paved an avenue for the preparation of disciplinary literacies, prioritizing it as a primary focus of K–12 literacy development (Litman et al., 2017).

"The hierarchical progression of disciplinary literacy may be problematic" (Spires et al., 2020, p. 12). Habits of mind are possessed and developed at an early age (Moje, 2008); these can be fostered and therefore enable students to negotiate the textual demands of sophisticated terminology, newly introduced text features, and varied writing styles. The need to connect literacy and content learning throughout K–12 classrooms is widely agreed upon; the ways to accomplish this in a traditional classroom context are debated. As Hargreaves and O'Connor (2018) discuss, more research is needed on how teachers can effectively collaborate within disciplinary literacy, especially in the elementary grades.

Not only are younger students expected to develop disciplinary literacy skills, but what constitutes equitable disciplinary literacy instruction also warrants further attention (Wrenn & Gallagher, 2021). Critical disciplinary literacy practices offer opportunities for teachers to highlight topics related to social justice through inquiry (Gabriel & Wenz, 2017). Williams and Martinez (Chapter 10, this volume) assert that intentions and beliefs don't always manifest in classroom practices. They describe how to provide "students [with] access to the specialized literacy practices of respective disciplines while simultaneously working toward making disciplinary scholars and practitioners accountable to the repertoires of practice, and communication of communities of color who have been ignored, erased and deemed deficient within many calls for disciplinary literacy instruction" (p. 194). Providing culturally relevant content connections and resources promotes authentic identity formation and language practices, as explored by Shriener in Chapter 5 (this volume), on creating spaces for integrative and responsive disciplinary literacy instruction.

→ PATHWAYS FORWARD: MULTILITERACIES, DIGITAL LITERACIES, AND CULTURALLY RESPONSIVE AND SUSTAINING PEDAGOGIES

In our work with teachers, we note that they often report familiarity with the term *content-area literacy*, but describe less recognition of the term *disciplinary literacy* (Kane et al., 2021). Yet, in surveys of their self-efficacy related to knowledge and practices that are related to disciplinary literacy, teachers report confidence in enacting many of these instructional practices (Kane et al., in press). This may be because many of the precepts that undergird disciplinary literacy similarly undergird other major theories related to effective literacy instruction (Kane & Savitz, 2022). By making these intersections more explicit, work in disciplinary literacy can be both expanded and enriched. Thus, in thinking about the future of disciplinary literacy, we draw parallels, especially, between what scholarship in multiliteracies and in culturally responsive and sustaining pedagogies might mean for the future of disciplinary literacy.

More than 25 years ago, the New London Group (1996) published the seminal piece "A Pedagogy of Multiliteracies," in which they coined the term *multiliteracies*. In the intervening years, the idea of multiliteracies has often been glossed as the need to expand our understanding of texts—and indeed of literacy itself. Specifically, the New London Group (1996) argued that students need opportunities to make meaning not only of traditional text-based forms, which rely primarily on linguistic representations, but also of other semiotic systems, including the visual, spatial, gestural, auditory, and multimodal. Because of its focus on multimodal semiotic systems, the theory of multiliteracies has been deeply influential in the study of digital literacies: As Leander and Boldt (2013) have described, "More than any other text, 'A Pedagogy of Multiliteracies' streams powerfully through doctoral programs, edited volumes, books, journal reviews, and calls for conference papers, as the central manifesto of the new literacies movement" (p. 23).

Although the theory of multiliteracies has been a major contribution to literacy studies more generally, it has not necessarily been central to the development of disciplinary literacy as a subfield. Yet, a deeper look at the underpinnings of multiliteracies—and its attendant pedagogical approaches—resonates with work in disciplinary literacy and certainly stands to strengthen it. Specifically, the theory of multiliteracies' focus on multiple modalities has important implications for disciplinary literacy—or, perhaps better stated, disciplinary literacies. As we have noted, disciplinary literacy is an outgrowth of content-area literacy strategies, and research on both content-area and disciplinary literacy has been roundly critiqued for narrow interpretations of both literacy and text. In their review of how content-area literacy textbooks treated literacy in mathematics, Siebert and Draper (2008) pointed out that these textbooks often implicitly (and sometimes explicitly) defined literacy only in terms of reading print text, and often included pedagogical advice that undervalued, ignored, or violated epistemological assumptions embedded in mathematics as a discipline. More recently, Hinchman and O'Brien (2019) warned that, like content-area literacy before it, disciplinary literacy runs the risk of paying too little attention to the epistemological assumptions that underpin disciplinary work. In light of these critiques, work on multiliteracies becomes even more poignant. If disciplinary literacy is, as a field, to attend more carefully to disciplinary epistemologies and processes of knowledge production, then it must also take seriously what the theory of multiliteracies posits: that "text" must be understood as constituted by a variety of often overlapping and multimodal semiotic systems, including the linguistic, spatial, auditory, gestural, and visual.

That is, research in disciplinary literacies must seek to understand—and devise ways to teach—students how to make meaning across the multiple, often multimodal, and increasingly digital text types that constitute disciplinary work. In this vein, research by Ivar Bråten and his colleagues (2020) is promising: It supports the field to better understand students' sense making about multiple and multimodal texts, broadly defined. This work dovetails with work in disciplinary literacy in important ways and highlights an important role for disciplinary literacy instruction. Specifically, Bråten and colleagues (2020) review an expanding research base that has found that, if students are to make sense of multiple, multimodal texts, they require epistemic stances on knowledge that assume knowledge is open-ended, constructed, and available for interpretation and reinterpretation. As we have described, one of the central goals of disciplinary literacy teaching is to support students to better understand processes of knowledge production. We note, then, that when students participate in disciplinary forms of inquiry and learn about discipline-specific processes of knowledge production, students may have opportunities to see firsthand that knowledge building is an uncertain social process of construction and reinterpretation.

This focus on knowledge production and critique also aligns with another important direction for future research in disciplinary literacies: how disciplinary literacy can become a catalyst for social justice and educational equity in the ways its advocates have described (e.g., Moje, 2007; Colwell, 2018; Kane & Savitz, 2022). The New London Group (1996) wrote their seminal work on multiliteracies at a time when the "old, monocultural, nationalistic sense of 'civic'" was in decline (p. 69). They argue, as have others (Gutierrez et al., 2009; Milner, 2020; Alim & Paris, 2017), that the role of schooling in our capitalistic society has been to require, perpetuate, and police "one cultural and linguistic standard" (p. 69). Research continues to point out how detrimental this goal is for those outside the linguistic and cultural mainstream—not only does it strongly limit students' access to social goods, such as economic opportunity and career advancement (Bucholz et al., 2017; Gee, 2009; Kinloch, 2017; New London Group, 1996), it also has potentially severe affective and cognitive effects on students' learning opportunities (e.g., Nasir et al., 2021).

However, if disciplinary literacy is not careful, it has the potential to become yet another instantiation of the mainstream, exclusive cultural and linguistic standards that many of its advocates seek to broaden. It is true that major advocates of disciplinary literacy have seen disciplinary literacy instruction as a potential means through which students might learn how knowledge is produced so that they might also learn how to critique those means of knowledge production that serve to marginalize and disempower (e.g., Moje, 2007; see also Colwell et al., 2018; Kane & Savitz, 2022). As Moje (2007) has noted:

> Disciplinary literacy theory and research—regardless of particular perspective—suggests possibilities for the development of rigorous subject-matter knowledge. This subject-matter knowledge is developed as a function of the development of ability to produce and represent knowledge in multiple forms, the ability to analyze how others have represented knowledge and therefore to assess truth claims, and with that analytic power in hand, the ability to challenge long-standing— even mainstream—claims to knowledge and, ultimately, to produce new knowledge that will benefit society. (p. 33)

Importantly, this is also a central tenet of culturally responsive and sustaining pedagogies: that educators should use language to connect with learners and to provoke engagement, critical thought, and participation in content associated with lived worlds. In Chapter 12 (this volume), Wilder and Manderino explain how disciplinary literacy might be taught in ways that avoid reinstating the status quo and equip students with the linguistic and literacy practices they need. The goal, as they highlight, is to support students to understand how knowledge is constructed in the disciplines and to critique those processes of knowledge production in pursuit of the goal of greater social equity and improved life chances for people who have been historically marginalized.

Another important area for disciplinary literacies to broach in the coming years is interdisciplinarity. As Dunkerley-Bean and Bean (2016) have pointed out, "an effective 21st century curriculum emphasizes connections, connections among the subjects taught and connections between school subjects and real life" (p. 20). A noticeable omission in content-area literacy and disciplinary literacy discussions is the increasing need for curricula that cross over disciplinary boundaries (Damico & Baildon, 2011) to address societal issues and problems that require an interdisciplinary perspective (Dunkerley-Bean & Bean, 2016). As Ian O'Byrne (Chapter 13, this volume) points out, serious attention to multiliteracies is one essential step in this direction.

Yet, if disciplinary literacy is to reach these admittedly lofty goals, it must make its way out of the academy and into PreK–12 schools. We believe that the following chapters provide a wealth of information for PreK–12 educators and higher education professionals alike with a comprehensive account of disciplinary literacy in core content-area classrooms, disciplinary literacy in other areas, opportunities and challenges in disciplinary literacy, and updated research methodologies and information on teaching teachers.

REFERENCES

Alim, H. S., & Paris, D. (2017). What is culturally sustaining pedagogy and why does it matter? In D. Paris & H. S. Alim (Eds.), *Culturally sustaining pedagogies: Teaching and learning for justice in a changing world* (pp. 1–25). Teachers College Press.

Anders, P. L., & Guzzetti, B. J. (1996). *Literacy instruction in the content areas.* Harcourt Brace.

Berson, I., & Berson, M. (2013). Getting to the core: Using digital resources to enhance content-based literacy in the social studies. *Social Education, 2*(5), 102–106.

Bråten, I., Braasch, J. L. G., & Salmeron, L. (2020). Reading multiple and non-traditional texts: New opportunities and new challenges. In E. B. Moje, P. P. Afflerbach, P. Enciso, & N. K., Lesaux (Eds.), *Handbook of reading research* (Vol. 5., pp. 79–98). Routledge.

Brozo, W. G., Moorman, G., Meyer, C., & Stewart, T. (2013). Content area reading and disciplinary literacy: A case for the radical center. *Journal of Adolescent and Adult Literacy, 56*, 353–357.

Bucholz, M., Casillas, D. I., & Lee, J. S. (2017). Language and culture as sustenance. In D. Paris & H. S. Alim (Eds.), *Culturally sustaining pedagogies: Teaching and learning for justice in a changing world* (pp. 43–60. Teachers College Press.

Cheek, E. H., Jr., & Cheek, M. C. (1983). *Reading instruction through content reading.* Merrill.

Colwell, J. (2018). Selecting texts for disciplinary literacy instruction. *The Reading Teacher, 72*(5), 631–637.

Coyne, P., Pisha B., Dalton, B., Zeph, L., & Cook Smith, N. (2012). Literacy by design: A universal design for learning approach for students with significant intellectual disabilities. *Remedial and Special Education, 33*(3), 162–172.

Dalton, B. (2014). E-text and e-books are changing the literacy landscape. *Phi Delta Kappan, 96*(3), 38–43.

Dalton, B., & Palincsar, A. (2013). Investigating text-reader interactions in the context of supported e-text. In R. Azevedo & V. Aleven (Eds.), *International handbook of metacognition and learning technologies* (pp. 533–544). Springer.

Dalton, B., Pisha, B., Eagleton, M., Coyne, P., & Deysher, S. (2002). *Engaging the text: Reciprocal teaching and questioning strategies in a scaffolded learning environment* (Final report to the U.S. Department of Education, Office of Special Education Programs). CAST.

Dalton, B., Proctor, C. P., Uccelli, P., Mo, E., & Snow, C. E. (2011). Designing for diversity: The role of reading strategies and interactive vocabulary in a digital reading environment for 5th-grade monolingual English and bilingual students. *Journal of Literacy Research, 43*(1), 68–100.

Damico, J. S., & Baildon, M. (2011). Content literacy for the 21st century: Excavation, elevation, and relational cosmopolitanism in the classroom. *Journal of Adolescent and Adult Literacy, 55*, 232–243.

Dobbs, C. L., Ippolito, J., & Charner-Laird, M. (2016). Layering intermediate and disciplinary literacy work: Lessons learned from a secondary social studies teacher team. *Journal of Adolescent and Adult Literacy, 60*(2), 131–139.

Dobbs, C. L., Ippolito, J., & Charner-Laird, M. (2017). *Investigating disciplinary literacy: A framework for collaborative professional learning.* Harvard Education Press.

Duhaylongsod, L., Snow, C. E., Selman, R. L., & Donovan, M. S. (2015). Toward disciplinary literacy: Dilemmas and challenges in designing history curriculum to support middle school students. *Harvard Educational Review, 85*(4), 587–608.

Dunkerly-Bean, J., & Bean, T. W. (2016). Missing the savoir for the connaissance: Disciplinary and content area literacy as regimes of truth. *Journal of Literacy Research, 48*(4), 448–475.

Gabriel, R., & Wenz, C. (2017). Three directions for disciplinary literacy. *Educational Leadership, 74*(5), 1–8. Retrieved from *www.ascd.org/el/articles/three-directions-for-disciplinary-literacy.*

Gee, J. P. (2009). *Social linguistics and literacies: Ideology in discourses* (3rd ed.). Routledge.

Goldman, S. R., Britt, M. A., Brown, W., Cribb, G., George, M., Greenleaf, C., . . . Project READI. (2016). Disciplinary literacies and learning to read for understanding: A conceptual framework for disciplinary literacy. *Educational Psychologist, 51*(2), 219–246.

Gravel, J. W. (2018). Going deep: Leveraging universal design for learning to engage all learners in rich disciplinary thinking in ELA. *Teachers College Record: The Voice of Scholarship in Education, 120*(3), 1–40.

Gray, W. S. (1961, February). Looking ahead in reading. *Educational Digest, 26*, 26–28.

Gutierrez, K. D., Morales, P. Z., & Martinez, D. (2009). Re-mediating literacy: Culture, difference, and learning for students from nondominant communities. *Review of Research in Education, 33*, 212–245.

Hargreaves, A., & O'Connor, M. T. (2018). *Collaborative professionalism: When teaching together means learning for all.* Corwin.

Heller, R. (2010). In praise of amateurism: A friendly critique of Moje's "Call for Change" in secondary literacy. *Journal of Adolescent and Adult Literacy, 54*, 265–273.

Hiebert, E. H. (2017). The texts of literacy instruction: Obstacles to or opportunities for educational equity? *Literacy Research: Theory, Method, and Practice, 66*(1), 117–134.

Hiebert, E. H. (2020). *Teaching words and how they work: Small changes for big vocabulary results.* Teachers College Press and Scholastic.

Hinchman, K. A., & O'Brien, D. G. (2019). Disciplinary literacy: From infusion to hybridity. *Journal of Literacy Research, 51*(4), 525–536.

Howell, E., Barlow, W., & Dyches, J. (2021). Disciplinary literacy: Successes and challenges of professional development. *Journal of Language and Literacy Education, 17*(1), 1–26.

International Literacy Association. (2017). *Literacy leadership brief: Content area and disciplinary literacy: Strategies and frameworks.* Author. Retrieved from *www.literacyworldwide.org/docs/default-source/where-we-stand/ila-content-area-disciplinary-literacy-strategies-frameworks.pdf?sfvrsn=e180a58e_6.*

Jacobs, V. A. (2008). Adolescent literacy: Putting the crisis in context. *Harvard Educational Review, 78*, 7–39.

Kaefer, T. (2020). When did you learn it?: How background knowledge impacts attention and comprehension in read-aloud activities. *Reading Research Quarterly, 55*(S1), S173–S183.

Kane, B. D., Morrison, J. D., Aldrich, C., Savitz, R., Ming, K., O'Byrne, W. I., & Lily, T. (2021). Disentangling content-area and disciplinary literacy: A metacognitive approach to professional development. *Literacy Matters, 21*, 77–84.

Kane, B. D., & Savitz, R. (2022). Disciplinary literacy and culturally sustaining pedagogies: Potential and tension. In S. Cantrell, D. Walker-Dalhouse, & A. Lazar (Eds.), *Culturally sustaining pedagogy: Developing socially just literacy teaching practices* (pp. 53–74). Teachers College Press.

Kane, B. D., Savitz, R., Brown, C., Morrison, J. D., & O'Byrne, W. I. (in press). Teachers' self-efficacy in content-area and disciplinary literacy. *Journal of Literacy Research.*

Kervin, L., Mantei, J., & Leu, D. J. (2017). Repositioning online reading to a central location in the language arts. In D. Lapp & D. Fisher (Eds.), *Handbook of research on teaching the English language arts* (pp. 327–358). Taylor & Francis.

Kinloch, V. (2017). "You ain't making me write": Culturally sustaining pedagogies and Black youths' performances of resistance. In D. Paris & H. S. Alim (Eds.), *Culturally sustaining pedagogies: Teaching and learning for justice in a changing world* (pp. 25–42). Teachers College Press.

Leander, K., & Boldt, G. (2013). Rereading "A pedagogy of multiliteracies": Bodies, texts, and emergence. *Journal of Literacy Research, 45*(1), 22–46.

Lee, C. D., & Spratley, A. (2010). *Reading in the disciplines: The challenges of adolescent literacy.* Carnegie Corporation of New York.

Litman, C., Marple, S., Greenleaf, C., Charney-Sirott, I., Bolz, M. J., Richardson, L. K., . . . Goldman, S. R. (2017). Text-based argumentation with multiple sources: A descriptive study of opportunity to learn in secondary English language arts, history, and science. *Journal of the Learning Sciences, 26*, 79–130.

McKenna, M. C., & Robinson, R. D. (1990). Content literacy: A definition and implications. *Journal of Reading, 34*(3), 184–186.

Milner, H. R. (2020). *Start where you are, but don't stay there: Understanding diversity, opportunity gaps, and teaching in today's classrooms* (2nd ed.). Harvard Education Press.

Moje, E. B. (2007). Developing socially just subject-matter instruction: A review of the literature on disciplinary literacy teaching. *Review of Research in Education, 31*(1), 1–44.

Moje, E. B. (2008). Foregrounding the disciplines in secondary literacy teaching and learning: A call for change. *Journal of Adolescent and Adult Literacy, 52*(2), 96–107.

Moje, E. B. (2010), Response: Heller's "in praise of Amateurism: A friendly critique of Moje's 'call for change' in secondary literacy." *Journal of Adolescent and Adult Literacy, 54*, 275–278.

Moje, E. B. (2015). Doing and teaching disciplinary literacy with adolescent learners: A social and cultural enterprise. *Harvard Educational Review, 85*(2), 254–278.

Moje, E. B., Dillon, D. R., & O'Brien, D. (2000). Reexamining roles of learner, text, and context in secondary literacy. *Journal of Educational Research, 93*(3), 165–180.

National Council of Teachers of English. (2011). *Literacies of disciplines: A policy research brief.* Author.

National Governors Association Center for Best Practices & Council of Chief State School Officers. (2010). *Common Core State Standards for English language arts and literacy in history/social studies, science, and technical subjects.* Authors. Retrieved from *www.corestandards.org/assets/CCSSI_ELA%20Standards.pdf.*

Nasir, S. N., Lee, C. D., Pea, R., & McKinney de Royston, M. (2021). Rethinking learning: What the interdisciplinary science tells us. *Educational Researcher, 55*(8), 1–9.

New London Group. (1996). A pedagogy of multiliteracies: Designing social futures. *Harvard Educational Review, 66*(1), 60–92.

Shanahan, C., & Shanahan, T. (2014). Does disciplinary literacy have a place in elementary school? *The Reading Teacher, 67*(8), 636–639.

Shanahan, T. (2012a). The death of content area reading: Disciplinary literacy.

Retrieved from *https://search.ucf.edu/#?client=UCF_Main&proxystylesheet=UCF_Main&q=death%20of%20content%20reading.*

Shanahan, T. (2012b, January 12). Disciplinary literacy is not the new name for content area reading. Retrieved from *www.shanahanonliteracy.com/2012/01/disciplinary-literacy-is-not-new-name.html.*

Shanahan, T. (2021, August 17). *Disciplinary literacy goes to elementary school.* Shanahan on Literacy, Reading Blog. Reading Rockets. Retrieved from *http://readingrockets.org/blogs/shanahan-literacy/disciplinary-literacy-goes-elementary-school.*

Shanahan, T., & Shanahan, C. (2008). Teaching disciplinary literacy to adolescents: Rethinking content-area literacy. *Harvard Educational Review, 78,* 40–59.

Siebert, D., & Draper, R. J. (2008). Why content-area literacy messages do not speak to mathematics teachers: A critical content analysis. *Literacy Research and Instruction, 47*(4), 229–245.

Smith, N. B. (1965). *American reading instruction.* International Reading Association.

Spires, H. A., Kerkhoff, S. N., Graham, A. C. K., Thompson, I., & Lee, J. K. (2018). Operationalizing and validating disciplinary literacy in secondary education. *Reading and Writing, 31,* 1401–1434.

Spires, H. A., Kerkhoff, S. N., & Paul, C. M. (2020). *Read, write, inquire: Disciplinary literacy in grades 6–12.* Teachers College Press.

Thorndike, E. L. (1917). Reading as reasoning: A study of mistakes in paragraph reading. *Journal of Educational Psychology, 8,* 323–332.

Trainin, G., Hayden, H. E., Wilson, K., & Erickson, J. (2016). Examining the impact of QuickReads technology and print formats on fluency, comprehension, and vocabulary development of elementary students. *Journal of Research on Educational Effectiveness, 9,* 93–116.

Wrenn, M., & Gallagher, J. L. (2021). Getting critical with disciplinary literacy: A read aloud strategy. *Social Studies Research and Practice, 16*(1), 1–15.

Wright, T. S., & Cervetti, G. N. (2017). A systematic review of the research on vocabulary instruction that impacts text comprehension. *Reading Research Quarterly, 52*(2), 203–226.

DISCIPLINARY LITERACIES IN CORE CONTENT-AREA CLASSROOMS

Teaching and Learning Literary Literacy

Emily C. Rainey
Corey A. Humphrey
Gianina Morales

Disciplinary literacy refers to the specialized ways that people working within academic and professional fields use language and texts to inquire and communicate. Language and text use vary by field due to differences in each community's purposes and histories of development (Moje, 2007, 2015). Disciplinary literacy research and teaching focus on these specialized ways with language and texts, which enable, for instance, evaluation of scientific claims based on knowledge of how those claims were generated (Lee & Spratley, 2010).

In this chapter, we consider the unique language- and text-based practice of literary analysis, or *literary literacy*. Like history, chemistry, and other disciplinary communities, the field of literary studies has been an area of interest for disciplinary literacy researchers, and specifications of literary literacy have been translated to K–12 teaching and learning, especially for the English language arts (ELA) classroom. Here, we distinguish among the school domain of ELA, the scholarly field of English, and English as a spoken language. The larger field of English, especially as indicated through scholarly activity and university programs and departmental structures, may be said to include literature, linguistics, composition and rhetoric, and theater arts, among others. Although the school domain of ELA may include aspects of literature, linguistics, composition and rhetoric, and theater arts, it also can include, for example, reading and writing instruction, forms of remedial instruction, and high-stakes test preparation. The English language is not synonymous with literary studies; literary studies is a field that spans the globe and includes many language systems.

As others have argued, we believe that it matters how children and youth are invited into various ways of knowing, being, and doing (e.g., Graff & Birkenstein-Graff, 2009); this includes how we represent the histories and evolving purposes of scholarly and professional communities to students. Specifically regarding English education, we believe that bringing a disciplinary literacy lens to considerations of K–12 ELA teaching and learning can be a powerful tool for identifying areas of unproductive misalignment between what we tend to do in classrooms, especially in the name of academic preparation and college readiness, and what we could instead do to more fully support students' literacies, including their literary literacy and epistemic agency.

In what follows, we first offer an overview of efforts to specify literary literacy, and then we highlight specific studies of the teaching and learning of literary literacy. We end with concerns and critiques of disciplinary literacy and offer implications for research and practice.

LITERARY LITERACY

What Is Literary Literacy?

Literary literacy is the practice of generating interpretive and critical knowledge with texts within a literature-focused interpretive community. We focus our attention on the community of literary studies, a scholarly community of people seeking to generate interpretive and critical knowledge through their work with texts and with one another, although we acknowledge and value the activity of many others who engage with literary texts. Literary scholarship has tended to center the analysis of novels, short stories, folk tales, and other written narrative and poetic genres; more and more, however, it also includes other cultural and historical texts, such as historical artifacts, digital media, religious texts, and visual art (Rainey, Storm, & Morales, in press; Storm & Rainey, 2022). Although shared interests in specific texts, genres, authors, or time periods may bind together networks of literary scholars, these networks may also be forged and bound by shared approaches to a broader range of texts or other dimensions of practice, such as shared theoretical perspectives.

The field of literary studies has long been represented and shaped from within by literary scholars and theorists. Interested in the study of readers, writers, and literacy, social scientists have also explored and sought to represent literary habits, processes, and practices with texts. Drawing on these bodies of work, we assert a set of key dimensions of literary literacy practice. As we will show, contemporary literary literacy seems to involve:

- working in community with others to build and extend literary knowledge
- establishing productive puzzles, questions, or frames for extended work, often through an inductive process with one or more texts
- using a range of interpretive strategies that enable recursive consideration of one or more texts
- attending to social, cultural, historical, and political contexts of texts, readers, and authors
- invoking and extending theory and other scholarly arguments
- generating and asserting preferred readings (i.e., interpretive and critical claims) of one or more texts and justifying the approaches used to develop those readings

The following sections address these dimensions of literary literacy.

Empirical Study of Literary Scholars

Since the 1980s, education researchers have sought to trace the specialized meaning-making processes and practices of groups of professionals as they read texts of their field, often in comparison with less experienced or younger readers. These studies have consistently revealed that literary meaning-making involves specialized ways of noticing and attending to the text and that literary reading is distinct from other discipline-specific ways of reading, such as those of history. For example, Graves and Frederiksen (1991) studied the reading processes of two senior English faculty and six sophomore students enrolled in university-based English literature courses. Participants read a three-page excerpt of *The Color Purple* by Alice Walker and thought aloud during and after their reading. The two literary scholars seemed to read in notably different ways from the undergraduate students. Overall, the scholars tended to make inferential comments and analyze the function of textual elements, whereas the students tended to repeat or closely paraphrase the text. The scholars situated the text in time and geographic location; they also focused on effects of specific language or linguistic structures, which they understood as creations of the author. The students did not tend to refer to the author or the relationship between the author and reader; instead, they tended to solely focus on events and character descriptions found within the text itself.

Dorfman (1996) compared interpretive strategies of 10 graduate students of English literature enrolled at a British university and 10 undergraduate students in a technical field of study. Participants were asked to read and respond to science fiction, modern British fiction, and postmodern fiction short stories. After reading, they answered short-answer and Likert scales questions. Compared with the undergraduates, the graduate students offered textual analyses that were more aligned with the literary community, they showed more interest in stories they did not especially like, and they offered extended interpretations even for stories they did not immediately and fully understand.

In another study of literary reading processes, Peskin (1998) examined how eight English PhD candidates and eight high school/undergraduate students read poetry. Participants read two poems and thought aloud as they sought to make meaning. The doctoral candidates engaged in extended reasoning about the poems to consider poetic significance and form and meaning. Specific strategies included using cues in the structure, language, and rhyme and rhythm, and titles of the poems; scanning for patterns; noting binary oppositions; and creating pencil representations of the poems. The less experienced readers tended to either come to an initial reading and then close off additional possibilities or deliberately move through the poem to establish some grasp of what it meant but stop short of interpretive analysis. Additionally, the doctoral candidates were more likely to express appreciation of the poetry they read, whereas the younger students more frequently expressed frustration.

In each of these studies (see also Reynolds & Rush, 2017; Zeitz, 1994), the more specialized readers of literature read inferentially and symbolically, noting structural and linguistic choices made by the author and expecting that those choices could shape the meaning to be made with the texts. They also seemed to appreciate or enjoy their reading more than the less experienced readers. Together, these studies identify some of the interpretive strategies that are useful for generating literary interpretation through recursive engagement with texts, and they begin to reveal some of the ways of reasoning with texts that are specific to literary studies.

Working from a sociocultural perspective, Rainey (2017) documented the social and problem-based nature of scholars' literary literacy practice. In her study of 10 American literature professors' and doctoral candidates' reading and reasoning with literary works, she found that all 10 participants understood their work as situated within a larger community and sought to identify and pursue puzzles as central dimensions of their practice. For instance, one scholar asked of Toni Morrison's *Beloved*, "It seems like *Beloved* ends twice. Why does it end twice, and what would happen to *Beloved* if we didn't get this extra short little chapter to readjust our sense of what the book is ending with? That's a puzzle" (p. 61). Another scholar asked how Whiteness functioned in Hemingway's short story "A Day's Wait." These scholars often generated puzzles inductively, beginning by reading closely—what one scholar called "careful listening"—in order to notice key dimensions of the text worthy of continued exploration.

Scholars also noticed strangeness and patterns in form and language; considered social, historical, political, and cultural contexts of texts, authors, and readers; and invoked scholarly conversations and theory. Ultimately, they used these practices flexibly to move toward establishing a preferred reading or claim of the text. These results complement previous studies of close reading moves employed by literary scholars, as they begin to show how scholars themselves understand their text-based moves as interconnected with the larger purposes they bring to their work and their communities of participation.

Rhetorical Analyses of Literary Scholarship

Rhetorical analyses of literary scholarship have added to our collective understanding of literary literacy. Fahnestock and Secor (1991) examined published articles in key literary journals from 1978 to 1982. They detected five special topoi (i.e., warrants or unstated premises held by a specific discourse community), which they asserted described the literary discourse community of the time:

1. *Appearance/reality.* The critic points out a surface meaning and then closely reads to uncover a deeper meaning.
2. *Paradigm.* The critic overlays a conceptual template onto a literary text to impose order and meaning.
3. *Ubiquity.* The critic points out and interprets a ubiquitous pattern.
4. *Paradox.* The critic points out and interprets duality.
5. *Contemptus mundi.* The critic articulates despair over the condition of modern society.

Directly adding to this work, Wilder (2005) analyzed 28 literary articles published from 1999 to 2001. Comparing her results to those of Fahnestock and Secor (1991), Wilder confirmed the continued prevalence of four of the original topoi, and she found that *Contemptus mundi* had nearly disappeared. Wilder also identified three additional topoi that seemed to have emerged since the early 1980s:

1. *Context.* The critic uses historical, social, and political contexts in their argument.
2. *Mistaken critic.* The critic argues that previous criticism has misunderstood the work in some way.
3. *Social justice.* The critic advocates for social change.

Most recently, Banting (2023) sampled a new set of 28 pieces of literary criticism, this time from among articles published in 2015 within one of 20 influential journals; Banting's results suggest the rhetorical act of *contributing to scholarly understanding* is a key characteristic of literary scholarship. These findings are useful indicators of a coherent community of practice of literary studies. They also remind us that disciplinary communities shift and evolve; for example, whereas social justice might not have been an explicit concern evident in the scholarship of the early 1980s, Wilder's (2005) work suggests that it became relatively prominent by the early 2000s.

Treatments of Literary Practice from within English Studies

A chief matter for literary scholarship is the evolution and use of theory. Tyson's (2015) guide to contemporary cultural theory makes the case for the indispensable role of theory in literary criticism and details critical theories most commonly used in contemporary literary analysis. Arguing that "there is no such thing as a non-theoretical interpretation," Tyson represents literary criticism as work that seeks to explain the production, meaning, design, and beauty of literary work (p. 4). She notes that some critical theories, such as feminism and postcolonial criticism, "involve a desire to change the world for the better." When we use these theories to analyze texts for their "deliberate or inadvertent promotion of, for example, sexist, classist, racist, heterosexist, or colonialist values . . . [they enable us] to understand how these repressive ideologies operate" (p. 6).

Richter (2000) offers a historical framing for the increasing concern with theory in literary studies. He argues that literary study is in the midst of a paradigm shift whereby the enabling assumptions that made earlier scholarship possible have begun to come undone. In the absence of clear and shared norms and values, theory becomes essential for debating and asserting fundamental values. As such, he writes, the field has "fallen into a state of theory," in which "we can hardly begin to talk without first presenting our approach to fundamental issues. What we have to say makes sense, after all, only when the problem or question is framed in a certain way" (p. 10). Richter notes parenthetically that given the tremendous importance of theory based on the state of the field, contemporary authors of scholarly essays frame their work by situating themselves, their theories and assumptions, and their approaches—acts that were not necessarily needed or expected in earlier decades and that have required increasingly specialized use of language.

These and other works (e.g., Eagleton, 2008) indicate the centrality of theory for literary study, as well as the important changes that literary studies scholars have brought about in the field over time. As the scholarly landscape continues to evolve, it is reasonable to expect that literacy practice would shift—this dynamic nature of literary literacy is illustrated by Richter's note that "framing" moves matter more and occur more frequently in contemporary scholarship than they did in the past. Questions of how scholars understand their own field and its boundaries are also evidenced in scholarly work. These points should make us somewhat wary of attempts to represent embodied, evolving scholarly practice through lists of moves, processes, or even practices.

TEACHING LITERARY LITERACY

Although some studies have tended to highlight the unique stances and literacy habits of more experienced readers as compared with less experienced readers, other studies have shown that even very young children are capable of engaging in metaphorical thinking and interpretive reasoning with texts (e.g., Goldman et al., 1984; Johnson & Goldman, 1987). Furthermore, multiple studies have shown that students can learn more specialized literary practice when supported to do so. In this section, we review key pieces that shine light on promising approaches for supporting students' literary literacy: explicitly teaching moves, processes, and conventions of literary interpretation and argumentation; establishing interpretive purposes; honoring and leveraging students' many resources; and supporting students' evaluation of disciplinary norms, practices, and conventions.

Explicitly Teaching Literary Interpretation and Argumentation

Although there are some risks to specifying that which is a dynamic and evolving cultural practice, there are indications that students can benefit from instruction that explicitly supports their learning of specialized moves, processes, and conventions of literature. Multiple studies have sought to explicitly teach students symbolic interpretation. One study tested the effects of explicitly teaching strategies for symbolic interpretation of poetry to ninth-grade students (Peskin et al., 2010). Partnering with a teacher-collaborator, the team developed a series of lessons with scaffolded opportunities to practice symbolic reasoning with poems. The teacher taught these lessons to one class of ninth graders, and he taught a second class of ninth graders a unit on poetry as he typically would have. In a culminating assessment, students were asked to read "Poem" by William Carlos Williams and write a response to the question "What do you think this poem is about?" Approximately 40% of students in the treatment group gave symbolic interpretations, compared to no students in the control group. Building on this effort, the authors tested a 2-week intervention designed to teach symbolic interpretation with students in grades 6, 9, and 12 (Peskin & Wells-Jopling, 2012). Across all three grade levels, the students who received explicit instruction on how to notice and interpret symbolism in poetry were likelier to make interpretive statements than students who did not receive such instruction. Furthermore, students receiving the explicit instruction also indicated higher levels of enjoyment of reading poems than their peers.

In another study, Wilder and Wolfe (2009) sought to introduce undergraduate students to literary topoi (Fahnestock & Secor, 1991; Wilder, 2005) and other markers of literary discourse to test the extent to which students' quality of argument would improve and whether students' perceptions of enjoyment would be negatively affected by learning dimensions of literary analysis. They taught literary topoi and other moves of literary reasoning and argumentation to nine sections of an undergraduate Writing about Literature course, and they compared students' writing and perceptions to students in seven other sections of the course. There were three major results: (1) Students in the treatment sections used more topoi in their written arguments than students in the control sections; (2) a group of English faculty without knowledge of the study design rated the essays of students in the treatment sections higher than the essays of the control group on overall quality, sophistication of argument, and organization and coherence; and (3) students in the treatment group indicated similar levels of personal engagement to those reported by the control group. Students in the treatment group also agreed that special topoi instruction helped them understand what counts as an argument in literature and that the instruction influenced how they wrote about literature. This quasi-experimental study shows the potential of explicitly teaching conventions of argumentation characteristic of literary discourse and—along with Peskin & Wells-Jopling's (2012) findings—begins to offer reassurance that such instruction need not interfere with students' personal enjoyment of reading.

Establishing Interpretive Purposes

One particular form of support that is foundational for interpretive reasoning is establishing interpretive purposes. Studies have shown that even small shifts in task or language can meaningfully shape students' interpretive reasoning with texts. In a pair of studies, McCarthy and Goldman (2015) sought to verify the hypothesis that less experienced readers of literature—those who typically would be most likely to summarize the plot of a text rather than its potential symbolic meanings—would express more interpretive responses if the task instructions explicitly invited interpretation. Across these two studies of more than 100 undergraduates each, participants received one of four sets of directions to guide their essay writing after reading a focal text: plot-oriented instructions (i.e., asking participants to consider what happened in the story); argument-oriented instructions (i.e., asking participants to decide between two interpretations of the story); theme-oriented instructions (i.e., asking students to articulate a theme of the text), and ambiguous instructions (i.e., asking students to consider what the story was about overall). Students' responses under the plot and ambiguous conditions were mostly literal retellings. In contrast, the argument and theme condition essays tended to include interpretation. McCarthy and Goldman concluded that a difference in task instructions can elicit interpretive reasoning in students, suggesting that a purposefully framed task is a powerful form of scaffolding.

Building on this work, Levine (2019) tested the effect of particular types of sentence stems on secondary students' interpretive reasoning. Levine hypothesized that the discourses of school—rather than students' interpretive limitations—might account for students' common responses to texts, particularly their tendency to summarize the plot or offer uplifting clichés or morals despite conflicting textual content. To test this hypothesis, students were introduced to an alternative: prompts that used everyday language to support their interpretation. Participants included 185 eighth-, ninth-, and eleventh-grade students drawn from three schools. After reading a short excerpt from a novel in their English classes, students were given one of three sentence stems:

- "Reading this story suggests that the world can be a place where ____________" (everyday)
- "By the end, this story seems to have a mostly positive/negative outlook on life, because it suggests that ____________" (everyday)
- "Some of my interpretations of themes in this story are ____________" (characteristic of school-based assessments and discourse)

Results showed that students who were given sentence stems using everyday language were significantly more likely to construct thematic interpretations than students who were given the sentence stem that used the word *themes*. These results echo those of McCarthy and Goldman (2015): Even small changes to the task language and purposes can result in substantially different forms of reasoning by students. Establishing interpretive purposes for reading literature and communicating those purposes in ways that students understand are essential for cultivating students' literary literacy.

Honoring and Leveraging Students' Resources

Work in literacy and English education has increasingly centered the language and literacy resources that youth bring to their reading and writing, including their rich forms of cultural knowledge and practice and social and emotional resources. Lee's (2006, 2007) *cultural modeling* framework is one notable contribution to this line of work. Her work begins by recognizing that youth have many resources for considering figurative and symbolic meaning in popular culture texts, such as sophisticated ways of engaging with music lyrics and videos, but often their knowledge about what, why, and how they use these resources is tacit. Cultural modeling is an instructional process for making those strategies explicit, a first step toward applying those strategies when reading and interpreting unfamiliar texts in the English classroom. Lee (2007) reports a 3-year study of instructional change in the English department of an urban high school in the Midwest. The cultural modeling approach led to increases in students' interpretive reasoning with familiar and unfamiliar canonical texts. These findings highlight the power of identifying and leveraging students' social, linguistic, and cultural repertoires—in this case, African American English and everyday cultural practices such as signifying.

More recently, building on this work, the Project READI team has developed and studied instructional units for teaching and learning literary interpretation in high school (Hall et al., 2016). The units, taught over several years to ninth-, eleventh-, and twelfth-grade students, addressed the disciplinary concepts of symbolism, argumentation, annotation, close reading, and the theme of coming of age. The units intentionally scaffolded these concepts using cultural data sets from students' everyday lives. Reports indicate that students overwhelmingly benefit from examining cultural texts of interest to them and translating moves of literary analysis from cultural datasets to less familiar texts. For example, a study of ninth-grade students within this project found that the students produced more interpretive statements after receiving explicit instruction on how to analyze symbolism than they did prior to the instruction (Sosa et al., 2016). This study traced changes in students' writing about and discussion of literary texts over the course of a 5-week unit designed to support their interpretive reasoning. The unit began by introducing students to visual images of symbols from everyday life (e.g., hearts, roses) and videos of pop culture songs. As students became more metacognitive about their reasoning processes (noticing potential symbols and making claims of meaning based on associations and what the text says), they moved to interpreting symbolism within longer and more unfamiliar texts. Together, this line of work is a powerful indicator that honoring and leveraging students' cultural and everyday resources matters and that such approaches can be combined with the explicit teaching of literary reasoning moves.

Another type of resource that youth bring to literary interpretation is feeling. Even though students may not immediately identify the interpretive meaning of texts, they do regularly use affective appraisal to interpret everyday experiences (e.g., appraising the "good" or "bad" of an experience or the positive valence of a compliment). Researchers have explored how affective appraisal might support literary interpretation (Levine,

2014; Levine & Horton, 2013, 2015). Similar to Lee's (2007) premise, these studies seek to make explicit to students what they already may do or be inclined to do as a step toward constructing thematic interpretations. Levine and Horton (2013) reported the results of a month-long intervention that shared and routinely practiced an affective evaluation strategy with twelfth-grade students. The experimental group was taught a strategy for identifying emotionally suggestive language in poems, considering moods and tones of whole texts, and supporting those interpretations. Pre- and posttests showed significant shifts in the experimental group's reasoning from literal descriptive statements to thematic and supported interpretations. Subsequent studies (Levine, 2014; Levine & Horton, 2015) have further supported the authors' hypothesis that the explicit teaching of affective evaluation strategies improves students' understanding of literary texts and seems to foster their thematic interpretations of literature.

Supporting Students' Critical Consideration of Disciplinarity

Most of the extant work seeking to relate disciplinary literacy to the teaching of literature has focused on supporting students' development of interpretive and close reading strategies. However, another emergent line of work seeks to both teach and trouble disciplinary practice. This work uses literary literacy teaching as a context for supporting students to critically evaluate disciplinary norms, practices, and conventions and determine their own stances in relation to them.

Recent work has sought to support students' consideration of the inherently political nature and function of curricula and the literary canon (Dyches, 2018a, 2018b; Dyches & Gunderson, 2021). Dyches (2018a) asked high school seniors to examine the traditional canon in their British Literature class. Students read texts that introduced ongoing debates about the literary canon, and they discussed issues such as what the canon prioritizes and whose voices are absent from it. Students critically analyzed the Common Core State Standards and their own high school's English graduation requirements. Finally, students completed a *restorying* assignment where they rewrote a piece from the traditional canon using the perspective of an underrepresented group. For instance, one student restoried *Romeo and Juliet* as an interracial couple who begin a national movement by tweeting about their inability to be together with the hashtag #lovehasnobounds. These efforts invited students to learn about and critique aspects of disciplinary practice and the ways that disciplinary activity was represented in their English curriculum.

Another emerging line of work has sought to support students' engagement with an expansive range of texts and alongside their own reflections about the extent to which they find literary analysis useful in their lives.

Storm (2020) conducted a qualitative study in his untracked public high school English classroom. He explored the literary reading, writing, and reasoning of his students when they were supported to analyze power, privilege, and oppression through routines of close reading. Based on his analysis of his students' work, he argued that youth can learn to both use disciplinary tools valued by a dominant culture of power and simultaneously transform those tools to reorient them toward justice.

Relatedly, Storm and Rainey (2018) describe the pedagogical routine #LitAnalysis4Life developed and used by Storm weekly in his high school English classroom. Each week, students bring in a text from their own life that is of importance to them (e.g., a text message thread, a movie clip). The class reads it multiple times and uses various literary literacy practices to analyze form and meaning. These practices include noticing strangeness, identifying literary elements, noticing patterns, and applying critical lenses. Then, students consider multiple interpretations in a student-led seminar discussion. In these seminars, students sometimes discuss how their identities, values, and goals relate to other literary scholars; this stage in the routine gives students space to evaluate and critique disciplinary norms and determine whether they will employ, modify, or reject them. In the example offered, students watched a 30-second viral video of a young person dancing by a pool that had been spreading through social media and their school. Most students had seen the video and thought it was funny. Through the discussion and analysis routine, students explored new layers of meaning in the video, culminating in critiques that the focal dancer, who presented as a young woman of color, was being Othered by the White-presenting individuals watching and filming her at the pool and by the way in which the video was captured, edited, and distributed through social media channels. One student concluded that she no longer regarded the video as funny and had decided to stop sharing it with her friends. Disciplinary literacy does not require students to repudiate the texts of their lives; yet, this student's conclusion offers a powerful example of disciplinary literacy teaching and learning in action. This pedagogical routine offers an example of how students may be introduced to meaningful forms of literary literacy that can enable their critical consideration of texts and the world.

CONCLUSIONS AND IMPLICATIONS

In this chapter, we sought to build on efforts to synthesize what literary literacy involves and how it might be taught (Deane, 2020; Lee et al., 2016; Shanahan & Shanahan, 2017). We began by asserting the potential of disciplinary literacy teaching and learning in K–12 classrooms. Of particular note for literacy researchers, our review points to the need for research that would strive to develop and refine theories to support our continued collective efforts. The complex relationships among the many fields (or subfields) of English and the school domain of ELA draw attention to the muddiness of what does or does not count as a "discipline," the challenges of establishing which disciplines, fields, and other communities we privilege in schools (and determining the extent to which we privilege them), and the need to further conceptualize youths' relationships to those communities.

One important set of considerations involves how disciplinary communities have systematically excluded minoritized groups of people and legitimized their harm, while also co-opting literacies borne of insurgent, indigenous, feminist, and transnational knowledge systems, to name a few (e.g., Brandt, 2008; Downing & Sosnoski, 1995; Thomas et al., 2020). These perspectives matter for our continued progress in literacy education and in particular for disciplinary literacy scholarship and teaching. As social constructions, disciplines are never neutral, and they are reflective of larger social and political realities and motivations; moreover, they largely represent Westernized forms of knowledge that have become so dominant that it can be difficult to see beyond them. Based on these and other points, some argue that disciplines and their reproduction are forms of colonization (Patel, 2016). Although we maintain that a disciplinary literacy frame can support students' exploration of these tensions and ideas—especially when students are given extended opportunities to evaluate and critique aspects of disciplinary practice and determine their own stances, and most especially within literary studies, which itself increasingly centers questions of knowledge, power, and meaning through textual analysis—our review reveals that most disciplinary literacy work with students has not yet focused on these possibilities.

Relatedly, we must interrogate how the academy as formalized by university structures and arrangements relates to any given discipline. To the extent that we wish to represent and support disciplinary ways of knowing, being, and doing in K–12 classrooms, we wonder how we might look outside of university-based communities to extend our conceptualizations of disciplinarity. Such approaches would meaningfully contribute to literacy education research, which has often equated disciplinary practice with the activity of doctoral students and professors. And even if we do also maintain an interest in understanding academic scholarly practice and its continued evolution, how can we attend to the increasingly interdisciplinary nature of this practice? Continuing to grapple with relationships among disciplinarity, interdisciplinarity, transdisciplinarity, and postdisciplinarity will matter for our continued progress.

Additionally, there is much work to be done to conceptualize youths' relationships to disciplinary practice, however defined. Such work might continue to press toward supporting youths' epistemic agency by prioritizing ways that youth could be invited to examine and evaluate disciplinary norms, conventions, and goals with the possibility of modifying, remixing, or refusing them. As we previously noted, such possibilities are not antithetical to disciplinary literacy and they have been called for in some disciplinary literacy scholarship (Moje, 2015), but they have not typically been included in empirical work as legitimate outcomes of disciplinary literacy instruction.

Of particular note for practitioners, these patterns point to the potential for using disciplinary literacy scholarship as a resource for engaging in ongoing reflection about what is prioritized in the ELA classroom, why, and to what ends. Patterns in disciplinary practice do not necessarily need to drive K–12 instruction. But, especially where there are curricular or instructional efforts employed in the name of academic or college readiness, then syntheses of disciplinary literacy scholarship invite questions that could support decision making. For example, assessment regimes privileging the five-paragraph essay are somewhat misaligned with contemporary literary argumentation, which often unfolds an argument and culminates in a main assertion in the conclusion. Such a difference in essay organization and structure is not simply about layout on the page; it also represents an inductive approach to analysis that ideally would be available to learners. Furthermore, assessment-driven activity itself largely conflicts with sociocultural understandings of disciplinary work as social, evolving, and motivated by the longstanding and pressing questions and commitments of real people. In these ways, considering patterns of particular disciplines and fields can enable educators to nuance literacy goals and instruction and push against initiatives that would misrepresent or narrowly represent scholarly purposes and practice. Specifically, if literary studies involves dimensions we have traced—recursively considering texts, working in community with others to build and extend literary knowledge, invoking and extending critical theory, and attending deeply to the contexts of texts, readers, and authors—then how might students be supported to do this kind of work? What routines and structures of school would need to be shifted to better enable such work?

Still further, educators might consider how they could use literary literacy teaching as a context for supporting students' examination of literary studies as one community among many other disciplines and fields, and, widening the scope again, as part of a Westernized system of knowledge that does not come close to representing the breadth of available ways of knowing. Such instructional approaches could begin to "right size" the disciplines and invite students' experimentation and decision making in relation to them, complementing other ongoing efforts in English education to enliven and expand students' literacy learning opportunities.

REFERENCES

Banting, S. (2023). Humanistic knowledge-making and the rhetoric of literary criticism: Special topoi meet rhetorical action. *Written Communication, 40*(1), 175–209.

Brandt, C. B. (2008). Scientific discourse in the academy: A case study of an American Indian undergraduate. *Science Education, 92*(5), 825–847.

Deane, P. (2020). *Building and justifying interpretations of texts: A key practice in the English language arts* (Report ETS RR-20-20). Educational Testing Service.

Dorfman, M. H. (1996). Evaluating the interpretive community: Evidence from expert and novice readers. *Poetics, 23*, 453–470.

Downing, D. B., & Sosnoski, J. J. (1995). Working with narrative zones in a postdisciplinary pedagogy. *Narrative, 3*, 271–286.

Dyches, J. (2018a). Critical canon pedagogy: Applying disciplinary inquiry to cultivate canonical critical consciousness. *Harvard Educational Review, 88*(4), 538–564.

Dyches, J. (2018b). Investigating curricular injustices to uncover the injustices of curricula. *High School Journal, 101*(4), 236–250.

Dyches, J., & Gunderson, M. P. (2021). "I learned the rules": Using a critical disciplinary literacy model to foster disciplinary apprenticeship. *Journal of Adolescent and Adult Literacy, 64*(4), 379–387.

Eagleton, T. (2008). *Literary theory: An introduction* (anniversary ed.). University of Minnesota Press.

Fahnestock, J., & Secor, M. (1991). The rhetoric of literary criticism. In C. Bazerman & J. Paradis (Eds.), *Textual dynamics of the professions: Historical and contemporary studies of writing in professional communities* (pp. 76–96). University of Wisconsin Press.

Goldman, S. R., Reyes, M., & Varnhagen, C. K. (1984). Understanding fables in first and second languages. *NABE Journal, 8*(2), 35–66.

Graff, G., & Berkenstein-Graff, C. (2009). An immodest proposal for connecting high school and college. *College Composition and Communication, 61*(1), W409–W416.

Graves, B., & Frederiksen, C. H. (1991). Literary expertise in the description of a fictional narrative. *Poetics, 20*(1), 1–26.

Hall, A., Sosa, T., Levine, S., Lee, C. D., & Goldman, S. R. (2016). *Iterative design and implementation of literature modules in high school classrooms* (Project READI Technical Report #13). Retrieved from *http://projectreadi.org*.

Johnson, D. F., & Goldman, S. R. (1987). Children's recognition and use of rules of moral conduct in stories. *American Journal of Psychology, 100*(2), 205–224.

Lee, C. D. (2006). 'Every good-bye ain't gone': Analyzing the cultural underpinnings of classroom talk. *International Journal of Qualitative Studies in Education, 19*(3), 305–327.

Lee, C. D. (2007). *Culture, literacy and learning: Taking bloom in the midst of the whirlwind.* Teachers College Press.

Lee, C. D., Goldman, S. R., Levine, S., & Magliano, J. P. (2016). Epistemic cognition in literary reasoning. In J. A. Greene, W. A. Sandoval, & I. Bräten (Eds.), *Handbook of epistemic cognition* (pp. 165–183). Routledge.

Lee, C. D., & Spratley, A. (2010). *Reading in the disciplines: The challenges of adolescent literacy*. Carnegie Corporation of New York.

Levine, S. (2014). Making interpretation visible with an affect-based strategy. *Reading Research Quarterly, 49*(3), 283–303.

Levine, S. (2019). Using everyday language to support students in constructing thematic interpretations. *Journal of the Learning Sciences, 28*(1), 1–31.

Levine, S., & Horton, W. S. (2013). Using affective appraisal to help readers construct literary interpretations. *Scientific Study of Literature, 3*(1), 105–136.

Levine, S., & Horton, W. (2015). Helping high school students read like experts: Affective evaluation, salience, and literary interpretation. *Cognition and Instruction, 33*(2), 125–153.

McCarthy, K. S., & Goldman, S. R. (2015). Comprehension of short stories: Effects of task instructions on literary interpretation. *Discourse Processes, 52*, 585–608.

Moje, E. B. (2007). Developing socially-just subject matter instruction: A review of the literature on disciplinary literacy teaching. *Review of Research in Education, 31*, 1–44.

Moje, E. B. (2015). Doing and teaching disciplinary literacy with adolescent learners: A social and cultural enterprise. *Harvard Educational Review, 85*(2), 254–278.

Patel, L. (2016). *Decolonizing educational research: From ownership to answerability*. Routledge.

Peskin, J. (1998). Constructing meaning when reading poetry: An expert-novice study. *Cognition and Instruction, 16*(3), 235–263.

Peskin, J., Allen, G., & Wells-Jopling, R. (2010). "The educated imagination": Applying instructional research to the teaching of symbolic interpretation of poetry. *Journal of Adolescent and Adult Literacy, 53*(6), 498–507.

Peskin, J., & Wells-Jopling, R. (2012). Fostering symbolic interpretation during adolescence. *Journal of Applied Developmental Psychology, 33*, 13–23.

Rainey, E. C. (2017). Disciplinary literacy in English language arts: Exploring the social and problem-based nature of literary reading and reasoning. *Reading Research Quarterly, 52*(1), 53–71.

Rainey, E. C., Storm, S., & Morales, G. (in press). What trends in contemporary literary studies have to offer English education. *English in Education*.

Reynolds, T., & Rush, L. (2017). Experts and novices reading literature: An analysis of disciplinary literacy in English language arts. *Literacy Research and Instruction, 56*(3), 199–216.

Richter, D. H. (2000). *Falling into theory: Conflicting views on reading literature* (2nd ed.). Bedford.

Shanahan, C., & Shanahan, T. (2017). Disciplinary literacy. In D. Lapp & D. Fisher (Eds.), *Handbook of research on teaching in the English language arts* (pp. 281–308). Routledge.

Sosa, T., Hall, A. H., Goldman, S. R., & Lee, C. D. (2016). Developing symbolic interpretation through literary argumentation. *Journal of the Learning Sciences, 25*(1), 93–132.

Storm, S. (2020). Black words matter: Bending literary close reading toward justice. In J. Dyches, B. Sams, & A. S. Boyd (Eds.), *Acts of resistance: Subversive teaching in the English language arts classroom* (pp. 7–21). Myers Education Press.

Storm, S., & Rainey, E. C. (2018). Striving toward woke English teaching and learning. *English Journal, 107*(6), 95–101.

Storm, S., & Rainey, E. C. (2022). Designing for criticality: Cultivating textual practice for a pluralistic society. *English Leadership Quarterly, 45*(2), 6–9.

Thomas, E. E., Bean-Folkes, J., & Coleman, J. J. (2020). Restorying critical literacies. In E. B. Moje, P. P. Afflerbach, P. Enciso, & N. K. Lesaux (Eds.), *Handbook of reading research* (Vol. V, pp. 324–335). Routledge.

Tyson, L. (2015). *Critical theory today: A user-friendly guide* (3rd ed.). Routledge.

Wilder, L. (2005). "The rhetoric of literary criticism" revisited: Mistaken critics, complex contexts, and social justice. *Written Communication, 22*, 76–119.

Wilder, L., & Wolfe, J. (2009). Sharing the tacit rhetorical knowledge of the literary scholar: The effects of making disciplinary conventions explicit in undergraduate writing about literature courses. *Research in the Teaching of English, 44*(2), 170–209.

Zeitz, C. M. (1994). Expert-novice differences in memory, abstraction, and reasoning in the domain of literature. *Cognition and Instruction, 12*(4), 277–312.

CHAPTER 3

Disciplinary Literacy in Mathematics

Keri-Anne Croce

Mathematical understandings are developed and employed globally through communication. Consider a series of engagements that start with a verbal conversation between a financial analyst and a client. The client may state to his financial analyst that his goal is to retire at age 65. The financial analyst and client may clarify some information verbally. The client may mail written supporting documents that an administrative assistant then sorts upon receipt. The financial analyst and her colleagues may engage in oral discussions or use sign language to deliberate written financial projections that they have read. The client may sign into an online portal to view the financial analyst's recommendations. These communications help facilitate mathematical understandings. In order to engage in mathematical problem solving in professional environments, problems must be defined, possible solutions considered, and solutions communicated (Croce & McCormick, 2020). This suggests that mathematical thinking cannot be implemented without language engagements that involve reading, writing, oral dialogue, sign language, gestures, or physical actions. These engagements may manifest themselves differently depending on the participants and contexts. Since there are a vast number of participants and contexts that may be involved in mathematical engagements, much has yet to be explored within disciplinary literacy in mathematics. For instance, if we refer back to the previous example, how do the mathematical engagements change if the financial analyst is a developing French/Spanish bilingual and lives in Switzerland and the client is a biologist who speaks Spanish and lives in Mexico? Although studies of mathematical practices across societies have led to the disruption of the belief that mathematics is universal (Sfard, 2021), researchers are still examining disciplinary literacy in mathematics across cultures. While disciplines have their own ways of using texts (Shanahan et al., 2011), little is known about how language diversity informs mathematical engagements across communities (Edmonds-Wathen, 2019). As we begin to explore the nature of communication, different theories arise to explain mathematical engagements.

As researchers develop understandings of what mathematical engagements look like globally, educators are considering how to prepare students to participate in multiple communities. Referring back to the example described at the start of this chapter, we can consider the effect of hiring a recent college graduate to join the financial analyst's office team of colleagues. How does the college graduate transition into communicating with colleagues while problem solving, as opposed to communicating solutions to clients? Before students graduate, should universities, high schools, middle schools, and elementary schools facilitate access to language exchanges in professions that use mathematics? How should classrooms be structured to prepare students for different environments? This chapter will both provide descriptions of the many elements that shape disciplinary literacy in mathematics, as well as offer implications for pedagogy and research.

While disciplinary literacy in mathematics refers to the specialized literacy practices within a given discipline (Moje, 2015; Shanahan et al., 2011), it is important to consider mathematical engagements in a variety of contexts. In order to understand different literacy practices, we can focus on different types of texts such as written, oral language, signed language, physical and spatial. The first section of this chapter explores how mathematical texts have been defined. Building on these conversations, the chapter then examines the sociopolitical dimensions of mathematical engagements. These discussions transition into a conversation detailing how educational communities might empower students to produce and reflect on mathematical texts. The chapter then reflects on the ways in which assessment influences how individuals view mathematical engagements. Finally, this chapter discusses implications for pedagogy and proposes pathways for future research.

DEFINING MATHEMATICAL TEXTS

I refer to a *mathematical text* as a platform that has the potential to engage participants. Mathematical texts might be written, orally spoken, signed, physical, or spatial. While Sfard (2021) positions mathematics as storytelling, how those stories are told and interpreted may be unique to different subcommunities within a discipline (Ball & Lacey, 1984). Disciplines are domains or cultures in which certain texts are read for distinct purposes (Moje, 2015), and engaging with these texts requires distinct kinds of literacy practices (O'Brien et al., 1995). Halliday (1978) asserts that people are socialized to develop a mathematical register within a specific setting for specific purposes, yet Pimm (2021) proposes that some individuals may have personal mathematical registers that cross languages. Since language has situated meanings to members of a community, it can be difficult to describe to outsiders the nature of language used by insiders of a group (Gee, 2005; Heath, 1996). As Moschkovich (2021) reminds us, " . . . mathematical activity is not a unitary category but is manifested in different ways in different settings. Moreover, mathematical activity may not be immediately evident to the participants or to the analyst but, instead, is un-covered during analysis" (p. 63). Building on Moschkovich's ideas, we can infer that multiple communities may hold conflicting values as to how mathematical texts are defined. Due to the presence of conflicting perspectives of mathematical texts, it impossible to bring together a unified definition of each category of mathematical text. Instead, this chapter describes how individuals in a variety of settings attempt to communicate through different types of mathematical texts.

Written Mathematical Texts

Written mathematical texts are often specific to a context and set of participants. For example, a recipe details measurement and requires a reader to engage in mathematical thinking. Instructions on a seed packet present measurements and require a reader to engage in mathematical thinking. While both of these examples are written mathematical texts, they may be very different in tone or syntax. Studies focusing on the literacy practices of academics in the field of mathematics (Shanahan et al., 2011) and the practices of adults who use mathematics in their professions (Croce & McCormick, 2020) have found that individuals outside of classrooms utilize a wide variety of mathematical texts that hold specific meaning to them. One way to start a discussion of mathematical texts is by looking at mathematic textbooks. Textbooks are mathematical texts commonly situated uniquely within classroom settings. The next section investigates mathematic textbooks globally and addresses how textbooks may or may not create a bridge between subcommunities of practice in professional fields and classrooms.

Mathematic Textbooks: A Global Perspective

Globally, textbooks are often used in classrooms as a resource for instruction in mathematics (Ding, 2016). When students read a mathematic textbook, they are observing the author's realization of an idea (Sfard, 2008). Different countries may have different approaches to helping students develop mathematical reasoning (Stevenson & Nerison-Low, 2002). For example, fractions have been introduced to students in Korea, Japan, the United States, Cyprus, Taiwan, and Ireland during different school years (Delaney et al., 2007; Son, 2011; Watanabe, 2001, 2006). While Irish and Cypriot mathematic textbooks have included prepartitioned representations of fractions, Taiwanese textbooks use these representations as well as linear representations, volumetric representations, and discrete sets (Delaney et al., 2007). To teach fractions, Japanese textbooks mostly utilize measurement contexts, while forgoing area models or discrete models (Watanabe, 2006). In contrast, Korean textbooks include a balanced use of area models, discrete set models, and measurement models (Son, 2011). Contexts presented in textbooks may also vary. For example, textbooks in Uganda provide commercial contexts, such as banking or factory production (Namukasa et al., 2010), while Irish textbooks have been found to not provide any context at all in some instances (Delaney et al., 2007). This indicates that there is no global approach to the presentation of mathematical topics in textbooks (Schmidt et al., 1997).

A feature of many mathematic textbooks is the word problem. Students' development of disciplinary literacy in mathematics across the globe is often measured through responses to word problems written by others (Adams & Lowery, 2007; Schleppegrell, 2007). A mathematic word problem usually involves taking a situation and changing it (Johnson et al., 2011). A reader of a word problem may have to figure out what kind of change has to occur to get something from one state to another, or determine how to replicate a transformation within a different situation. While Johnson et al. (2011) assert that this requires precision in language, Siegel and Borasi (1992) indicate that mathematicians should be encouraged to explore their arguments and thinking. Gresalfi et al. (2009) argue that teachers should create environments that allow students to arrive at the wrong answers but still be considered competent at mathematics. Debates continue as to the purposes and constructions of word problems.

Mathematic textbooks often possess separate discourses from those used in communities outside of classrooms. Devlin (2010) maintains that textbooks frequently lay out the process steps that students should use to solve a problem, denying students a chance to learn through exploration. This would suggest that many textbooks do not model the language that mathematicians or other professionals use when determining how to solve a problem. Mathematicians have expressed concern that students cannot differentiate between the languages in textbooks and the languages that are necessary in the field of mathematics (Solomon & O'Neil, 1998). Mathematic textbooks have also been found to exclude populations or present groups of individuals within a limited set of roles in society (Parise, 2021), further distancing textbooks from discourses used in communities. Wiesner et al. (2020) recommend that future studies consider how mathematic textbooks do or do not encourage literacy practices in disciplines.

Orally Spoken and Signed Mathematical Texts

Verbal texts, or speech, involved in mathematical engagements are not neutral but instead are informed by social, cultural, and political forces (Vetter & Schieble, 2021). For many colonized countries, there may be many dominant languages used by students but only one officially designated language for learning and teaching (Phakeng et al., 2018). Within Kenya and Catalonia, the home languages of students may not be the language of instruction used during verbal discussions in classrooms; yet, research suggests that students feel more agency when educators draw from students' funds of knowledge (Moll, 2019). Learners' participation in mathematical discourses is shaped by many complex overlying systems (Hunter & Civil, 2018). For example, Hunter and Anthony (2011) describe how drawing on the cultural capital and beliefs of Pasifika students creates opportunities for all students to engage in equitable exchanges that center on mathematics. Barwell (2020) maintains that students are socialized into mathematics and language during socialization events that are embodied by language and discourse. Speakers may assign converging and diverging purposes to this language (Gee, 2005). Researchers have investigated what they label as informal versions of students' mathematical thinking, as well as the influence of teacher talk on students' discourse (Barwell, 2020; Moschkovich & Zahmer, 2018; Planas, 2021). Verbal texts reflect not just the values of the participants but also stakeholders outside the classroom.

Research has analyzed how teachers attend to verbal texts constructed in classrooms during mathematical engagements. Mathematical registers allow individuals to articulate mathematical symbols using language (Pimm, 2021); yet, teachers continue to reflect on their role in helping students create verbal mathematical texts. Barwell (2020) describes language-positive classrooms as locations where socialization practices support students as they participate in mathematical discourses. He notes that language-positive classrooms have attributes such as drawing on students' home languages and engaging in explicit conversations about language. In contrast, Barwell discusses language-neutral classrooms where language is not a focus of instruction. Teachers seeking to study language practices in classrooms might consider discourse analysis as a methodology. Discourse analysis has been used to investigate verbal texts (Gee, 2005). Verbal texts may be analyzed within a specific moment in time or across situations over time (Vetter & Schieble, 2021).

Signed languages also present forms of mathematical texts. Signed languages are not universal but are instead languages with their own syntactic rules created by different communities (Krause, 2019; Lucas et al., 2001). Studies have addressed the intricacy of coordinating the learning of a mathematical idea simultaneously with the introduction of a sign that reflects this idea (Goldin-Meadow et al., 2012; Gürefe, 2018; Krause, 2018). Signing avatar technology has been proposed as support for students' development of mathematics vocabulary and mathematical concepts (Vesel & Robillard, 2013); however, there is sparse research that examines the differences across sign language communities participating in mathematical engagements.

Physical and Spatial Mathematical Texts

In the first paragraph of this chapter, I mentioned the mathematical engagements that might occur after a client makes a comment to a financial analyst regarding his goal to retire at age 65. A set of subsequent actions are demonstrated by the administrative assistant who sorts the client's documents into piles. The act of physically sorting involves critical thinking (Bloom, 1956). The client sends each document because he believes that it provides mathematical information that may contribute to the solving of a problem. The administrative assistant reads each document, interprets the document's purpose, and determines the document's category. The action of sorting is classified as a physical mathematical text since sorting presents a representation of meaning-making (classification). Asher (1982) uses the term *total physical response* to describe how physical actions represent meaning across genres such as mathematics. Future studies might focus on potential differences across communities as they use physical action to convey meaning during mathematical engagements.

Studies have analyzed how students use gestures to engage in mathematical interactions in classrooms (Bakos & Pimm, 2020; Novack & Goldin-Meadow, 2017) and when using technology (Barwell, 2020; de Freitas, 2018). This type of research emphasizes the use of the term *gesture* as opposed to *action* (Alibali et al., 2019; Arzarello et al., 2015). Gestures form types of mathematical texts. While individuals may create gestures in a conversation that express their own personal meanings, technology often requires precise gestures as responses to texts. Two traders on a stock market floor may create different hand motions to communicate to others an increase or decrease in a stock. In contrast, many technical applications require predetermined responses to texts such as finger taps (clicks), or horizontal movements (swipes). In this way, technology is altering relationships between written mathematical texts and gestures.

The study of spatial texts within mathematical engagements is a relatively new field of research. Scollon and Scollon (2003) introduce the idea of *geosemiotics*, arguing that physical/social influences impact interpretations of texts. As an example, the researchers argue that geosemiotics allows for the exploration of how urban planning design influences textual relationships. There is also a movement to employ spatially sensitive literacy research methods (Nichols, 2014). Within this area, researchers may consider examining the relationship between mathematical problems and spatial contexts. Sharing written, orally spoken, signed, or physical texts virtually also creates types of spatial relationships that may influence mathematical engagements. In 2020, the circumstances of COVID-19 altered the spatial texts of mathematical engagements for schools as well as many individuals who use mathematics in their professions. This draws attention to the need for research that addresses spatial relationships within mathematical engagements.

SOCIOPOLITICAL DIMENSIONS OF DISCIPLINARY LITERACY IN MATHEMATICS

Disciplinary literacy in mathematics has been framed as a civil rights issue in the United States and around the world (Julie, 2006; Moses & Cobb, 2001). Researchers have examined mathematical and racial identities of students in a variety of contexts as well as equitable mathematical pedagogy (Langrall, 2020; Moses & Cobb, 2001). Mathematics engagements in schools sometimes do not reflect the beliefs of indigenous students or immigrant teachers (Meaney, 2002; Seah, 2002). Parents have also verbalized perspectives on the relationship between literacy, mathematics, and equity (Gutstein, 2006; Martin, 2006). Studies have explored how inequities within power structures shape what mathematical language looks like in classrooms (Barajas-López & Larnell, 2019; Tate, 1994). The placement of mathematics with distinct contexts has become a focus internationally (Julie, 2006) and has informed views of literacy practices.

Both ethnomathematics and critical mathematics pedagogy describe how culture and politics inform mathematics. Ethnomathematics links mathematical engagements with sociocultural and political practices (D'Ambrosio, 1987). D'Ambrosio (1997) indicates that a belief in the universality of mathematics inhibits consideration of the ways that different cultures form mathematics and how mathematics takes shape. Ethnomathematics advances the study of the ways in which societies and cultures influence what is considered a mathematical idea (Powell & Frankenstein, 1997). Critical mathematics pedagogy proposes examination of the ways in which power structures support inequities through factors such as resource distribution (Frankenstein, 1983). Future research might build on ethnomathematics and critical mathematics pedagogy to study mathematical engagements in multiple contexts.

EDUCATIONAL COMMUNITIES SUPPORTING THE DEVELOPMENT OF DISCIPLINARY LITERACY

For years, teachers and researchers have debated how to influence the mathematical engagements in which students participate. Discussions have focused on how teachers should scaffold students' understandings of languages to be used in mathematical engagements in classroom discussions (Fang, 2012). Researchers have considered whether students should draw on their knowledge of languages used outside classrooms in order to engage in discussions inside classrooms (Setati & Adler, 2000). Mathematics classrooms themselves have also been considered as distinct sites of communication (Morgan, 2021). A recent movement within disciplinary literacy suggests that instruction should be influenced by the knowledge of experts (Shanahan et al., 2011). Some researchers have examined how the knowledge generated from observing professionals can be applied to classrooms (Fang & Chapman, 2020), or how language intertwines among researchers and students in classrooms (Pimm, 2021). Other approaches have observed how students redefine themselves through apprenticeships (Gutiérrez, 2008). The following section considers how educational communities can support students during mathematical engagements.

The use of the term *apprenticeship* within disciplinary literacy has taken on different meanings. For some, the term is used to situate relationships between teachers and students (Moje, 2015). Schoenbach et al. (2012) propose that teachers act as guides for students while reading written mathematical texts in a type of apprenticeship. For others, apprenticeships can draw students into domain-specific methods (Collins, 2006). Research has analyzed how apprenticeships can support students as they examine literacy in particular professions (Enderson & Colwell, 2021). Croce and McCormick (2020) propose that students participate in specific language communities. Within these language communities, professionals who use mathematics in their jobs are positioned as specialists/mentors and students are positioned as student apprentices. Under the mentorship of the professionals, the student apprentices observe and/or participate in language exchanges that occur among professionals or between professionals and clients. Some are concerned that apprenticeships might address too narrow a focus, providing students with skills that may become obsolete (Decker, 2019). Consideration must be given as to how apprenticeships are selected to support students during mathematical engagements. Classroom teachers may create other opportunities for students to draw on linguistic experiences developed in apprenticeships. Linguistic inquiry and discourse analysis (LIDA) offers opportunities for students to advance their language practices (Croce & McCormick, 2020). Within LIDA, the teachers position students to engage with a "client." A *client* is defined as any individual seeking change, such as a principal or custodian. Students may experiment with language observed in apprenticeships in order to define a problem with a client, explore solutions with colleagues, and communicate solutions to clients. Educators can consider how apprenticeships and methodology such as LIDA may give students a foundation of support for mathematical engagements.

ASSESSMENT AND DISCIPLINARY LITERACY IN MATHEMATICS

By developing an understanding of the uniqueness of assessment within disciplinary literacy in mathematics, educators may influence how students view mathematical engagements. This section focuses on assessment practices across multiple types of mathematical texts in educational environments. While changing methods and theory related to assessment necessitate teachers who are assessment-literate (Lee & Son, 2015), little research explores how teachers use assessment to measure students' development of disciplinary literacy in mathematics (Gillis & Van Wig, 2015). This research is important because teachers may feel pressure to use data to improve their instruction in mathematics (Cai et al, 2020) and communication serves as a foundation for instruction within mathematics. The following section presents what is known about assessment of disciplinary literacy in mathematics within higher, secondary, middle, and elementary education settings.

Differences among disciplinary assessment cultures may exist in higher education (Ylonen et al., 2018). Within the discipline of mathematics, researchers have evaluated what constitutes productive feedback (Esterhazy, 2018). Research has examined how assessment tools may influence student performance in higher education. For example, preservice mathematical teachers' beliefs about peer feedback have been investigated (Alqassab et al., 2019). This research challenges educators to think about encouraging preservice mathematical teachers to partner with educators to design assessment criteria. Calibration tasks have also been used to encourage students to develop the ability to give feedback as they reflect on a range of assignments created by others (Knight et al., 2019). Additionally, some argue for a reevaluation of the types of texts used within assessments, such as the call for the use of modified essays in medical school (Fortun & Tempest, 2020). This research suggests that educators seek to strengthen the connection between assessment and instruction.

Within secondary and middle school settings, educators have struggled to determine how to reflect on assessment results. Stanovich and Stanovich (2003) propose that testing can be helpful to calibrate instructional methods but interpreting results requires sensitivity to context. Methodology such as problem-based learning presents students with problems to solve that have a real-world context (Prince & Felder, 2006), but few assessment tools exist that solely focus on identifying students' literacy development in mathematics. The Strategic Content Literacy Assessment (SCLA; Alvermann et al., 2013) has been offered as a means to measure students' abilities to read and comprehend texts appropriate to different disciplines. Future research may provide educators with more assessment tools that specifically measure secondary and middle school students' methods of communicating mathematics.

Within elementary schools, many educators have been encouraged to differentiate instruction but not assessment of disciplinary literacy in mathematics (Croce, 2017). Sociocultural theory addresses the different ways that parents engage in problem solving in the world (González et al., 2005). Since individuals process information and determine outcomes based on cultural norms, decision making involving mathematics is not standardized (Croce, 2020). Morgan (2006) proposes that when students are only allowed to choose answers from multiple-choice options on tests, they are prevented from fully exploring their identities. Observation of children's mathematical activities in natural settings might be used as a form of assessment in addition to required standardized assessments (Sitabkhan et al., 2018). Educators should not assume that learning products must be the same for all students (Krause, 2019). More research should focus on investigating ways of problem solving across communities. This research may inform assessment of disciplinary literacy in mathematics.

IMPLICATIONS FOR PRACTICE AND RESEARCH

Educators must consider that students participate in mathematical engagements for different purposes. As students in schools are subjected to high-stakes standardized testing assessments that utilize mathematical texts, students must also be prepared to participate in different literacy environments across classrooms and in communities outside of classrooms. For example, university students must pass certification exams in their chosen professions, while also preparing to participate in mathematical engagements with clients and colleagues. Educators have the daunting task of considering how to help students navigate all of these environments. The literature reviewed in this chapter explores ways for educators to support disciplinary literacy in mathematics in distinct settings. Unfortunately, research has not addressed how teachers might balance all of the different purposes and goals for disciplinary literacy in mathematics.

The term *mathematical engagements* describes how individuals inside, outside, and between communities communicate a wide range of mathematical texts. This is the essence of disciplinary literacy in mathematics. More research is needed in order to understand the nature of written, orally spoken, signed, physical, or spatial mathematical texts inside, outside, and between communities. Educators have begun to focus on the ways that apprenticeships can support mathematical engagements across communities. As educators consider positioning students in language communities with professionals who use mathematics, the role of assessment is also being reevaluated. In addition, as educators consider focusing mathematics instruction on world issues such as climate change and ecology (Colesa et al., 2020), persuasion may also play an important role in mathematical engagements in the future.

Future pedagogy may focus on encouraging students to observe what they notice about how mathematics is communicated. Mathematical engagements that are already occurring between students and community members may become a focus of classroom discussions. Students may engage in retrospective analysis of their own literacy practices in multiple settings. As students are given opportunities to apprentice in different language communities, they might develop metacognition and observe how their own literacy practices are similar to or different from the literacy practices of others. While it has been recommended that researchers evaluate the role that textbooks play in encouraging literacy practices (Wiesner et al., 2020), research also needs to analyze the mathematical texts that students already produce and transact with when living in their communities (González et al., 2005). Teachers and researchers might evaluate decisions related to mathematical text choices, as well as how mathematical texts are positioned in classrooms. Technology has also created new opportunities for students to explore how spatial texts embody mathematical engagements. In the future, students may explore geosemiotics, allowing them to investigate texts in the social/physical world.

When students are empowered to take ownership of their learning, they are more likely to view mathematics as a reasoning tool both inside and outside of classrooms (Speranzo & Tilema, 2019). Students' feelings of empowerment may depend on how multilingualism is positioned in classrooms. There is very limited research on the influence of trilingualism during mathematics teaching and learning (Phakeng et al., 2018). Since an increasing number of students are becoming multilingual, future studies may consider the influence of multilingualism on mathematical engagements between students and community members. As students engage in retrospection, their observations could lead to new understandings of mathematical engagements across multiple communities.

This chapter demonstrates that there are many exciting opportunities to continue developing understandings of disciplinary literacy in mathematics. Table 3.1 presents an overview of some of the questions addressed throughout this chapter. Table 3.2 documents some of the implications of the discussions presented in this chapter. Collaborations among students, educators, and educators/researchers will continue to move the field in new directions.

TABLE 3.1. Questions to Consider When Examining Disciplinary Literacy in Mathematics

Questions	Sample resources that address these questions
What is a mathematical text? How do mathematical texts differ?	Croce (2017, 2020)
Do textbooks create a bridge between communities of practice in professional fields and classrooms?	Devlin (2010); Solomon & O'Neil (1998); Parise (2021); Wiesner et al. (2020)
Do different countries have different approaches to structuring mathematical textbooks?	Stevenson & Nerison-Low (2002); Schmidt et al. (1997)
What are the many approaches to responding to a word problem?	Johnson et al. (2011); Siegel & Borasi (1992)
What shapes learners' participation in verbal mathematical discourses?	Hunter & Civil (2018); Barwell (2020); Gee (2005); Moschkovich & Zahmer (2018); Planas (2021); Pimm (2021); Vetter & Schieble (2021)
How can educators coordinate the learning of a mathematical idea simultaneously with the introduction of a sign that reflects that idea?	Goldin-Meadow et al. (2012); Gürefe (2018); Krause (2018)
How are gestures used during mathematical engagements in classrooms?	Bakos & Pimm (2020); Novack & Goldin-Meadow (2017); Alibali et al. (2019); Arzarello et al. (2015)
How do physical/social contexts inform interpretations of mathematical texts? This is also known as the study of geosemiotics.	Scollon & Scollon (2003); Nichols (2014)
How does the placement of mathematics within distinct contexts inform development of disciplinary literacy in mathematics?	Julie (2006); Moses & Cobb (2001); Langrall (2020); Meaney (2002); Seah (2002); Gutstein (2006); Martin (2006); Barajas-López & Larnell (2019); Tate (1994)
How do ethnomathematics and critical mathematics pedagogy describe how cultures and politics inform mathematics?	D'Ambrosio (1987, 1997); Powell & Frankenstein (1997)
How can students develop disciplinary literacy through mathematical engagements that occur between students, professionals, and clients within language communities?	Croce & McCormick (2020)
What are the differences and similarities between disciplinary assessment cultures in elementary, middle, high school, and higher educational settings?	Alvermann et al. (2013); Stanovich & Stanovich (2003); Prince & Felder (2006); Alqassab et al. (2019); Knight et al. (2019); Fortun & Tempest (2020); Sitabkhan et al. (2018); Croce (2020)

TABLE 3.2. Implications of the Discussions in This Chapter

- Disciplinary literacy in mathematics addresses how individuals engage in *mathematical engagements*. The term describes how individuals inside, outside, and between communities communicate a wide range of mathematical texts.
- More research is needed to understand the nature of written, orally spoken, signed, physical, or spatial mathematical texts inside, outside, and between communities.
- Educators might consider that students participate in mathematical engagements for different purposes. Future research might address how educators may balance all of the different purposes and goals for disciplinary literacy in mathematics.
- Educators might reflect on the role that persuasion may play in future mathematical engagements.
- Educators may focus on encouraging students to observe what they notice about how mathematics is communicated. Mathematical engagements that are already occurring between students and community members may become a focus of classroom discussions. Students may engage in retrospective analysis of their own literacy practices in multiple settings.
- Educators and researchers might focus on the ways that apprenticeships can support mathematical engagements across communities.
- As students are given opportunities to apprentice in different language communities, they might develop metacognition and observe how their own literacy practices are similar to or different from the literacy practices of others.
- Future research might reimagine the role of assessment within disciplinary literacy in mathematics.
- Educators might evaluate decisions related to mathematical text choices, as well as how mathematical texts are positioned in classrooms.
- Educators might consider how technology and virtual environments have also created new opportunities for students to explore how spatial texts inform mathematical engagements.

REFERENCES

Adams, T., & Lowery, R. (2007). An analysis of children's strategies for reading mathematics. *Reading & Writing Quarterly*, *23*(2), 161–177.

Alibali, M. W., Nathan, M. J., Boncoddo, R., & Pier, E. (2019). Managing common ground in the classroom: Teachers use gestures to support students' contributions to classroom discourse. *ZDM: International Journal on Mathematics Education*, *51*(2), 347–360.

Alqassab, M., Strijbos, J., & Ufer, S. (2019). Preservice mathematics teachers' beliefs about peer feedback, perceptions of their peer feedback message, and emotions as predictors of peer feedback accuracy and comprehension of the learning task. *Assessment & Evaluation in Higher Education*, *44*(1), 139–154.

Alvermann, D. E., Gillis, V. R., & Phelps, S. F. (2013). *Content area reading and literacy: Succeeding in today's diverse classroom*. Pearson.

Arzarello, F., Robutti, O., & Thomas, M. (2015). Growth point and gestures: Looking inside mathematical meanings. *Educational Studies in Mathematical Education*, *90*(1), 19–37.

Asher, J. (1982). *Learning another language through actions: The complete teachers' guidebook*. Sky Oaks Productions.

Ball, S., & Lacey, C. (1984). Subject disciplines as the opportunity for group action: A measured critique of subject sub-cultures. In A. Hargreaves & P. Woods (Eds.), *Classrooms and staffrooms: The sociology of teachers and teaching* (pp. 234–244). Open University Press.

Bakos, S., & Pimm, D. (2020). Beginning to multiply with dynamic digits: Fingers as physical-digital hybrids. *Digital Experiences in Mathematical Education*, *6*(3), 145–165.

Barajas-López, F., & Larnell, G. (2019). Unpacking the links between equitable teaching practices and standards for mathematical practice: Equity for whom and under what conditions? *Journal for Research in Mathematics Education*, *50*(4), 349–361.

Barwell, R. (2020). Learning mathematics in a second language: Language positive and language neutral classrooms. *Journal for Research in Mathematics Education*, *51*(2), 150–178.

Bloom, B. (1956). *Taxonomy of educational objectives: Handbook I: Cognitive domain*. McKay.

Cai, J., Morris, A., Hohensee, C., Hwang, S., Robison, V., Cirillo, M., . . . Hiebert, J. (2020). Timely and useful data to improve classroom instruction. *Journal for Research in Mathematical Education, 51*(4), 387–398.

Colesa, A., Jones, K., & Black, L. (2020). Towards the next 21 years of research in mathematics education. *Research in Mathematics Education*, *22*(1), 1–2.

Collins, A. (2006). Cognitive apprenticeship. In R. K. Sawyer (Ed.), *The Cambridge handbook of the learning sciences* (pp. 47–60). Cambridge University Press.

Croce, K. (2017). *Navigating assessment with multilingual learners*. Information Age.

Croce, K. (2020) Processing the world through mathematical reasoning: The sociocultural contexts of readers and writers. In R. Meyers & K. Whitmore (Eds.), *Reclaiming literacies as meaning making: Manifestations of values, identities, relationships, and knowledge* (pp. 231–239). Routledge.

Croce, K., & McCormick, M. (2020). Developing disciplinary literacy in mathematics: Learning from professionals who use mathematics in their jobs. *Journal of Adolescent and Adult Literacy*, *63*(4), 415–423.

D'Ambrosio, U. (1987). Reflections on ethnomathematics. *International Study Group in Mathematics Newsletter*, *3*(1), 3–5.

D'Ambrosio, U. (1997). Ethnomathematics and its place in history and pedagogy of mathematics. In A. Powell & M. Frankenstein (Eds.), *Ethnomathematics: Challenging eurocentrism in mathematics education* (pp. 13–24). State University of New York Press.

de Freitas, E. (2018). The biosocial subject: sensor technologies and worldly sensibility. *Discourse: Studies in the Cultural Politics of Education, 39*(2), 292–308.

Decker, D. (2019). Student perception of higher education and apprenticeship alignment. *Education Sciences, 9*(86), 1–14.

Delaney, S., Charalambous, C. Y., Hsu, H.-Y., & Mesa, V. (2007). The treatment of addition and subtraction of fractions in Cypriot, Irish, and Taiwanese textbooks. In J. H. Woo, H. C. Lew, K. S. Park, & D. Y. Seo (Eds.), *Proceedings of the 31st Conference of the International Group for the Psychology of Mathematics Education* (Vol. 2, pp. 193–200). Korea Society of Educational Studies in Mathematics.

Devlin, K. (2010). The Pascal–Fermat correspondence: How mathematics is really done. *The Mathematics Teacher, 103*(8), 578–582.

Ding, M. (2016). Opportunities to learn: Inverse relations in U.S. and Chinese textbooks. *Mathematical Thinking and Learning: An International Journal, 18*(1), 45–68.

Edmonds-Wathen, C. (2019). Linguistic methodologies for investigating and representing multiple languages in mathematics education research. *Research in Mathematics Education, 21*(2), 119–134.

Enderson, M., & Colwell, J. (2021). Considering possibilities to promote disciplinary literacy instruction in mathematics. *Journal of Adolescent and Adult Literacy, 64*(6), 683–692.

Esterhazy, R. (2018). What matters for productive feedback? Disciplinary practices and their relational dynamics. *Assessment and Evaluation in Higher Education, 43*(8), 1302–1314.

Fang, Z. (2012). Approaches to developing content area literacies: A synthesis and a critique. *Journal of Adolescent and Adult Literacy, 56*(2), 103–108.

Fang, Z., & Chapman, S. (2020). Disciplinary literacy in mathematics: One mathematician's reading practices. *Journal of Mathematical Behavior, 59*, 100799.

Fortun, J., & Tempest, H. (2020). A case for written examinations in undergraduate medical education: Experiences with modifies essays. *Assessment & Evaluation in Higher Education, 45*(7), 926–939.

Frankenstein, M. (1983). Critical mathematics education: An application of Paulo Freire's epistemology. *Journal of Education, 165*(4), 315–339.

Gee, J. (2005). *An introduction to discourse analysis: Theory and method*. Routledge.

Gillis, V., & Van Wig, A. (2015). Disciplinary literacy assessment: A neglected responsibility. *Journal of Adolescent and Adult Literacy, 58*(6), 455– 460.

Goldin-Meadow, S., Shield, A., Lenzen, D., Herzig, M., & Padden, C. (2012). The gestures ASL signers use tell us when they are ready to learn math. *Cognition, 123*(3), 448–453.

González, N., Moll, L., & Amanti, C. (2005). *Funds of knowledge: Theorizing practices in households, communities, and classrooms*. Routledge.

Gresalfi, M., Martin, T., Hand, V., & Greeno, J. (2009). Constructing competence: An analysis of student participation in the activity systems of mathematics classrooms. *Educational Studies in Mathematics, 70*(1), 49–70.

Gürefe, N. (2018). The role of gestures in mathematical discourse of hard-hearing students: Prism example. *Acta Didactica Napocensia, 11*(3–4), 125–140.

Gutiérrez, K. (2008). Developing a sociocritical literacy in the third space. *Reading Research Quarterly*, *43*(2), 148–164.

Gutstein, E. (2006). "The real world as we have seen it": Latino/a parents voices on teaching mathematics for social justice. *Mathematical Thinking and Learning*, *8*(3), 331–358.

Halliday, M. A. K. (1978). *Language as social semiotic: The social interpretation of language and meaning.* University Park Press.

Heath, S. B. (1996). *Ways with words: Language, life, and work in communities and classrooms.* Cambridge University Press.

Hunter, R. K., & Anthony, G. (2011). Forging mathematical relationships in inquiry-based classrooms with Pasifika students. *Journal of Urban Mathematics Education*, *4*(1), 98–119.

Hunter, R., & Civil, M. (2018). Introduction. In R. Hunter, M. Civil, B. Herbel-Eiermann, N. Planas, & D. Wagner (Eds.), *Mathematical discourse that breaks barriers and creates space for marginalized learners* (pp. vii–x). Sense.

Johnson, H., Watson, P., Delahunty, T., McSwiggen, P., & Smith, T. (2011). What it is they do: Differentiating knowledge and literacy practices across content disciplines. *Journal of Adolescent and Adult Literacy*, *55*(2), 100–109.

Julie, C. (2006). Mathematical literacy: Myths, further inclusions and exclusions. *Pythagoras*, *64*, 62–69.

Knight, S., Leigh, A., Davila, Y., Martin, L., & Krix, D. (2019). Calibrating assessment literacy through benchmark tasks. *Assessment and Evaluation in Higher Education*, *44*(8), 1121–1132.

Krause, C. (2018). Embodied geometry: Signs and gestures used in the deaf mathematics classroom: The case of symmetry. In R. Hunter, M. Civil, B. Herbel-Eisenmann, N. Planas, & D. Wagner (Eds.), *Mathematical discourse that breaks barriers and creates space for marginalized learners* (pp. 171–193). Sense.

Krause, C. (2019). What you see is what you get?: Sign language in the mathematics classroom. *Journal for Research in Mathematics Education*, *50*(1), 84–97.

Langrall, C. (2020). 2013–2016: Reflections on perceptions of JRME. *Journal for Research in Mathematical Education, 51*(5), 530–534.

Lee, J., & Son, J. (2015). Two teacher educators' approaches to developing preservice elementary teachers' mathematics assessment literacy: Intentions, outcomes, and new learning. *Teaching and Learning Inquiry*, *3*(1), 47–62.

Lucas, C., Bayley, R., Valli, C., & Rose, M. (2001). *Sociolinguistic variation in American Sign Language.* Gallaudet University Press.

Martin, D. (2006). Mathematics learning and participation as radicalized forms of experience: African American parents speak on the struggle for mathematics literacy. *Mathematical Thinking and Learning: An International Journal*, *8*(3), 197–229.

Meaney, T. (2002). Symbiosis or cultural clash?: Indigenous students learning mathematics. *Journal of Intercultural Studies*, *23*(2), 167–187.

Moje, E. (2015). Doing and teaching disciplinary literacy with adolescent learners: A social and cultural enterprise. *Harvard Educational Review*, *85*(2), 254–278.

Moll, L. (2019). Elaborating funds of knowledge: Community-oriented practices in international contexts. *Literacy Research: Theory, Method, and Practice, 68*(1), 130–138.

Morgan, C. (2021). Conceptualizing and researching mathematics classrooms as sites of communication. In N. Planas, C. Morgan, & M. Schutte (Eds.), *Classroom research on mathematics and language* (pp. 101–116). Routledge.

Morgan, C. (2006). What does social semiotics have to offer mathematics education research? *Educational Studies in Mathematics, 61*, 219–245.

Moschkovich, J. (2021). Learners' language in mathematics classrooms: What we know and what we need to know. In N. Planas, C. Morgon, & M. Schütte (Eds.), *Classroom research on mathematics and language: Seeing learners and teachers differently* (pp. 60–76). Routledge.

Moschkovich, J., & Zahmer, W. (2018). Using the academic literacy in mathematics frameworks to uncover multiple aspects of activity during peer mathematical discussions. *ZDM Mathematics Education, 50*(4), 999–1011.

Moses, R., & Cobb, C. (2001). *Radical equations: Math literacy and civil rights.* Beacon Press.

Namukasa, I., Quinn, M., & Kaahwa, J. (2010). School mathematics education in Uganda: Its successes and its failures. *Procedia: Social and Behavioral Studies, 2*(2), 3104–3110.

Nichols, S. (2014). Geosemiotics. In P. Albers, T. Holbrook, & A. Flint (Eds.), *New Methods of Literacy Research* (pp. 177–192). Routledge.

Novack, M., & Goldin-Meadow, S. (2017). Gesture as representational action: A paper about function. *Psychonomic Bulletin and Review, 24*(3), 652–665.

O'Brien, D. G., Stewart, R. A., & Moje, E. B. (1995). Why content literacy is difficult to infuse into the secondary school: Complexities of curriculum, pedagogy, and school culture. *Reading Research Quarterly, 30*(3), 442–463.

Parise, M. (2021). Gender, sex, and heteronormativity in high school statistics textbooks. *Mathematics Education Research Journal, 33*(2), 757–785.

Phakeng, M., Planas, N., Bose, A., & Njurai, E. (2018). Teaching and learning mathematics in trilingual classrooms. In R. Hunter, M. Civil, B. Eisenmann, N. Planas, & D. Wagner (Eds.), *Mathematical discourse that breaks barriers and creates space for marginalized learners* (pp. 277–293). Sense.

Pimm, D. (2021). Language, paralinguistic phenomena and the (same-old) mathematics register. In N. Planas, C. Morgon, & M. Schütte (Eds.), *Classroom research on mathematics and language: Seeing learners and teachers differently* (pp. 22–40). Routledge.

Planas, N. (2021). How specific can language as resource become for the teaching of algebraic concepts? *ZDM: Mathematics Education, 53*(2), 277–288.

Powell, A., & Frankenstein, M. (1997). Considering interactions between culture and mathematical knowledge. In A. Powell & M. Frankenstein (Eds.), *Ethnomathematics: Challenging Eurocentrism in mathematics education* (pp. 119–128). State University of New York Press.

Prince, M. J., & Felder, R. M. (2006). Inductive teaching and learning methods: Definitions, comparisons, and research bases. *Journal of Engineering Education, 95*(2), 123–138.

Scollon, R., & Scollon, S. (2003). *Discourses in place: Language in the material world.* Routledge.

Schmidt, W. H., McKnight, C. C., Valverde, G., Houang, R. T., & Wiley, D. E. (1997). *Many visions, many aims: A cross-national investigation of curricular intentions in school mathematics*. Kluwer.

Schleppegrell, M. (2007). The linguistic challenges of mathematics teaching and learning: A research review. *Reading and Writing Quarterly*, *23*(2), 139–159.

Schoenbach, R., Greenleaf, C., & Murphy, L. (2012). *Reading for understanding: How reading apprenticeship improves disciplinary learning in secondary and college classrooms*. Jossey-Bass.

Seah, W. (2002). The perception of, and interaction with, value differences by immigrant teachers of mathematics in two Australian secondary classrooms. *Journal of International Studies*, *23*(2), 189–210.

Setati, M., & Adler, J. (2000). Between languages and discourses: Language practices in primary multilingual mathematics classrooms in South Africa. *Educational Studies in Mathematics*, *43*(3), 243–269.

Sfard, A. (2008). *Thinking as communicating: Human development, the growth of discourses, and mathematizing*. Cambridge University Press.

Sfard, A. (2021). Bewitched by languages: Questions on language for mathematics education research. In N. Planas, C. Morgon, & M. Schütte (Eds.), *Classroom research on mathematics and language: Seeing learners and teachers differently* (pp. 41–59). Routledge.

Shanahan, C., Shanahan, T., & Misischia, C. (2011). Analysis of expert readers in three disciplines: History, mathematics, and chemistry. *Journal of Literacy Research*, *43*(4), 393–429.

Siegel, M., & Borasi, R. (1992). Toward a new integration of reading in mathematics instruction. *Focus on Learning Problems in Mathematics*, *14*(2), 18–36.

Sitabkhan, Y., Platas, L. M., & Ketterlin-Geller, L. R. (2018). Capturing children's mathematical knowledge: An assessment framework. *Global Education Review*, *5*(3), 106–124.

Solomon, Y., & O'Neil, J. (1998). Mathematics and narrative. *Language and Education, 12*(3), 210–221.

Son, J. (2011). A global look at math instruction. *Teaching Children Mathematics, 17*(6), 360–370.

Speranzo, L., & Tilema, E. (2019). Designing for voice and agency. *Mathematics Teaching in the Middle School, 24*(7), 400–405.

Stanovich, P. J., & Stanovich, K. E. (2003). *Using research and reason in education: How teachers can use scientifically based research to make curricular and instructional decisions*. National Institute for Literacy.

Stevenson, H., & Nerison Low, R. (2002). *To sum it up: Case studies of education in Germany, Japan and the United States* (ERIC Document ED463240). National Institute on Student Achievement, Curriculum and Assessment, U.S. Department of Education.

Tate, W. (1994). Race, retrenchment, and the reform of school mathematics. *Phi Delta Kappan, 75*(6), 477–485.

Vesel, J., & Robillard, T. (2013). Teaching mathematics vocabulary with an interactive signing math dictionary. *Journal of Research on Technology in Education*, *45*(4), 361–389.

Vetter, A., & Schieble, M. (2021). Approaches to discourse analysis in language and literacy research. In M. Mallette & N. Duke (Eds.), *Literacy research methodologies* (pp. 121–140). Guilford Press.

Watanabe, T. (2001). Let's eliminate fraction from primary curricula! *Teaching Children Mathematics*, *8*(2), 70–72.

Watanabe, T. (2006). The teaching and learning of fractions: A Japanese perspective. *Teaching Children Mathematics*, *12*(7), 368–374.

Wiesner, E., Weinberg, A., Fulmer, E., & Barr, J. (2020). The roles of textual features, background knowledge, and disciplinary expertise in reading a calculus textbook. *Journal for Research in Mathematics Education*, *51*(2), 204–233.

Ylonen, A., Gillespie, H., & Green, A. (2018). Disciplinary differences and other variations in assessment cultures in higher education: Exploring variability and inconsistencies in one university in England. *Assessment & Evaluation in Higher Education*, *43*(6), 1009–1017.

Promoting Science Literacy through Reading

A Disciplinary Literacy Approach

Zhihui Fang
Natalie Colosimo

Science permeates practically every facet of our daily lives. Becoming scientifically literate is essential to not only our personal well-being but also the prosperity and security of our nation. Science literacy can be understood from a fundamental sense and a derived sense (Norris & Phillips, 2003). The fundamental sense of science literacy refers to the ability to access, comprehend, evaluate, and produce science texts. The derived sense of science literacy concerns knowledge about key concepts, big ideas, core practices, and unifying themes in science. Its development is dependent on the fundamental sense of science literacy. That is, the ability to comprehend, critique, and compose science texts is essential to becoming "knowledgeable, learned and educated in science" (Norris & Phillips, 2003, p. 224).

It is now widely recognized that reading—or, more broadly, literacy—is not an adjunct to the practice of science, but an essential component of engaging in science (Yore, 2004). In fact, reading is one of the most common activities performed by scientists. Scientists spend a considerable amount of time reading journal articles and other sources (books, documents, notes, blogs, webpages, newspapers) to synthesize information, gain new ideas, evaluate claims, seek explanations, and deepen understanding. They review the work of others to scrutinize its conceptual underpinnings, to assess its logic of argument and quality of evidence, to determine what questions or topics to investigate, to make predictions about what to expect from the investigation, and to offer evidence-based explanations or arguments. As Osborne (2002) aptly put it, science without reading is akin to a ship without a sail or a car without an engine.

This privileging of reading in science means that science educators must give prominence to reading in science teaching and learning (Patterson et al., 2018; Wellington & Osborne, 2001). Recent national standards in science education, such as the Next Generation Science Standards (NGSS Lead States, 2013), recognize the centrality of reading to science education, calling on science teachers to promote language use and to support reading development in service of scientific inquiry, learning, and sense making (Lee et al., 2013). The Common Core State Standards (CCSS; National Governors Association & Council of Chief State School Officers, 2010), likewise, emphasize the essential role of reading in disciplinary learning, noting that students should demonstrate increasing proficiency and sophistication in reading disciplinary texts to support knowledge acquisition and communication. Empirical research (e.g., Cervetti et al., 2012; Fang & Wei, 2010; Romance & Vitale, 2001) has shown that reading enhances content understanding, promotes inquiry and conceptual change, contributes to knowledge building, and cultivates scientific habits of mind. Medium to high correlations have been reported between reading and academic achievement in science courses, with students who struggle with reading often performing poorly in science (August et al., 2009; Cromley et al., 2010; O'Reilly & McNamara, 2007; Reed et al., 2016).

THE CHALLENGES OF SCIENCE READING

Despite the importance of reading to science and science learning, many schoolchildren struggle with science reading, failing to meet the state or national standards in science and literacy. According to the 2019 National Assessment of Educational Progress (NAEP) reading assessment, only 35% of fourth graders, 34% of eighth graders, and 37% of twelfth graders are able to read grade-level texts at a proficient level (*nationsreportcard.gov/highlights/reading/2019*). Children from economically disadvantaged and linguistically minoritized backgrounds are disproportionately represented in this struggling population. Those who have reading difficulties tend to have serious trouble with the study of science (and other content areas) because scientific knowledge is presented in school largely through written texts. Only 36% of fourth graders, 35% of eighth graders, and 22% of twelfth graders scored at or above proficient on the 2019 NAEP science assessment (*nationsreportcard.gov/highlights/science/2019*).

One of the challenges confronting children in science reading is the expository nature of science texts. Unlike narrative texts (i.e., stories), to which children are exposed early and often in and out of school, science texts feature new discourse patterns that are generally less familiar and hence more intimidating to children (Fang, 2005, 2006). Specifically, narrative texts typically present topics or themes (e.g., friendship, love, family, honesty, bravery) that are near and dear to children; follow a story grammar (e.g., setting, sequence of events, complication, resolution) about which children have well-developed schemas; and use language patterns that are close to those children use in their everyday social interactions with friends and family members (Fang, 2008; McNamara et al., 2011). In other words, children often have extensive experience, relevant background knowledge, and requisite language skills to process and understand what is described in stories. Science texts, on the other hand, present new content and technical concepts that children are beginning to learn in the science class, contain implicit or abstract logical-semantic relations that can be difficult for children to interpret, infuse authorial points of view in subtle ways, and use language patterns that are dense and complex (Fang, 2006; Halliday & Martin, 1993). As such, they place greater processing demands on reading and understanding, requiring readers to have the content knowledge, academic language skills, and literacy strategies that are specific to science. That is, students need to develop new knowledge, skills, and habits of mind to effectively engage with science texts.

A THEORY OF TEXT COMPREHENSION

To address the challenges of science reading, it is important to first understand what reading involves and what it takes to comprehend and understand a text. Reading is now widely understood to be an active, complex process of constructing meaning that involves interaction between the skills and cognitive processes of the reader and the discursive characteristics of a text (Pearson et al., 2020). This *construction–integration* model of text comprehension (Kintsch, 1998) suggests that the extent to which a reader understands a text is influenced by at least four factors (Fang, 2008). The first is the reader's familiarity with text language and text genre. Fluency with text language at the word, phrase, and sentence levels enables efficient processing of text and contributes substantially to comprehension. Research (e.g., Lonigan et al., 2018; Uccelli et al., 2015) has consistently demonstrated a significant, positive relationship between language skills and reading ability among both first- and second-language learners. Similarly, knowledge of text genres (e.g., narrative vs. informational) impacts comprehension in that readers who understand the schematic structure and linguistic features of a text tend to perform better on comprehension and recall tasks than those who do not (Denton et al., 2015). In short, familiarity with text characteristics facilitates mental representations of textual propositions, resulting in a text base model (Kintsch, 1998), which is then integrated with the reader's preexisting schemata.

The second factor is the reader's prior, or background, knowledge about the topic of the text. This knowledge includes both everyday knowledge about our social/cultural lifeworlds and domain-specific knowledge about specialized topics. Every text makes lexicogrammatical choices that are inherently ambiguous and takes for granted the reader's familiarity with a wide range of unspoken and unwritten facts about the natural and social worlds (Hirsch, 2006). It is prior knowledge that enables the reader to clarify potentially ambiguous words/phrases or sentences, draw inferences, fill gaps, make connections, establish conceptual coherence, and attain a deeper understanding of the text (Willingham, 2017). In other words, prior knowledge helps the reader construct a situation model (Kintsch, 1998) of what the text is about, including its events, actions, and circumstances.

The third factor impacting comprehension is use of cognitive strategies such as inferring, summarizing, questioning, verifying, and predicting. These strategies help the reader activate prior knowledge, sustain mental attention, focus on task-relevant goals, suppress irrelevant information, monitor and evaluate text understanding, and regulate reading behaviors for the purpose of constructing meaning (Almasi & Fullerton, 2012; Arrington et al., 2014). They facilitate integration of text information with the reader's prior knowledge to form a coherent mental representation of the meaning of the text (Kintsch, 1998). Effective use of cognitive strategies, however, hinges on the extent to which the reader understands the text language and the text genre, is familiar with the text topic, and has the motivation to engage with the reading task (Fang, 2008).

Fourth, readers' motivation and engagement also influence the comprehension outcomes of their reading. When readers are motivated to read, they become more engaged with the plots, ideas, and arguments presented in the text; this, in turn, results in better overall understanding of the text (Barber & Klauda, 2020). Texts on topics that relate to readers' experiences, are meaningful to their lives, or pique their interests tend to be more appealing and have the potential to engender deeper engagement with the text. Because motivation resides in the interaction between the reader and the text (Turner & Paris, 2005), readers who are more familiar with the text topic and the text language/genre and confident in their reading ability are likely to be more motivated to read the text and become more engaged while reading, which, in turn, leads to better comprehension outcomes (Wolters et al., 2014).

To summarize, a broad and complex array of skills, strategies, knowledge, and disposition interact in synergic ways to bring about an understanding of text. As the knowledge students are expected to engage with becomes more specialized and complex over the years of schooling, the texts they are expected to read also become more abstract, dense, and complex. Successful comprehension of these texts requires progressively more advanced language skills, mature cognitive strategies, and specialized content knowledge, as well as discipline-relevant experiences and motivation (Fang, 2020).

A DISCIPLINARY LITERACY PERSPECTIVE ON SCIENCE READING

Like reading in other contexts, science reading comprehension also depends on readers' background knowledge, language proficiency, and use of cognitive strategies. However, the nature of knowledge encoded in science texts, the complexity of language that presents this knowledge, and the habits of mind needed to process the technical content, dense language, and abstract logical-semantic links make science reading uniquely different from everyday reading. Specifically, science aims to construct theorized interpretations of the universe. As such, it produces knowledge that is distilled from our concrete experience with the physical world. This knowledge tends to be more technical, abstract, systematic, hierarchically organized, and transcendent than the commonsense knowledge with which we live our everyday lives. For example, we commonly refer to small gnawing animals with strong incisors and no canine teeth collectively as *rats*, but in science (biology) they belong to a family of mammals called *rodents*, or technically Rodentia, that also includes mice, gundis, squirrels, chipmunks, hamsters, beavers, porcupines, guinea pigs, gophers, degus, and jerboas. Rodentia itself is an order in a hierarchy of classification that includes magnorder (*boreoeutheria*), superorder (*euarchontoglires*), granorder (*euarchonta*, *glires*), and order (*lagomorpha*, *rodentia*).

Because of the nature of their work, scientists employ certain habits of mind in their social practice. These habits of mind include curiosity, skepticism, openness to new ideas, creativity, intellectual honesty, and ethical responsibility (National Research Council [NRC], 2012; NGSS Lead States, 2013). They inform the ways scientists read, write, talk, and think. For example, reading in science means more than just the ability to comprehend and recite information in the text; it also involves analyzing and evaluating what is read and drawing inferences based on the evidence presented and/or reasonable assumptions. As Wellington and Osborne (2001) pointed out, "To be capable of reading carefully, critically, and with a healthy skepticism is a vital component of being a scientist" (p. 42). Scientists must accurately assess the validity of knowledge claims, the quality of evidence, the logic of argument, and the coherence of claims in relation to the established body of knowledge in the field to produce and renovate knowledge (Patterson et al., 2018; Yore, 2004).

Studies of expert performance have yielded valuable information about how practicing scientists read while doing their work. Bazerman (1985), for example, observed seven physicists with varied specializations while they were conducting library searches and reading articles in their fields, and interviewed them about their reading processes. He found that the physicists conducted weekly library searches to stay current in the field and were purposeful when selecting materials to read. Specifically, the scientists selected materials for careful reading based on their current or future work and personal knowledge of the field, focusing in particular on work that was most closely related to their own. Once an article had been determined to be of interest, the physicists were just as selective in determining what portions of the article to read. Frequently, they would read only the materials that would provide them with more information about a topic or modify their current understandings of the topic; and they often read the article out of sequence, reading backward or jumping from section to section to raise or answer questions. In cases of comprehension challenges, the physicists weighed the amount of gain against the amount of effort in tackling the challenging materials. When encountering information that was unclear due to a lack of knowledge, they read freely and uncritically; however, when reading complicated material in anticipation of using it immediately in their own work, they first read for the gist and then conducted a second or third reading with a more critical stance.

Shanahan et al. (2011) focused on how chemists, as well as historians and mathematicians, interacted with texts in their field. They examined the ways these experts used sourcing, contextualization, and corroboration in their considerations of disciplinary texts. They also examined how text structure and visual elements influenced the ways these experts interacted with the text, the role of interest in their reading, and how they engaged in critiquing and rereading of the text. Through examination of data collected from individual interviews, think-alouds, and focus group meetings, the researchers found that the chemists had an approach to reading that could be characterized as flexible, pragmatic, and recursive. Specifically, they paid attention to authorship, author affiliation, citations, and publication outlet, using them to determine the quality and credibility of the text and whether they wanted to read it. They also took note of the time period of composition to determine the recency and, thus, the worth of the text. However, they did not seem to pay as much attention to corroboration as a way to reveal authorial stance or perspective. Instead, when they made comparisons across texts, their main purpose was to determine the relative value of the texts and to see if differences in experimental results could be attributed to differences in research methods and conditions. They used text structure to help build an understanding of ideas in the text, rather than for critique or interpretation. They attended to visual elements (e.g., graphs, charts, diagrams, equations) as much as they did prose, moving back and forth between the two sources of information as they sought to learn from and understand the text.

School science knowledge is presented in a range of discourse genres that catalogue the social practice of scientists. They include report, description, explanation, exposition, and discussion, among others. Each of these genres draws on a particular constellation of lexical, grammatical, and discursive features that makes it the kind of genre it is (Fang, 2010). These linguistic features also reflect the scientific habits of mind that are embodied in the work of scientists. They tend to be more technical, dense, abstract, and metaphoric than the lexicogrammatical features that characterize the ordinary language that constructs the commonsense knowledge and everyday habits of mind (Fang, 2012; Halliday, 2006; Halliday & Martin, 1993). Lexically, science uses specialist terminology to build technical taxonomies. Grammatically, science foregrounds verbs of relational process (e.g., *be*, *have*, *belong to*, *become*, *concern*, *deal with*, *weigh*, *measure*) that identify, define, classify, explain, or describe concepts and entities, such that its sentences often consist of two long noun phrases linked by a verb of relational process. Discursively, science features a tightly knit structure that facilitates information flow and argument development.

In the following excerpt from a science trade book (Chin, 2017), for example, technical terms such as *species*, *mammals*, *invertebrates*, *endemic*, *topography*, and *landscape* are used. Sentences 1, 3, and 4 (noted with a superscripted number in the extract below) each use a verb of relational process (*is*, *have*) that links noun phrases of varying complexities. They identify *Grand Canyon* as *home to thousands of species*, attribute *this wide variety of life* to *the canyon's topography*, and describe *its rugged landscape and . . . its great depth* as having *a significant effect on climate throughout the canyon*. Sentence 2 characterizes 29 species as *endemic to the canyon* through the use of the relational verb *is*, providing additional information that reinforces the message presented in Sentence 1. The nonfinite clause *meaning they don't live anywhere else on Earth* explains what *endemic to the canyon* in the main clause means. The beginning of Sentence 3, *this wide variety of life*, is a nominalization that refers to *thousands of species* in the predicate position of Sentence 1. The preposition *or* introduces an appositive that defines the technical term *topography*, thus avoiding the need for a separate sentence (*topography is a physical structure*) that may disrupt the flow of information and diffuse the focus of discussion. The beginning of Sentence 4, *its rugged landscape and . . . its great depth*, exemplifies the concept of topography introduced in the predicate position of Sentence 3. These ways of structuring text create a discursive flow that enables the author to effectively present information and advance argument.

> [1]Grand Canyon is home to thousands of species, including 373 birds, 92 mammals, 1,750 plants, and more than 8,000 invertebrates. [2]Twenty-nine species are endemic to the canyon, meaning they don't live anywhere else on Earth. [3]This wide variety of life is due to the canyon's topography, or physical structure. [4]Its rugged landscape and in particular its great depth have a significant effect on climate throughout the canyon.

In addition to language, modern science also draws on visual resources such as images, graphs, tables, diagrams, maps, and mathematics symbols to present its knowledge, ideas, and worldviews (Hand et al., 2016; Kress et al., 2001), resulting in what Lemke (2002) referred to as "science multimedia genres." These genres arise not only because they are "fit to the internal functional needs of the scientific community," but also because they "play a role in linking that community within the wider social, economic, and political institutions that make their continued existence possible" (Lemke, 2002, p. 28). In fact, today's science has become so heavily dependent on visual representations that it is difficult to imagine a science text without at least some visual elements. In many science texts, visual elements dominate.

The increasingly multimodal and multisemiotic nature of today's science texts results from both the limitations of language itself and the invention of new technologies. While language is a powerful tool for conceptualization and classification, it is not very effective in describing, for example, complex shapes, shades of color, degrees of temperature, or the trajectory of a rocket, for which visual and spatial-motor representations are much better suited (Lemke, 2002). The advent of digital technologies, such as color coding or graphing tools, has enabled writers to manipulate multimodal/multisemiotic resources to meet the communicative needs of science writers. These technologies provide new affordances that expand the meaning-making repertoires of scientists and at the same time facilitate science teaching/learning. For example, a linguistic description of a solid (e.g., *"Solid" is a state of matter with a definite shape and volume*) tends to be abstract, but a drawing of a solid affords meaning-making at the macroscopic level and the particle model of a solid affords thinking of matter at the microscopic or nano-level (Yeo & Nielsen, 2020).

The unique ways in which scientists think, read/write, and produce knowledge suggest that science is a specialized discourse community. Members within this community have shared purpose, goals, assumptions, values, worldviews, rhetorical conventions, stylistic practices, and other patterns of interaction; they establish and maintain a common set of concepts, principles, processes, standards, terminology, and genres for inquiries and debates within the discipline (Christie & Maton, 2011). From this perspective, then, induction into the scientific community involves learning both "the organization of knowledge" and the "intellectual and educational practices for its creation, teaching and learning" (Christie & Maton, 2011, p. 4). This means that a vital part of becoming scientifically literate entails learning to access, comprehend, evaluate, and produce science texts in discipline-legitimated ways.

A BLUEPRINT FOR IMPROVING SCIENCE READING ABILITY

Despite the importance of discipline-specific content knowledge, language skills, and habits of mind, they have been "incidental" or "underaddressed" aspects of school reading instruction (Pearson et al., 2020; Smith et al., 2021). Efforts to boost students' reading performance at the elementary, middle, or secondary level have been strikingly similar, remaining largely focused on the Fab Five—phonological awareness, phonics, fluency, vocabulary, and cognitive strategies—with the consequence that many students, especially those from economically disadvantaged and linguistically minoritized groups, continue to struggle in content-area reading and learning.

Understanding what the reading process involves and, more specifically, what is unique about science reading allows us to design reading instruction that is more focused and thus potentially more effective in addressing the challenges of science reading. In light of what was reviewed above, we believe teachers can address the challenges of science reading by helping students (1) build content knowledge about science, (2) develop science language proficiency and multimodal competence, and (3) learn to read like a scientist. Each of these components is elaborated below.

Building Science Content Knowledge

Content knowledge is knowledge about a specific and defined subject such as science. It is a subset of background, or prior, knowledge, which refers to all of the world knowledge the reader brings to the task of reading, including episodic (events), declarative (facts), and procedural (how-to) knowledge (Smith et al., 2021). The link between background knowledge and reading comprehension is a widely recognized and well-researched aspect of reading comprehension for the past four decades. Recent reviews of this body of research literature conclude the following: (1) High levels of background knowledge enable children to better comprehend a text, (2) the effect of knowledge is larger with expository texts than with narrative texts, (3) knowledge has a compensatory effect on comprehension, and (4) children tend to rely more heavily on prior knowledge than on the text when information in the text contradicts prior knowledge (Cervetti & Wright, 2020; Smith et al., 2021). These findings suggest that building knowledge should be considered foundational to improving students' reading proficiency in general and disciplinary reading ability in particular.

Given the robust relationship between background knowledge and comprehension, it is clear that explicitly building knowledge, especially domain-specific content knowledge, should be a key piece of school reading instruction (Hirsch, 2006; Willingham, 2017). One way to help build students' science content knowledge is to provide opportunities for them to read and discuss many texts on a variety of topics related to nature of science; physical science; life science; earth and space science; and engineering, technology, and applications of science. This variety can be found in science trade books.

Science trade books have several distinct advantages over traditional textbooks (Fang, 2010, 2013). First, they provide more contextualized, focused, current, and in-depth coverage of science content. As such, they tend to be more appealing and something that students will actually read. Second, science trade books are written at different reading levels and on many different topics. As such, they are better able to accommodate the needs of students with diverse backgrounds, interests, and reading levels. Third, science trade books portray science as it is practiced in the real world, showing how scientists formulate questions and seek answers to these questions through firsthand (e.g., hands-on experiments and observations) and secondhand (e.g., reading, writing) inquiries. As such, they are generally viewed as not only more authentic and motivating but also a powerful resource for building science content knowledge, developing science inquiry skills, understanding nature of science, and fostering scientific habits of mind.

Not all science trade books are created equal, however. They are of varied qualities. To find quality science trade books, teachers can consult the National Science Teachers Association (NSTA) Outstanding Science Trade Books for Students K–12, an annual list of about 40 quality science trade books for children and young adults compiled by the NSTA in cooperation with Children's Book Council. Books selected for inclusion in the list are judged to be scientifically accurate, up-to-date, engagingly written, attractively designed, logically organized, and devoid of stereotypes. They are sorted into topical areas, such as archaeology, anthropology, and paleontology; biography; earth and space science; environment and ecology; fiction; life science; physical science; science-related careers; and technology and engineering. They are also identified according to national science education standards. Additionally, the reading level for each book is identified: P = primary (K–2), E = elementary (grades 3–5), I = intermediate (grades 6–8), and A = advanced (grades 9–12). These levels are intended as a guide and not meant to limit the potential uses of the books.

Besides the NSTA list, other professional organizations have also created their own lists of quality science trade books. Among them are the AAAS/Subaru SB & F Prize for Excellence in Science Books, created by the American Association for the Advancement of Science, with support from Subaru America Inc., to celebrate outstanding science writing and illustration for children and young adults. The prize is awarded to four categories of books: children's science picture books, middle grade nonfiction science books, popular science for high school readers, and hands-on science/activity books. In addition, the National Council of Teachers of English established the Orbis Pictus Award for Outstanding Nonfiction for Children to recognize books that demonstrate excellence in the writing of nonfiction. Many science books won this award. Although only one award is given each year, up to five titles are recognized as Honor Books.

Finally, two award-winning science magazines, *Kids Discover* (*https://kidsdiscover.com*) and *Science News for Students* (*www.sciencenewsforstudents.org*), provide quality reading materials on science topics that schoolchildren may also find relevant and appealing. *Kids Discover* publishes high-interest nonfiction materials for children ages 6–14. Each issue focuses on a specific topic in science or social studies. The magazine has published many issues covering life science (e.g., five senses, brain, germs, cells, insects, flower, nutrition); earth science (e.g., climate, weather, oceans, glaciers, rocks, water); and physical and space science (e.g., atoms, energy, astronauts, planets, moon, simple machines). *Science News for Students* is a free online resource for middle and high school students that publishes award-winning journalism on research across the breadth of science, health, and technology fields, showing them how science really works, what scientists do, what goes into conducting first-class research and science projects, and how anyone can get involved with the work of science.

Teachers can engage students in reading these quality trade books by conducting unit studies, biographical studies, book studies, author studies, genre studies, and read-alouds (Fang, 2010). In unit studies, students read and discuss multiple science trade books on an important science topic or idea, hoping to deepen their understanding of the topic or idea. In biographical studies, students read and discuss biographies of scientists to deepen their understanding of nature of science and develop interest in pursuing science-related careers. In book studies, students form literature circles, reading, analyzing, sharing, and then exchanging a science book of personal interest or disciplinary significance. In author studies, students read and discuss multiple science books written by the same, often accomplished, author, learning how the author's background and life experience have shaped his or her writing style and creative process. In genre studies, students read and discuss several books belonging to the same genre, aiming to develop a deeper understanding of its social purpose and rhetorical moves, as well as its verbal and visual features. In read-alouds, teachers read a quality science book out loud, demonstrating effective reading strategies and engaging students in discussion about key ideas, important details, and powerful writing crafts in the book. To promote reading, teachers can set up a home science reading program (e.g., Fang et al., 2008), asking students to check out books regularly from the classroom/school library to read at home, complete a short reading response sheet (see Figure 4.1 for examples), and hold weekly discussions about these books in class or via an online forum.

Developing Science Language Proficiency and Multimodal Competence

Science language is a linguistic register functional for construing scientific knowledge and habits of mind. This language is technical, abstract, dense, formal, metaphoric, tightly knit, and complex, epitomizing the sort of academic language that students find foreign and challenging in disciplinary learning (Fang, 2006, 2021a; Fang & Schleppegrell, 2008). Research (e.g., DiCerbo et al., 2014; Uccelli et al., 2015) has suggested that academic language proficiency is a significant predictor of students' reading comprehension and that children from economically disadvantaged or linguistically minoritized backgrounds tend to score lower on academic language measures. This means that proficiency with science language is key to improving science reading comprehension. Despite its importance, science language is rarely an emphasis in science literacy instruction. Efforts to teach science language or, more generally, academic language have typically centered on science or academic vocabulary, with much less attention to other aspects of science language, such as dense noun phrases, which are a key and pervasive resource in scientific meaning-making (Biber & Gray, 2010; Fang et al., 2006, 2021; Halliday & Martin, 1993).

One way to develop students' science language proficiency is to provide explicit instruction about science language in authentic contexts of science reading so that they understand what science language looks like, what it means, what its discursive functions are, and why it is needed in scientific meaning-making. Such instruction can be provided during close reading sessions. Close reading is a method of reading texts that involves detailed analysis and thoughtful discussion of how language choices make meaning in ways that realize the purpose of the text and the author's intention (Fang, 2016; Fang & Chapman, 2015). A model of close reading that involves systematic analysis and discussion of language patterns in the text is called

Reading Response to Science Informational Text
Book Title and Author:
Your Name:
One big idea I have learned from the text:
One key scientific vocabulary word in the text. Explain what the word means in a sentence and/or with an illustration:
One juicy (grammatically complex and challenging) sentence from the text. Try to paraphrase by saying it in your own words:
One question I have after reading the text:

Reading Response to Scientist's Biography			
Book Title and Author:			
Your Name:			
Document the use of the inquiry process.		Note information on life locally, nationally, and internationally at the time the scientist lived.	Identify personal traits that you think contribute to the scientist's success. Explain how.
Sense a problem			
Hypothesize			
Experiment			
Evaluate			
Publish			

FIGURE 4.1. Sample reading response sheets. The first part is adapted from Fang et al. (2008); the second part from Fairweather and Fairweather (2010) and Monhardt (2005).

functional language analysis, or FLA (Fang, 2021b; Fang & Schleppegrell, 2008, 2010). FLA provides a guiding framework that enables students to explore what a text is about (experiential meaning), how a text is organized (textual meaning), and how the author infuses judgments and points of view (interpersonal meaning) by attending to the lexical, grammatical, and discursive choices the author made in constructing the text.

Follow-up language-based tasks can be designed to give students an opportunity to practice the linguistic features spotlighted during close reading sessions, further cementing their understanding of and control over these features. Fang (2010) described a range of such tasks at the levels of word (e.g., morphemic analysis, vocabulary think chart, conception definition word map, word sort); phrase (e.g., noun deconstruction, building noun trains, noun search, definition game); sentence (sentence combining and syntactic anatomy); and discourse (e.g., sentence completion, noticing textual signposts, paraphrasing). Several principles are worth keeping in mind when designing these tasks: (1) Use authentic examples from the texts students are reading and writing, (2) make explicit links between the language feature being introduced and how it works in the text students are reading/writing, (3) explain the linguistic features through examples, not dictionary definitions or lengthy abstract explanations (Fang, 2021b; Myhill et al., 2013).

Scientific meaning is typically made in some combination of words, images, graphs, and mathematics signs. There is "close and constant integration and cross-contextualization" among various semiotic modalities in science texts, making it both normal and necessary to interpret the verbal text in relation to other semiotic formations, and vice versa (Lemke, 2004, p. 39). This means it is also important to consider students' multimodal competence in science reading. In other words, developing students' ability to effectively navigate multimodal/multisemiotic textual environments is key to comprehension of science multimedia genres. According to Lemke (2002), "Advanced scientific literacy means both using advanced literacy skills specific to scientific activity and making specialized scientific meanings that cannot be made without using some language, in conjunction with other semiotic resources" (p. 42).

Scholars have suggested ways multimodal competence can be fostered in conjunction with science language proficiency. Lemke (2004) recommended that science educators create partnerships with verbal literacy educators and with visual media educators to promote more explicit attention to teaching students how to read science multimedia genres. More specifically, he encouraged teachers to (1) make more use of gestural and visual representations and numerical tables and graphs in their instruction, and (2) provide opportunities for students to not only do hands-on science and talk and write science in words, but also draw, tabulate, graph, geometrize, and algebrize science in all possible combinations. He additionally highlighted the importance of (1) helping students understand the conventions that connect verbal text with visual images, and (2) giving students practice in translating back and forth among verbal accounts, mathematical expressions and calculations, schematic diagrams, abstract graphs, and hands-on actions. Similarly, Tang and Putra (2018) suggested giving students practice in making observations and translating inscriptions from one form to another in the process of conducting experiments and collecting data, such as modeling an experimental procedure and translating the procedure into a flowchart that students can then use to guide their experiment.

The process through which meanings are transformed from one semiotic system (e.g., language) to another (e.g., visual) is called *resemiotization*. One useful tool for resemiotization is *sketchnote*. Sketchnote is "a visual thinking form that integrates notes and sketches to explain scientific topics" (Fernandez-Fontecha et al., 2018, p. 7). It is a multimodal complex made up of language and visual resources. Using sketchnotes, teachers and students can create a visual representation of complex scientific content in their texts. This renders abstract, complex ideas more accessible and digestible, facilitates reading comprehension, and promotes visual thinking and multimodal competence. More activities for infusing the use of multimodal representation in science classrooms can be found in Hand et al. (2016).

Learning to Read Like a Scientist

Viewing science reading from a disciplinary literacy lens requires that students learn to read science texts like a scientist. Science texts are not repositories of immutable facts. They communicate scientists' interpretations of the universe through "motivated conjunctions of form and meaning" (Kress, 2003, p. 169). As Lemke (2002) has argued, scientific texts are not just about matters of fact and explanation; they make meaning about "desirability, importance, permissibility, expectedness, and all the other value dimensions" (p. 28). From this perspective, then, science texts are never neutral: They are imbued with authorial intentions, beliefs, attitudes, and values. Given the constructed nature of science texts and scientific knowledge, it is important that students adopt a critical stance in science reading, paying close attention to not only what evidence (if any) is used and the quality of the evidence but also how this evidence is presented, linguistically and/or visually, to support a particular claim or argument.

While it may be argued that not all students will be future scientists, there is still a need for them as citizens to develop this critical reading ability. We are living in the age of science, and no one can live a productive, fulfilling life without at least some interaction with science. Current issues related to science often appear as headlines in newspapers, websites, and other media outlets, from stories of Rover's landing on Mars and Hurricane Ian's destructive power to health news about the Coronavirus and calls to combat global warming and cyberterrorism. These reports can distort the original source by, for example, omitting potentially important details or evidence, twisting logic, diminishing substantive claims, overextrapolating or overgeneralizing research results, foregrounding applications, or taking things out of context. Having the ability to detect these distortions or inconsistencies is critical to maintaining an informed citizenry and a vibrant democracy. Developing this critical reading ability is especially important in the current sociopolitical climate, where what counts as science, evidence, facts, or news is being debated with intense heat and considerable rancor.

One approach to developing critical reading in science is to read multiple texts on the same topic or the same text from different perspectives. Students should have opportunities to analyze, evaluate, problematize, and transform texts on a regular basis, interrogating the values, points of view, prejudices, and ideologies underpinning the text. Teachers can have students read supplementary texts that cover topics or issues glossed over or avoided in traditional science textbooks. They can also have students read multiple texts on the same topic to gain insights into how different authors present the same topic from different angles and with different interpretations. For example, Ivermectin, a drug often used to treat parasites in animals, was touted in some media circles as a promising treatment for COVID-19, even though the Food and Drug Administration has cautioned against its use for COVID-19. Without the ability to think critically about what is presented in the media and the disposition to check one source against another and weigh the evidence, students may be victimized by misinformation.

When reading a text, students can learn to ask and respond to such questions as these: (1) What is the author's background and affiliation? (2) Who/what sponsors the publication? (3) Who/what is or is not represented in the text and why? (4) What evidence is provided to support a claim or argument? (5) What is the quality of this piece of evidence, and how was it generated? (6) Is the evidence sufficiently relevant, credible, and complete? (7) Whose interest is best served by the message of the text? (8) How are various groups/individuals positioned by the text? (9) How do particular content, discourse genres, methodology, and mode of inquiry become privileged and acquire power in science? (10) How does such privileging affect access, equity, and learning? (11) What action might you take on the basis of what you have learned? (Behrman, 2006). For multimodal texts, students can, in addition, discuss why a certain image (e.g., graph, chart, table, diagram, map) is included or excluded, where the image came from, how the image is positioned in relation to verbal text, what is foregrounded or backgrounded in the image, and whether the image enhances, supplements, or contradicts the message in verbal text.

Teachers can also promote critical reading by encouraging students to make connections between what they read in the text and what they see in their everyday lifeworlds. For example, when reading texts on erosion, the teacher can ask students to examine the erosion that exists on their school grounds (Alvermann & Wilson, 2011). Students can obtain background information about their campus through old photographs, interviews, newspaper clippings, or televised footages. They can analyze these verbal and visual texts to better understand the environment in which they live. They can also create images of their campus before and after erosion, interview various members of the community to elicit their reactions to the state of the campus, and compare/contrast opinions across groups. In short, connecting what is read to students' immediate surroundings can deepen their engagement with the text topic and their understanding of the text content while at the same time stimulating their interest in science and developing science literacy.

Another way to foster critical reading ability in science is to promote critical language awareness, that is, to help students become aware of how language choices in science texts—such as nouns (e.g., ***some** scientists, deforestation*); adjectives (e.g., *at an **alarming** 8.5% per decade*); verbs (e.g., *hypothesize, claim, conclude, suggest*); modal verbs (***will** double, **might** alter*); adverbs (e.g., *have **gradually** changed, is **somewhat** problematic, declined **significantly***); and prepositional phrases (e.g., ***In the past 2 million years,** there have been many major ice ages*)—present knowledge, infuse points of view, construe precision, moderate or boost claims, and facilitate discursive flow (Fang et al., 2019; Román & Busch, 2015; Zhu & Fang, 2019). During close reading, teachers can highlight a range of lexical, grammatical, and discursive features that express affect, judgment, or appreciation (e.g., *Influenza A viruses are **constantly** changing, making it possible on **very rare** occasions for non-human influenza viruses to change in such a way that they can infect people **easily** and spread **efficiently** from person to person*); convey degree of certainty, usuality, normality, or likelihood (e.g., *Increased sea levels **will** cause flooding of low-lying coastal areas. More storms **could** increase the damage caused to the state*); and bury agency to promote objectivity and to foreground ideas/concepts and background processes (e.g., *More than one-fourth of the world's coral reefs **have been lost** to **coastal development, pollution, overfishing, warm ocean temperatures,** and **other stresses** that are increasing*). These analyses help students uncover the hidden messages in the text, gain a more nuanced understanding of authorial voice, expand their linguistic repertoires for making-meaning in more purposeful and effective ways, and develop a critical orientation in text reading (see Martin & White, 2005). They can become an integral part of science literacy instruction.

A HEURISTIC FOR TEACHING READING IN SCIENCE

Reading is not just a cognitive activity; it is also a social process because every act of reading takes place in a specific context for a specific purpose. For this reason, Patterson et al. (2018) recommended that reading in science class be done with specific goals defined by the practices of doing science (e.g., developing conceptual understanding, identifying cause–effect relations, constructing explanations, engaging in argument from evidence, understanding how scientists use language to present information and logical reasoning), and that teachers make the goals of reading in science explicit to their students. This section describes a heuristic that science (or reading) teachers can use to help build science content knowledge, develop science language proficiency and multimodal competence, and promote scientific habits of mind in the process of conducting science inquiries.

The heuristic, captured in Figure 4.2, is called the five E's, or enquiry–engage–examine–exercise–extend (Fang et al., 2019; Fang, 2020, 2021b). It places *enquiry* in the center of the instructional cycle, inviting students to explore a question or issue that is of personal interest and/or disciplinary significance in a unit of study through a variety of activities and tasks that are authentic to the discipline and meaningful to students. A key component of these social practices is the use of texts. As students *engage* with these texts, they utilize the strategies scientists use to help them make sense of these texts (e.g., predicting, inferring, setting purpose, questioning, skimming, rereading, evaluating, storying, verifying, cross-checking, visualizing, drawing inferences, summarizing, paraphrasing, taking notes, making connections). Challenging and important portions of these texts are then selected for close reading. During close reading, students *examine* how authors use language (and other semiotic resources) to present information, structure text, infuse points of view, engage with and position the reader, and express epistemic commitment to knowledge claims. Next, *exercises* are designed to help students cement their understanding of—as well as develop their facility in using—key or unfamiliar features of science language and scientific habits of mind. In the end, students write to *extend* and communicate their understanding of the focal topic and target genre by using the linguistic/semiotic resources and habits of mind highlighted in the unit.

To illustrate how this heuristic works, we describe a middle school science unit on humidity and the water cycle in which students *enquire* into scientific questions (e.g., What is humidity? What is the water cycle? What

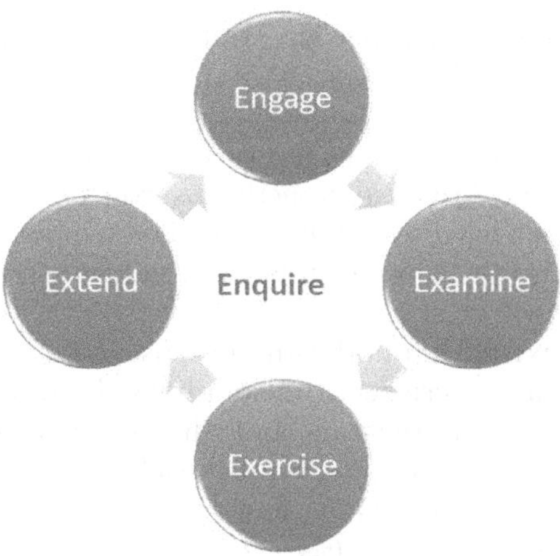

FIGURE 4.2. Five E's pedagogical heuristic (Fang et al., 2019, p. 8). Copyright © 2019 Emerald Publishing, Inc. Reprinted by permission.

is the relationship between humidity and the water cycle? How does humidity affect the health of people, animals, and plants?) through both firsthand (hands-on investigations) and secondhand (reading/talking/writing) experiences. The unit was developed by a team of science and literacy teacher educators at the University of Florida to serve as a model for preservice teachers who were required to plan disciplinary literacy instruction that integrates reading/literacy and science (Hershfield & Fang, 2015). Relevant science standards addressed in this model unit include science/engineering practices (e.g., asking questions and defining problems, developing and using models, planning and carrying out investigations, using mathematics and computational thinking, engaging in argument from evidence, evaluating and communicating knowledge); disciplinary core ideas (e.g., the role of water in the earth's surface processes, weather and climate, global climate change); and crosscutting concepts (e.g., cause–effect, systems and system models, stability and change). It also addresses the literacy standards in the CCSS, such as (1) cite specific textual evidence to support analysis of science and technical texts (RST.6–8.1); (2) determine the central ideas or conclusions of a text (RST 6–8.2); (3) determine the meaning of symbols, key terms, and other domain-specific words and phrases as they are used in specific scientific or technical context; (RST.6–8.4); (4) compare and contrast the information gained from experiments, simulations, video, or multimedia sources with that gained from reading a text on the same topic (RST.6–8.9); and (5) read and comprehend science/technical texts in the grades 6–8 text complexity band independently and proficiently (RST6–8.10).

To start the unit, the teacher has students in small groups discuss the questions posed in the following scenario:

> "You take a short walk outside. It is early in the morning and the temperature is only 80° Fahrenheit. Nonetheless, you are sweating. Why? Now you go into your luxury mobile home. The temperature in the mobile home also reads 80° Fahrenheit, but you suddenly feel cool. Why?"

This gets students excited about the unit because it relates the topic (humidity) to their personal experience. It also allows the teacher to assess how much students know about the topic and whether there are misunderstandings about the topic. After discussion, the teacher asks each group to complete two experiments over the next few days, one on humidity (see Figure 4.3) and the other on water cycle (see *https://old.miniscience.com/projects/watercycle/index.html*). Students record and graph their findings from the experiments and discuss what they found.

Firsthand experiences like these help students develop initial conceptual understanding of humidity and water cycle and at the same time get them

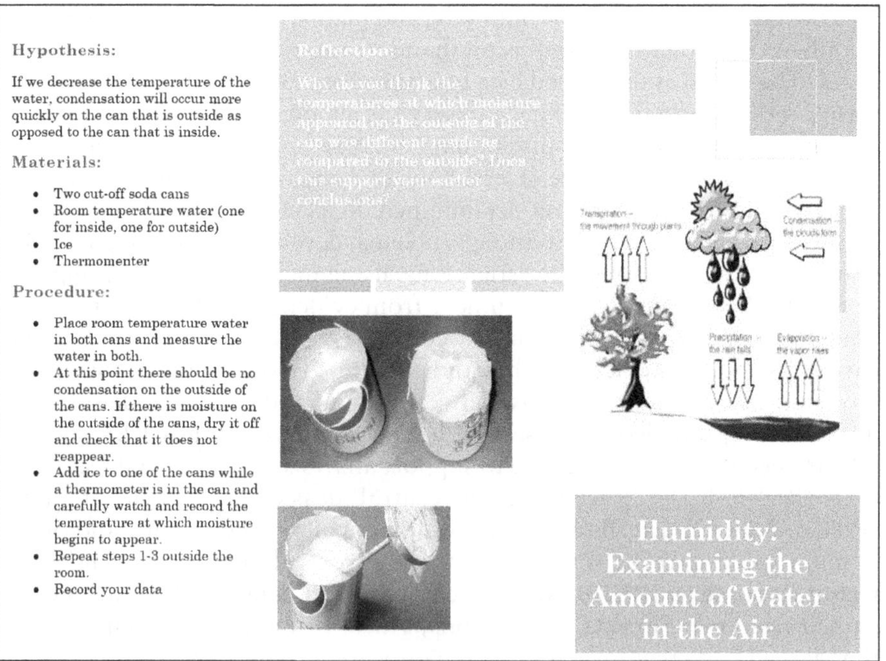

FIGURE 4.3. Science experiment 1.

interested in exploring the topic. To further develop their understanding of the key concepts in the unit, the teacher *engages* students in reading-related texts on the topic. These texts come from traditional textbooks, trade books, magazines, and websites, varying in text difficulty such that the easier texts help build background knowledge and motivation for the reading of more challenging texts. Some of these texts are used for class read-alouds, when the teacher models how to read like a scientist, using the same strategies that scientists use to read carefully, critically, and with a healthy skepticism. Other texts are for independent reading, when students are expected to take notes, ask questions, make connections, weigh evidence, evaluate statements, and draw inferences as they read. Students also get to share their understanding, questions, and wonderings in a small group and/or with the whole class. Through reading and discussing these texts, students increase their content knowledge about humidity and the water cycle and gain exposure to the sort of language that constructs the content.

The next step in the five E's heuristic involves selecting challenging text excerpts for close reading. The teacher selects an excerpt (see Figure 4.4) from a science textbook (Ahrens, 1999, p. 112), reading it two times, the first for general understanding and the second with a functional-critical focus on language and image, *examining* how lexical, grammatical, and

A change in relative humidity *can be brought about* in *two primary ways*:

1. by changing the air's water vapor content, and
2. by changing the air temperature.

In Fig. 4,11a, we can see that *an increase in the water vapor content of the air* (*with* no change in air temperature) *increases the air's relative humidity. The reason for this increase resides in the fact that, as* more water vapor molecules are added to the air, there is *a greater likelihood* that some of the vapor molecules will *stick together and condense. Condensation* takes place in saturated air. *Therefore, as* more and more water vapor molecules are added to the air, the air *gradually* approaches saturation, *and* the relative humidity of the air increases. *Conversely, removing water vapor* from the air decreases *the likelihood of saturation, which* lowers the air's relative humidity. *In summary, with* no change in air temperature, adding water vapor to the air increases the relative humidity; removing water vapor from the air lowers the relative humidity.

These changes in relative humidity are important in determining *the amount of evaporation from vegetation and wet surfaces.* If you water your lawn on a hot afternoon, *when* the relative humidity is low, much of the water will evaporate quickly from the lawn, instead of soaking into the ground. Watering the same lawn in the evening or during the early morning, *when* the relative humidity is higher, will cut down the evaporation and increase *the effectiveness of the watering.*

FIGURE 4.4. Sample textbook excerpt for close reading (Ahrens, 1999, p. 112).

visual choices present meaning in more or less transparent ways relevant to the intended reader of the text.

For example, the teacher discusses the obvious issue of technical vocabulary such as *molecules*, *saturation*, *condensation*, and *relative humidity*, as well as general academic vocabulary (e.g., *reside, approach, conversely, determine*). She also draws students' attention to less obvious but equally important text features (italicized in the text), as outlined in Table 4.1. Reading text closely and critically this way deepens students' understanding of the text content and makes them become more aware of the ways scientists use language and visuals to fashion meaning in discipline-legitimated ways.

Next, the teacher highlights nominalization, one of the most important and pervasive resources used in scientific meaning-making. Using examples from the close reading excerpt and other texts students have read, the teacher explains how nominalization allows the author to summarize and distill information, bury agency, create technicality, and facilitate discursive flow. She also designs sentence completion *exercises*, such as the example below, to show students how nominalization works:

> As the air cools during the night, the relative humidity increases. Normally, the highest relative humidity occurs in the early morning, during the coolest part of the day. As the air warms during the day, the relative humidity decreases, with the lowest values usually occurring during the warmest part of the afternoon. __________ are important in determining the amount of evaporation from vegetation and wet surfaces. [*Answer*: These changes (in relative humidity)]

Finally, the teacher has students write a text that (1) explains how humidity relates to the water cycle and/or (2) discusses how humidity impacts the health of humans, animals, or plants. They go through the writing process of brainstorming, drafting, revising, editing, and publishing, with an emphasis on revision, where students focus on how verbal and visual choices realize the purpose of their text and present its content. A writing sample from the National Geographic website (*www.nationalgeographic.org/encyclopedia/humidity*) is shared with the class and analyzed and critiqued with respect to its content, organization, and style, as well as language choices, so that students understand what is expected of them for the assignment. This task clarifies, enhances, and *extends* students' conceptual understanding while also providing an opportunity for them to apply some of the verbal/visual skills and habits of mind highlighted in the unit.

As a whole, the unit creates experiences that engage students in three-dimensional learning as recommended by the NGSS. It offers students the

TABLE 4.1. Focal Text Features and Teacher Comments during Close Reading

Focal text features	Teacher comments
can be brought about	• "Why is passive voice, instead of active voice, used here?" • "What is the actor being buried?" • "Why is agency backgrounded?" • "The modal verb *can* here denotes possibility, not ability, meaning that it is possible to bring about a change in relative humidity."
two primary ways	• "What are some other, primary or minor, ways of bringing about change in relative humidity beyond the two mentioned in the text?"
In Figure 4.11a	• "Where does the figure come from? Does the author indicate the source? Is the source reliable?" • "What information is presented in the graph?" • "Does this information match what is described in the verbal text?" • "What information is highlighted or left out in the verbal text? Why?"
we	• "To whom does this pronoun refer? Does it refer to the author, the reader, the author and the reader, or the scientific community in general? It is likely used here as a way of engaging the reader and invoking a sense of community and shared responsibility between the author and the reader." • "In scientific and academic writing, it is becoming more common for the author to embrace a more direct and egalitarian relationship with readers (through the use of the first-person plural *we*) in order to engage and persuade them."
an increase in the water vapor content of the air	• "This is a long noun phrase with *increase* as the head, and *in the water vapor content of the air* is a prepositional phrase serving as a qualifier specifying what increases."
with no change in air temperature	• "The use of the preposition *with* conflates condition and temporality, meaning 'if/when there is no change in air temperature.' "
an increase vs. increases	• "The word *increase* is used as a noun and a verb in the same sentence."
the air's relative humidity	• "This possessive noun phrase can also be reworded using a prepositional phrase, as in 'the relative humidity of the air.' Normally, the possessive is used when the possessor is animated. Here, the possessor *air* is not an animated entity, however."

(*continued*)

TABLE 4.1. *(continued)*

Focal text features	Teacher comments
The reason . . . resides in . . .	• "This is one way of expressing causation within the same clause. The conjunction *because* could have been used, but it will require two clauses (main clause + subordinate clause) to express the same logical meaning." • "*Reside in* is equivalent to the linking verb *is*. It identifies the cause of the increase."
this increase	• "The phrase (demonstrative + noun) is a nominalization referring to the clause *increases the air's relative humidity* in the previous sentence. Its use facilitates the transition from one sentence to the next. This is one way discursive flow is created in science writing."
the fact that . . .	• "This is a complementary noun clause, with *the fact* serving as a nominalization that distills the ideas presented in the subsequent clauses: *as more water vapor molecules are added to the air, there is a greater likelihood that some of the vapor molecules will stick together and condense*."
a greater likelihood	• "This is a nominalization that could have been expressed in more everyday language as 'is more likely.' " • "What does *likelihood* mean? Does it mean 25% chance, 60% chance, 80% chance, or 95% chance?"
stick together and condense . . . Condensation . . .	• "*Condensation* here is a nominalization of *stick together and condense* in the preceding clause. It distills a process (*stick together and condense*) into a technical concept, making it the subject of the ensuing sentence. This is how scientists create technical terminology and information flow at the same time in text construction."
Therefore	• "This adverb indicates causality. What comes after the word is the effect, but can the cause be pinpointed? The cause is usually indicated in the sentence(s) or even paragraph(s) preceding it. Exactly which sentence(s) indicate(s) the cause here?"
as more and more water vapor molecules are added to the air . . .	• "The conjunction *as* conflates condition (*if*), temporality (*when*), and causality (*because*) at the same time. This sort of ambiguity benefits disciplinary insiders because they have the requisite background knowledge to resolve it."
the air gradually approaches saturation,	• "The adverb *gradually* is a hedging device used to increase precision in scientific meaning-making. It tells us saturation is not reached in a jiffy." • "Scientific and academic writing generally privileges caution, possibility, and delimited claims over certainty. This stance is achieved through the use of a variety of hedging devices, such as modal verbs (e.g., *could*, *might*), verbs (e.g., *appear to*, *suggest*, *surmise*), nouns (e.g., *assumption*, *likelihood*, *possibility*), adverbs (e.g., *approximately*, *usually*, *hypothetically*, *maybe*), adjectives (e.g., *probable*, *tentative*, *questionable*), and phrases (e.g., *to our knowledge*, *in some sense*, *to a certain extent*)."

(continued)

TABLE 4.1. *(continued)*

Focal text features	Teacher comments
and the relative humidity of the air increases.	• "The conjunction *and* implies causality, with the cause expressed in the preceding clause *the air gradually approaches saturation* and the effect in the clause following *and*."
conversely	• "This adverb indicates that the author is going to present something that is in opposition to what has just been discussed."
Removing the water vapor from the air decreases the likelihood of saturation.	• "Agency is buried here via the use of a gerund phrase (*removing the water vapor*) as the subject of the sentence and a nominalization (*the likelihood of saturation*) as the object of the sentence. This is the kind of compact syntax that scientists privilege—two noun phrases joined by a verb. It enables authors to reason logically (in this case, causally) within, rather than between, clauses." • "What or who removes the water vapor from air? How is the water vapor removed from air? What gets saturated? What is the degree of probability in getting saturated?"
which lowers the air's relative humidity	• "This is a nonrestrictive relative clause. But what does the pronoun *which* refer to? Does it refer to *the likelihood of saturation* or the idea expressed in the entire clause *removing the water from the air decreases the likelihood of saturation*? This kind of writing benefits experts but disadvantages students who may not have the requisite background knowledge to make the right inference."
In summary	• "This phrase signals that the author is ready to sum up what has just been discussed. So pay attention; this is likely where I can find the main idea of the paragraph."
with no change in air temperature . . .	• "The prepositional phrase is a metaphoric expression of what would normally be presented in a clause. It buries the logical meaning that would have become evident if a clause is used. Is the logical relationship being expressed here conditional (***if*** *no change in air temperature occurs*), temporal (***when*** *no change in air temperature occurs*), causal (***because*** *no change in air temperature occurs*), or a conflation of all three?" • "Again, this is how scientists reason logically within, rather than between, clauses. This kind of writing creates ambiguity that benefits disciplinary insiders."
These changes	• "This phrase is a nominalization that refers to the changes in relative humidity described in the preceding paragraph." • "Scientists use nominalizations like this one to summarize and distill previously presented information so that they can further discuss the idea."

(continued)

TABLE 4.1. *(continued)*

Focal text features	Teacher comments
the amount of evaporation from vegetation and wet surfaces	• "This is a long noun phrase with nominalizations (*amount*, *evaporation*) embedded. It enables scientists to compact information for within-clause logical reasoning. In more everyday language, the same information is usually expressed as 'how much water evaporates from vegetation and wet surfaces.' "
when	• "The adverb *when* in the last two sentences of the last paragraph is used to introduce a nonrestrictive relative clause that provides extra, often nonessential, information about *a hot afternoon* and *the early morning*, respectively." • "This is another way scientists create dense sentence and at the same time stay focused on the main idea. Had each adverbial clause introduced by *when* been rewritten into an independent clause, the information it presents would have become equal in importance to the information presented in the main clause of the original sentence. This rewording would result in diffusion of focus and disruption of information flow."
the effectiveness of the watering	• "This is a highly abstract noun phrase with two nominalizations (*effectiveness*, *the watering*) embedded. The phrase *the watering* refers to the process of watering the lawn described in the beginning of the sentence." • "The use of nominalizations increases abstraction but at the same time facilitates the construction of compact sentences with 'abstract/long noun phrase (as subject) + verb + abstract/long noun phrase (as object)' structure. This is one main reason students feel turned off when reading science texts. In everyday language, the same amount of information is spread out in more clauses, making it easier to process and comprehend."

opportunity to engage in some of the same *practices* that scientists use in scientific inquiry, including asking questions, carrying out investigations, reading relevant sources, analyzing and interpreting data, reasoning with evidence, constructing explanations, and communicating information. It allows students to see how *crosscutting concepts*, such as cause–effect and pattern, are essential to understanding not only life sciences but also earth science. Equally important, students are able to learn some of the *core ideas* about weather, climate, and the environment by reading/discussing science texts and engaging in science practices.

CONCLUSION

Reading plays a pivotal role in science learning. It helps students identify questions or problems for inquiry, gain information on the topic and process of inquiry, consolidate understanding of core concepts and ideas, evaluate competing explanations of scientific phenomena, enhance understanding of epistemology of science, develop scientific habits of mind, and learn the language for construing and communicating scientific understanding (Goldman et al., 2016). To become scientifically literate, students need to develop the ability to read science texts carefully, deeply, critically, and with a heathy skepticism. This development work seems best suited for science teachers because, as Lemke (2002) has argued, they seem better prepared to teach science reading than are reading teachers, at least in the sense that they could acquire the necessary reading concepts in far less time than reading teachers would require to master the necessary scientific ones.

It is worth noting, however, that preparing science teachers for reading instruction is by no means an easy undertaking, for, as research (Fang et al., 2008; Patrick & Fang, 2022) has shown, they, too, may struggle with the sometimes technical content of reading (e.g., understanding the cognitive processes underpinning and the procedures for teaching a reading strategy, understanding the forms and functions of science language, learning a linguistic metalanguage for text exploration) and require ongoing support to design and deliver an integrated science-reading curriculum. The beliefs and attitudes many science teachers hold toward reading—such as "Science is primarily an empirical (hands-on) subject, with reading serving only a supportive role"; "I am not an English teacher; it's not my job to teach reading"; or "Reading is an optional extra; I can wait until I have time in my curriculum to teach it"—could likewise present a barrier to their development of expertise in reading instruction. Finally, the existing school structure and culture (e.g., compartmentalized curriculum, lack of incentives for cross-disciplinary collaboration, lack of support for sustained and focused professional development) may not be conducive to the promotion of reading and reading instruction in science classrooms.

Addressing these challenges requires concerted efforts from science teachers, science teacher educators, school/district administrators, curriculum developers, and national/state policy makers to make reading a more prominent and integral part of the science curriculum. Central to these efforts is a reconceptualization of the relationship between reading and science. Instead of seeing reading as merely a handmaiden in service of science, science educators need to view reading as a constitutive part of science and an essential component of the content of science that must be taught and learned in school. Science teachers who embrace this new perspective will be more eager to develop knowledge of reading and expertise in reading instruction and thus better positioned to promote science literacy through reading. One promising approach to promoting science literacy is by regularly engaging students in reading and discussion of texts on science-related topics and at the same time conducting close reading sessions that explicitly teach students how to read like a scientist and draw their attention to how verbal and visual choices shape meaning in genre-specific, discipline-legitimated ways. That is, a disciplinary literacy approach that emphasizes the building of science content knowledge, development of science language skills and multimodal competence, and cultivation of scientific habits of mind in the context of authentic science inquiries is more likely to succeed in improving students' science reading ability and raising their science literacy achievement.

REFERENCES

Ahrens, C. D. (1999). *Meteorology today: An introduction to weather, climate, and the environment* (6th ed.). Brooks Cole.

Almasi, J., & Fullerton, S. (2012). *Teaching strategic processes in reading* (2nd ed.). Guilford Press.

Alvermann, D., & Wilson, A. (2011). Comprehension strategy instruction for multimodal texts in science. *Theory into Practice*, *50*(2), 116–124.

Arrington, C., Kulesz, P., Francis, D., Fletcher, J., & Barnes, M. (2014). The contribution of attentional control and working memory to reading comprehension and decoding. *Scientific Studies of Reading*, *18*, 325–346.

August, D., Branum-Martin, L., Cardenas-Hagan, E., & Francis, D. (2009). The impact of an instructional intervention on the science and language learning of middle grade English language learners. *Journal of Research on Educational Effectiveness*, *2*(4), 354–376.

Barber, A., & Klauda, S. (2020). How reading motivation and engagement enable reading achievement: Policy implications. *Policy Insights from the Behavioral and Brain Sciences*, *7*(1), 27–34.

Bazerman, C. (1985). Physicists reading physics: Schema-laden purposes and purpose-laden schema. *Written Communication*, *2*(1), 3–23.

Behrman, E. (2006). Teaching about language, power, and text: A review of classroom practices that support critical literacy. *Journal of Adolescent and Adult Literacy*, *49*, 490-498.

Biber, D., & Gray, B. (2010). Challenging stereotypes about academic writing: Complexity, elaboration, explicitness. *Journal of English for Academic Purposes*, *9*(1), 2–20.

Cervetti, G., Barber, J., Dorph, R., Pearson, D., & Goldschmidt, P. (2012). The impact of an integrated approach to science and literacy in elementary school classrooms. *Journal of Research in Science Teaching*, *49*(5), 631–658.

Cervetti, G., & Wright, T. (2020). The role of knowledge in understanding and learning from text. In E. Moje, P. Afflerbach, P. Enciso, & N. Lesaux (Eds.), *Handbook of reading research* (Vol. 5, pp. 237–260). Routledge.

Chin, J. (2017). *Grand Canyon*. Roaring Book Press.

Christie, F., & Maton, K. (2011). *Disciplinarity: Functional linguistic and sociological perspectives*. Bloomsbury.

Cromley, J., Snyder-Hogan, L., & Luciw-Dubas, U. (2010). Reading comprehension of scientific text: A domain-specific test of the direct and inferential mediation model of reading comprehension. *Journal of Educational Psychology, 102*(3), 687–700.

Denton, C., Enos, M., York, M., Francis, D., Barnes, M., Kulesz, P., . . . Carter, S. (2015). Text processing differences in adolescent adequate and poor comprehenders reading accessible and challenging narrative and informational text. *Reading Research Quarterly, 50*, 393–416.

DiCerbo, P., Anstrom, K., Baker, L., & Rivera, C. (2014). A review of the literature on teaching academic English to English language learners. *Review of Educational Research, 84*(3), 446–482.

Fairweather, E., & Fairweather, T. (2010). A method for understanding their method: Discovering scientific inquiry through biographies of famous scientists. *Science Scope, 33*(9), 23–30.

Fang, Z. (2005). Science literacy: A systemic functional linguistics perspective. *Science Education, 89*(2), 335–347.

Fang, Z. (2006). The language demands of science reading in middle school. *International Journal of Science Education, 28*(5), 491–520.

Fang, Z. (2008). Going beyond the Fab Five: Helping students cope with the unique linguistic challenges of expository reading in intermediate grades. *Journal of Adolescent and Adult Literacy, 51*(6), 476–487.

Fang, Z. (2010). *Language and literacy in inquiry-based science classrooms, grades 3–8*. Corwin and NSTA Press.

Fang, Z. (2012). The challenges of reading disciplinary texts. In T. Jetton & C. Shanahan (Eds.), *Adolescent literacy in the academic disciplines: General principles and practical strategies* (pp. 34–68). Guilford Press.

Fang, Z. (2013). Disciplinary literacy in science: Developing science literacy through trade books. *Journal of Adolescent and Adult Literacy, 57*(4), 274–278.

Fang, Z. (2016). Teaching close reading with complex texts across content areas. *Research in the Teaching of English, 51*(1), 106–116.

Fang, Z. (2020). Toward a linguistically informed, responsive, and embedded pedagogy in secondary literacy instruction. *Journal of World Languages, 6*(1–2), 70–91.

Fang, Z. (2021a). *Demystifying academic writing: Genres, moves, skills, and strategies*. Routledge.

Fang, Z. (2021b). *Using functional grammar in English literacy teaching and learning*. Foreign Language Teaching and Research Press.

Fang, Z., Adams, B., Gresser, V., & Li, C. (2019). Developing critical literacy through an SFL-informed pedagogical heuristic. *English Teaching: Practice and Critique, 18*(1), 4–17.

Fang, Z., & Chapman, S. (2015). Enhancing English learners' access to disciplinary texts through close reading practices. In M. Daniel & M. Kouider (Eds.), *Research and practice that makes a difference in English learners' success* (pp. 3–18). Rowan & Littlefield.

Fang, Z., Gresser, V., Cao, P., & Zheng, J. (2021). Nominal complexities in school children's informational writing. *Journal of English for Academic Purposes, 50*.

Fang, Z., Lamme, L., Pringle, R., Patrick, J., Sanders, J., Zmach, C., . . . Henkel, M. (2008). Integrating reading into middle school science: What we did, found, and learned. *International Journal of Science Education, 30*(15), 2067–2089.

Fang, Z., & Schleppegrell, M. (2008). *Reading in secondary content areas: A language-based pedagogy*. University of Michigan Press.

Fang, Z., & Schleppegrell, M. J. (2010). Disciplinary literacies across content areas: Supporting secondary reading through functional language analysis. *Journal of Adolescent and Adult Literacy. 53*(7), 587–597.

Fang, Z., Schleppegrell, M., & Cox, B. (2006). Understanding the language demands of schooling: Nouns in academic registers. *Journal of Literacy Research. 38*(3), 247–273.

Fang, Z., & Wei, Y. (2010). Improving middle school students' science literacy through reading infusion. *Journal of Educational Research, 103*(4), 262–273.

Fernandez-Fontecha, A., O'Halloran, K., Tan, S., & Wignell, P. (2018). A multimodal approach to visual thinking: The scientific sketchnote. *Visual Communication, 18*(1), 5–29.

Goldman, S., Britt, M., Brown, W., Cribb, G., George, M., Greenleaf, C., . . . Project READI. (2016). Disciplinary literacies and learning to read for understanding: A conceptual framework for disciplinary literacy. *Educational Psychologist, 51*(2), 219–246.

Halliday, M. (2006). *The language of science* (J. Webster, Ed.). Continuum.

Halliday, M., & Martin, J. (1993). *Writing science: Literacy and discursive power.* University of Pittsburgh Press.

Hand, B., McDermott, M., & Prain, V. (2016). *Using multimodal representations to support learning in the science classroom.* Springer.

Hershfield, S., & Fang, Z. (2015). *Humidity and water cycle.* A science unit developed for Project ADePT Summer Institute, University of Florida, Gainesville, FL.

Hirsch, E. D. (2006). *The knowledge deficit: Closing the shocking education gap for American children.* Houghton Mifflin.

Kintsch, W. (1998). *Comprehension: A paradigm for cognition.* Cambridge University Press.

Kress, G. (2003). *Literacy in the new media age.* Routledge.

Kress, G., Jewitt, C., Ogborn, J., & Tsatsarelis, C. (2001). *Multimodal teaching and learning: The rhetorics of the science classroom.* Continuum.

Lee, O., Quinn, H., & Valdes, G. (2013). Science and language for English language learners in relation to next generation science standards and with implications for common core state standards for English language arts and mathematics. *Educational Researcher, 42*(4), 223–233.

Lemke, J. (2002). Multimedia semiotics: Genres for science education and science literacy. In M. Schleppegrell & C. Colombi (Eds.), *Developing advanced literacy in first and second languages* (pp. 21–44). Erlbaum.

Lemke, J. (2004). The literacies of science. In E. W. Saul (Ed.), *Crossing borders in literacy and science instruction: Perspectives on theory and practice* (pp. 33–47). International Reading Association and NSTA Press.

Lonigan, C., Burgess, C., & Schatschneider, C. (2018). Examining the simple view of reading with elementary school children: Still simple after all these years. *Remedial and Special Education, 39*, 260–273.

Martin, J., & White, P. (2005), *The language of evaluation: Appraisal in English.* Palgrave.

McNamara, D., Ozuru, Y., & Floyd, R. (2011). Comprehension challenges in the fourth grade: The roles of text cohesion, text genre, and readers' prior knowledge. *International Electronic Journal of Elementary Education*, *4*(1), 229–257.

Monhardt, R. (2005). Reading and writing nonfiction with children: Using biographies to learn about science and scientists. *Science Scope*, *28*(6), 16–19.

Myhill, D., Jones, S., Watson, A., & Lines, H. (2013). Playful explicitness with grammar: A pedagogy for writing. *Literacy*, *47*(2), 103–111.

National Governors Association Center for Best Practices & Council of Chief State School Officers. (2010). *Common core state standards for English language arts and literacy in history/social studies, science, and technical subjects.* Authors.

National Research Council. (2012). *A framework for K–12 science education: Practices, crosscutting concepts, and core ideas.* National Academies Press.

NGSS Lead States. (2013). *Next generation science standards: For states, by states.* National Academies Press.

Norris, S., & Phillips, L. (2003). How literacy in its fundamental sense is central to scientific literacy. *Science Education*, *87*(2), 224–240.

O'Reilly, T., & McNamara, D. (2007). The impact of science knowledge, reading skill, and reading strategy knowledge on more traditional "high stakes" measures of high school students' science achievement. *American Educational Research Journal*, *44*(1), 161–196.

Osborne, J. (2002). Science without literacy: A ship without a sail? *Cambridge Journal of Education*, *32*(2), 203–218.

Patrick, J., & Fang, Z. (2022). High school science teachers learning to teach reading through a functional focus on language: Toward a grounded theory of teacher learning. In L. Seah, R. Silver, & M. Baildon (Eds.), *The role of language in content pedagogy: A framework for teachers' knowledge* (pp. 61–85). Springer.

Patterson, A., Roman, D., Friend, M., Osborne, J., & Donovan, B. (2018). Reading for meaning: The foundational knowledge every teacher of science should have. *International Journal of Science Education*, *40*(3), 291–307.

Pearson, D., Palincsar, A., Biancarosa, G., & Berman, A. (2020). *Reaping the rewards of the Reading for Understanding Initiative.* National Academy of Education.

Reed, D., Petscher, Y., & Truckenmiller, A. (2016). The contribution of general reading ability to science achievement. *Reading Research Quarterly*, *52*(2), 253–266.

Román, D., & Busch, K. (2016). Textbooks of doubt: Using systemic functional analysis to explore the framing of climate change in middle-school science textbooks. *Environmental Education Research*, *22*(8), 1158–1180.

Romance, N., & Vitale, M. (2001). Implementing an in-depth expanded science model in elementary schools: Multi-year findings, research issues, and policy implications. *International Journal of Science Education*, *23*(4), 373–404.

Shanahan, C., Shanahan, T., & Misischia, C. (2011). Analysis of expert readers in three disciplines: History, mathematics, and chemistry. *Journal of Literacy Research*, *43*(4), 393–429.

Smith, R., Snow, P., Serry, T., & Hammond, L. (2021). The role of background knowledge in reading comprehension: A critical review. *Reading Psychology, 42*(3), 214–240.

Tang, K., & Putra, G. (2018). Infusing literacy into an inquiry instructional model to support students' construction of scientific explanations. In K. Tang & K. Danielsson (Eds.), *Global development in literacy research for science education* (pp. 281–300). Springer.

Turner, J., & Paris, S. (2005). How literacy tasks influence children's motivation for literacy. In Z. Fang (Ed.), *Literacy teaching and learning: Current issues and trends* (pp. 31–39). Merrill.

Uccelli, P., Galloway, E., Barr, C., Meneses, A., & Dobbs, C. (2015). Beyond vocabulary: Exploring cross-disciplinary academic-language proficiency and its association with reading comprehension. *Reading Research Quarterly, 40*, 337–356.

Wellington, J., & Osborne, J. (2001), *Language and literacy in science education.* Open University Press.

Willingham, D. (2017). *The reading mind: A cognitive approach to understanding how the mind reads.* Jossey-Bass.

Wolters, C., Denton, C., York, M., & Francis, D. (2014). Adolescents' motivation for reading: Group differences and relation to standardized achievement. *Reading and Writing, 27*, 503–533.

Yeo, J., & Nielsen, W. (2020). Multimodal science teaching and learning. *Learning: Research and Practice, 6*(1), 1–4.

Yore, L. (2004). Why do future scientists need to study the language arts. In W. Saul (Ed.), *Crossing borders in literacy and science instruction* (pp. 71–94). International Reading Association.

Zhu, S., & Fang, Z. (2019). Has the prose quality of science textbook improved over the past decade?: A linguistic perspective. *Journal of World Languages, 5*(2), 113–131.

Integrative, Culturally Responsive Disciplinary Literacy Instruction in Social Studies

Tamara Shreiner

Social studies is a complex subject area. According to the National Council for the Social Studies (NCSS, 2021), the subject draws its content and practices from a multitude of disciplines. These disciplines include a core of history, geography, economics, and political science, as well as anthropology, archaeology, law, philosophy, psychology, religion, sociology, and the humanities, mathematics, and natural sciences. Using an interdisciplinary approach to teach a school subject is a lofty task in and of itself. But add to that the overarching goal of helping "young people develop the ability to make informed and reasoned decisions for the public good," and it becomes even more challenging. Yet, educating students for citizenship through an integrative approach has been the charge of social studies educators since it emerged as a school subject in the first two decades of the 20th century (Cremin, 1965; Halvorsen, 2006). And it continues to be the charge today. In 2013, NCSS published the *College, Career, and Civic Life (C3) Framework for Social Studies State Standards*, a document intended to "frame the ways students learn social studies content" and to help states upgrade their social studies standards "to include the application of knowledge within the disciplines of civics, economics, geography, and history" (p. 6). The framework emphasizes disciplined inquiry, as well as imparting to students the "disciplinary concepts and practices" that will give them the "capacity to know, analyze, explain, and argue about interdisciplinary challenges in our social world" (p. 6). In short, the C3 Framework stresses the importance of disciplinary literacy—acquiring the specialized knowledge and skills necessary for reading and writing in each of the core disciplines of social studies—for addressing complex civic and political issues.

Teaching and integrating disciplinary literacy practices from across disciplines must feel like a daunting task to teachers. Despite evidence that disciplinary literacy instruction results in positive learning gains for students (e.g., De La Paz et al., 2014; Dobbs et al., 2016; Monte-Sano & De La Paz, 2012; Reisman, 2012), it has failed to become a norm within social studies classrooms (Hynd-Shanahan, 2013; Nokes, 2010). Yet, as this chapter will argue, an integrative approach to teaching disciplinary literacy in social studies is possible. Despite differences in their specializations, disciplines across the social studies share practices that can serve as points of convergence, allowing teachers to maintain the integrity of the disciplines while addressing problems that require interdisciplinary solutions.

At the same time, this chapter challenges assumptions that teaching integrative disciplinary literacy is, by itself, enough for teachers to achieve the civic aims of social studies. Rather, to prepare all students for the challenges of civic life, we must prioritize culturally responsive disciplinary literacy (hereafter, CRDL), expanding interest and access to students who have been traditionally excluded from the discourse communities of the disciplines. The disciplines themselves have their own cultures—their own specialized language and discourse practices, in which certain kinds of texts are read and written for specific purposes and audiences (Moje, 2015). Teaching disciplinary literacy unveils this culture for students, inviting students to engage in the discourse community's specialized inquiry and literacy practices. However, to be culturally responsive, educators must also be deliberate in inviting into the disciplinary culture students who have been traditionally marginalized, while at the same time, respecting, honoring, and sustaining the cultural identities and assets that students bring with them. To teach CRDL, educators must give students opportunities to produce knowledge outside of the accepted canon, to ask questions of the assumptions held in the disciplines, and to push back on knowledge the disciplines have produced (Moje, 2015).

Moje (2015) offers a heuristic for deliberately incorporating disciplinary literacy into the classroom, and its components offer several opportunities for culturally responsive pedagogy (Colwell et al., 2021). The first step of Moje's (2015) "four E's" entails regularly *engaging* students in the practices of the disciplines, thereby providing students with a window into the disciplinary community's culture. Next, Moje argues, teachers should *elicit* student knowledge and engineer inquiry-based learning experiences. In addition, teachers should allow their students to closely *examine* disciplinary words and the ways people in the disciplines use words, and, finally, *evaluate* when and under what circumstances disciplinary language is useful. Conceiving of disciplinary literacy instruction in this way provides a pathway to CRDL in that it allows for academic success, honors students' cultures while using their cultures as a vehicle for learning, and encourages students to engage the world and others critically (Colwell et al., 2021).

This chapter uses Moje's heuristic to guide discussion and illustration of integrative, culturally responsive disciplinary literacy practices in social studies. It begins with a description of literacy practices in each of the core disciplines that make up social studies, before describing ways to integrate these literacies in service of addressing interdisciplinary social studies problems. The chapter then presents considerations for engineering culturally responsive disciplinary literacy practices that take into consideration students' knowledge and interests, provide opportunities for students to examine discipline-specific words and uses of words, and evaluate when disciplinary language is and is not useful.

ENGAGING STUDENTS IN THE DISCIPLINARY LITERACIES OF THE SOCIAL STUDIES

The first component of Moje's (2015) heuristic for teaching disciplinary literacy is regularly engaging students in discipline-specific practices. This requires that teachers recognize a discipline's specific ways of reading, writing, speaking, thinking, and reasoning (Fang & Coatoam, 2013; Moje, 2015; Shanahan & Shanahan, 2008). Unfortunately, few teachers have had coursework sufficient for recognizing literacy practices in even one of the core social studies disciplines of history, geography, civics, and economics, let alone all four (Martell, 2013; Nokes, 2010; Segall & Helfenbein, 2008). Thus, the following sections provide an overview of disciplinary literacy practices in each of the core disciplines, before providing suggestions for how teachers might integrate their practices.

Historical Literacy

Historians ask questions about the past in an attempt to accurately reconstruct and explain events and processes that are available to us only through the remnants of the past (Gaddis, 2002). They question what was important in the past, what has changed and continued over the course of time, whether things have changed for better or worse, what motivated actors in the past, what caused particular events and processes, what arose as the result of particular events and processes, and how the chaos and complexity of the past can be organized to help us make sense of it (Gaddis, 2002; Levesque, 2008).

To answer their questions, historians analyze, interpret, and use a variety of primary and secondary sources, both verbal and visual (Nokes, 2012). They work with books, manuscripts, personal correspondence, diaries and journals, newspapers, political cartoons, music, motion pictures, oral histories, sound recordings, photographs, prints, paintings, maps, charts, graphs, and more. While some of their work with evidence is done in libraries and archives, they also work with digitized collections and datasets, and technologies such as geographic information systems (GIS) or text mining and data visualization software.

Literate practices in history begin with an understanding that history is interpretation based on remnants from the past, that historical accounts differ across time and space, and that interpretations are dependent on individual authors' biases and worldviews. Historically literate individuals employ historical empathy and perspective, and draw on ideas about significance, change, continuity, causes, and consequences (Lee, 2005; Levesque, 2008; Nokes, 2012). When approaching a piece of evidence, historians take account of the type of source they are working with, whether primary or secondary, record or remnant. This initial step will help them decide how to approach and analyze the information (Leinhardt & Young, 1996). Historians source the information, which involves identifying the author and their biases and motivations, when the document was produced, and where the document was produced (Leinhardt & Young, 1996; Rouet et al., 1997; Wineburg, 1991). And they contextualize, which involves zooming out from the immediate context of the document and considering what other events occurred at the time, as well as what preceded and followed the event represented by the document (Leinhardt & Young, 1996; van Drie & van Boxtel, 2008; Wineburg, 1991). Historians engage in a close textual reading of documents, considering the meaning of words and passages, connecting the documents to their background knowledge and historical theories, and making inferences (Leinhardt & Young, 1996). They also corroborate documents, checking for internal consistencies, comparing them with other documents, and looking for discrepancies in information among documents (Leinhardt & Young, 1996; Rouet et al., 1997; Wineburg, 1991). In working with multiple texts, historians recognize that all documents have biases and limitations but that these limitations do not necessarily render the document useless (Rouet et al., 1997; Wineburg, 1991).

Writing is an essential means of communication in history, whether in a book, article, editorial, or blog, though speaking at conferences, or in social media, podcasts, or documentaries are also common practices. Historical writing is a cyclical process of finding evidence, fitting it together through writing, and identifying gaps in available evidence. Rather than ignoring available counterevidence that does not fit an argument, historians account for contrary evidence by adjusting their claims (Monte-Sano, 2010; Schneider & Zakai, 2016). While writing or otherwise communicating arguments, historians weave together a meaningful and coherent story, supporting claims with evidence that has been vetted through a process of sourcing, contextualizing, and corroborating (Schneider & Zakai, 2016). Because their evidence is often multimodal, so, too, is their communication, as they integrate images, maps, timelines, tables, graphs, or diagrams to contextualize, support, or extend a historical argument or explanation (Shreiner, 2020).

Geographic Literacy

Geographers ask questions about past and present, and about the natural and human world. Because of their specializations in both the physical and the human, they are well positioned to ask questions concerning the relationship between human societies and the natural environment, or about ways location affects human actions or developments in human societies. The questions geographers ask are wide-ranging from both a spatial and temporal perspective, and are held together by their concern with spatial relationships, processes, and patterns (de Blij, 2012).

Geographers work with maps, globes, aerial photographs, satellite data, and censuses to reason about past and contemporary problems (de Blij, 2012; Johnson et al., 2011; Morin, 2012; National Geographic Society, 2016; National Research Council, 1997). They use several technologies to collect, analyze, and display data, including GIS, remote sensing, and global positioning systems (GPS). Because they look for connections not only between physical locations, but also between physical locations and human activities, geographers use written texts, photographs of locations and people, magazines, local news sources, surveys, interviews, and focus groups to understand human behaviors (Johnson et al., 2011).

Geographers understand and apply geospatial concepts from simple (e.g., location, direction, distance) to complex (e.g., distortion, projection, interpolation) (Golledge et al., 2008; Lobben & Lawrence, 2015). They use spatial reasoning to evaluate patterns, distributions, diffusions, circulations, interactions, juxtapositions, changes and continuities, and relationships across space and time (de Blij, 2012; Gersmehl, 2014). Maps help mediate geographers' and their audience's spatial understanding of the world by modeling vast spaces that humans can never directly experience (Uttal & Sheehan, 2014). But reading maps means recognizing their limitations as well as affordances. Geographers understand that maps are imperfect two-dimensional representations of three-dimensional space that present spatial data in a structured and scaled way (Golledge et al., 2008). They further recognize that maps are partial representations of space, created by individuals who intend to represent space within a particular frame, and whose interpretations of space can be influenced by information available at the time a map was made and by their motivations and biases (Gregg & Leinhardt, 1994). Geographers also recognize that maps are distorted, and understand why and to what degree they are distorted based on the scale of the map and the projection type (e.g., Mercator, Robinson). This understanding allows them to overcome the distortion and use maps as representational systems for reasoning about the earth's surface (Golledge et al., 2008). Reasoning with maps also requires recognizing the symbol system used to communicate data on the map, the relationships among symbols, and how the map is layered with physical, political, historical elements (Bausmith & Leinhardt, 1998; Gregg & Leinhardt, 1994; Uttal & Sheehan, 2014). Understanding the system used to communicate information on a map allows geographers to make meaningful connections among the layers of the map, draw inferences, and reason about a problem (Bausmith & Leinhardt, 1998).

Geographers write reports, books, and articles to communicate their findings, but they also present their data visually as maps, graphs, and charts. For example, geographers create digital maps by overlaying aerial or satellite images with data like population density or distribution. These maps are then integrated with other information in written and oral reports or policy recommendations for governments, businesses, and the general public (de Blij, 2012).

Economic Literacy

Economists ask questions about a wide range of topics, including education, health care, energy, economic development, and the environment, to understand and solve problems at various levels of society. They also address questions related to the cost of products, employment levels, exchange rates, taxes, or inflation. Economic inquiry might entail investigations of historical economic events like the Great Depression or the 1970s oil crisis, or more recent events like the Great Recession of 2008 (Akhan, 2015; Anthony et al., 2015; Miller & Vanfossen, 1994).

Economic literacy requires understanding of a large number of economic concepts, such as choice, opportunity costs, inflation, poverty, and recession (Council for Economic Education, 2010; Miller & Vanfossen, 2008). Economists apply these concepts when analyzing economic developments or to work with visual representations of economic data, including time series or line graphs that show how economic variables change over time, or scatterplots that show relationships between economic variables (Council for Economic Education, 2010; Goodwin et al., 2017). Furthermore, economists use economic reasoning guided by understanding of concepts such as choice and opportunity costs to analyze economic policy and decision making (Niederjohn & Schug, 2008; Schug, 1996). Economists frame economic problems by considering historical and contemporary context and intentions (Council for Economic Education, 2010; Goodwin et al., 2017; Niederjohn & Schug, 2008). They can develop a theoretical framework for the problem and apply relevant economic models, concepts, principles, and facts to determine a policy's likely consequences, or to explain the actual consequences. In assessing consequences, economists develop a complex causal chain, using if–then scenarios, and returning to policy goals (Miller & Vanfossen, 1994).

Economists communicate theoretical explanations of economic phenomena through models, highlighting some aspects of reality while ignoring others or assuming all other variables remain constant. These models might be in the form of simplified stories, images, figures, graphs, or equations (Goodwin et al., 2017). Writing is also an important aspect of economic literacy, particularly writing that integrates visual representations of data, like graphs and charts. Economists write journal articles, newspaper articles, reports, and policy recommendations, often advising governments, businesses, and individuals on actions they should take.

Civic Literacy

The school subject of civics is a branch of political science, and deals specifically with the rights and responsibilities of citizenship. As Journell et al. (2015) have argued, civics has not typically been framed as "a discipline in which students use specific tools and ways of thinking that mimic those used by professionals within that discipline" (p. 30). However, the American Political Science Association (APSA) has weighed in on civic or political literacy since at least the early 1970s when they formed a committee on precollegiate education (American Political Science Association Committee on Pre-Collegiate Education, 1971). Referring to civics and government courses as "political science education," the authors of the report offered recommendations that students should develop "the capacity to think about political phenomena in conceptually sophisticated ways; an understanding of, and skill in the process of social scientific inquiry; [and] a capacity to systematically analyze political decisions and values" (p. 442). Since that time, scholars have defined civic literacy as understanding history, law, governmental processes, and current events, and being able to use such knowledge to reason about political problems and participate in civic life (Carnegie Corporation of New York & CIRCLE, 2003; Partnership for 21st Century Learning, 2007). A key part of civic literacy, then, is identifying social and political problems, and how such problems affect different individuals (Epstein, 2014).

In reasoning about civic and political issues, civically literate people can use a variety of texts, including policy papers and statutes, survey and polling data, voter registration data, election results, graphs of political trends and relationships, case studies, newspaper articles, and opinion pieces (Barbour & Wright, 2015). They are versed in political theory and the history of political thought, and analyze and use texts like the U.S. Constitution, The Federalist Papers, Supreme Court cases, and historical accounts (Shreiner, 2009).

When working with evidence around civic issues, civically literate people are careful to source and contextualize historical and contemporary documents to consider underlying values and assumptions, question authors' claims and assertions, and analyze political significance and implications (Barbour & Wright, 2015; Shreiner, 2014). When using visual representations of data to address an issue, civically literate people apply similar heuristics: considering the source, exploring contextual factors at play when data were gathered, questioning the methodologies, and critically evaluating the arguments implied by the data (Shreiner, 2009, 2014). They recognize citizens' rights and responsibilities, and evaluate the legitimacy of governing units in exercising certain powers (Freeden, 2008). Civically literate people also understand the significance of values and principles that form the foundation of democratic societies. They know that people can have different conceptions of the same value (e.g., justice as fairness vs. justice as desert) and that real-life situations sometimes involve tensions between core political values (e.g., justice and liberty), thereby requiring prioritization of certain values over others (e.g., justice over liberty) (Freeden, 2008; Swift, 2019). Furthermore, civically literate people recognize and can articulate different conceptions of the "good life," and competing viewpoints, arguments, and claims in society (Freeden, 2008).

While writing in different formats and using multiple modalities is as important in civics or political science as other disciplines, oral arguments have perhaps greater import for political scientists than other disciplinary experts. Reasoning in public, with the public, and about public issues is a core practice both studied and practiced in political science, as is individual and collaborative deliberative decision making (Shreiner, 2009).

Integrating the Disciplinary Literacies of Social Studies

The C3 Framework is explicit in its recommendations to integrate the disciplines of social studies in pursuit of civic aims. A challenge for teachers, then, is constructing lessons that teach disciplinary literacy from across the disciplines in an authentic and coherent way, while avoiding an overcommitment of time to "cover" each disciplinary perspective separately. One way that teachers can integrate the disciplines is to focus on commonalities in disciplinary practices. Moje (2015) argues that all disciplines, in and outside of social studies, share six literate practices: (1) problem framing; (2) working with data; (3) using varied media to produce and consult multiple texts; (4) analyzing, summarizing, and synthesizing findings; (5) examining and evaluating claims; and (6) communicating claims orally and in writing. These common practices can serve as points of unification across the disciplines.

Social studies teachers can integrate the disciplines by first considering topics from different disciplinary perspectives, and then looking for places where the disciplines might overlap or complement each other in framing questions about topic. Consider a topic like immigration, which is both of public interest and one that all core social studies disciplines address. Historians might begin inquiry by framing a question about the history of immigration among a certain ethnic group, about the ways that people have reacted to immigrants at different times, or about how immigration policies and their consequences have changed over time. Geographers might be interested in why people are migrating and where they are migrating to, or in studying global diasporas that result from migration. Economists, on the other hand, might be interested in the economic reasons for migration and whether migration is good for a national or the global economy. A political scientist might focus on analyzing contemporary and historical policies, or draw on conceptions of citizenship and explore how immigration is connected to democratic values.

All these discipline-specific lenses and inquiries could be fused in a single, compelling question posed to students in a U.S. history or other social studies class, such as "Who should the United States welcome across and within its borders?" Supporting questions could then draw on the various disciplinary perspectives. Which groups have immigrated to the United States, and why did they migrate? What were the experiences of different immigrant groups when they arrived and settled in the United States? How have immigration policies throughout United States history shaped migration patterns and the treatment of immigrants? How have different immigrant groups affected U.S. culture, politics, and economics? Alternatively, a teacher could allow students to focus on one group of migrants, and explore similar historical, geographic, economic, and political questions related to the group.

Another common feature among experts in the social studies disciplines is that they apply disciplinary tools and concepts in using and critically analyzing a variety of information, and in a variety of modalities. While different disciplines place value on particular types of information, there are also commonly valued sources across the social studies disciplines. These sources include historical and contemporary policy documents; data and statistics; maps, graphs, and charts; interviews; and scholarly secondary sources. In studying immigration to address the questions described above, both the historian and political scientist might examine U.S. Census Bureau data on changes in immigrant demographics, analyze primary source policy documents, and consult secondary accounts to better understand how other scholars have interpreted changes in policies. The geographer and economist might analyze data maps documenting human movement across the globe, and examine graphs that show contextual factors for migration patterns such as changes in national economies or in the number of regional conflicts.

Based on Moje's (2015) observations of common practices, experts across all the disciplines would also use varied media and technologies to gather these data and to report their findings. A historian, for example, might go from reading a print book to using text-mining software to analyze and visually display the use of particular words or phrases and connections between them. A geographer could go from using GIS and maps to analyze population patterns, to interviewing people who live in the area or reading oral histories to better understand people's experiences in both their country of origin and destination. An economist may spend the first half of her day preparing a report for a government official, before logging into her computer to write her popular blog. In any case, experts across the disciplines often use a combination of "low-tech" and "high-tech" tools to investigate their questions and communicate their conclusions.

Students trying to answer the question "Who should the United States welcome across and within its borders?" would be well served, then, by moving beyond a textbook to examine information in a variety of formats and with a variety of technologies. They could read secondary sources for background on immigration, but they can also examine primary source sets from the Library of Congress (n.d.) or Digital Public Library of America (n.d.), or videos of personal histories such as those at the University of Minnesota's Immigration Research Center (2021). And they can view data visualizations of migration trends such as those featured at the Migration Policy Institute (2021) or work with demographic data from the U.S. Census Bureau to make their own graphs, charts, or data maps. Furthermore, they could use tools like Google Earth to trace the path of migrants, or to view physical and cultural characteristics in a migrant's country of origin.

To answer questions that they have posed about a particular topic, disciplinary experts analyze data, summarize and synthesize their findings, and evaluate their own claims and the claims of others (Moje, 2015). When analyzing evidence, the skills of sourcing, contextualizing, closely reading, and corroborating evidence are common reading practices across social studies disciplines (Shreiner, 2014). Disciplinary experts also research claims that others have made in relation to the topics they are studying, and are prepared to interrogate their research methods, gaps in their evidence or perspectives, and their underlying biases (Bain, 2006). At the same time, disciplinary experts are prepared to recognize gaps or weaknesses in their own research or body of evidence, carefully hedging claims based on these reflections (Moje, 2015). These are practices that can and should be integrated into social studies instruction, and are key to providing students with access to disciplinary literacy. Students need to understand the process behind the texts or data representations that they read, so they are better equipped to view others' work with a discerning and critical eye (Hullman & Diakopoulos, 2011; Irgens et al., 2020; Moje, 2015).

Finally, all disciplinary experts in the social studies construct evidence-based arguments and explanations. Importantly, it is not uncommon for experts in the social studies disciplines to communicate in multiple modalities, including oral, graphic, written, digital, static, and dynamic. Nor is it uncommon for disciplinary experts to communicate to different audiences. Academics write traditional academic articles and books, and give presentations at conferences, but they also communicate through podcasts, websites, blogs, and digital projects. No matter the form, the evidence that they are using to support their case is explicit and well documented. They make their evidence accessible because they know that their peers and audience will evaluate their claims, as they do when others make claims. Again, students should have opportunities to communicate their conclusions in multiple formats. They can and should practice writing for an academic audience, for policymakers, and for the public.

ADVANCING CULTURALLY RESPONSIVE DISCIPLINARY LITERACY IN SOCIAL STUDIES

Teaching disciplinary literacy is important because it gives students access to the language and culture of disciplines as they exist within the current social order, so they can both enter and challenge the fields that produce knowledge (Moje, 2015). Conceiving of disciplinary literacy teaching as a way to potentially challenge the status quo through a critical lens makes it a form of culturally responsive teaching (Gay, 2018; Ladson-Billings, 1995). It is through the other three facets of Moje's four E's—*eliciting/engineering*, *examining*, and *evaluating*—that disciplinary literacy instruction in social studies can become CRDL.

Eliciting and Engineering

As they move through grade levels, students will encounter disciplinary texts that are increasingly technical, dense, abstract, hierarchically structured, and multimodal (Fang, 2012). Yet, they will enter the social studies classroom at different reading and writing levels, and with different background knowledge for decoding text. Furthermore, students will enter the classroom with their own experiences, cultural tools, and funds of knowledge that will determine how they make meaning of the information that they encounter (Barton & Levstik, 2004; Gay, 2018; Wade & Moje, 2000). CRDL teaching requires teachers to elicit not only students' academic knowledge, but also their skills and experiences, and use them to engineer learning experiences that will support students' work with academic language and multimodal texts (Moje 2015). It requires recognizing that a student's academic racial, ethnic, religious, gender, or other identity will influence the epistemological stance he or she takes toward information, the connections he or she makes, and his or her judgments about the trustworthiness and usefulness of information (Buehl, 2011; Epstein, 2008; Harris et al., 2016; Moje, 2007).

Several scholars (e.g., Choi, 2013; Colwell, 2018; Epstein et al., 2011; Franquiz & Salinas, 2011; Kucan et al., 2018) have made recommendations for designing CRDL instruction in social studies. Beginning with the questions that frame inquiry, one suggested approach is designing inquiry around questions of local and personal interest, or engaging students in inquiry through place-based education (Kucan et al., 2018). To make sure students can access information sources, Moje (2015) encourages teachers to incorporate content-area literacy strategies such as reciprocal teaching (Palincsar & Brown, 1984), questioning the author (Beck & McKeown, 2002), and word generation (Snow et al., 2009) to support students' reading of disciplinary texts. Information sources should also represent a wide range of text types, modalities, and purposes, including artifacts, cartoons, documentaries, maps, graphs, photographs, paintings, primary sources, and trade books (Colwell, 2018; Moje, 2015). Colwell (2018) points out that texts should offer multiple perspectives, allow students to question the traditional textbook narratives, and place value on minority or less focal viewpoints. Epstein et al. (2011) have argued that the inclusion of narratives showing the multifaceted nature of diversity, and the complexity of race and racism have the potential to improve students' understanding of marginalized groups' collective agency in history, and enhance their understanding of the complex and systemic nature of racism. And Fránquiz and Salinas (2011) have argued that students' English literacy and historical thinking skills can be improved through a curriculum that teaches academic vocabulary, checks and builds background knowledge, accepts responses in students' native or second language, scaffolds learning with primary source documents, cultivates historical thinking through document-based questions, and plans for meaningful interactions that will inspire the writing of an identity text.

Examining and Evaluating

While several of the aforementioned scholars emphasize the importance of academic vocabulary, Moje (2015) takes this recommendation a step further by encouraging teachers to have students "examine the meanings of words, phrases and symbols in a given subject area or discipline and the ways that people use language in the discipline under study" (p. 267). In addition, she encourages teachers to "engage students in evaluating why, when, and how disciplinary discourses are useful and why, when, and how they are not useful" (p. 268). Together, argues Moje (2015), these two steps function to make visible the discourse practices of the disciplines, and assist students in taking on the discourse practices. At the same time, they help learners know when and how to navigate into and out of a discipline's discourse practices, depending on audience and circumstances.

Evaluating academic vocabulary is important, not only because students need to know the dictionary definitions of words they read, but also because, as Fang (2012) argues, academic language "constructs and reflects different kinds of knowledge in ways that are functional for each discipline" (p. 36) As a result, "grammatical features of text change as the knowledge they encode" changes across the disciplines (Fang, 2012, p. 36). Arguments and explanations in history texts, for example, tend to be challenging for students because of the density of generic, abstract language used to represent groups of people, things, and places. Buehl (2011) points out that history texts are laden with conceptual vocabulary like *industrialization*, *urbanization*, *political parties*, *power*, and *justice* that embody "extensive webs of relationships" (p. x). There are also multiple historical references to names, events, and titles that are also conceptual because they are supposed to represent particular ideas, values, and significant developments. Furthermore, historians tend to use so-called nominalizations, whereby they convert adjectives into nouns to package a series of events into a single thing (e.g., the Great Depression, the Industrial Revolution) or they construe a specific action (e.g., *colonize*) into a noun (e.g., *colonization*) that can then be modified with adjectives that present a particular perspective or argument (e.g., *ruthless colonization*; Fang, 2012; Schleppegrell, 2013). Finally, history texts may be chronological, but they may also juxtapose chronology with causal explanations and arguments indicated through nouns (e.g., *reason*, *effects*); verbs (e.g., *make*, *lead to*); and prepositional phrases (e.g., *for*, *through*, *from*; Fang, 2012).

Decoding information in social studies disciplines is further complicated by the fact that "text" in the social studies can take many forms. Data visualizations such as maps, graphs, charts, and timelines, for example, are typically included to help readers imagine what is described in the prose, to augment the text, or to provide information not developed in the prose (Buehl, 2011; Fang, 2012; Shreiner, 2018). Yet, readers can face several challenges when trying to interpret, analyze, and integrate data visualizations (Duke et al., 2013; Maltese et al., 2015; Roberts et al., 2013; Shah & Hoeffner, 2002). Reading data visualizations involves discrete steps, including identifying important visual features, sorting out conceptual relations represented by these features, and determining how a visualization is connected to and serves a purpose within the surrounding text (Shah & Hoeffner, 2002). Research indicates that the more visual elements a student notices in a data visualization, the better he or she is able to read the data visualization and use it to reason about social studies questions (Shreiner, 2019). Comprehension can also be hindered by factors like the reader's understanding of graphical conventions and the content related to the data (Maltese et al., 2015).

Teachers can examine language and symbol systems or other visual elements with students by having them work with texts within the social studies disciplines, and discuss why words and symbols are being used in the ways that they are. It is also important for students to have opportunities to write and speak with disciplinary language, and to work with and visualize data—engaging in the discourse practices of the disciplines (Moje, 2015). Moreover, students should have opportunities to construct modes of communication for different audiences, including letters, newspaper articles, historical fiction, poetry, lyrics, policy recommendations, infographics, or blogs. Teachers will then be able to discuss with students the changes in language that need to be made based on context and audience, help students unpack vocabulary that is difficult to understand, support students in rewording or explaining disciplinary concepts in their own words, or in providing illustrations or examples to help others understand. At the same time, teachers can acknowledge with students that there are different ways to communicate with friends, family, and others that are effective and valuable. Disciplinary discourse has a purpose, but so do other kinds of discourse.

Teaching integrative, culturally responsive disciplinary literacy is not easy to do, especially for new teachers (Colwell et al., 2021). While there are a variety of teaching resources to help social studies teach disciplinary literacy, they do not necessarily provide guidance on how to teach integrative, culturally responsive disciplinary literacy. The 4E's heuristic combined with attention to common practices shared by the disciplines provides a useful framework for planning social studies instruction. Teachers can engage students in the cultural practices of the disciplines, while recognizing students as apprentices to the disciplines with backgrounds and perspectives that add value to disciplinary inquiry and knowledge.

REFERENCES

Akhan, N. E. (2015). Economic literacy levels of social studies teacher candidates. *World Journal of Education, 5*(1), 25–39.

American Political Science Association Committee on Pre-Collegiate Education. (1971). Political education in the public schools: The challenge for political science. *Political Science and Politics, 4*(3), 431–479.

Anthony, K. V., Smith, R. C., & Miller, N. C. (2015). Preservice elementary teachers' economic literacy: Closing gates to full implementation of the social studies curriculum. *Journal of Social Studies Research, 39*, 29–37.

Bain, R. B. (2006). Rounding up unusual suspects: Facing the authority hidden in the history classroom. *Teachers College Record, 108*, 2080–2114.

Barbour, C., & Wright, G. C. (2015). *Keeping the republic: Power and citizenship in American politics*. SAGE.

Barton, K. C., & Levstik, L. S. (2004). *Teaching history for the common good*. Erlbaum.

Bausmith, J. M., & Leinhardt, G. (1998). Middle-school students' map construction: Understanding complex spatial displays. *Journal of Geography, 97*, 93–107.

Beck, I., & McKeown, M. G. (2002). Questioning the author: Making sense of social studies. *Educational Leadership, 60*(3), 44–47.

Buehl, D. (2011). *Developing readers in the academic disciplines*. International Reading Association.

Carnegie Corporation of New York & CIRCLE. (2003). *The civic mission of schools*. Carnegie Corporation of New York.

Choi, Y. (2013). Teaching social studies for newcomer English language learners: Toward culturally relevant pedagogy. *Multicultural Perspectives, 15*(1), 12–18.

Colwell, J. (2018). Selecting texts for disciplinary literacy instruction. *The Reading Teacher, 72*(5), 631–637.

Colwell, J., Gregory, K., & Taylor, V. (2021). Examining preservice teachers' perceptions of planning for culturally relevant disciplinary literacy. *Journal of Teacher Education 72*(2), 195–208.

Council for Economic Education. (2010). *Voluntary national content standards in economics* (2nd ed.). Author.

Cremin, L. A. (1965). *The transformation of the school: Progressivism in American education, 1876–1957*. Vintage Books.

de Blij, H. (2012). *Why geography matters: More than ever*. Oxford University Press.

De La Paz, S., Felton, M., Monte-Sano, C., Croninger, R., Jackson, C., Deogracias, J. S., & Hoffman, B. P. (2014). Developing historical reading and writing with adolescent readers: Effects on student learning. *Theory and Research in Social Education, 42*(2), 228–274.

Digital Public Library of America. (n.d.). *Primary source sets*. Retrieved September 15, 2022, from *https://dp.la/primary-source-sets*.

Dobbs, C. L., Ippolito, J., & Charner-Laird, M. (2016). Layering intermediate and disciplinary literacy work: Lessons learned from a secondary social studies team. *Journal of Adolescent and Adult Literacy, 60*(2), 131–139.

Duke, N. K., Martin, N. M., Norman, R. R., Knight, J. A., & Roberts, K. L. (2013). Beyond concepts of print: Development of concepts of graphics in text, preK to grade 3. *Research in the Teaching of English, 48*(2), 175–203.

Epstein, S. E. (2014). *Teaching civic literacy projects: Student engagement with social problems, grades 4–12*. Teachers College Press.

Epstein, T. (2008). *Interpreting national history: Race, identity, and pedagogy in classrooms and communities*. Routledge.

Epstein, T., Mayorga, E., & Nelson, J. (2011). Teaching about race in an urban history class: The effects of culturally responsive teaching. *Journal of Social Studies Research, 35*(1), 2–21.

Fang, Z. (2012). The challenges of reading disciplinary texts. In T. L. Jetton & C. Shanahan (Eds.), *Adolescent literacy in the academic disciplines* (pp. 34–68). Guilford Press.

Fang, Z., & Coatoam, S. (2013). Disciplinary literacy: What you want to know about it. *Journal of Adolescent and Adult Literacy, 56*, 627–632.

Franquiz, M. E., & Salinas, C. S. (2011). Newcomers developing English literacy through historical thinking and digitized primary sources. *Journal of Second Language Writing, 20*, 196–210.

Freeden, M. (2008). Thinking politically and thinking about politics: Language, interpretation, and ideology. In D. Leopold & M. Stears (Eds.), *Political theory: Methods and approaches* (pp. 196–215). Oxford University Press.

Gaddis, J. L. (2002). *The landscape of history: How historians map the past.* Oxford University Press.

Gay, G. (2018). *Culturally responsive teaching: Theory, research, and practice.* Teachers College Press.

Gersmehl, P. (2014). *Teaching geography.* Guilford Press.

Golledge, R., Marsh, M., & Battersby, S. (2008). A conceptual framework for facilitating geospatial thinking. *Annals of the Association of American Geographers, 98*(2), 285–308.

Goodwin, N., Nelson, J. A., & Harris, J. M. (2017). *Useful economic tools and concepts.* Retrieved from *www.ase.tufts.edu/gdae/education_materials/modules/Useful_Macroeconomic_Tools_and_Concepts.pdf.*

Gregg, M., & Leinhardt, G. (1994). Mapping out geography: An example of epistemology and education. *Review of Educational Research, 64*, 311–361.

Halvorsen, A.-L. (2006). *The origins and rise of elementary social studies education, 1884 to 1941.* PhD dissertation, University of Michigan, Ann Arbor.

Harris, L. M., Halvorsen, A.-L., & Aponte-Martinez, G. J. (2016). "[My] family has gone through that": How high school students determine the trustworthiness of historical documents. *Journal of Social Studies Research, 40*(2), 109–121.

Hullman, J., & Diakopoulos, N. (2011). Visualization rhetoric: Framing effects in narrative visualization. *IEEE Transactions on Visualization and Computer Graphics, 17*(12), 2231–2240.

Hynd-Shanahan, C. (2013). What does it take?: The challenge of disciplinary literacy. *Journal of Adolescent & Adult Literacy, 57*(2), 93–98.

Immigration History Research Center. (2021). *Immigration stories.* University of

Minnesota. Retrieved September 15, 2022, from *https://cla.umn.edu/ihrc/immigrant-stories.*

Irgens, G. A., Knight, S., Wise, A. F., Philip, T. M., Olivares, M. C., van Wart, S., . . . Kahn, J. B. (2020). *Data literacies and social justice: Exploring critical data literacies through sociocultural perspectives.* Paper presented at the 14th International Conference of the Learning Sciences: The Interdisciplinarity of the Learning Sciences, ICLS 2020, Nashville, TN.

Johnson, H., Watson, P., Delahunty, T., McSwiggen, P., & Smith, T. (2011). What it is they do: Differentiating knowledge and literacy practices across content disciplines. *Journal of Adolescent and Adult Literacy, 55*(2), 100–109.

Journell, W., Beeson, M. W., & Ayers, C. A. (2015). Learning to think politically: Toward more complete disciplinary knowledge in civics and government courses. *Theory and Research in Social Education, 43*(1), 28–67.

Kucan, L., Rainey, E., & Cho, B.-Y. (2018). Engaging middle school students in disciplinary literacy through culturally relevant historical inquiry. *Journal of Adolescent and Adult Literacy, 63*(1), 15–27.

Ladson-Billings, G. (1995). But that's just good teaching!: The case for culturally relevant pedagogy. *Theory into Practice, 34*(3), 159–165.

Lee, P. J. (2005). Putting principles into practice: Understanding history. In J. Bransford & S. Donovan (Eds.), *How students learn history, mathematics, and science in the classroom* (pp. 31–78). National Academies Press.

Leinhardt, G., & Young, K. M. (1996). Two texts, three readers: Distance and expertise in reading history. *Cognition and Instruction, 14*(4), 441–486.

Levesque, S. (2008). *Thinking historically: Educating students for the twenty-first century.* University of Toronto Press.

Library of Congress. (n.d.). *Immigration and relocation in U.S. history.* Retrieved September 15, 2022, from *www.loc.gov/classroom-materials/immigration.*

Lobben, A., & Lawrence, M. (2015). Synthesized model of geospatial thinking. *The Professional Geographer, 67*(3), 307–318.

Maltese, A. V., Harsh, J. A., & Svetina, D. (2015). Data visualization literacy: Investigating data interpretation along the novice-expert continuum. *Journal of College Science Teaching, 45*(1), 84–90.

Martell, C. (2013). Learning to teach history as interpretation: A longitudinal study of beginning teachers. *Journal of Social Studies Research, 37*, 17–31.

Migration Policy Institute. (2021). *Migration data hub.* Retrieved September 15, 2022, from *www.migrationpolicy.org/programs/data-hub/us-immigration-trends.*

Miller, S. L., & Vanfossen, P. J. (1994). Assessing expertise in economic problem solving: A model. *Theory and Research in Social Education, 22*(3), 380–412.

Miller, S. L., & Vanfossen, P. J. (2008). Recent research on teaching and learning pre-collegiate economics. In L. S. Levstik & C. Tyson (Eds.), *Handbook of research in social studies education* (pp. 284–304). Routledge.

Moje, E. B. (2007). Developing social just subject-matter instruction: A review of literature on disciplinary literacy teaching. *Review of Research in Education, 31*, 1–44.

Moje, E. B. (2015). Doing and teaching disciplinary literacy with adolescent learners: A social and cultural enterprise. *Harvard Educational Review, 85*, 254–301.

Monte-Sano, C. (2010). Disciplinary literacy in history: An exploration of the historical nature of adolescents' writing. *Journal of Learning Sciences, 19*, 539–568.

Monte-Sano, C., & De La Paz, S. (2012). Using writing tasks to elicit adolescents' historical reasoning. *Journal of Literacy Research, 44*(3), 273–299.

Morin, K. M. (2012). Geographical literacies and their publics: Reflections on the American scene. *Progress in Human Geography, 37*(1), 3–9.

National Council for the Social Studies. (2013). *College, career, and civic life (C3) framework for social studies state standards: Guidance for enhancing the rigor of K–12 civics, economics, geography, and history*. Author.

National Council for the Social Studies. (2021). About NCSS. Retrieved September 6, 2022, from *www.socialstudies.org/about*.

National Geographic Society. (2016). *What is geo-literacy?* Author. Retrieved September 28, 2022, from *http://nationalgeographic.org/media/what-is-geo-literacy*.

National Research Council. (1997). *Rediscovering geography: New relevance for science and society*. National Academies Press.

Niederjohn, M. S., & Schug, M. C. (2008). Can students learn economics in U.S. history? *Journal of Private Enterprise, 23*(2), 167–176.

Nokes, J. D. (2010). Observing literacy practices in history classrooms. *Theory and Research in Social Education, 38*(4), 515–544.

Nokes, J. D. (2012). *Building students' historical literacies: Learning to read and reason with historical texts and evidence*. Taylor & Francis.

Palincsar, A. S., & Brown, A. L. (1984). Reciprocal teaching of comprehension-fostering and comprehension-monitoring activities. *Cognition and Instruction, 1*(2), 117–175.

Partnership for 21st Century Learning. (2007). *Framework for 21st century learning*. Retrieved from *www.p21.org/about-us/p21-framework*.

Reisman, A. (2012). Reading like a historian: A document-based history curriculum intervention in urban high school. *Cognition and Instruction, 30*(1), 86–112.

Roberts, K. L., Norman, R. R., Duke, N. K., Morsink, P., Martin, N. M., & Knight, J. A. (2013). Diagrams, timelines, and tables—oh, my!: Fostering graphical literacy. *The Reading Teacher, 67*(1), 12–23.

Rouet, J.-F., Favart, M., Britt, M. A., & Perfetti, C. A. (1997). Studying and using multiple documents in history: Effects of discipline expertise. *Cognition and Instruction, 15*(1), 85–106.

Schleppegrell, M. J. (2013). Exploring language and meaning in complex texts. *Perspectives on Language and Literacy, 39*(3), 37–40.

Schneider, J., & Zakai, S. (2016). A rigorous dialectic: Writing and thinking in history. *Teachers College Record, 118*(1), 1–36.

Schug, M. C. (1996). Introducing children to economic reasoning: Some beginning lessons. *Social Studies, 87*(3), 114–118.

Segall, A., & Helfenbein, R. J. (2008). Research on K–12 geography education.

In L. S. Levstik & C. Tyson (Eds.), *Handbook of research in social studies education* (pp. 259–283). Routledge.

Shah, P., & Hoeffner, J. (2002). Review of graphic comprehension research: Implications for instruction. *Educational Psychology Review, 14*(1), 47–69.

Shanahan, T., & Shanahan, C. (2008). Teaching disciplinary literacy to adolescents: Rethinking content-area literacy. *Harvard Educational Review, 78*, 40–59.

Shreiner, T. L. (2009). *Framing a model of democratic thinking to inform teaching and learning in civic education* (Proquest Publication No. 3354111). PhD dissertation, University of Michigan, Ann Arbor.

Shreiner, T. L. (2014). Using historical knowledge to reason about contemporary political issues: An expert-novice study. *Cognition and Instruction, 32*(4), 313–352.

Shreiner, T. L. (2018). Data literacy for social studies: Examining the role of data visualizations in K–12 textbooks. *Theory and Research in Social Education, 46*, 194–231.

Shreiner, T. L. (2019). Students' use of data visualizations in historical reasoning: A think-aloud investigation with elementary, middle, and high school students. *Journal of Social Studies Research, 43*(4), 389–404.

Shreiner, T. L. (2020). Turning on the historian's macroscope: A call to foreground the teaching and learning of data visualizations in world history education. *World History Connected, 17*(1).

Snow, C. E., Lawrence, J. F., & White, C. (2009). Generating knowledge of academic language among middle school students. *Journal of Research on Educational Effectiveness, 2*, 325–344.

Swift, A. (2019). *Political philosophy: A beginner's guide for students and politicians*. Polity Press.

Uttal, D. H., & Sheehan, K. J. (2014). The development of children's understanding of maps and models: A prospective cognition perspective. *Journal of Cognitive Education and Psychology, 13*(2), 188–200.

van Drie, J., & van Boxtel, C. (2008). Historical reasoning: Towards a framework for analyzing students' reasoning about the past. *Educational Psychology Research in Social Education, 20*(2), 87–110.

Wade, S. E., & Moje, E. B. (2000). The role of text in classroom learning. In M. L. Kamil, P. B. Mosenthal, P. D. Pearson, & R. Barr (Eds.), *Handbook of reading research* (pp. 609–627). Routledge.

Wineburg, S. (1991). On the reading of historical texts: Notes on the breach between school and academy. *American Educational Research Journal, 28*(3), 495–519.

DISCIPLINARY LITERACIES IN OTHER AREAS

Disciplinary Literacy and Physical Education

Kavin M. Ming

As the students filed into the classroom, the instructor could feel the nervous energy rising up in her body. It was the first time that she would be teaching this undergraduate content-area reading and writing course, and she didn't know what to expect. This course had a wide variety of majors that represented content areas across all core and related arts subjects. As the students took their seats, she looked at their faces to gauge their level of excitement. Like the diverse representation of subject areas, so, too, were the mixed expressions. After attending to the first-day housekeeping tasks, she began the class with the following opening question: "How do you believe literacy will influence the teaching of your content?" A few hands went up, and students responded with answers such as "It will give me ideas for getting students to read the material I will give them" and "It will help me know how to make my lessons more interesting." One of the three physical education majors in the class raised her hand and said, "I'm not sure that I will have any time for literacy because that is going to take away from the time that my students will be active. My advisor told me that I need to take this class in order to graduate." The instructor knew that she was about to undertake the task of dispelling the myth that literacy is an "add-on"—just another time-consuming task that content-area teachers had to fulfill. Her goal was to help this group realize that literacy serves as an aid in supporting teachers to deliver their content with fidelity. More importantly, she would show them how literacy can be tailored, in discipline-specific ways, to meet the unique requirements of each subject. She grew excited about the challenge.

Literacy is the ability to identify, understand, interpret, create, communicate, and compute, using printed and written materials associated with varying contexts (UNESCO, 2017). It is an essential component of the academic experience, spanning all curricula. A variety of national reform efforts, including the 2001 No Child Left Behind Act and the 2009 Race to the Top, have emphasized the importance of improved student literacy achievement across the grade levels (Shimon, 2004). Juxtaposed with this goal is the notion that physical education is often considered a literacy-free zone where students expel energy and only engage in movement-related activities (Guerrero, 2015). According to Buell and Whittaker (2001), when physical education teachers maintain that class time should be used solely for movement, it perpetuates the myth that physical activity is isolated from education. On the contrary, physical education fosters increased cognitive performance as teachers capitalize on students' interest in this content by allowing them to explore new concepts, analyze ideas, and draw conclusions (Gage, 2011; Mears, 2003; Palinscar & Brown, 1984; Weinstein & Erickson, 2011).

A key purpose of physical education instruction is to create learners who are knowledgeable, thoughtful, and skillful when learning about and performing physical education content (James & Manson, 2015). When students read, write, think, and communicate in the physical education classroom, it enhances their performance as they are able to reflect on their learning. It also helps them to make connections between physical education activities and aspects of their lives outside of the classroom (Buell & Whittaker, 2001). Research conducted by Connor-Kuntz and Dummer (1996) indicates that literacy in the physical education classroom positively impacts students' motor skill development and knowledge of language concepts as early as the preschool years. Landers and colleagues (2001) hypothesize that physical education presents opportunities to develop thinking and reasoning skills because children are naturally imaginative and creative. They believe that the skills students learn in physical education can be applied in other academic subjects and other areas of their lives, allowing them to become lifelong learners and lifelong agents of movement.

DISCIPLINARY LITERACY AND PHYSICAL EDUCATION

As outlined in the UNESCO (2017) definition, literacy is a broad concept that encompasses a wide range of skills. Disciplinary literacy narrows this focus to target requisite literary practices that underscore the knowledge base within different disciplines (Costa & Kallick, 2008). It is considered to be the ways of reading, writing, thinking, and communicating in the disciplines through the use of discipline-specific strategies (Gillis, 2014; Shanahan & Shanahan, 2012). It does not use literacy as a separate tool to learn the concepts within a content area, but rather incorporates strategies as an essential component within each learning task (Castelli et al., 2015). It provides students with opportunities to participate in meaningful experiences that are unique to specific content areas (Moje, 2011). Research on this topic has been largely focused on the four core academic subjects: English language arts, mathematics, science, and social studies, resulting in an emphasis on cognitive processes (Wickens et al., 2015). These four content areas have traditionally employed the use of conventional text that more readily enables the seamless infusion of literacy.

Physical education requires an expansion on the concept of cognitive processes to encompass both cognitive and physical activities. This type of disciplinary literacy is known as physical literacy, a concept that was developed in the early 21st century (Roetert & MacDonald, 2015). It is a goal of physical education and is defined as the ability to "move with competence in a wide variety of physical activities that benefit the development of the whole person" (Mandigo et al., 2009, p. 28). Whitehead (2013), one of the leading researchers in the field of physical literacy, outlines trends and concerns in the area of physical health and fitness that have influenced the rise in the idea of physical literacy. She notes that there is less of an emphasis on physical activity once individuals leave school; there is an increase in sedentary pursuits, and there is an increase in obesity and stress-related conditions. Research conducted by the World Health Organization (2020) illustrates that, globally, one in four adults do not meet the global recommendations of physical activity.

Physical literacy has four domains: (1) physical fitness (endurance, strength, balance, flexibility); (2) motor behavior (gross motor skill proficiency); (3) physical activity (behaviors performed several times per week); and (4) psychosocial/cognitive factors (knowledge, feelings, and attitudes (Lloyd et al., 2012). These help to form the characteristics, knowledge, behaviors, and understanding of what is required for a healthy and active lifestyle (Gabbani, 2001). When teachers approach instruction within this context, students learn that physical literacy is not a moment in time. Instead, it is their lived experience that they practice each day based on their thoughts and behaviors (Longmuir & Tremblay, 2016): "It is an inclusive concept accessible to all, and represents a unique journey for each individual" (Physical Literacy, 2015). That is, each individual engages in the four domains of physical literacy to the extent that his or her abilities, physical health, and environmental factors allow. Because physical literacy takes into account the needs, abilities, thoughts, and feelings of each student, teaching with the learner in mind will improve students' confidence as they develop awareness of their physical abilities and basic mobility skills (Basoglu, 2018).

"Age-appropriate guidelines and standards provide a structure that forms the basis for a physically literate lifestyle" (Roetert et al., 2017). Based on this principle, physical literacy has been adopted into the SHAPE America 2014 National Standards and grade-level outcomes for K–12 physical education, with the goal being "to develop physically literate individuals who have knowledge, skills, and confidence to enjoy a lifetime of healthful physical activity" (SHAPE America, 2013, p. 1). The standards include five broad competencies along with grade-level outcomes that provide specific targets for learning. These five competencies and select grade-level outcomes are outlined in the literacy strategies section of this chapter to demonstrate how teachers can use content-area literacy strategies to achieve physical literacy in the physical education classroom. Collectively, the goal of physical literacy, the five broad national standards, and the grade-level outcomes convey the idea that physical literacy is a multifaceted experience that occurs within and beyond the school environment (Roetert & MacDonald, 2015). Incorporating physical literacy into the national standards provides educators with the context for producing physically literate students who will have the tools for making physical activity an ongoing part of their everyday lives. Important to the discussion of disciplinary literacy in physical education is the fact that an individual does not need to specialize in one specific sport to be physically literate, but may participate in a variety of sporting or physical activities to exhibit an active and healthy lifestyle. As physical educators emphasize the idea that there are multiple activities, within and outside of the school day, that allow students to exhibit the knowledge, skill, and confidence needed to lead a healthy physical lifestyle, it reinforces the notion that physical literacy is a broad concept relevant to all learners. Thus, disciplinary literacy in this field requires students to engage in both thought and action (movement) to fully participate in the discipline. Students gain the full experience of the physical education discipline when they have opportunities to move, converse, engage in active writing, consult relevant text, and observe models of good practice (Wickens et al., 2015).

There are many opportunities for students in the physical education classroom to demonstrate cognitive, linguistic, social, and kinesthetic skills. Students communicate as they share their ideas and opinions, evaluate the viewpoints of others, and express their emotions in a range of social and physical activities. They use their listening skills to ensure that they have a clear understanding of physical requirements and are able to participate effectively in classroom conversations, discussions, and debates. They access and interpret spoken, audio, written, and multimodal texts. These texts are wide-ranging and include news and magazine articles, reports, diagrams, pictures, charts, graphs, maps, videos, demonstrations, and academic texts. They must also understand the language of movement and movement sciences. This understanding enables them to critically analyze their own and others' movements to provide explicit feedback that they can effectively communicate to others (Australian Curriculum, Assessment, and Reporting Authority, n.d.).

In physical education, there is a major emphasis on movement, with students being generally expected to move 70% of the time (SHAPE America, 2014). With this focus on movement, the outcomes selected for each grade span (elementary school, middle school, and high school) are influenced by the stages of motor development. At the elementary school level, students must demonstrate competence in fundamental motor skills and selected combinations of skills; use basic movement concepts in dance, gymnastics, and small-sided practice tasks; identify basic health-related fitness concepts; exhibit acceptance of self and others in physical activities; and identify the benefits of a physically active lifestyle. At the middle school level, students must apply tactics and strategies to modified game play; demonstrate fundamental movement skills in a variety of contexts; design and implement a health-enhancing fitness program; participate in self-selected physical activity; cooperate with and encourage classmates; accept individual differences and demonstrate inclusive behaviors, and engage in physical activity for enjoyment and self-expression. At the high school level, students must demonstrate the ability to plan and implement different types of personal fitness programs; demonstrate competency in two or more lifetime activities; describe key concepts associated with successful participation in physical activity; model responsible behavior while engaged in physical activity; and engage in physical activities that meet the need for self-expression, challenge, social interaction, and enjoyment (SHAPE America, 2013). Hence, it is essential that physical education teachers consider the multiple modalities needed to shape the cognitive, linguistic, social, and kinesthetic requirements in this discipline. They can do this by examining their program design as well as the teaching and learning activities that will make up daily instructional practice (Roetert et al., 2017). Following this investigation, they intentionally select tools (literacy strategies) that correlate with lesson objectives to ensure maximum engagement across the grade levels.

LITERACY STRATEGIES THAT SUPPORT PHYSICAL LITERACY

Physical literacy is an important concept on which physical education teachers can draw as they create their instructional content. To illustrate how teachers can adapt content-area literacy strategies in discipline-specific ways to teach in the physical education classroom, nine examples of literacy strategies, based on select SHAPE America 2014 National Standards, are discussed. Three strategies are discussed at each level—elementary, middle, and high school—that address the knowledge, skills, and confidence that physical education teachers work to build as they support the development of physically literate individuals. Specifically, these strategies were selected to demonstrate how teachers target students' cognitive, linguistic, social, and kinesthetic skills. They include an activity log, steps in a process, self-assessment, exit slip, checklist with reflection, quick write, guide, double-entry journal, and rubric.

Elementary Education

Standard 3. The physically literate individual demonstrates the knowledge and skills to achieve and maintain a health-enhancing level of physical activity and fitness.

Knowledge Outcome: Standard 3-S3.E1.3a: Physical Activity Knowledge (grade 3). Charts participation in physical activities outside physical education class.

Link to Physical Literacy for This Outcome: Students adopt physical activity as a lifestyle.

Discipline-Specific Use of an Activity Log: An activity log is a tool used to describe and document weekly activity along multiple dimensions such as activity type and duration (Garcia et al., 1997). Figure 6.1 provides an example of this instrument. At the beginning of the academic year, one of the teacher's goals will be to have third-grade students engage in as much movement as possible outside of the classroom. Thus, she could provide them with what she will call a physical activity log that enables them to document their physical activities outside of the classroom, reflect on their performance, and incorporate their parents into the learning experience. She will ask students to set goals for their weekly movement, and when she collects the logs, she will engage them in a conversation, individually and collectively, that gives them the opportunity to discuss their performance across the week and consider opportunities for improved performance.

Standard 1. The physically literate individual demonstrates competency in a variety of motor skills and movement patterns.

Skill Outcome: Standard 1-S1.E26.4: Manipulative (grade 4). Combines traveling with the manipulative skills of dribbling, throwing, catching, and striking in teacher- and/or student-designed small-sided practice–task environments.

Day of week	Example activities (walk, bike, swim)	Number of minutes	Reflection on day's accomplishments	Parent's initials
Sunday				
Monday				
Tuesday				
Wednesday				
Thursday				
Friday				
Saturday				
Total number of minutes				

FIGURE 6.1. Physical activity log.

Link to Physical Literacy for This Outcome: Students develop an awareness of the metacognitive processes needed to support the learning of a new skill.

Discipline-Specific Use of Steps in a Process: Students learn one sequential text pattern during their first 6 years at school (Dymock & Nicholson, 1999). They acquire the skill of putting events in a series of progressive events. The string pattern, a type of sequential structure, presents an activity in chronological order (Calfee & Patrick, 1995). Before fourth-grade students participate in dribbling the ball on the basketball court, the teacher uses her knowledge of steps in a process to provide a running commentary on each step while modeling the steps. This enables the students to observe the action while hearing what is required for the action to occur. The teacher would say the following as she demonstrates each movement:

- "First, I spread my fingers around the ball to have a good grip."
- "Second, I bend my knees to make sure that I stay low to the ground."
- "Third, as I bounce the ball, I make sure that I pound it with force and know where the ball bounces."
- "Fourth, as I dribble, I keep the ball from my defender."
- "Fifth, I keep my eyes on the court so that I can pass the ball correctly."
- "Then, as I dribble, I change my speed to throw off my defenders."
- "Finally, I pass the ball."

Standard 5. The physically literate individual recognizes the value of physical activity for health, enjoyment, challenge, self-expression, and/or social interaction.

Confidence Outcome: Standard 5-S5.E2.2: Challenge (Grade 2). Compares physical activities that are challenging and can build confidence.

Link to Physical Literacy for This Outcome: Students reflect on their strengths and weaknesses before they engage in physical activity.

Discipline-Specific Use of Self-Assessment: Self-assessment is a process by which students monitor and evaluate their thinking and ability. As students identify discrepancies between current and desired performance, they can work with teachers to identify strategies to support improved understanding and skills (McMillan & Hearn, 2008). Before completing a second-grade unit on movement with a purpose, the teacher asks students to assess their ability using a self-assessment chart, as shown in Figure 6.2. The teacher lets students know that they can include more than one activity in each choice. He analyzes the collective responses to determine which activities he will target during the unit to help build students' confidence and level of performance.

Middle School

Standard 3. The physically literate individual demonstrates the knowledge and skills to achieve and maintain a health-enhancing level of physical activity and fitness.

Knowledge Outcome: Standard 3-S3.M1.7: Physical Activity Knowledge (grade 7). Identifies barriers related to maintaining a physically active lifestyle and seeks solutions for eliminating those barriers.

Link to Physical Literacy for This Outcome: Students consider environmental factors that hinder continued engagement in physical activity and identify ways to solve the problem to ensure daily activity.

Discipline-Specific Use of an Exit Slip: An exit slip is a brief, written comment used toward the end of class to gauge a student's knowledge about the current or upcoming topic as well as assess the effectiveness of instruction (Leigh, 2012). As a means of bringing the lesson to a close, the teacher asks students to write, for several minutes, in response to one or more prompts. These responses can remain private or they can be shared with the class. Students write on 3″ × 5″ cards, on notebook paper, or on a Padlet wall. In the seventh-grade physical education classroom, the teacher could ask students to complete an exit slip to get an idea of challenges that they currently face in maintaining a physically active lifestyle and to then help them navigate potential solutions.

Your Feelings	Activities
Directions: Place the following activities in the table to show how you feel about each one: skipping, galloping, throwing, catching, balancing, climbing, running, hopping, dancing. You can place more than one activity in each choice.	
5 Really easy	
4 A bit easy	
3 Average (in the middle)	
2 A bit challenging	
1 Really challenging	

FIGURE 6.2. Self-assessment.

Name: *Ron Taylor*

Grade: *7*

Physical Activity Knowledge Exit Slip

Question: *What are three barriers you face that are preventing you from maintaining a physically active lifestyle, and what ideas do you have for removing those barriers?*

Response: *In my life, I am up against these barriers: lack of time to exercise, lack of motivation, and lack of energy. However, I think that there are some things I can do to stay active. I can find activities that don't take up a lot of time, like jump rope and jumping jacks, find a group of people to work out with, like a workout group on YouTube, and work out first thing in the morning when my energy is higher.*

The teacher uses students' responses to determine the direction of the lesson as it relates to physical activity knowledge, and thinks about ways to motivate students to stay active.

Standard 4. The physically literate individual exhibits responsible personal and social behavior that respects his- or herself and others.

Skill Outcome: Standard 4-S4.M2.8: Personal Responsibility (grade 8). Uses effective self-monitoring skills to incorporate opportunities for physical activity in and out of school.

Link to Physical Literacy for This Outcome: Students develop daily habits to ensure physical activity in all contexts.

Discipline-Specific Use of a Checklist with Reflection: An informal assessment, such as a checklist, is a set of predetermined categories that enable students to know the specific criteria against which the teacher will judge their performance (Vacca et al., 2017). When creating a checklist, the teacher should know, beforehand, the benchmarks that will determine success. In addition, to foster critical thinking and self-examination, the teacher can adapt the checklist to incorporate students' written input. While teachers typically use checklists to observe student performance, older students can use them to monitor their own behaviors. Figure 6.3 provides an example of a checklist that eighth-grade students can use to self-monitor their physical activity in and out of school. The teacher can give students a checklist at the end of each week for use throughout the subsequent week, and then provide them with instructions for using this tool, such as placing the instrument in a convenient location, entering information on the checklist immediately after engaging in an activity, setting periodic reminders throughout the day to review the checklist, and submitting it on the days specified by the teacher.

Standard 5. The physically literate individual recognizes the value of physical activity for health, enjoyment, challenge, self-expression, and/or social interaction.

Confidence Outcome: Standard 5-S5.M4.6: Self-Expression and Enjoyment (grade 6). Describes how moving competently in a physical setting creates enjoyment.

Link to Physical Literacy for This Outcome: Students identify the affective benefits of physical activity.

Discipline-Specific Use of Quick Writes: According to Driessens and Parr (2020), quick writes are short, often timed, written responses to a prompt for which students write as quickly as they can, with a focus on the content rather than conventions (e.g., grammar, spelling, punctuation). They can be used in a variety of ways including before the lesson to activate students' prior knowledge, during the lesson to assess engagement with the content, and after the lesson to allow reflection on learning (Rief, 2002). Quick writes provide opportunities for students to think critically as they analyze ideas and question information in formulating their written responses (Kovalik & Kovalik, 2007). To introduce the topic of movement competence, the sixth-grade teacher can ask students to write for 3 to 5 minutes about one physical activity in which they are proficient, and explain how engaging in that activity brings enjoyment. A student could respond to the prompt in the following way:

Simone Kennedy

Quick Write: *Movement Competence*

I am great at salsa dancing. I started taking dance lessons at the age of 5, and my favorite type of dance has been the salsa. My dance teacher says that I have excellent ability. I like it because it is lively, happy, has lots of foot movements, and requires me to be coordinated. When I dance, I feel like my muscles are awake and my mind is clear. I also enjoy being with my friends when we dance in class and when we dance at parties.

High School

Standard 3. The physically literate individual demonstrates the knowledge and skills to achieve a health-enhancing level of physical activity and fitness.

Directions:
Place a √ in the box if you engaged in the activity for 5–15 minutes.
Place a √√ in the box if you engaged in the activity for 16–30 minutes.
Place a - in the box if you did not engage in the activity.

Sample activities	Sunday	Monday	Tuesday	Wednesday	Thursday	Friday	Saturday
Weight training							
Resistance training							
Hiking							
Jogging							
Dancing							
Aerobic activity							
Other (fill in)							

Week's Reflection:
How would you describe your physical activity for the week?

Provide a justification for your description.

FIGURE 6.3. Physical activity checklist.

Knowledge Outcome: Standard 3-S3.H13.L1. Designs and implements a nutrition plan to maintain an appropriate energy balance for a healthy, active lifestyle.

Link to Physical Literacy for This Outcome: Students recognize that health is a multifaceted experience that includes the foods one eats.

Discipline-Specific Use of a Guide: One definition of guide is "to direct or influence the course of action of someone or something" (Oxford Languages, n.d.). In the field of literacy education, there are several types of guides that direct student learning, some of which include reading guides, anticipation guides, and three-level comprehension guides. In the field of physical education, a nutrition guide serves a similar purpose. It provides evidence-based food and beverage recommendations for Americans across the lifespan. The goal of these recommendations is to promote health and prevent chronic disease (U.S. Department of Health and Human Services, 2021). To help students demonstrate their knowledge of the importance of healthy eating habits, the high school physical education teacher asks them to individually create a nutrition guide that outlines the main food groups and track their intake of these foods. The teacher provides students with the five food groups as outlined by the U.S. Department of Agriculture (2021), and asks them to research the daily serving size and example foods for each category. The teacher adapts the guide to include a section where students monitor their food intake in relation to the guidelines for their age. To monitor students' implementation of the plan, the teacher collects their guides at specified periods throughout the semester. Figure 6.4 shows a sample nutrition guide and Day 1 of a student's response to the guide.

Standard 4. The physically literate individual exhibits responsible personal and social behavior that respects him- or herself and others.

Skills Outcome: Standard 4-S4.H1.L1: Personal Responsibility. Employs effective self-management skills to analyze barriers and modify physical activity patterns appropriately, as needed.

Link to Physical Literacy for This Outcome: Students practice accountability by working with partners to monitor their physical activity.

Discipline-Specific Use of Double-Entry Journal Writing: A double-entry journal is a two-columned academic journal that allows students to document their responses to a variety of topics that are conceptually connected. To create this journal, they divide either their loose-leaf or notebook paper into half lengthwise. They juxtapose their ideas by responding to the prompts in each column of the journal (Vacca et al., 2017). In the high school physical education classroom, as students learn about personal

Student Name: Jonathan Henry *Grade:* 10th			
My Plan			
Food type	Daily serving (girls) 14–18 years	Daily serving (boys) 14–18 years	Examples
Fruits	1½–2 cups	2–2½ cups	Apple, banana, orange, strawberry, pineapple, mango, raisins, grapes, pear, grapefruit
Vegetables	2½–3 cups	2½–4 cups	Broccoli, spinach, carrots, sweet potatoes, kidney beans, lentils, avocado, corn, mushrooms, lettuce
Grains	6–8 oz	6–10 oz	Brown rice, oatmeal, quinoa, cereal, whole grain bread, grits, pasta, popcorn
Protein	5–6½ oz	5½–7 oz	Salmon, sardines, tuna, tilapia, chicken, turkey, eggs, nuts, seeds, soy products
Dairy	3 cups	3 cups	Cheese, milk, calcium-infused soymilk, yogurt, sour cream, butter, cottage cheese
Daily servings taken from *www.myplate.gov.*			

My Performance		
Food type	How much did I eat?	How was my eating today?
Sunday	Fruits: 2 cups Vegetables: 1 cup Grains: 8 oz Protein: 6 oz Dairy: 3 cups	Overall, I started the week well. I ate sufficient amounts in all except for one category, vegetables. I will work to do a better job with this food group tomorrow.
Monday		
Tuesday		
Wednesday		
Thursday		
Friday		
Saturday		

FIGURE 6.4. Nutrition guide.

responsibility, the teacher asks them to create a double-entry journal where they document barriers to physical activity in the first column and self-management skills to combat those barriers. The teacher pairs students with an "accountability buddy" with whom students check in to make sure that they are using their self-management skills to maximize opportunities for physical activity. Figure 6.5 is an example of this kind of journal.

Standard 1. The physically literate individual demonstrates competency in a variety of motor skills and movement patterns.

Confidence Outcome: Standard 1-S1.H1.L1: Lifetime Activities. Demonstrates competency and/or refines activity-specific movement skills in two or more lifetime activities (outdoor pursuits, individual-performance activities, aquatics, net/wall games or target games.

Link to Physical Literacy for This Outcome: Students demonstrate mastery of movement skills.

Discipline-Specific Use of Rubrics: Rubrics are tools used to provide students with consistent guidelines about the expectations for their performance. They can be designed for use by either the teacher or the student, and the categories found in rubrics range from simple to comprehensive. There are several types of rubrics that include holistic rubrics, analytic rubrics, and weighted trait rubrics. Holistic rubrics provide a list of criteria that relate to a particular grade or point total. Analytic rubrics categorize an assignment's score into individual traits on which the assignment

Barriers to Physical Activity	Self-management skills
Lack of equipment	I can find activities that do not require equipment, such as running, hiking, push-ups, squats, lunges, planks, dancing, crunches, and burpees.
Lack of energy	I can make sure to get enough rest by going to bed at a reasonable time each night. I can also make sure to eat a balanced diet and drink plenty of water.
Lack of motivation	I can track my progress to see how well I am doing, and I can get some friends in join in my activities.
Lack of time	I can break up my workout into two manageable chunks: doing the first 15 minutes of exercise before I go to school, and the second 15 minutes when I get home.

FIGURE 6.5. Double-entry journal.

is graded. Weighted trait rubrics assign greater values to some traits over others (Vacca et al., 2017). The high school teacher of the aquatics team can assess students' mastery of the freestyle swim stroke by using a holistic rubric to score their performance. The holistic rubric is appropriate for this activity as the teacher must observe several movements that occur simultaneously and in rapid succession of each other and quickly score those movements. Figure 6.6 provides an example of an adapted version of a holistic rubric that was created by Keller (2021) that could be used to score students as they engage in freestyle swim.

Score 5 (All nine of the components are present.)

- Head is in neutral position.
- Body is horizontal and legs do not sink.
- Head and body roll to the side simultaneously.
- Body rolls from side to side over the cycle.
- Exhales while face is in the water.
- Uses a high elbow position.
- Extends recovering arm at half the distance of a full extension.
- Uses a two-beat kick for longer-distance swimming.
- During recovery, keeps hands flat and parallel to the water surface with your palm facing down.

Score 4 (Seven of the nine components are present.)

- Head is in neutral position.
- Body is horizontal and legs do not sink.
- Head and body roll to the side simultaneously.
- Body rolls from side to side over the cycle.
- Exhales while face is in the water.
- Uses a high elbow position.
- Extends recovering arm at half the distance of a full extension.
- Uses a two-beat kick for longer-distance swimming.
- During recovery, keeps hands flat and parallel to the water surface with your palm facing down.

Score 3 (Five of the nine components are present.)

- Head is in neutral position.
- Body is horizontal and legs do not sink.
- Head and body roll to the side simultaneously.
- Body rolls from side to side over the cycle.
- Exhales while face is in the water.
- Uses a high elbow position.
- Extends recovering arm at half the distance of a full extension.
- Uses a two-beat kick for longer-distance swimming.
- During recovery, keeps hands flat and parallel to the water surface with your palm facing down.

(continued)

FIGURE 6.6. Freestyle swim rubric.

Score 2 (Three of the nine components are present.)
- Head is in neutral position.
- Body is horizontal and legs do not sink.
- Head and body roll to the side simultaneously.
- Body rolls from side to side over the cycle.
- Exhales while face is in the water.
- Uses a high elbow position.
- Extends recovering arm at half the distance of a full extension.
- Uses a two-beat kick for longer-distance swimming.
- During recovery, keeps hands flat and parallel to the water surface with your palm facing down.

Score 1 (One of the nine components is present.)
- Head is in neutral position.
- Body is horizontal and legs do not sink.
- Head and body roll to the side simultaneously.
- Body rolls from side to side over the cycle.
- Exhales while face is in the water.
- Uses a high elbow position.
- Extends recovering arm at half the distance of a full extension.
- Uses a two-beat kick for longer-distance swimming.
- During recovery, keeps hands flat and parallel to the water surface with your palm facing down.

FIGURE 6.6. *(continued)*

IMPLICATIONS

For Practice

As teachers use the SHAPE America 2014 National Standards to guide their teaching, they must consider the standard, the learner, the task, and the time to make their instruction most effective. First, teachers must work to unpack the standards by analyzing the language to determine what students are expected to know and be able to do at each grade level. This analysis will help them as they consider the basic skills that students will need as they create lessons that meet the requirements of the standards. It will also enable them to develop formative and summative assessments that align with the objectives of their lessons. Building-level administrators should provide opportunities for teachers to collaborate with colleagues within the discipline as they work to gain a deep understanding of the standards. In a content area like physical education, where there may be only one teacher in the building, efforts for cross collaboration across schools must be considered.

Second, because physical literacy takes into account the needs, abilities, thoughts, and feelings of each student, teachers must clearly communicate that there are occasions in which students' performance will be compared to others, such as in competitive sports. However, as they promote the healthy development of the whole person, teachers emphasize that each student is unique, and proficiency levels are based solely on their individual abilities. Students learn that they are to compare their performance only to their prior performance. To meet individual learner needs, teachers must provide explicit instruction, ensure opportunities for guided and independent practice, and provide timely feedback. They must also consider how accommodations for diverse student populations will be seamlessly integrated into instruction.

Third, teachers must have an awareness of literacy strategies, understand the role that these strategies play in supporting student learning, and determine their use outside of the classroom to support lifelong healthy behaviors. Physical education teachers are experts in their content area, not in literacy strategy instruction. Some of them have not had the opportunity to learn about literacy strategies that they can use to support the development of students' physical literacy. Thus, they must seek opportunities to gain knowledge of a wide array of literacy strategies for use in their content area. They can enroll in a content-area or disciplinary literacy graduate-level course, seek out professional development opportunities at the school or district level, work with their school's literacy coach to gain ideas, and read articles through professional organizations or online. As they build their strategy "toolkit," they must select strategies for use that most closely support the requirements of the standard to ensure that students have opportunities to build their knowledge, skill, and confidence in and out of the classroom.

Fourth, teachers must consider the time it takes to infuse literacy strategy instruction into their lessons. The typical length of a physical education lesson varies from school to school and from district to district. One time period that is used at the elementary school is 30 minutes per class, and at the secondary level it may be 90 minutes per class if students are on a block rotation. As teachers work within these time limits, they must consider that one of the expectations of the SHAPE America 2014 National Standards is for students to move 70% of the time. In the elementary setting, for example, if teachers have groups of students for 30 minutes, they should aim to keep them engaged in physical activity for 21 of those minutes. Time-efficient techniques for integrating literacy strategies into lessons could include (1) breaking up one literacy strategy across multiple lessons, and having students complete a portion of the strategy during each lesson; (2) considering classroom routines that minimize the time it takes to distribute/collect materials and transition from one activity to the next; (3)

employing strategies that require minimal amounts of time to implement; and (4) encouraging the implementation of literacy strategies outside of the classroom session to ensure additional practice time.

For Research

The concept of physical literacy is fairly new, as its inception has occurred within the last 20 years. As such, the many aspects of this idea need continued investigation. Because it takes the whole learner into account, it requires physical education teachers to consider the multiple facets of students' daily experiences. Research to address the following questions may help further our understanding of this idea. First, because the idea of physical literacy is in its infancy, research that highlights how it supports the healthy development of the whole person will help to strengthen the case for why it should be incorporated into the physical education curriculum. Second, the goal of the SHAPE America 2014 standards is to develop learners who have the knowledge, skills, and confidence to enjoy a lifetime of physical activity. Answering the question about whether there are specific personal characteristics and/or environmental factors that more clearly enhance student success beyond the classroom will enable physical educators to foster those characteristics and help to create those environments that will lead to success beyond the classroom. Third, research that shows the correlation between exposure to physical literacy in the early grades and continued commitment to these habits as students move into the upper grades and as they transition into adulthood may provide physical educators with the incentive to engage in, and reinforce, physical literacy behaviors in the early years. Fourth, as our classrooms become increasingly diverse, research on how to support students with disabilities, and students from culturally and linguistically diverse backgrounds as they acquire the knowledge, skills, and competence to make physical activity a part of their lifestyle will provide physical educators with the tools for creating relevant and meaningful lessons for these populations. Fifth, physical education teachers are encouraged to seek out knowledge about literacy strategies that can be seamlessly integrated into the physical education classroom. Many of the strategies currently in the literature are examples of how content-area literacy strategies can be used to meet disciplinary goals. Thus, research on effective content-area literacy strategies that correlate with instruction in physical literacy will provide them with the tools that could, in turn, help to build their confidence to teach this information. Finally, instruction is improved when teachers are able to use carefully crafted assessments that are aligned with the goals of their lessons. Research on assessment tools that enable students to demonstrate their knowledge, skills, and confidence in the area of physical literacy will allow teachers to tailor their lessons to specifically meet students' needs.

CONCLUSION

In the past 20 years, the field of physical education has adopted the concept of physical literacy as the guideline by which individuals engage in physical activity that benefits the whole person. The SHAPE America 2014 National Standards have operationalized this concept to help physical educators develop students' knowledge, skills, and confidence that will enable them to enjoy a physically healthy lifestyle during the school years and beyond. Content-area literacy strategies can be used in discipline-specific ways to support physical educators in meeting grade-level outcomes that target physical literacy goals. To ensure the smooth and effective integration of literacy strategies into the physical education curriculum, knowledge of the standards, the learners, the literacy strategies, and the time that physical educators will need as they plan and implement instruction must be considered so that appropriate supports can be provided. Ongoing research on the importance of physical literacy, learner characteristics and environmental factors, early exposure to physical literacy and ongoing commitment to healthy practices, diverse student physical literacy needs, relevant content-area literacy strategies and assessments will help to improve physical literacy practices in schools and in the broader community.

REFERENCES

Australian Curriculum, Assessment, and Reporting Authority. (n.d.). *Literacy learning progression and health and physical education*. Retrieved August 27, 2021, from *https://australiancurriculum.edu.au/media/3656/literacy-hpe.pdf.*

Basoglu, U. D. (2018). The importance of physical literacy for physical education and recreation. *Journal of Education and Training Studies*, *6*(4), 139–142.

Buell, C., & Whittaker, A. (2001). Enhancing literacy in physical education. *Journal of Physical Education, Recreation and Dance*, *72*(6), 32–37.

Calfee, R. C., & Patrick, C. L. (1995). *Teach our children well: Bringing K–12 education into the 21st century*. Stanford Alumni.

Castelli, D. M., Barcelona, J. M., & Bryant, L. (2015). Contextualizing physical literacy in the school environment: The challenges. *Journal of Sport and Health Sciences*, *4*(2), 156–163.

Connor-Kuntz, F. J., & Dummer, G. M. (1996). Teaching across the curriculum:

Language-enriched physical education for preschool children. *Adapted Physical Activity Journal, 13*(3), 302–315.

Costa, A. L., & Kallick, B. (Eds.). (2008). *Learning and leading with habits of mind: 16 essential characteristics for success.* Association for Supervision and Curriculum Development.

Driessens, S., & Parr, M. (2020). Rewriting the world: Quick writes as a space for critical literacy. *The Reading Teacher, 73*(4), 415–426.

Dymock, S. J., & Nicholson, T. (1999). *Reading comprehension: What is it? How do you teach it?* New Zealand Council for Educational Research.

Gabbani, F. (2001). Physical education-physical literacy kinesthetic intelligence. *Physical and Health Education Journal, 67*(1), 2.

Gage, F. (Ed.). (2011). Exercise training increases size of hippocampus and improves memory. *Proceedings of the National Academy of Sciences of the USA, 108*(7), 3017–3022.

Garcia, A. W., George, T. R., Coviak, C., Antonakos, C., & Pender, N. J. (1997). Development of the child/adolescent activity log. A comprehensive and feasible measure of leisure-time physical activity. *International Journal of Behavioral Medicine, 4*(4), 323–338.

Gillis, V. (2014). Disciplinary literacy. *Journal of Adolescent and Adult Literacy, 57*(8), 614–623.

Guerrero, M. (2015). Literacies in health and physical education. *Literacy Learning: The Middle Years, 23*(3), 50–56.

James, A., & Manson, M. (2015). *Physical education: A literacy-based approach.* Sagamore.

Keller, C. (2021). Freestyle swimming—10 tips to improve your technique. *Enjoy Swimming.* Retrieved August 29, 2021, from *www.enjoy-swimming.com/freestyle-swimming-technique.html.*

Kovalik, D. L., & Kovalik, L. M. (2007). Language simulations. The blending space for writing and critical thinking. *Simulation and Gaming, 38*(3), 310–322.

Landers, D. M., Maxwell, W., Butler, J., & Fargan, L. (2001). Developing thinking skills in physical education. In A. L. Costa (Ed.). *Developing minds: Resource book for teaching thinking* (pp. 343–351). Association for Supervision and Curriculum Development.

Leigh, S. R. (2012). The classroom is alive with the sound of thinking: The power of the exit slip. *International Journal of Teaching and Learning in Higher Education, 24*(2), 189–196.

Lloyd, R. S., Oliver, J. L., Meyers, R. W., Moody, J. A., & Stone, M. H. (2012). Long-term athletic development and its application to youth weightlifting. *Strength and Conditioning Journal, 34*(4), 55–66.

Longmuir, P. E., & Tremblay, M. S. (2016). Top 10 research questions related to physical literacy. *Research Quarterly for Exercise and Sport, 87*(1), 28–35.

Mandigo, J., Francis, N., Lodewyk, K., & Lopez, R. (2009). Physical literacy for educators. *Physical Education and Health Journal, 75*(3), 27–30.

McMillan, J. H., & Hearn, J. (2008). Student self-assessment: The key to stronger student motivation and higher achievement. *Educational Horizons*, *87*(1), 40–49.

Mears, B. (2003). The ABCs of effective reading integration. *Teaching Elementary Physical Education*, *14*(5), 36–39.

Moje, E. B. (2011). Developing disciplinary discourses, literacies, and identities: What's knowledge got to do with it? In M. G. L. Bonilla & K. Englander (Eds.). *Discourses and identities in contexts of educational change* (pp. 49–74). Peter Lang.

Oxford Languages. (n.d.). *Oxford Languages and Google.* Retrieved July 28, 2021, from *https://languages.oup.com/google-dictionary-en.*

Palinscar, A. S., & Brown, A. L. (1984). Reciprocal teaching of comprehension-fostering and comprehension-monitoring activities. *Cognition and Instruction*, *1*(4), 117–175.

Physical Literacy. (2015). *Canada's physical literacy consensus statement 2015.* Retrieved September 3, 2021, from *https://physicalliteracy.ca/physical-literacy/consensus-statement.*

Rief, L. (2002). Quick-writes: Leads to literacy. *Voices from the Middle*, *10*(1), 50–51.

Roetert, E. P., Kriellaars, D., Ellenbecker, T. S., & Richardson, C. (2017). Preparing students for a physically literate life. *Journal of Physical Education, Recreation, and Dance*, *88*(1), 57–62.

Roetert, E. P., & MacDonald, L. C. (2015). Unpacking the physical literacy concept for K–12 physical education: What should we expect the learner to master? *Journal of Sport and Health Science*, *4*(2), 108–112.

Shanahan, T., & Shanahan, C. (2012). What is disciplinary literacy and why does it matter? *Topics in Language Disorders Journal*, *32*(1), 7–18.

SHAPE America. (2013). *Grade-level outcomes for K–12 physical education.* Author.

SHAPE America. (2014). *National standards and grade-level outcomes for K–12 physical education.* Human Kinetics.

Shimon, J. (2004). Content literacy in physical education: The use of word association charts. *Strategies: A Journal for Physical and Sport Educators*, *17*(6), 7–9.

UNESCO. (2017). *Sustainable development goals.* Institute for Statistics. Retrieved August 25, 2021, from *http://uis.unesco.org/en/glossary-term/literacy.*

U.S. Department of Agriculture. (2021). *Back to the basics. All about MyPlate food groups.* Retrieved August 4, 2021, from *www.usda.gov/media/blog/2017/09/26/back-basics-all-about-myplate-food-groups.*

U.S. Department of Health and Human Services. (2021). *About the dietary guidelines.* Retrieved August 4, 2021, from *https://health.gov/our-work/food-nutrition/about-dietary-guidelines.*

Vacca, R. T., Vacca, J. L., & Mraz, M. (2017). *Content area reading: Literacy and learning across the curriculum* (12th ed.). Pearson Education.

Weinstein, A. M., & Erickson, K. I. (2011). Healthy body equals healthy mind. *Journal of the American Society on Aging*, *35*(2), 92–98.

Whitehead, M. (2013). The history and development of physical literacy. *ICSSPE Bulletin*, *65*, 22–28.

Wickens, C. M., Manderino, M., Parker, J., & Jung, J. (2015). Habits of practice: Expanding disciplinary literacy frameworks through a physical education lens. *Journal of Adolescent and Adult Literacy*, *59*(1), 75–82.

World Health Organization. (2020). *Physical activity*. Retrieved September 3, 2021, from *www.who.int/news-room/fact-sheets/detail/physical-activity*.

Disciplinary Literacy in the Visual Arts

Jennifer D. Morrison

It seemed innocuous enough when I decided my Advanced Placement language and literacy students needed an engaging and instructional, yet different, unit following their completion of the AP exam in May. Three weeks of the school year remained, and I didn't want to see them go to waste. I had recently read a book on Alfred Hitchcock and attended a workshop on film analysis, so I began to teach my students about the art of film production—the visual and auditory choices directors make to impact a viewing audience, the techniques directors use, and the language associated with the medium. With *Notorious*, we discussed Hitchcock's use of the Dutch tilt, high-angle shots, and checkerboard floors (an allusion to chess) to visually indicate a character was in danger. We examined the initial montage of Baz Luhrmann's *Romeo + Juliet* considering how he established audience positioning through his use of crosscuts, objective shots, zoom-ins, zoom-outs, voice-overs, nondiegetic sounds, and visual metaphors. This process was not about just watching a movie in an English class; it was about considering how directors and artistic producers think about the subject of their films, the discourse in which they engage, and the skills they employ to create their art form.

I later realized that while I was drawing some parallels between directors' craft and writers' craft, my intention was not to equate the two, but to instead recognize the distinct language, concepts, tools, skills, and competencies of each discipline: literature as a subset of the language arts and film as a subset of the visual arts. I was in the infancy of my understanding of disciplinary literacy in the visual arts. Since then, I have spent significant time working to understand how artists, designers, and filmmakers practice their craft and engage in meaning-making processes within their fields. This chapter attempts to share some of those insights into key issues related to disciplinary literacy in the visual arts, to provide an overview of what literacy looks like in the field, and to offer instructional practice suggestions for building visual arts disciplinary literacy with students.

In this chapter, *visual arts* is defined as the fine arts commonly taught in K–12 schools that are primarily visual in nature, including drawing, painting, sculpture, printmaking, photography, design (e.g., clothing, interior), ceramics, crafts, film production, graphic and digital arts, and architecture. While the term visual arts sometimes encompasses the performative arts of drama or dance, these fields will be addressed in Chapter 8 of this volume. Additionally, this chapter acknowledges the multisensory nature of visual arts—that they engage olfactory, aural, tactile, and emotional senses, not just visual ones (Eisner, 2004; Jarvis, 2011).

CONSEQUENTIAL ISSUES AND QUESTIONS IN VISUAL ARTS

In the time since Shanahan and Shanahan (2008) and Moje (2008) called for content-area literacy to be reexamined in terms of disciplinary literacy, research in this area has disproportionately focused on the four core subjects of English, mathematics, social studies, and science, with very little focus on specialist areas including not only visual arts but also library sciences, performing arts, business and career technology, world language, and physical education. This privileging of core subject areas can be problematic for specialist teachers who seek to implement disciplinary literacy concepts since they are generally left to apply generic reading and writing strategies without guidance or consideration of their specific contents' demands (Chandler-Olcott, 2017). It can also be problematic because it privileges certain literacy forms and epistemologies over others, with alphabetic language superseding musical and dance notation, digital code, and visual image. As has been seen internationally as well as in the United States, historical and continued emphasis on standardizing and testing reading literacy and numeracy has "led to the visual arts being consigned to the margins of curricular practice" (Jarvis, 2011, p. 307).

One of the biggest issues with trying to consolidate research on literacy in visual arts is that while there are studies examining how these two fields can interact collaboratively, visual arts is almost always positioned, similar to how Chandler-Olcott (2107) claimed physical education is positioned, as "literacy's handmaiden" (p. 149). While there has been some attempt to explore what literacy looks like in the visual arts, much of the literature about visual arts and literacy falls into one of two categories. First, the literature tends to focus on how the visual arts can reinforce literacy skills developed in other classes for the benefit of achieving higher test scores or future employment. For example, Dehner (2018) provides "5 ways to bring literacy into the art classroom" including exit slips, sequence writing, and curating an art-based library. The suggestion is that visual arts does not have its own literacy practices and therefore must "borrow" from other areas to meet the expectation of externally imposed literacy performance levels. While these strategies can be beneficial, they are often suggested as "tack-ons" that check off boxes of literacy performance rather than serving to unpack the specific ways visual artists create, disseminate, and evaluate knowledge and the unique ways in which these practices "are instantiated in [the discipline's] use of language" (Shanahan & Shanahan, 2008, p. 48). While exit slips and art libraries can be beneficial for students to begin building arts literacy, they do not in and of themselves address the journey of students becoming deep practitioners of artistry.

The second categorization is that the literature linking visual arts and literacy tends to promote application of the visual arts as instructional tools in other content areas. For example, Cappello and Lafferty (2015) looked at the role photography could play in students' development of scientific literacy, specifically geology. Students were engaged in the Visual Thinking Strategy and performed both receptive and productive activities to help them in reading and taking photographs. However, the focus of the study, as with so many others that feature the use of visual arts, was not on the visual arts themselves, but on the core content course (in this case, science). Academic vocabulary focused on "sedimentary rock" and conceptual understanding zeroed in on taking photographs of everyday instances of minerals. While the authors argued that the participating students had engaged in visual literacy because they looked at and produced photographs, there was no apparent unpacking of the terminology and conceptual understanding of photographs and photography in their own right. Looking at a photograph and taking a photograph but engaging in discussion about geology is not effectively building literacy in the visual arts; it is using visual tools to teach science concepts. Teaching through the use of images does not equate to developing visual arts literacy.

Too often, the visual arts are seen as a vehicle through which to learn core content material. While this integration can be a very powerful process in learning biology, history, or math, it can also devalue the arts if they are seen only as supports for other disciplines instead of being highly valued as their own discipline. My entry point may have been through my privileged art form—literary writing—but I quickly realized the depth and breadth of disciplinary literacy across the many subfields of visual arts, and by engaging in film analysis, I began to recognize the highly specialized nature of film as an art form that derived as a "natural outgrowth" from filmmakers' and directors' epistemologies and creation of knowledge (Shanahan & Shanahan, 2008, p. 9).

Because of this marginalization of visual arts, teaching interns and novice teachers have often not seen explicit literacy instruction in their disciplines and are often not equipped to unpack the language, skills, and concepts of disciplinary literacy (Buelow et al., 2018). They become engulfed in what Wiggins and McTighe (2005) call "the expert blind spot" whereby individuals within the field make assumptions about what novices know, understand, are able to do, and are able to be. What is obvious to the content-area expert—the teacher—is not obvious to novices—students—and mislearning, misunderstanding, confusion, frustration, and low motivation can subsequently occur.

HOW IS LITERACY PRACTICED IN THE VISUAL ARTS?

Because visual artists engage in disciplinary literacy in ways different from their core content-area counterparts, it is important to understand the distinctions in how literacy is practiced. This section explains several key underpinnings to visual arts practice that shape how disciplinary literacy should be taught in arts courses. Visual art literacy is multimodal, social, multifaceted, and being reshaped by digital tool development. A brief discussion on variations in visual arts literacy recommendations based on student grade level ends the section.

Visual Arts Literacy as Inherently Multimodal

Frequently in research on disciplinary literacy, literacy is defined as something similar to this: "Literacy is not simply knowing how to read and write a particular script but applying this knowledge for specific purposes in specific contexts of use" (Scribner & Cole, 1981, as cited in Smagorinsky, 2014, p. xiii) or "a multifaceted concept that cannot be taught solely within one discipline (typically English) and then exported wholly for use in others," requiring "teachers in each discipline to emphasize what makes their work unique and how their ways of reading and writing require special knowledge" (Smagorinsky, 2014, pp. xiii, xiv). One of the key issues in the discussion of visual arts disciplinary literacy is the assumption that disciplinary literacy largely hinges on the ways professionals *read* and *write* within their fields. This definition has broadened to include "reasoning (which encompasses speaking and doing)" (Lent & Voigt, 2019, p. 3); "thinking skills expressed through language" (Wolsey & Lapp, 2017,

p. 10); and "what it means to *learn* in the subject areas and what counts as knowledge in the disciplines that undergird those subjects" (Moje, 2008, p. 99, italics in original). Moje's variation is most in alignment with subject areas such as visual arts where the predominant means of communication and expression are not necessarily rooted in alphabetic words (read, written, spoken, heard, or enacted). Instead of focusing on merely the way language is used within the discipline, we also need to consider that literacy in the disciplines is the ability to make meaning of a text and that texts are something about which meaning needs to be made regardless of their medium or mode.

Alphabetic and phonemic semiotics are highly privileged as forms of communication in school and academia because they have historically been the source of transmitted knowledge. For us to step away from this conception, we need to consider what it might be like to live in a world where reading and writing as we know it are not possible or even permissible. In Margaret Atwood's (2019) *The Testaments*, Agnes has grown up in the theocratic Gilead where women's eyes are gouged or fingers are cut off for reading and writing. Agnes is chosen to be one of the few young women given access to learning to read books, but she struggles to "translate the black insect marks into words" and asks, "What's an A?" while her friend rambles through her initial primer (p. 242). It is not until the letters, words, and sentences are compared to musical notation, painting, and embroidery that Agnes is able to make meaning of the texts she is presented with. "Becka said that writing was almost the same as [embroidering and painting]—each letter was like a picture or a row of stitching, and it was also like a musical note; you just had to learn how to form the letters and then how to attach them together" (p. 298). For her, the privileged visual "languages" were those of art (painting and stitchery) and music (read, heard, and performed). In the absence of written alphabetic language, these became her means of expression and communication, and she was unable to comprehend alphabetic semiotics until she could access them through her existing schema of artistic literacies.

While artists *do* read and write print-based texts in the form of discipline-based periodicals, artistic critique, artist statements, and screenplays, much of their literacy interaction derives from multimodal texts. They must "read" photographs and paintings, clay and canvas, digital and moving images; they "write" or communicate through production of social media images, printmaking, water colors, and moving image stills. Some artists must even be able to "read" and interpret unusual canvases such as skin. After an interview with a tattoo artist, one of my students once discussed how the artist had seen a wide variety of skin types from those "who take care of their skin with lotion to those who have 'alligator skin'" (student paper, 2018). The tattoo artist's interpretation of a customer's skin condition impacted whether or not he was able to tattoo the customer's desired design, what colors of ink to use, and how to adapt the image to meet the customer's request while also meeting dermal constraints.

Visual arts is multimodal by its very nature and, depending upon the subfield, installation, or approach, integrates any combination of visual, aural, tactile, kinesthetic, gestural, proxemic, paralinguistic, textual, spatial, and even olfactory modes (Barton, 2013; Jarvis, 2011). It is not enough to merely decode the discipline's words; with multimodal text, we must also be able to decode images, understand how images and words work together as well as comprehend what they look like within practice. For example, in my classes, I ask students to follow the instructions they are given auditorily. Those instructions are "Virabhadrasana I, Prasarita Padottanasana, Trikonasana, Parivrtta Trikonasana" (Morrison, 2018). When students do not understand the Sanskrit words, I present the same instructions in English: "Warrior I, Intense Leg Stretch, Triangle, Reverse Triangle." While students can decode the words—they understand the concept of a triangle or warrior—most are not able to connect the words to the kinesthetic actions that must be performed to implement these yoga poses. This is because the task for this yoga sequence (and for the visual arts) is not just to acquire information from a text but "rather to embody it in dynamic three-dimensional space, as it unfolds over time, in concert with other individuals" (Chandler-Olcott, 2017, p. 151).

For us to truly value and honor the disciplinary literacy of those individuals who study and create art, we must reframe conceptions of literacy within visual arts as predominantly print-based. It is important we begin considering what it is to "unprivilege" read and written text; we must afford greater attention to the multimodal nature of specialist subjects, their habits of practice, and methods of knowledge generation in order to justly instruct disciplinary literacy in the visual arts.

Visual Arts Literacy as a Social Practice

The idea that Chandler-Olcott (2017) raises—that literacy in specialist contents is often performed in concert with others—pushes the concept of disciplinary literacy into a sociocultural context. While art making can be perceived as personal and individual, it is often situated within larger interactive communities. Barton (2013) argues that a key component of visual arts literacy is for students to be able to engage in critical thinking whereby "students can actually set really complex problems themselves to solve" (p. 14). This problem-solving stance is critical to what Tucker-Raymond et al. (2016) call "making" literacies, which are inherently socially oriented and treat "individual learning as part of the greater, interconnected whole" (p. 210).

Additionally, with the integration of digital tools with art literacy, artists increasingly interact with online communities where they can swap strategies for design and production, and with social media where they can share finished products to an online audience (Tucker-Raymond et al., 2016). Tucker-Raymond et al. (2016) share a case study of Naeem (the paper's fourth author), who engages in designing and creating a book cover. He drew from instructions and recommendations shared to online platforms to help him in the engineering of the project; then he shared his own instructions, photographs, design constraints, decisions, and results with other "makers" within the Instructables online community (*www.instructables.com*), serving as a teacher. This example shows how members of a "knowledge ecosystem" (p. 209) can help to build disciplinary literacy through discussion and enactment. Artistic making is not necessarily a solo expedition.

Visual Arts Literacy as Multifaceted

Art education is closely associated with teaching students the elements of design, considered the creative building blocks for visual artists and graphic designers to create mood, evoke feelings, establish a focal area, and position the viewer in ways the artist desires (MasterClass, 2021). These elements include: color, line, value, space, shape, form, and texture. While these elements are foundational to all forms of visual arts, how they play out, are combined, and even defined vary, depending upon the subfield in which an artist is operating. This is also true for the principles of design—or the ways an artist organizes elements within an artwork—which include balance, contrast, movement, emphasis, pattern, proportion, and unity.

In addition to the elements and principles of design, each subfield of the visual arts has its own language, skills, and concepts. While these may intertwine and overlap for many artists (Picasso was both a sculptor and painter), each area still has its specific language and skills. While printmaking requires individuals to understand terms like *matrix* as well as processes such as etching and lithography, architecture involves different language (*facade*, *parlante*) and skills (drafting) to successfully enact that may or may not align with other fields. This means that just as it is important to recognize the contextualized meaning of vocabulary and concepts within the general visual arts, it is also important to engage in effective intradisciplinary communication to ensure clarity of meaning within specific subfields.

One of the key components multiple researchers identify as defining literacy in visual arts is an individual's knowledge of and ability to choose from multiple mediums in order to create art (Barton, 2013; Buelow et al., 2018; Eisner, 2004; Jarvis, 2011):

> In the arts it is plain that in order for a work to be created, we must think within the constraints and affordances of the medium we elect to use. . . . Painting with watercolor makes certain visual qualities possible that cannot be created with oil paint. The artist's task is to exploit the possibilities of the medium in order to realize aims he or she values. Each material imposes its own distinctive demands and to use it well we have to learn to think within it. (Eisner, 2004, p. 8)

Role of Digital Development in Visual Arts

Recent developments in digital practices have shifted the field of visual literacy and its education. Digitization has created entire new art fields, such as graphic design; it has also reconceptualized more traditional art forms, such as the use of computer-generated imagery (CGI) in filmmaking. As technology develops, so, too, do the possibilities for artistic representation, which, in turn, impacts our conceptualization of art. As Eisner (2004) states, "Artists have learned to think within materials such as neon tubing and plastic, day glow color and corfam steel. . . . Each new material offers us new affordances and constraints and in the process develops the ways in which we think" (p. 8). As computers become more sophisticated and readily available (think of the high-level cameras and editing tools now on smartphones), the ability to create and innovate in new ways increases exponentially, as does the capability for anyone to create art. Spalter and van Dam (2008) point to a cultural shift from print media and traditional video to ubiquitous digital image creation and dissemination incomparable to any previous time in history. While students may appear to be highly proficient in visual technologies, often they are not well versed in the principles of digital tools nor skilled in evaluating the media produced from them. The authors subsequently recommend expanding conceptions, and subsequent instruction, of visual literacy to include digital visual literacy (DVL) defined as the ability to (1) "critically evaluate digital visual materials," (2) "make decisions on the basis of digital visual representations of data and ideas," and (3) "use computers to create effective visual communications" (Spalter & van Dam, 2008, p. 94).

> As quickly as technology is evolving, it is imperative to remember disciplinary literacies that rely solely on print resources are no longer sufficient to fully convey complex and multilayered meanings, as learning in the digital age traverses digital/print, in- and out-of-school, face-to-face, and virtual communication. Digital literacies are critical to fully access the literacies required for disciplinary learning. (Manderino & Castek, 2016, p. 80)

As digital literacies integrate with arts literacies, the lines between them continue to blur. Disciplinary literacy in visual arts begins to also include competencies in choosing and using tools, such as Photoshop, Affinity, Krita, and even simple filters on phone cameras in the process of learning art discourse and art making.

Visual Arts in Differing Grade Levels

Much of the literature on disciplinary literacy as a whole to this point has focused on adolescents, largely due to the developmental progression of vocabulary, literacy attainment, and reading purpose. Wolsey and Lapp (2017) adapted Shanahan and Shanahan's (2008) literacy pyramid by tipping it on its side and splitting it to show a continuum of literacy specialization across grade levels. Through this diagram, Wolsey and Lapp show that while disciplinary literacy can be and is addressed in elementary grades, it is logically further along the developmental continuum as students gain greater foundations in reading basics and more content-area specialization.

However, some work discusses disciplinary literacy in the visual arts with younger children. It tends to focus more on art making, inquiry, and exploration and less on attainment of vocabulary and concepts (see, e.g., Jarvis, 2011). However, there is a shift in this perspective. Shanahan and Shanahan (2014) discuss how the Common Core State Standards' emphasis on informational text in the primary grades means elementary students are encountering disciplinary differences earlier and "as such, the informational text demands serve as a precursor to the disciplinary reading to follow" (p. 637). Buelow et al. (2018) argue that elementary students' disciplinary literacy in the visual arts can be supported "through first-hand experience in manipulating an art medium, using complex text to explain the vocabulary, and a graphic organizer to scaffold and organize their thinking" (p. 247). Discussion strategies can be used to reinforce learning and socially construct their understanding of artistic elements and principles, just as they often are with older students. One recommendation the authors make is to ensure sufficient time is provided to address student knowledge gaps that may be based on their background knowledge, preferences, identities, skills, and dispositions. This will allow the teacher to support students in "build[ing] and bridg[ing] their own knowledge" (p. 248).

One issue that arises in younger grades is that in an environment where budget cuts often result in greater cutting back of specialized art teachers, general education teachers, who may not have deep disciplinary knowledge in the visual arts, are tasked with teaching students to think like artists. In such cases, visual arts can easily become an add-on or supplement to the core/tested disciplines and more about crafting than true artistic expression and honoring the deep disciplinary literacy of the visual arts (Jarvis, 2011).

EFFECTIVE WAYS TO SUPPORT STUDENT DEVELOPMENT IN VISUAL LITERACY

Repeatedly, researchers in this area identify three key prongs for developing students' disciplinary literacy in visual arts: (1) building knowledge of technical language and its associated practices; (2) learning to respond to and critique others' artworks; and (3) performing as artists (see, e.g., Barton, 2013; Buelow et al., 2018; Eisner, 2004). This section will discuss concrete practices that can help students develop these skills. While all three prongs are needed to build disciplinary literacy, they are not necessarily hierarchical and should be taught together through both deductive and inductive approaches. That being said, Barton (2013) argues that when students' initiation into the discourse of understanding and critiquing art informs artistic expression, students become more literate in the arts.

Building Knowledge of Technical Language and Practices

Adaptation of Existing "Reading" Strategies to Multimodal and Nonprint Texts

One suggestion Gross (2020) makes to improve students' visual arts disciplinary literacy is to adapt Vacca et al.'s (2016) before, during, and after (B-D-A) reading instructional framework to the art classroom. While students may actually read a print text about an artist or artistic theory, they also must be able to "read" nonprint texts—sculpture, film, photographs, lithographs. Therefore, we need to reframe our thinking from B-D-A reading to B-D-A text interactions. The same support students receive before, during, and after interacting with a traditional text should be enacted before, during, and after interacting with multimodal and nonprint texts as well.

What might this look like? Common before strategies include preteaching vocabulary through word splashes or concept cards, making predictions, or building anticipation with questions or an anticipation guide. All of these approaches can be implemented with nonprint text. Before viewing a film clip, teachers may preteach terms like *subjective shot* and *objective shot* to help students identify these elements, or teachers may prime students to think about how they feel when the director uses each type of shot. They may also provide a graphic organizer, such as a Frayer model (or four-square), that helps students develop a conceptual understanding of terms such as subjective or objective shots.

Other strategies can provide scaffolding for students as they learn to grapple with and articulate their ideas within the discipline's literacies. Sentence frames and templates can assist students in using specific language and structures associated with writing artists' statements, recording an art critique, or discussing art. These are particularly beneficial for students with special needs who might require greater guidance in addressing required writing and discussion prompts (Gross, 2020). Mentor texts that model for students how artists, art critics, museum curators, designers, and filmmakers discuss their work are also beneficial for initiating students into the field. These mentor texts may be traditional print texts, but they may also be a videotaped conversation between artists or multimodal online Web articles that utilize hyperlinks, images, and embedded text.

Learning to Respond to and Critique Others' Artwork

It is not enough to know the terminology and components associated with specific visual arts subfields. "Being literate in aesthetic discourse is a crucial component of students' practice in making meaning through art" (Shenfield, 2015, p. 48). A strategy often used to encourage deep, thoughtful analysis is the *close reading*, which helps students examine a text critically. Table 7.1 shows how the close reading steps of a traditional print text (as stated in Wolsey & Lapp, 2017) can be adapted for a two-dimensional artwork and a film clip. The PACE Guide helps identify text complexity qualitatively through consideration of a text's provocativeness, ambiguity, complexity, and emotion (Strong et al., 2001).

As seen in Table 7.1, the close reading framework may be adapted so students can more closely examine two- and three-dimensional work and film texts, and analyze the artist's or director's craft in creating his or her art. This examination of mentor texts, practice in using disciplinary terminology, and discussion of artists' craft builds a foundation for students to then engage in critique and artistic production.

Not only do adapted B-D-A text interaction strategies—such as a close reading, read-alouds, chunking, annotation, and graphic organizers—help students to gain disciplinary language and to think about artistic concepts, many of these activities "fall into the premaking category of visual arts in the classroom" (Gross, 2020, p. 162) that students can build upon when it comes time for them to engage in their own art-making processes.

Students as Assessors and Evaluators

As students gain disciplinary literacy in visual art subfields, they can become the creators of performance-based rubrics and scoring guides on projects. Often, these evaluative tools are designed by teachers; however, allowing students to create rubrics and scoring tools to establish criteria for success based on explicit disciplinary literacy instruction helps them to internalize and apply the language, concepts, and dispositions they have

TABLE 7.1. Close Reading Adaptation for Two-Dimensional Artwork and Film

Traditional print text	Two-dimensional artwork (painting or photograph)	Film clip
Select a complex text that relates to instructional purpose (use Lexile levels to help with this).	Select a complex text that relates to instructional purpose (use PACE Guide).	Select a complex text that relates to instructional purpose (use PACE Guide).
Provide priming questions: What are you thinking as you read? What words do you not know? What techniques is the author using? What is the author's message? What is the text's impact on the reader?	Provide priming questions: What do you see? What is the mood of the piece? How does the art piece make you feel? What techniques is the artist using? What is the artist's purpose for these choices? What is the artwork's impact on the observer?	Provide priming questions: What do you see? How does the film clip make you feel? What techniques is the director using? What is the director's purpose for these choices? What is the film's impact on the viewer?
Number the paragraphs.	Divide the painting into quadrants.	Segment the clip using time stamps.
Independent reading (use paragraph numbers to chunk text for greater analysis).	Independent viewing (use quadrants to chunk text for greater analysis).	Independent viewing (use time stamps to chunk text for greater analysis).
Text annotation—writing on paper; using Wikki-Stix to "mark" papers.	Text annotation—using sticky notes and virtual sticky notes; using digital tools such as Diigo or those internal to PDF, Adobe, Google.	Text annotation—using storyboarding; using digital tools such as Hudl, VoiceThread, or screen-recording apps.
Partner sharing—discussion with language frames.	Partner sharing—discussion with language frames.	Partner sharing—discussion with language frames.
Rereading (independent, student-led, or teacher-led) with analysis of how the text was written and the writer's craft.	Reexamining (independent, student-led, or teacher-led) with analysis of how the artwork was created and the artist's craft.	Reviewing (independent, student-led, or teacher-led) with analysis of how the film clip was created and the director's craft.
Discussion to reinforce academic vocabulary and interpretation.	Discussion to reinforce academic vocabulary and interpretation.	Discussion to reinforce academic vocabulary and interpretation.
Written extension, reflection, explanation of the piece, or demonstration of the skill/concept through writing.	Written extension (art critique or analysis), reflection, explanation of the piece, or demonstration of the skill/concept through art performance.	Written extension (film critique or analysis), reflection, explanation of the piece, or demonstration of the skill/concept through filmography.

learned. It is through students' ability to describe and evaluate an artwork's form, using terminology such as unity, balance, theme, line, tension, and texture as well as identifying and evaluating an artist's intent, that students gain literacy in the arts as "aesthetic discourse becomes an integral part of the students' practice in making meaning through art" and they are encouraged to "view things in 'uncustomary ways'" (Barton, 2013, p. 3, 4). Student-created rubrics and scoring guides also may be applied to artwork that students view as well as what they themselves create. One example would be a group of students engaged in a study of Surrealism. First, the teacher would provide instruction regarding the language (*iconography, automatism*), characteristics (*figure/shape distortion*), and individuals (Frida Kahlo) associated with the Surrealist movement. Once students are taught the explicit characteristics and language associated with Surrealism, and then shown various representative works from artists like Salvador Dali, Joan Miro, Vladimir Kush, and Chris Buzelli, they may be asked to create a scoring guide, similar to the one in Figure 7.1, that identifies the degree to which various paintings, sculptures, or installations demonstrate the characteristics of Surrealism. The teacher would share a variety of artworks—perhaps in a gallery setting—and ask students to score these artworks based on their Surrealist characteristics. Students would then engage in small-group and whole-group discussions to explain and justify their scoring choices.

By establishing a scoring guide such as the one in Figure 7.1, students not only internalize the language and concepts of the form, they also begin to discern levels of characteristic application and engage in rich discourse about the degree to which different artists mix, match, blend, privilege, and understate different aspects of the form. Through this kind of critical thinking about the artwork, they become more skilled at recognizing greater nuanced composition that can then serve to inform their own art-making processes.

Performing as Artists

It is not enough for students to read about, look at, and talk about art to gain disciplinary literacy; they must also engage in its creation (Buelow et. al., 2018; Eisner, 2004; Jarvis, 2011). Jarvis (2011) recommends children's "art skills need to be constantly practiced alongside a much wider and varied diet of visual artwork by contemporary artists as well as modern artists, of art work being seen in the gallery/museum and examples by visiting artists, . . . craftworkers, and designers" (p. 315). It, therefore, becomes important to create a learning environment that not only exposes students to a wide range of artistic styles, but also a wide range of artistic mediums where children can "experiment and explore, where children can follow

For each characteristic listed below, indicate the degree to which the following art pieces demonstrate that characteristic. Be able to justify your decisions.

1 Does not demonstrate the characteristic at all.
2 Somewhat demonstrates the characteristic.
3 Moderately demonstrates the characteristic.
4 Highly demonstrates the characteristic.

Characteristic	Painting 1 (René Magritte, *The Double Secret*)	Painting 2 (Frida Kahlo, *The Broken Column*)	Photograph (Man Ray, Rayograph)	Painting 3 (Vladimir Kush, *African Sonata*)	Sculpture (Salvador Dali, *Venus de Milo with Drawers*)
Dreamlike sequence; use of symbolism	1 2 3 4	1 2 3 4	1 2 3 4	1 2 3 4	1 2 3 4
Distorted figures and shapes	1 2 3 4	1 2 3 4	1 2 3 4	1 2 3 4	1 2 3 4
Unusual combinations of ordinary objects	1 2 3 4	1 2 3 4	1 2 3 4	1 2 3 4	1 2 3 4
Personal iconography	1 2 3 4	1 2 3 4	1 2 3 4	1 2 3 4	1 2 3 4
Spirit of spontaneity (automatism)	1 2 3 4	1 2 3 4	1 2 3 4	1 2 3 4	1 2 3 4
Visual puns	1 2 3 4	1 2 3 4	1 2 3 4	1 2 3 4	1 2 3 4

FIGURE 7.1. Sample student-generated evaluative tool for Surrealism. From Graciela's (the author's student) final class project in 2018.

their instincts, and literally 'play,' where children can learn to juxtapose disparate elements, media, and materials" (Jarvis, 2011, p. 316).

Artist Statement: Process, Not Just Product

As stated earlier, the visual arts are multimodal and performative; however, artists *do* engage in discipline-specific reading, writing, and communicating practices, and in performing as artists, students need to engage in those same practices. A key practice in visual arts is the artist statement, in which artists explain their process and rationale for the artwork they have created. From an educational standpoint, having students write artist statements does a couple of things: First, it helps students to reinforce and synthesize specific language and concepts of not only the discipline but also the subfield in which they are engaging. Second, it encourages self-reflective discourse where they can articulate the decisions they made, why they made them, and what may have inspired their work—including previous exposure to others' art forms and theoretical underpinnings. Third, it permits students to self-assess, to discern "with an open mind and no regrets" (Jarvis, 2011, p. 316) what they have done in the process of artistic practice. It is imperative for teachers to allow students the space to focus on process as well as product because it is through the process—through "frustrating encounters and love affairs with the materials of one's craft" (Jarvis, 2011, p. 316); through the posing of problems and experimenting with mediums; through the happy accidents, aggravating defeats, and resultant growth from both—that students are initiated into the arts discipline. Writing about their process encourages students to self-reflect and consider alternative possibilities for their artwork.

Joan Didion (1976) once stated, "I write entirely to find out what I'm thinking, what I'm looking at, what I see and what it means. What I want and what I fear" (p. 2). The same sentiment has been shared by artists such as Susan Rothenberg, who claimed, "I'm not a clear thinker, but I find things out by stumbling upon them," or Francis Bacon, who insisted, "I had no intention to do this picture [*Painting* of 1946]; I never thought of it that way. It was like a continuous accident mounting on top of another" (as cited in Jarvis, 2011, pp. 315–316). These quotes indicate that artists often do not know how their work will turn out—it is the process and the thinking that occurs during the process where growth and learning result, not in the final product. Providing students of all ages with environments that allow for creative risk-taking, that eschew preconceived notions of what must be accomplished to learn art, as well as opportunities to self-reflect and self-assess through the use of artist statements, journaling, blogs, or vlogs, gives them the scaffolding to find problems, to solve them, to experiment, and to still articulate the multiple levels of disciplinary literacy that avail themselves in visual arts. Through such exploration, students then become not just problem-solvers, but problem-finders, engaging in authentic inquiry rooted in visual arts disciplines.

Creating Space for Inquiry

Buelow et al. (2018) claim that because disciplinary literacy instruction should intend to build understanding of a discipline's knowledge construction rather than simply transmitting knowledge, inquiry is a crucial component of visual arts literacy attainment. That space for inquiry can be student-generated, where students encounter problems and then seek to find solutions to them (Tucker-Raymond et al., 2016); can derive from the experimentation with materials, tools, and media (Jarvis, 2011); or can be framed through a problem-posing approach to curriculum that teachers design and implement through the use of big ideas and essential questions or by juxtaposing texts within a unit and calling into question assumed ideas or beliefs. Wiggins and McTighe (2005) define *big ideas* as fundamental, comprehensive ideas that embody broad subject-specific or cross-subject concepts, are core to human understanding, and are "chosen especially for their power to explain phenomena" (p. 67). These can also be seen as "themes" that bring together seemingly disparate texts. To support students' inquiry into a theme, the authors recommend using *essential questions*, which they describe as the big, important, "so what" questions of the world that help students and educators "uncover" the curriculum in meaningful and purposeful ways. Using big ideas and essential questions in visual arts allows students to not only explore a wide range of artwork to build their disciplinary literacy, but also engage in "notions of literacy [that] include how individuals interact within a complex sociocultural system and the discourse in which the art is created and perceived" (Handerhan, 1993, as cited in Shenfield, 2015, p. 47).

For example, as represented in Figure 7.2, images of French protests on climate change, break dancing, text-based street art, a Banksy mural, a speech by women's rights activist Malala Yousafzai, and track and field athlete Raven Saunders protesting at the Tokyo Olympics can all be brought together under the big idea/theme of resistance with essential questions such as: What does it mean to resist? How do people show resistance? How can art function as a conduit, catalyst, or expression of resistance? What are ways in which artists demonstrate resistance? Such curricular framing is important because it provides relevancy for examining artwork and prevents what Williams (2016) calls "passive exposure" (p. 12) to images that can reify and reinforce existing sociocultural biases and stereotypes. Instruction in visual arts disciplinary literacy must include ways that help students "deal with conflicting messages, to make judgements in the absence of rule, to cope with ambiguity, and to frame imaginative solutions to the problems we face" (Eisner, 2004, p. 9).

Integration with Critical Literacy

Perhaps no other discipline lends itself as nimbly to engagement with critical literacy as the visual arts. Within a single wordless picture, entire stories and arguments can be made. Images are powerful messengers. Critical literacy questions issues of power and status quo. While critical analysis focuses on uncovering artistic intentionality, critical literacy asks viewers

FIGURE 7.2. Images reflecting the big idea/theme of resistance. All images are in the public domain.

to consider the text "within a matrix of social, political, and historical power relations and in relation to the search for a more just world" (Morrison, 2020, p. 11). The first prong of critical literacy requires viewers to consider their personal identities and "imbue text with meaning rather than extracting meaning from it" (Cervetti et al., 2001, para. 1). Asking students to respond to artwork from a personal vantage point, but also from a societal one, where norms are questioned and the status quo is disrupted, is at the heart of artwork. For example, the photograph pictured in Figure 7.3 shows Isaias Mata's mural entitled *500 Años de Resistencia* painted in 1992 on the side of St. Peter's Parish in the Mission District in San Francisco, which is known for its public art spaces and street murals. Helping students to understand the context for this mural can help them to develop critical literacy in the visual arts. Given the mural's title and painting date, it can easily be inferred that this mural refers to Columbus. That in itself may not be enough for students to recognize the piece's significance. However, understanding that the Mission District is the Latin portion of San Francisco, with *mercados* and *bodegas* and often Spanish-only signage, can bring its significance to light. Conquistadors with gas masks and skull faces; horses with red, glowing eyes; spears raised; and

FIGURE 7.3. Mural on St. Peter's Parish Church, San Francisco. Photographs by the author.

fires burning all tell a very different—and much more violent—narrative from the usual "Columbus discovered America" myth still perpetuated through our national holiday and historical instruction. Additionally, the use of gas masks, an icon of 20th-century warfare, indicates this conquering of Latin culture is not limited to 500 years ago but continues into the current day. Overarching the conquistadors is a Mayan/Aztec god (perhaps Quetzalcoatl or Tezcatlipoca) who swoops down to protect his people from the invaders, or in an alternative interpretation, has been martyred in a Christ-like way, demonstrating the crucifixion of Indigenous culture. Helping students to unpack cultural, societal, historical, and political iconography engages them in visual text analysis and imbues their own lived experiences into these texts. Students are then better able to question the dominant narrative, gaining not only disciplinary literacy in the arts, but also relevancy for the artwork, which can encourage students to take action in striving for a more socially just world—the second prong of critical literacy.

CONCLUSION

In a society that privileges forms of knowledge that are standardized, efficient, and "rigorous," visual arts' creative, intuitive, sensory-based processes are often marginalized and undervalued. However, "not everything knowable can be articulated in propositional form. The limits of our cognition are not defined by the limits of our language" (Eisner, 2004, p. 7). It is, therefore, imperative to recognize and value the means of expression and communication beyond language that the visual arts provide. They are not merely vehicles through which to learn the academic language of geology or to garner better reading literacy test scores. Instead, "the Arts have not only a distinct body of knowledge but also ways of expressing [this knowledge]" (Barton, 2013, p. 17) that is valuable in its own right. Disciplinary literacy in the visual arts not only constitutes understanding and enacting this body of knowledge, but also realizing the larger sociocultural landscape in which it operates and, increasingly, influences the actions and dispositions of individuals who experience it.

REFERENCES

Atwood, M. (2019). *The Testaments*. Doubleday.

Barton, G. (2013). The arts and literacy: What does it mean to be arts literate? *International Journal of Education and the Arts*, *14*(18), 1–21. Retrieved from *www.ijea.org/v14n18*.

Buelow, S., Frambaugh-Kritzer, C., & Au, C. (2018). Communicating like an artist: Disciplinary literacy instruction in the elementary visual arts. *Literacy Research and Instruction*, *57*(3), 232–254.

Cappello, M., & Lafferty, K. E. (2015). The roles of photography for developing literacy across the disciplines. *The Reading Teacher*, *69*(3), 287–295.

Cervetti, G., Pardales, M. J., & Damico, J. S. (2001). A tale of differences: Comparing the traditions, perspectives, and educational goals of critical reading and critical literacy. *Reading Online*, *4*(9).

Chandler-Olcott, K. (2017, September). Disciplinary literacy and multimodal text design in physical education. *Literacy (UKLA)*, *51*(3), 147–153.

Dehner, M. (2018). 5 ways to bring literacy into the art classroom [blog]. *The Art of Education*. Retrieved from *http://theartofeducation.edu/2018/12/10/5-ways-to-bring-literacy-into-the-art-classroom*.

Didion, J. (1976). Why I write. *The Essay Experience*. Retrieved from *http://theessayexperiencefall2013.qwriting.qc.cuny.edu/files/2013/08/%E2%80%9CWhy-I-Write%E2%80%9D-by-Joan-Didion.pdf*.

Eisner, E. W. (2004, October). What can education learn from the arts about the practice of education? *International Journal of Education & the Arts*, *5*(4), 1–11.

Gross, K. M. (2020). Visual arts content literacy: A partnership between art educators and special educators. *Teaching Exceptional Children*, *52*(3), 157–165.

Jarvis, M. (2011). What teachers can learn from the practice of artists. *International Journal of Arts and Design Education*, *30*(2), 307–317.

Lent, R. C., & Voigt, M. M. (2019). *Disciplinary literacy in action: How to create and sustain a school-wide culture of deep reading, writing, and thinking.* Corwin Literacy.

Manderino, M., & Castek, J. (2016). Digital literacies for disciplinary learning: A call to action. *Journal of Adolescent and Adult Learning*, *60*(1), 79–81.

MasterClass. (2021, May 11). *Elements of design: Understanding the 7 elements of design*. Retrieved from *www.masterclass.com/articles/elements-of-design-explained#the-elements-of-design*.

Moje, E. B. (2008). Foregrounding the disciplines in secondary literacy teaching and learning: A call for change. *Journal of Adolescent & Adult Literacy*, *52*(2), 96–107.

Morrison, J. D. (2018). Disciplinary literacy in the "othered" courses: Valuing the related arts' and physical education's literacies. Paper presented at the SCCTE Conference, Kiawah Island, SC.

Morrison, J. D. (2020). Dually critical: Blending Liberal-Humanist critical reading with Freirean critical literacy. *Talking Points*, *32*(1), 10–19.

Shanahan, C., & Shanahan, T. (2014). Does disciplinary literacy have a place in elementary school? *The Reading Teacher*, *67*(8), 636–639.

Shanahan, T., & Shanahan, C. (2008). Teaching disciplinary literacy to adolescents: Rethinking content-area literacy. *Harvard Educational Review*, *78*(1), 1–21.

Shenfield, R. (2015). Literacy in the arts. *Literacy Learning: The Middle Years*, *23*(1), 47–53.

Smagorinsky, P. (2014). Introduction. In P. Smagorinsky (Ed.), *Teaching dilemmas and solutions in content-area literacy grades 6–12* (pp. ix–xvii). Corwin Press.

Spalter, A. M., & van Dam, A. (2008). Digital visual literacy. *Theory into Practice*, *47*, 93–101.

Strong, R. W., Silver, H. F., & Perini, M. J. (2001). *Teaching what matters most: Standards and strategies for raising student achievement*. ASCD.

Tucker-Raymond, E., Gravel, B. E., Wagh, A., & Wilson, N. (2016). Making it social: Consider the purpose of literacy to support participation in making and engineering. *Journal of Adolescent & Adult Literacy*, *60*(2), 201–211.

Vacca, R., Vacca, J., & Mraz, M. (2016). *Content area reading: Literacy and learning across the curriculum*. Pearson.

Wiggins, G., & McTighe, J. (2005). *Understanding by design* (2nd ed.). ASCD.

Williams, J. (2016). Art education with attitude. *Journal of Social Science Education*, *15*(4), 7–13.

Wolsey, T. D., & Lapp, D. (2017). *Literacy in the disciplines: A teacher's guide for grades 5–12*. Guilford Press.

Disciplinary Literacy in the Performing Arts

Rachelle S. Savitz
Alison E. Leonard

Our lives are steeped in the performing arts—from the music we listen to; shows, movies, concerts, and performances we watch; to the media we consume. We engage in the performing arts in our daily lives in small ways when we sing along to the song playing in the background and dance to its beat, or recite the lines from our favorite shows and movies. We participate in the performing arts in more extensive ways through our social pastimes and cultural and religious traditions. Even more, the performing arts signify a vital part of our economies. The Arts and Cultural Production Satellite Account (ACPSA) reported that arts and cultural organizations contributed $877.8 billion (4.5%) to the nation's gross domestic product (GDP) in 2017 (Americans for the Arts, 2021; National Endowment for the Arts, 2021). On a personal level, the performing arts also promote positive physical, psychological, social, spiritual, and cultural well-being and health. Yet, despite the multitude of roles that the performing arts play in our personal and professional lives, the performing arts remain relegated to electives or "specials" within education contexts. The performing arts, typically defined as dance, drama/theater, and music, often are thought of as pursuits for only a talented few or as hobbies outside the general curriculum despite their inclusion in national and state curricula. That said, the performing arts' role in arts integration contexts in general education PreK–5 classrooms may, in fact, play an increasingly prevalent role in PreK–12 education.

Interestingly, the performing arts are well positioned in the realm of literacy, despite largely remaining marginalized in schools. While some attention is paid to disciplinary literacies in music (Buehl, 2017), theater (Draper et al., 2010), and dance and drama (Frambaugh-Kritzer et al., 2015), there is a dearth of discussions of the performing arts, particularly dance and drama, within the realm of disciplinary literacy and its relevant scholarship and literature. It is important to note that while arts integration in secondary contexts remains relatively rare, more resources are emerging in the literature about opportunities to utilize the arts within other disciplines (Leonard, 2021; Leonard & Cridland-Hughes, 2020; Macro & Zoss, 2019).

As educators in the performing arts, we have both questioned what disciplinary literacy in the performing arts means since what we do in the performing arts is essentially literacy. As artistic and aesthetic forms of communication and expression, individually as disciplines, dance, drama, and music require and rely on multiple forms of literacy and literacy skills. Dance, drama, and music include vocabulary that is embodied, performed knowledge in which performers act as both object and subject, the artist and the art. When we think of the performing arts, we often think about an end goal of preparing for and then presenting a performance as there is the assumption of a performer and an audience (Prendergast, 2004). Whether the audience is your classmate or a theater of spectators, the performing arts assumes a relationship between the performer and audience in time and space and with respect to a creative pursuit. Performing can be defined broadly as acting, moving, playing, pretending, speaking/singing, and engaging in rituals and tasks. Moreover, an entire and rather complex discipline dedicated to studying all kinds of performances called performance studies broadly defines performance as taking "place both in doing and showing doing" (Schechner, 2020, p. 4). In this way, performing in the arts involves paying attention to what is performed and how it is performed.

Whether honing technical skills in the performing arts or utilizing them through arts integration, the act of performing in small ways when we share something with a friend or in large ways in presenting on stage becomes essential. Through the performing arts, the performers and the audience write and read, speak and listen to and through a multitude of multimodal texts from the body, gestures, and movements to sounds, music, and musical and written/spoken texts (Dils, 2007; Leonard et al., 2016). By engaging in multimodal literacy practices, students must decipher and interpret meanings across diverse and intertwined modes and texts.

To represent knowledge and communicate in multimodal literacy contexts, such as in the performing arts, one must make artistic, aesthetic, and interpretive choices, transmediating knowledge, based on the affordances and limitations of these varied modes and texts (Leonard et al., 2015).

Therefore, through the performing arts, the opportunities for rich, complex teaching and learning across a multitude of texts are possible, despite practitioners in performing arts education not always explicitly referring to forms of literacy in the arts. In this way, the performing arts aligns with Universal Design for Learning (UDL) because they serve as multiple means of representation, action, and engagement to provide access to a myriad of diverse learners with extensive ways to construct and demonstrate knowledge and learning (Silverstein, 2020).

What counts as text in the performing arts may refer to traditional texts, such as reading a biographical sketch of an artist, a performance critique, or a play, but also relates to scores, choreographic maps, scene designs, or even the music and musical performance itself, dance, or play. In disciplines outside of education, such as performance studies, the concept of a text expands to not merely include performance but also questions whether written text can also perform (Browning, 2018). There are numerous forms of texts and multiliteracies (Alvermann et al., 2010; Provenzo et al., 2014) that require us to reconceptualize our definitions about texts and literacy, considering what students are doing, such as producing, creating, or making sense of something. The focus is then on how students interact with the texts and the way in which they perform can be read as text (Broomhead, 2010; Moxley et al., 2012; Worthen, 2007). Furthermore, the tension lies more in examining the authoritative structures and societal assumptions that determine who gets to decide what is a text versus arguing for what is defined as a text (Worthen, 2007). In the past, one might interpret the discussion of literacy and dance, for example, as distancing itself from the arts (Dils, 2007), whereas they are connected.

Examining disciplinary literacy within the performing arts in education involves integrating the habits and practices of performing arts disciplines across many subjects and disciplines in general education settings, particularly in PreK–8 settings and those engaged in specialized, more technical performing arts coursework in secondary and higher education contexts. The National Core Arts Standards involve four so-called anchor standards that relate to artistic processes and support reflective and interpretive processes that can easily be connected to what we consider "literacy":

1. Creating (i.e., generating, conceptualizing, organizing, developing, refining, completing artistic work)
2. Performing/Presenting/Producing (i.e., selecting, analyzing, interpreting, developing, refining techniques, conveying meaning for the presentation of artistic work)
3. Responding (i.e., perceiving, analyzing, interpreting intent and meaning, applying criteria to evaluate artistic work)

4. Connecting (i.e., synthesizing and relating knowledge and personal experiences, relating artistic ideas and works with societal, cultural, and historical context to deepen understanding) (National Coalition for Core Arts Standards [NCCAS], 2014)

While the National Core Arts Standards and state arts standards often pertain to the arts disciplines individually, there is much room for inter- and cross-disciplinary collaborations. Similar to core classrooms, a place exists for blending content-area literacy with the literacy skills needed for these specific areas. There is a need to keep in mind that the performing arts have a heavy focus on "critical thinking, critical making, and performing," as "creativity and critique are core elements of artistic thinking and habits of mind" (Zygouris-Coe, 2015, p. 39).

In this chapter, we will focus on the performing arts disciplines of dance, drama, and music. However, within each of those disciplines are a range of styles, genres, practices, and potential ways of integrating them within, across, and through other disciplines. Perhaps just as importantly, there may be ways in which this chapter might also relate to disciplinary literacy within the visual arts if engaging in art installations that bridge the visual arts and performance experiences (e.g., Van Gogh: The Immersive Experience). In this way, when we talk about dance, drama, and music in education, we acknowledge a broad spectrum of practices and genres and potential applications for educators and scholars within the realms of disciplinary literacy.

WHAT ARE THE PERFORMING ARTS?

The performing arts, typically defined as dance, drama/theater, and music, are often taught by arts specialists in PreK–12 schools and can also be part of an integrated arts curriculum in general education classrooms. However, typically, dance and drama/theater are not as widely available in most PreK–12 schools, whereas music often is. As students progress through PreK–12 schools and into higher education, the performing arts tend to play more peripheral roles or ones of choice when students elect to take courses in the genres of dance, drama, or theater, or playing in the band or singing in the choir, rather than mandated curriculum.

Dance

Dance in education in PreK–12 schools for early childhood students can include creative dance classes/activities where there is a focus on learning about and through the elements of dance (body, action, space, time, and energy) as forms of creative expression and self-expression, physical development, and inquiry (Green Gilbert, 2015). In middle and high school contexts where disciplines are more siloed, dance may be used for conceptual understanding. However, in early and elementary contexts, dance is frequently integrated into general education by utilizing gestures and movements to explore curricular concepts, sometimes with musical accompaniment and song, to focus energy through interactive videos, such as GoNoodle, or as a unit in physical education class. While dedicated classes for dance are still relatively rare in most PreK–12 schools, some may have dance classes with dance education specialists who follow the National Core Arts Standards or state's standards that typically involve curriculum-related creating dance, performing/presenting/producing, responding to dance performance, and making connections across dance genres and other disciplines. Districts and schools often employ a dance artist-in-residence or teaching artists to teach shorter units or guest-teach, focusing on various genres or setting or collaborating with students on choreography. Dance technique classes are typically taught in informal settings outside of PreK–12 schools; however, some high schools include dance techniques as elective courses. PreK–12 dance classes and artist-in-residence programs may infuse influences and activities related to more of dance, such as African, Asian, Latin rhythm; creative and contemporary modern, ballet, jazz/musical theater, tap, and hip-hop; social and line dancing, ballroom, and folk.

Drama

Like dance, dedicated classes in drama in education in PreK–12 schools are rare, typically in early and elementary schools. In contrast, a drama or theater class or club in secondary education for middle school or high school is more common. Drama typically refers to process-oriented learning activities to deepen understanding of self and others focused on exploration, play, critical thinking, fostering creativity, expression, and communication that bring together "cognitive, emotional, and kinesthetic domains that make us human" (van de Water et al., 2015, p. 8). Although drama activities may lead to the performance or sharing of creative work, theater typically focuses on creating or staging a final performance for an audience. While theater may have a director and performers, drama involves a facilitator and participants. Another way to think about it is that theater often involves participating in drama activities to prepare for roles, whereas drama may involve a performance, but the primary purpose or goal is experiential. In earlier grades, guest teaching artists or an artist-in-residence from a local theater company (Anderson & Risner, 2014), or even the staging and performance of a play facilitated by a classroom teacher within a class or school are more typical. Like dance, drama activities infused into general education classrooms have become even more commonplace (Macro & Zoss, 2019). Within the realm of drama in education, we include theater (plays, musical theater, opera); reader's theater; dramatic storytelling; spoken word poetry; improvisation and improv games; and drama activities, such as role play, tableau, and simulations, many that also involve creative movement/dance, sound explorations, and music.

Music

Of the three major performing arts disciplines, music in education is the most prevalent for all students in PreK–12 schools (Campbell, 2018). As is common in most K–5 schools, students attend music and visual arts classes taught by arts specialists in their regular curriculum. Then in elementary school through the middle and high school grades, elective instruction in band or orchestra becomes more common. In secondary contexts, choir and orchestra electives are frequently available for students, along with varied opportunities to play in the marching band, jazz bands, or pit orchestra in drama departments. Music performance classrooms "emphasize developing technical competence in music facility with a musical instrument or one's voices, reading musical notation, and contributing as a member of an ensemble" (Buehl, 2017, p. 218).

Similar to PreK–12 general education contexts for dance and drama, music plays an important role in arts integration opportunities through activities such as sound walks; the creation and singing of songs and raps for memorizing and learning content; using music for relaxation, focus, and visualization; and even through spoken word poetry (Donovan & Pascale, 2013). Music in education also involves "musicking": "the act of making music and to engaging as a participant in a musical event—as an active listener or as a dance whose movements respond to music's expressive qualities, rhythms" and technical qualities (Campbell, 2018, p. 5; Small 1998). Music of any form requires more than playing notes but also learning how to play music in a way that is expressive and tells a story (Buehl, 2017).

LITERACY AND THE PERFORMING ARTS

Literacy directly connects with communication as meaning is shared with words on paper and across multiple modalities and forms of communication (Buehl, 2017; National Council of Teachers of English [NCTE], 2005; Wilson & Chavez, 2014). Eisner (1997) aptly posits, "In order to be read, a poem, an equation, a painting, a dance, a novel, or a contract each requires a distinctive form of literacy . . . a way of conveying meaning through and recovering meaning from the form of representation in which it appears"

(p. 353). Yet, often, literacy educators are uncomfortable applying their literacy expertise to supporting and understanding literacy within the performing arts (Broomhead, 2010) due to a multitude of reasons, such as a dearth of training and professional development revolving around what literacy is and is not in the performing arts.

A significant component of the performing arts is being immersed in the learning *and* participation in each discipline, addressing four main elements of literacy: creating literacy, performing literacy, listening (and watching) literacy, and contemplating literacy (Moxley et al., 2012). As students explore dance, music, and theater, they learn to read; write (compose, design, create, choreograph); and speak/communicate (perform). Students become insiders in these performing and expressive arts and audience members and critical observers/listeners when they evaluate, analyze, and critique performances. Moreover, the performing arts invite and rely on this dual role of performers and audience members (Prendergast, 2004). What's more, if we consider that disciplinary literacy focuses on the reading, writing, listening, speaking of a discipline, we extend this general understanding to include the integration of content knowledge, experiences, and skills related to thinking critically and performing. Then as educators, we invite readers to consider as Dils (2007) aptly and thoughtfully asks:

> If movement [music, acting/performing] is considered a literacy, what might this do for children who have difficulty reading and writing, but not in expressing themselves physically [vocally, with instruments, in dance, in drama]? . . . What might be possible if we were prepared to consider fluency in nonverbal behavior and dance as other forms of literacy, equally important to our communication? Would this change our sense of who was succeeding in schooling and who was not? (pp. 100–101)

Another common misunderstanding when considering literacy within the performing arts is the difference between reading the notes on a staff or a choreography plan and assuming that such reading is enough. When artists learn music, dance, theatrical scenes, or participate in drama activities and games, they must learn to reflect through a performing lens relating to content and performing that content. Mastery of notes or dance moves is not the end: Artists must also interpret the intent and purpose behind each piece and song. Within the realm of arts integration/fusion, they reflect on the experience as individuals and as a collective, allowing students to engage within and reflect on content and techniques and social, cultural, political, and intersectionality of performance. Therefore, when tackling a new movement or piece, artists must not only learn how to read the many various musical symbols and notations, but also engage in "fleshing out a context and a story line" to "transcend" from reading to performing

(Buehl, 2017, p. 219). While contextualizing performance work or the creative process can come in the form of researching and providing context and background, this may also be done through arts analysis, critique, and reflection. Similar to the visual arts, in theater the role of critique, and in drama the role of reflection, are hallmarks of the creative and performative process (van de Water et al., 2015).

In addition, while classrooms have advocated for the use of culturally responsive and sustaining pedagogies to address inequitable instruction through curricula (Ladson-Billings, 2014, 2017; Muhammad, 2020; Paris, 2012), the same applies in the performing arts. The three central tenets of culturally responsive and sustaining pedagogies are that teachers should hold high academic expectations for students, support students to build their cultural competence, and help students develop a critical consciousness about the surrounding social and political world (Ladson-Billings, 1995). While many teachers may choose a piece based on difficulty, quality, or other factors related to student demographics and the time of year, there is also a critical need to consider critical pedagogies that, for example, utilize representation from various historical periods, genres of music, and styles of dance, theater, and music (Buehl, 2017), as well as diverse representation in terms of race, gender identity, among various subjectivities.

While performing arts disciplines and arts integration practices incorporate literacy in every sense of the word, it will be helpful for literacy educators to break down what this means precisely. Here, we will discuss how reading, writing, speaking, and listening can translate in each performing arts discipline.

Reading and Interpreting

Analysis in the performing arts parallels what we traditionally think of when analyzing more traditional texts in content-area classrooms, but with a unique flair. Each performing arts discipline has its own vocabulary and elements or forms (e.g., elements of music, dance, or drama). Just as with a traditional text, students explore these forms, what they observe/hear, why specific stylistic elements or forms were used. For example, how a dancer uses sharp and quick movements in contrast to flowing and slower movements might be observed, and then how those movements create contrast discussed. This process is akin to examining word choice, for example. To explore and analyze works in the performing arts from a literacy perspective, there is a need for deeper inquiry and a line of questioning to comprehend how to read and interpret a piece fully and thus help enhance students' performances. Students must assess the *how* and *why* when performing, not just the *what* of a piece. This type of analysis occurs before performing, but also during and after it, to consistently assess whether their interpretation and performing align with the intent of the artist, performer, or composer.

Lent and Voight (2019, p. 309) provide a thoughtful breakdown of disciplinary practices within various disciplines. Their list for reading characteristics in a music class can equally relate to other performing arts classrooms:

- Synthesize knowledge and personal experience.
- Connect artistic ideas and works with societal, cultural, and historical context.
- Understand specialized vocabulary such as harmony, rhythm, and timbre.
- Consider others' perspectives by reading reviews and critiques of concerts, musicals, and albums.
- Determine validity of sources and quality of evidence in critiques.
- Search for innovative processes.
- Compare their experiences to others by reading biographies, articles, blogs, and books.
- Apply theories of creativity to their own artistic processes.
- Find inspiration that fuels creativity.
- Learn the sonic properties and structural elements of musical instruments.

In other words, as students read and comprehend in the performing arts, literacy strategies and skills are required with performing arts teachers embodying the work of a literacy teacher. It is important to note that literacy and performing arts teachers are both engaging in the teaching of literacy, but a disconnect can exist between the two without effective communication to learn with and from one another. And most importantly, students should be asked to interpret and make meaning from aural, visual, and written texts that draw from various cultures, times, and locations (Mills & McPherson, 2015).

Spotlight on Music: Reading and Interpreting

In a music classroom, literacy involves reading musical notes on a staff, lyrics, improvisation, sight-reading, practice, memorization, composition, body movement, watching or listening to a performance, critiquing, and intentional use of expression and intonation (Brozo, 2017; Moxley et al., 2012). Another possible way that reading is embedded in the classroom is when students read about a musician, their life, music philosophy or beliefs, or reasons for writing a particular piece. This type of reading, especially if done prior to listening to musical masterpieces from the artist, provides a sense of previewing what students may hear at a performance (Brozo, 2017) and learning about the composer's intended message.

Reading and interpreting instrumental music are like learning how to read and interpret the English language (Hansen & Milligan, 2012; Runfola et al., 2012; Wolsey & Lapp, 2017). As Henry Wadsworth Longfellow stated, "Music is the universal language of mankind." Both require first mastering technical aspects, then learning to read, compose, and perform the artistic elements. Similar to learning how to read, the first few years of learning music emphasize pitch and rhythm (Wolsey & Lapp, 2017). Pitch is the actual sound made by an instrument, including vocal sounds, and rhythm is decided by symbols that denote specific notes, beats, and patterns. Musically, phonics is most readily associated with notes. Learning how each note of the musical alphabet has a particular frequency is important. Notes move up and down in stepwise and interval motion to create melodies. Children must also learn how sounds and symbols connect, such as with musical notation, where a symbol communicates the duration of how long or short to hold a note or rest (Moxley et al., 2012). For music, notes are the words. Students learn how to read notes, both in duration and pitch level, understanding how these two come together to make measures and phrases of music.

Phonemic awareness, as we know, is the ability for students to hear, identify, and manipulate phonemes. Students learn how to segment the sounds and blend them to form words. The awareness that music can be deconstructed into smaller parts is essential, as is the idea that students must learn how to manipulate the sounds. In an elementary music classroom, children often learn to listen to the sound of music before learning how to read music. They may hear low-pitched sounds and then high-pitched sounds or sounds that are held longer versus short and brief sounds (Runfola et al., 2012). After students learn these fundamental components, they then learn more specific artistic concepts, such as dynamics, articulation, diction, and other stylistic elements that relate to creating emotional expression and knowing the emotion to be performed as intended by the artist.

Music comprehension is as crucial as comprehension in an English classroom. Students must make sense of a piece and synthesize information and knowledge of the musical elements throughout the work to provide the appropriate expression when performing. Brozo (2017) shares the example of a twelfth-grade teacher directing students to read *Lohengrin* by Wagner before practicing and performing the opera so that they could gather needed knowledge of traditional story elements, such as character development, to learn the intentions behind Wagner's lyrics and words. This supported students' ability to determine how the music should be performed.

One form of analysis for students in a music classroom is to critique and evaluate a person's performance, their own or someone else's that they are watching. This requires students to use their knowledge about the piece and background to interpret and make judgments of the work. Students may review based on their interpretation and assess historical and cultural accuracy, critical thinking, and writing in a medium that is true to the performing arts outside of the classroom (Zygouris-Coe, 2015). This may occur simply to practice evaluating and assessing specific aspects of performance, such as the ability to follow the required stylistic notations or used to better one's performance to prepare for a concert or recital.

When we ask students to conduct a critique, we may first ask them to *identify* and *describe* the experience and description of the piece or performance. This may include a focus on subject matter, what they are seeing and hearing, the characters and story elements, and could even include historical and cultural context. Next, students *analyze* what they are experiencing, focusing on the elements of the discipline (i.e., dance, drama, and/or music) and how they are used specific to what they are seeing and hearing. For example, with dance, students will investigate and evaluate body, action, space, time, and energy. Building on the analysis, students then interpret by exploring what an artist or the artists might be trying to say to the audience, what messages are being conveyed. Finally, using the examples from the previous steps to *evaluate* the best, they consider the success of the piece or performance and how it compares to other pieces and performances in this same discipline and/or genre. While there are many types of critiques and resources available, here are a few questions to contemplate when beginning this type of work in the classroom. It is important to note that these are only examples as there are many ways to critique and evaluate the performing arts and elements within each. Therefore, it is crucial to provide a clear focus on what element or aspect students are critiquing so that they do not evaluate an entire performance all at once.

- How does the art compare to other work in its genre? How original is this work? Have your thoughts or feelings changed since your first impression? If so, what made you change your mind?
- What emotions does the music invoke? Do the melody and harmony sufficiently take the audience on the intended journey?
- How did the actor or actors use their bodies and voices to interpret and create their characters? Were their characterizations realistic and believable?
- What was the dancers' relationship to space? For example, how did they utilize the low, medium, and/or high movements in the vertical plane to convey meaning?

- How do the set design, lighting, and other theatrical elements convey mood, tone, and other story elements individually as well as in connection to what is being portrayed?
- What do you believe were the director's intent and purpose in creating this piece or performance? Provide evidence to support your claim.
- Would you recommend this play to others? Why or why not? Who is the intended audience?
- Does the work succeed or fail in your opinion? What specifically makes it a success or a failure?

Listening and Critiquing

In performing arts classrooms, as students read words, language, and music, they simultaneously translate and interpret the meaning behind the artist's intent. As musicians or dancers listen to music, they are inundated with various factors to listen for and interpret in their bodies: tone, mood, being in tune, and so on. For instance, have you ever stopped to consider how the tone of a piece you listen to communicates emotion and can even change your mood? This occurs because of the musical key used to build the melody and harmony throughout the piece. The key can be major or minor, with each prompting different emotions in the listener. Here are a few examples of songs and the key. Consider what emotion or feeling each piece elicits and how you respond when hearing this song.

- Pachelbel's *Canon in D Major*, often heard at weddings or during wedding scenes
- Hallelujah Chorus in Handel's *Messiah in D Major*, often heard at religious events or during momentous scenes
- Beethoven's *Symphony Number 5 in C Minor*, often heard in action scenes
- Mozart's *Requiem in D Minor*, often played at funerals and during somber scenes

Sounds create a mood, frequently during a scene or even a scene change. In drama activities, a soundscape may be created by using one's body and immediate surroundings, such as making the environment of a story being read or relating to a particular character or event. Listening and assessing behavior and actions play an integral role in drama and improvisation games.

While the key used in a song can support analysis related to an artist's purpose, so, too, does the tempo, as it influences and evokes different emotions (Bogert et al., 2016; Liu et al., 2018), with a faster tempo evoking feelings of happiness and excitement and a slower tempo causing more negative emotions, such as sadness and depression (Hunter et al., 2010). Typically, tempo is measured according to beats per minute (bpm) and is divided into prestissimo (>200 bpm), presto (168–200 bpm), allegro (120–168 bpm), moderato (108–120 bpm), andante (76–108 bpm), adagio (66–76 bpm), larghetto (60–66 bpm), and largo (40–60 bpm).

These few examples of elements demonstrate the need for students to critique and evaluate a person's performance, their own or someone else's that they are watching. This requires students to use their knowledge about the piece and its background to interpret and form judgments of the work. Students may review the performance based on their interpretation and assess its historical and cultural accuracy, critically thinking and writing in a medium that is true to the performing arts outside of the classroom (Zygouris-Coe, 2015). This may occur simply to practice evaluating and assessing specific aspects of performance, such as the ability to follow the required stylistic notations, or used to better one's performance to prepare for a concert or recital.

Some sample questions provided by Zygouris-Coe (2015, p. 40) that students may use when assessing a performance include the following:

- What do I see or hear?
- How did the musician, performer, or composer use harmony, rhythm, texture, color, and form in the piece?
- What did I think about the play, its direction, the acting, and the use of design elements (i.e., scenery, costumes, lighting, music/sound)?
- What is the message or story of this work?
- What artistic elements did the artist use to convey the message?
- What artistic elements stood out?
- Does the work hold together visually?
- What mood does this art communicate?

Writing and Composing

Often overlooked is the ability for students to compose and create themselves, going through the process of writing a play, developing a particular dance or choreography, and even composing their musical rendition of a piece or original musical piece. As students create their lyrics and music or write a short play, they become the sole deciders for what message and story they want to convey and how to express emotions with an audience. Regardless of which area of performing arts is involved, students will consider a range of perspectives and ways to communicate their intended message, feelings, emotions, and ideas within what they create or compose. Like writing an essay in a composition class, they create an outline and draft a concise piece, choosing their words and phrases carefully. As Wolsey and Lapp (2017) note, "Lyrics and songs are like sketches—the 'underdrawing' of a sketch, expressing a lyrical idea, pulling out the purest form of language, refine, refine, refine, refine, and layer, layer, layer, and revisit your original thoughts" (p. 45). This type of composing can occur within any grade level, such as creating hip-hop songs in the early grades (Meacham et al., 2019).

Another possibility is a student critiquing a performance, analyzing various stylistic interpretations, feelings, and the mood conveyed, how the story elements were developed, evaluating personal reactions to performances, and determining if the version in performance expressed its intended meaning and emotions. This type of writing connects with argumentative and persuasive writing as students use textual evidence or respond to teacher-identified criteria to evaluate and critique a piece or performance (Lent & Voight, 2019). Using their knowledge of artistic design and performance of the past provides the necessary information related to the details and facts of a genre and time portrayed and the historical and cultural context to accurately give meaning and value to their work (Buehl, 2017; Zygouris-Coe, 2015).

Writing in the performing arts could also consist of researching eras, genres, artists, works, or other ways to become more informed on the performance or play or to determine the author's craft, style, and choices. Students could research different genres and types of music, dance, or theater and investigate diverse cultural perspectives used and compare and contrast how stories and experiences are represented (Lent & Voight, 2019).

Spotlight on Dance: Writing and Composing

As Foster (2018) poignantly writes, "A body, whether sitting writing or standing thinking or walking talking or running screaming, is a bodily writing. Its habits and stances, gestures and demonstration . . . all these emerge out of cultural practices, verbal or not, that construct corporeal meaning" (p. 291). Choreographing and dancing in their representation of concepts, ideas, and expressions become a form of writing and composing. In the realm of disciplinary literacy, if we take Foster's words seriously, the possibilities in schools for embodied forms of writing and how educators might assess students' development of writing skills have enormous potential. In no way does this perspective replace the written word and development of those skills; however, a broader perspective on what skills could be involved in developing writing habits and practices might help educators support students who often struggle with traditional forms of writing and/or further challenge students to creatively expand their writing repertoire (Dils, 2007). Moreover, the writing process "begins not only when we put pen to paper, or fingers to the keyboard, but also in the way we are consciously embodied—the way we breathe, think, and feel in our bodies" (Cancienne & Snowbar, 2003, p. 248).

Writing as dancing and composing as choreographing can come in multiple forms in schools. From dance classes in schools taught by certified dance teachers or teaching artists to PreK–5 classes taught by education generalists or even disciplinary classes in other subjects in the middle grades and secondary schools, students have been able to represent knowledge through dance and the act of choreography. The National Core Arts Standards in Dance involve the entire creative process: (1) generating and conceptualizing artistic ideas in dance; (2) organizing and developing these ideas; and (3) refining and completing artistic work. Part of that creative process is also analyzing, evaluating, refining, and documenting one's work (National Core Arts Standards, 2014). This process parallels the standards for English language arts (ELA). For example, in Adams (2016), the correlations between dance choreography and early writing with kindergarteners as "the Common Core State Standards for English Language Arts (CCSS for ELA) standards recognize the developmental link among pictures, symbols, and letters in literacy acquisition" (p. 31). In the dance class, Adams's students brainstorm movement ideas; document plans for their dances using symbols, drawings, and words; and read and interpret the plans of their peers.

Dance choreography in schools can also lend itself to aiding in the assessment of literacy skills. Even more than intersecting knowledge across literacies as dance does as a multimodal form of literacy, it allows students to use critical thinking, symbolic understanding, conditional reasoning as a means to abstract knowledge, transferring concepts, ideas, and spoken and written language into movement, writing it with their bodies (Leonard et al., 2015). As noted previously, what a student knows and understands might not be easily deciphered through their speaking and writing, but much could be learned from what the student expresses through dance. Triangulating what and how students write with their bodies, how they might verbally describe their dancing, and how they map it out or depict it visually and via symbols and words can provide a larger picture of their literacy development.

Dance as writing can also play a role in how literacy and ELA educators utilize dance in their classrooms or collaborate with dance educators. Macro and Zoss (2019) provide multiple examples of how the arts can be integrated into secondary ELA contexts, including the visuals arts, music, drama, and spoken word poetry. Leonard and Cridland-Hughes (2019) provide a pedagogical example of integrating English, hip-hop, and choreography to analyze vernacular texts, such as lyrics in secondary education and preservice teaching contexts. Pulling together standards in ELA and dance, students and participants explore hip-hop lyrics by creating original choreography based on literal and abstract choreographic representations of the lyrics.

Performing and Participating

As we have discussed, the performing arts are multimodal as students move from one mode (music/sound/aural sense) to another, for example, to translate music into written or spoken language, requiring interpretation and expression of the original material in a new way (Wagoner, 2020). As Lent and Voight (2019) state, when students participate as performing artists, they are asked to "exhibit artistic skills in craft and technique during presentation and performance, interacting with others to realize a common vision, [and at times] seek to respond and react to the present moment through improvisation" (p. 310). Students must consistently assess their performance and determine the changes that are needed to appropriately convey intended meaning. This means listening, conversing, and interpreting together. Therefore, one crucial consideration when considering performing is pronunciation. Within these disciplines, the mere change in how a word is pronounced can impact the song's tone, meaning, and intent that the audience will hear. As mentioned, the intent and meaning form expression for the audience, so the slight change could create a different and unintended misinterpretation of a piece.

In terms of fluency, for example, in drama or theater class, repeated readings, writing and rehearsing scripts, developing characterizations, creating props and costumes, and making decisions about staging are a few of the examples where students can increase their fluency. Interestingly, in dance, while fluency in reading traditional texts can apply, fluency in the sense of accuracy, rate, and prosody can also relate to one's dance movements and technical skills in performing. While one might assume that fluency in dance only occurs within the realm of a dance specialist, a generalist might approach dance fluency as related to other curricular content in which a student is performing. For example, attending to how a student chooses to move to represent a concept, such as embodying characteristics of the states of matter (solid, liquid, or gas) in science class might involve a change of speed or representing different qualities of being light or heavy, affecting how their performance is read by their peers/teacher/audience. One additional note here is that by incorporating this type of repetition, students are strengthening their accuracy and prosody through practice, listening to others, and making modifications based on feedback related to inflection, pitch, accentuation, and other skills needed to successfully perform a piece of music (Rasinski, 2010).

Spotlight on Drama: Performing and Participating

Drama is inherently about learning. From creative drama, drama in education, improvisation, process drama, educational drama to drama and theater classes in education, drama-based teaching and learning focus on performance in informal and more formal ways as a means to explore communication and forms of expression. Participating in drama in education in its myriad of forms is also innately about literacy. "Drama fosters literacy because it allows students of any age to become part of the learning process" and plays a role in developing and shaping our identities (Macro, 2015, p. 338). Interestingly, as Sean Layne, Kennedy Center for the Performing Arts teaching artist, teaches, behavior is a literacy, and therefore, how we act and perform in schools can greatly benefit from drama in education strategies (Layne, 2017).

In the United States, there are two main drama methodologies practiced in education: linear and process-oriented drama. Linear drama methods tend to be more structured activities with a beginning, middle, and end that invite students to play and explore (van de Water et al., 2015). Often linear drama activities involve drama games and activities that include improvisation, storytelling, activities, tableau, or pantomime, whereas process-oriented drama methods involve more open-ended activities, such as role play, simulations, and creating/developing characters. In all these kinds of drama activities, literacy plays a role. Engaging in drama activities involves comprehension, language skills, points of view/perspectives, communication skills such as fluency, and multimodal forms of reading, writing, speaking, listening, and performing.

Then in a theater class setting or in an ELA course, the act of reading, analyzing, rehearsing, and performing a play is dependent on and involves developing literacy skills, such as critical literacy as one investigates a text (Donovan & Pascale, 2013). Reading, staging a reading, and performing a scene often require the same situation to be considered through different perspectives, deepening comprehension. For example, many PreK–12 classrooms incorporate reader's theater for students to practice fluency and engage in the practice of reading through a story or play using expressive and performative skills as they read.

For example, the act of play building involves practicing critical literacy and working with narrative, expository structures, and also persuasive writing and performing. Here, students can take what they have learned about reading and performing plays to work collaboratively to create an original one, demonstrating and weaving together multiple forms of literacy and literacy skills. For example, "[to] create the argument, the participants work collaboratively to link drama pieces thematically. The process begins by choosing a topic collaboratively, then improvising to explore the topic, framing the work, drafting a script, and finally rehearsing and performing" (Perry et al., 2013, p. 651). The act of creating and performing an original script invites students to make choices about setting, characters, narrative, and conflict. In doing so, students practice critical literacy in these choices, as Perry et al. (2013) note when students consider these questions: "Why does the person need to speak? What do they want to achieve by speaking? Where are they when they speak? In what ways might they be changed by the failed or successful encounter?" (p. 652). The range of literacy skills and modalities expands when you add in the staging and performance of the play with added blocking, choreography, and possibly music, extending the multimodal literacies involved.

The example of play building and moreover any drama activities also have that potential to serve as ways to engage and enrich learning for English-language learners, as well as a wide range of diverse learners and needs, including focusing on equity and inclusion (Donovan & Pascale, 2013; Perry et al., 2013; van de Water et al., 2015). Here, language exploration and development can be approached in ways that may empower students to make choices in how they engage in the activities, as well as how they communicate. Drama and theater are well positioned to practice the valuing of all individuals within a community and acknowledging the mutual interests and needs of individuals within that community, to include those performing and those behind the scenes. Within this perspective, giving an opportunity for all students to engage in drama and theater in small or expansive ways can open the possibilities for equitable literacy practices in schools as well.

CONCLUSION

As has been noted throughout this chapter, literacy is a crucial and inherent component of the performing arts. However, the traditional definition of literacy is limited to a strict relationship between reading and writing certain texts (Dunbar & Cooper, 2020). As this chapter demonstrates, literacy within the performing arts is expansive and spans multiple modalities and weaves together a myriad of literacy skills. In the four main literacy practices of (1) reading and interpreting, (2) listening and critiquing, (3) writing and composing, and (4) performing and participating, literacy in the performing arts can be defined and practiced through written textual, auditory, embodied, and visual forms. By providing a spotlight example of these practices, our intention is to explore what "literacy" looks like in each of these areas and how it differs depending on the type of performance. Through our instructional practice examples, we hope to help broaden the field of disciplinary literacy for educators seeking to infuse literacy practices with and through the performing arts and to collaborate with arts practitioners in schools.

REFERENCES

Adams, J. H. (2016). Dance and literacy hand in hand, *Journal of Dance Education, 16*(1), 31–34.

Alvermann, D. E., Phelps, S. F., & Gillis, V. R. (2010). *Content area reading and literacy: Succeeding in today's diverse classrooms* (6th ed.). Pearson.

Americans for the Arts. (2021). *Statement on arts, jobs, and the economy.* Retrieved from *www.americansforthearts.org/news-room/arts-mobilization-center/statement-on-arts-jobs-and-the-economy.*

Anderson, M. E., & Risner, D. (2014). *Hybrid lives of teaching artists in dance and theatre arts: A critical reader.* Cambia Press.

Bogert, B., Numminen-Kontti, T., Gold, B., Sams, M., Numminen, J., Burunat, I., . . . Brattico, E. (2016). Hidden sources of joy, fear, and sadness: Explicit versus implicit neural processing of musical emotions. *Neuropsychologia, 89*, 393–402.

Broomhead, P. (2010). (Re)imagining literacy for music classrooms. In R. J. Draper (Ed.), *(Re)imagining content-area literacy instruction* (pp. 69–81). Teachers College Press.

Browning, B. (2018, Summer). The performative novel. *TDR: The Drama Review 62*(2), 43–58.

Brozo, W. G. (2017). *Disciplinary and content literacy for today's adolescents* (6th ed.). Guilford Press.

Buehl, D. (2017). *Developing readers in the academic disciplines* (2nd ed.). Stenhouse.

Campbell, P. S. (2018). *Music, education, and diversity: Building cultures and communities.* Teachers College Press.

Cancienne, M. B., & Snowbar, C. N. (2003). Writing rhythm: Movement as method. *Qualitative Inquiry 9*(2), 237–253.

Dils, A. (2007). Why dance literacy? *Journal of the Canadian Association for Curriculum Studies, 5*(2), 95–113.

Donovan, L., & Pascale, L. (2013). *Integrating the arts across the content areas.* Shell Educational Publishing.

Draper, R. J., Broomhead, P., Jensen, A. P., Nokes, J. D., & Siebert, D. (Eds.). (2010). *(Re)imagining content-area literacy instruction.* Teachers College Press.

Dunbar, L., & Cooper, S. (2020). Speaking the same language: How the Kodály method promotes disciplinary literacy. *General Music Today, 34,* 14–20.

Eisner, E. W. (1997). Cognition and representation: A way to pursue the American dream? *Phi Delta Kappan, 78*(5), 348–353.

Foster, S. (2018). "Choreographing history." In J. R. Giesdorf & Y. Yong (Eds.), *The Routledge dance studies reader* (3rd ed., pp. 377–388). Routledge.

Frambaugh-Kritzer, C., Buelow, S., & Steele, J. S. (2015). What are disciplinary literacies in dance and drama in the elementary grades? *Journal of Language & Literacy Education, 11*(1), 65–87.

Green Gilbert, A. (2015). *Creative dance for all ages: A conceptual approach* (2nd ed.). Human Kinetics.

Hansen, D., & Milligan, S. A. (2012). Aural skills: At the juncture of research in early reading and music literacy. *Music Educators Journal, 99*(2), 75–80.

Hunter, P. G., Schellenberg, E. G., & Schimmack, U. (2010). Feelings and perceptions of happiness and sadness induced by music: Similarities, differences, and mixed emotions. *Psychology of Aesthetics, Creativity, and the Arts, 4*, 47–56.

Ladson-Billings, G. (1995). Toward a theory of culturally relevant pedagogy. *American Educational Research Journal, 32*(3), 465–491.

Ladson-Billings, G. (2014). Culturally relevant pedagogy 2.0: A.k.a. the remix. *Harvard Educational Review, 84*(1), 74–84.

Ladson-Billings, G. (2017). "Makes me wanna holler": Refuting the "culture of poverty" discourse in urban schooling. *Annals of the American Academy of Political and Social Science, 673*(1), 80–90.

Layne, S. (2017). *Acting right: Building a cooperative, collaborative, creative classroom community through drama.* Foresight Book Publishing.

Lent, R. C., & Voight, M. M. (2019). *Disciplinary literacy in action: How to create and sustain a schools-wide culture of deep reading, writing, and thinking.* Corwin Literacy.

Leonard, A. E. (2021). Using the *Journal of Dance Education* with secondary students. *Journal of Dance Education.*

Leonard, A. E., & Cridland-Hughes, S. (2019). Dancing vernacular: Integrating English, hip hop, and choreography for analyzing texts. *Journal of Dance Education, 20*(4), 234–239.

Leonard, A. E., Dsouza, N., Babu, S. B., Daily, S. B., Jörg, S., Waddell, C., . . . Boggs, K. (2015). Embodying and programming a "constellation" of multimodal literacy practices: Computational thinking, creative movement, biology, and virtual environment interactions. *Journal of Language and Literacy Education, 11*(2), 64–93.

Leonard, A. E., Hall, A. H., & Herro, D. (2016). Dancing literacy: Expanding children's and teachers' literacy repertoires through embodied knowing. *Journal of Early Childhood Literacy, 16*(3) 338–360.

Liu, Y., Liu, G., Wei, D., Li, Q., Yuan, G., Wu, S., . . . Zhao, X. (2018). Effects of musical tempo on musicians' and non-musicians' emotional experience when listening to music. *Frontiers in Psychology, 9*(21), 2118.

Macro, K. (2015). Drama as literacy: Perceptions of an interactive pedagogy. *Research in Drama Education: Journal of Applied Theatre and Performance, 20*(3), 337–339.

Macro, K. J., & Zoss, M. (2019). *A symphony of possibilities: A handbook for arts integration in secondary English language arts.* National Council of English Teachers.

Meacham, S. J., Meacham, S., Thompson, M., & Graves, H. (2019). Hip-hop early literacy in K–1 classrooms. *The Reading Teacher, 73*, 29–37.

Mills, J., & McPherson, G. E. (2015). Musical literacy: Reading traditional clef notation. In G. E. McPherson (Ed.), *The child as musician: A handbook of musical development* (pp. 177–192). Oxford Scholarship.

Moxley, K., Batcheller, J., Burditt, L., Gamble, S., Gumm, A. J., Paas, J., & Thurston, J. (2012). Learning with text in the arts. In T. L. Jetton & C. Shanahan (Eds.), *Adolescent literacy in the academic disciplines: General principles and practical strategies* (pp. 227–266). Guilford Press.

Muhammad, G. E. (2020). *Cultivated genius: An equity framework for culturally and historically responsive literacy.* Scholastic.

National Coalition for Core Arts Standards. (2014). *Dance at a glance.* Retrieved from *www.nationalartsstandards.org/sites/default/files/Dance%20at%20a%20Glance%20-%20new%20copyright%20info.pdf.*

National Council of Teachers of English. (2005). *Multimodal literacy.* Position statement. Retrieved from *https://ncte.org/statement/multimodalliteracies.*

National Endowment for the Arts. (2021). *During economic highs and lows, the arts are key segment of U.S. economy.* Retrieved from *www.arts.gov/about/news/2020/during-economic-highs-and-lows-arts-are-key-segment-us-economy.*

Paris, D. (2012). Culturally sustaining pedagogies: A needed change in stance, terminology, and practice. *Educational Researcher, 41*(3), 93–97.

Perry, M., Wessels, A., & Wager, A. C. (2013). From play building to devising in literacy education: Aesthetic and pedagogical approaches. *Journal of Adolescent & Adult Literature, 56*(8), 649–658.

Prendergast, M. (2004). "Playing attention": Contemporary aesthetics and performing arts audience education. *Journal of Aesthetic Education, 38*(3), 36–51.

Provenzo, E. F., Goodwin, A., Lipsky, M., & Sharpe, S. (Eds.). (2014). *Multiliteracies: Beyond text and the written word.* Information Age.

Rasinski, T. V. (2010). *The fluent reader: Oral and silent reading strategies for building fluency, word recognition, and comprehension* (2nd ed.). Scholastic.

Runfola, M., Etopio, E. A., Hamlen, K., & Rozendal, M. (2012). Effect of music instruction on preschooler's music achievement and emergent literacy achievement. *Bulletin of the Council for Research in Music Education, 192,* 7–27.

Schechner, R. (2020). *Performance studies: An introduction* (4th ed.). Routledge.

Silverstein, L. B. (2020, January 14). *Arts integration and universal design for learning: Explore the powerful alignment between arts integration and three principles that guide Universal Design for Learning (UDL).* The Kennedy Center. Retrieved from *www.kennedy-center.org/education/resources-for-educators/classroom-resources/articles-and-how-tos/articles/collections/arts-integration-resources/arts-integration-and-universal-design-for-learning.*

Small, C. (1998). *Musicking: The meanings of performing and listening.* University Press of New England.

Van de Water, M., McAvoy, M., & Hunt, K. (2015). *Drama and education: Performance, methodologies for teaching and learning.* Routledge.

Wagoner, C. L. (2020). Integrating literacy within the performance classroom. *Music Educators Journal, 106*(4), 24–29.

Wilson, A. A., & Chavez, K. J. (2014). *Reading and representing across the content areas.* Teachers College Press.

Wolsey, T. D., & Lapp, D. (2017). *Literacy in the disciplines: A teacher's guide for grades 5–12*. Guilford Press.

Worthen, W. B. (2007). Disciplines of the text: Sites of performance. In H. Bial (Ed.), *The performance studies reader* (2nd ed., pp. 10–25). Routledge.

Zygouris-Coe, V. I. (2015). *Teaching discipline-specific literacies in grades 6–12: Preparing students for college, career, and workforce demands*. Routledge.

Disciplinary Literacy in Computer Science

Amy Hutchison
Jamie Colwell

In recent years, awareness of the need to broaden participation in the field of computer science has increased. More specifically, there has been a push to provide exposure and opportunities to learn about computer science to girls and students of color (Code.org, 2028) and students with disabilities (Hutchison et al., 2021; Wille et al., 2017). One major approach to broadening participation has been to make computer science accessible to all students in K–12 education. As a result, new pedagogical approaches for teaching computer science are being tested and published on a regular basis. Some popular approaches include the Predict–Run–Investigate–Modify–Make (PRIMM) approach (Sentance et al., 2019); the Use–Modify–Create (UMC) approach (Lee et al, 2011); the TIPP&SEE approach (Franklin et al., 2020); and using literacy instruction as a mechanism for teaching coding (Hutchison et al., 2021). To supplement these approaches, we contend that computer science instruction can be made more accessible to students by viewing it through a disciplinary literacy lens. However, in expanding this accessibility through disciplinary literacy, we contend that disciplinary literacy as a concept may need to be viewed from a more nuanced perspective as computer science is often interdisciplinary in nature. In this chapter, we will (1) explain how disciplinary literacy is relevant for computer science instruction and how computer science specifically might be viewed through a disciplinary literacy lens, and (2) consider how computer science and computational thinking promote a dual-focus lens on disciplinary literacy.

THE RELEVANCE OF DISCIPLINARY LITERACY FOR COMPUTER SCIENCE

Although computer science is a burgeoning area of literacy research, the connections between approaches to computer science instruction and disciplinary literacy are recognizable. Computer scientists often use coding, algorithms, and problem solving in their everyday work practices, and computer science educators focus on these same concepts in computer science instruction. In this type of use and engagement, we believe disciplinary literacy is easily recognizable as an approach that may enhance computer science instruction. Indeed, disciplinary literacy places a strong focus on the use of disciplinary practices and engaging students in relevant real-world practices (Moje, 2008). However, in many K–12 classrooms, computer science, particularly related to coding, is often taught in isolation, with students practicing coding sequences through direct instruction to produce a desired teacher-selected outcome.

While computer scientists also use coding to create a desired output, coding is a part of a problem-solving process where a real-world need is determined, and coding is used to address that need. To more readily approach computer science in the manner in which it is used in real-world contexts with experts, which is a tenant of disciplinary literacy, we consider that disciplinary literacy in computer science may need to be considered from the perspective of the fundamental thinking processes required of computer scientists and how those processes may be applied to problem solving. For example, coding is used in many professional fields, such as aviation, artificial intelligence (AI), spacecraft design, marketing, health care, and financial trading. Arts-based areas of everyday life, such as social media and the music, also use coding. Considering the many real-world applications and how computer science is often integrated into other fields of study, a disciplinary literacy approach to studying computer science would have students engage in coding as a part of a larger problem-solving process and engage in authentic practices related to coding. For example, students might code a meditation app for happiness, which may be particularly useful in addressing stress, targeting stress alleviation in their lives.[1] Additionally, and importantly in our view, this type of approach would not only engage students in real-life practices, but it could also address socially relevant issues pertinent to students' lives and interests (Moje, 2015). By considering disciplinary literacy in computer science as disciplinary fundamental thinking processes, such as coding, specific to the discipline of computer science, teachers might be better able to integrate computer science in a more authentic, and thus disciplinary, manner.

---

[1] See, for example, *www.codespeaklabs.com/blog/code-a-happy-place-meditation-app*.

A benefit of considering disciplinary literacy from this perspective in computer science is that there are multiple K–12 computer science organizations (e.g., Code.org) promoting real-life applications to engage students and create interest in computer science. This promotion may better support teachers as they think about disciplinary literacy in computer science. Organizations such as Code.org provide multiple examples, modules, and planning tools to support disciplinary literacy-focused computer science in K–12 education. For example, elementary teachers can support students' learning about the ethical use of AI in ocean study to support and sustain healthy ocean life.[2] Specifically, students can use computer science skills to learn about programming and training AI to recognize and study different types of ocean life to classify species. While these types of learning activities involve disciplinary literacy in computer science, the authentic connection computer science creates here with the discipline of science (oceanography) highlights a unique feature of disciplinary literacy in computer science. Specifically, computer science is often used in other disciplines to solve real-world problems, and thus the thinking processes associated with computer science better align with disciplinary literacy than the sole study of computer science in a singular computer science class that students take in middle/high school or in a rote coding activity in elementary school.

A Dual-Focus Lens on Disciplinary Literacy in Computer Science

Certainly, there are times when computer scientists focus on coding and programming specific to computers and computer functions and that type of disciplinary literacy instruction could readily be integrated into a high school computer science elective class. However, particularly in today's technological context, computer science is more often used in other fields to find solutions to problems. Furthermore, computer science is rapidly becoming a prominent focus across K–12 education, not just in a singular elective in the upper grades. When K–12 students authentically use computer science from a disciplinary perspective, they consider how practices that computer scientists utilize might address and provide a solution for a real issue. Going back to the ocean example, if students were to use their computer science literacy skills to train AI to recognize, study, and classify different types of ocean life, they would have to consider both computer science practices and the skills and knowledge that an oceanographer would use, for example. It is in these combined practices of reading, training (a form of writing), and communicating their thinking that students engage in disciplinary literacy.

Considering this particularity of experts' use of computer science in

[2]See, for example, *https://studio.code.org/s/oceans/lessons/1/levels/1*.

real-world contexts, we believe it is important to consider what disciplinary literacy is specific to the field of computer science and that it may take a slightly different form in this particular discipline. However, we see this as a strength of computer science as it provides ample opportunities for computer science integration into K–12 learning as teachers can integrate computer science into other content areas and still retain a disciplinary literacy focus of learning. The following examples highlight this integration:

- Coding an avatar to engage in a literary heroic quest to conquer a real-world related issue
- Programming AI to water and fertilize a community garden
- Creating computer simulations to predict weather patterns

These are a just a few examples of how computer science disciplinary literacy might require a dual discipline focus, but we believe that this focus expands chances for its integration and creates powerful opportunities for all students to recognize the importance of computer science in everyday life and how it might help create positive social change. Furthermore, as computer science is a rapidly growing field, these connections provide space for students who may not have considered a future career in computer science to gain authentic experience in its practices.

The Role of Computational Thinking in Disciplinary Literacy in Computer Science

Up to this point, we have emphasized the role of coding in computer science. However, it is important to understand that computer science goes far beyond just coding and furthers the connections among computer science and literacy. Computer science has been defined in many ways, but, at its simplest, learning computer science involves understanding whether and how technology can be applied to solve real-word problems. Most importantly, computer science requires a high degree of computational thinking. Computational thinking is generally defined as "the conceptual foundation required to solve problems effectively and efficiently (i.e., algorithmically, with or without the assistance of computers) with solutions that are reusable in different contexts" (Shute et al., 2017, p. 151). Although there is not singular agreement on the components of computational thinking, the most commonly cited computational thinking skills are pattern recognition, sequencing, abstraction, decomposition, debugging, and algorithmic thinking (Shute et al., 2017). It is widely believed that computational thinking skills are broadly applicable beyond computer science (Berland & Wilensky, 2015), despite the fact that the term originated in reference to computer science. Computational thinking has been called "the most important skill that any child in the twenty-first century could acquire, with the same life skill, personal development, economic prospects, and even well-being and prosperity status as reading, writing and arithmetic" (Walker & Gleaves, 2018, p. 22). So, what do these computational thinking skills have to do with disciplinary literacy? We argue that computational thinking skills define the fundamental thinking processes that are the foundation of disciplinary literacy in computer science. In targeting these skills, disciplinary literacy in computer science may be more readily approached across disciplines. In the next few sections, we will consider each of the six computational thinking skills we have listed, their connections to literacy specific to English language arts (ELA; a focal area of instruction in K–5 learning), and how considering these skills as fundamental disciplinary literacy processes can support a disciplinary literacy approach particular to computer science.

Pattern Recognition

As it relates to computer science, pattern recognition can be defined as observing and identifying patterns, trends, and regularities in data, processes, or problems (Catete et al., 2018). Upon close examination, it's easy to recognize that the computational thinking skill of pattern recognition is akin to part of what we might ask students to look for or consider in a close reading of a text. For example, we often ask students to consider the structure of a text and to look for organizational patterns, patterns of word use, and patterns related to repetition, contradictions, and similarities. Although recognizing patterns within a text can be a key to understanding, simply recognizing patterns does not lead to a deep understanding of a text. The reader must also ask questions about why these patterns exist, what they tell us, and how they can apply these patterns to new contexts. Students also benefit by understanding where and why they may need to apply this skill again. Pattern recognition becomes important when studying textual patterns in creative works, such as poetry, to understand ideas the author wants to highlight or emphasize in the work. Additionally, in non-fiction, pattern recognition can help students understand how informational texts, which are often more difficult for young students to comprehend due to limited exposure (Duke, 2000), are structured so that students can predict and better organize information presented.

When we consider pattern recognition through a computer science disciplinary literacy lens, we must consider how this skill might be used in a classroom setting. Certainly, in the upper grades where computer science is often an elective stand-alone course, adolescents can engage in pattern recognition from a purer computational thinking and computer science perspective. They might use these computational thinking skills to build programs for which they identify patterns in the code and use the same patterns repeatedly to make the coding process more efficient. Similarly, they might debug an existing program by considering disruptions in patterns.

However, in earlier grades when students are engaging in pattern recognition, teachers may integrate such skills into core content or disciplinary instruction, which emphasizes the dual-discipline focus common when considering disciplinary literacy in computer science and, in turn, computational thinking. Although this type of computational thinking often has nothing to do with computers or programming as it would in a computer science classroom, it does lay the groundwork for students to begin thinking analytically about patterns. Pattern recognition might also be integrated in a disciplinary literacy perspective in other content areas.

Economics. Students may engage in forecasting to predict future economical outcomes based on past data. These predictions would be based on studying patterns in economic trends and encourage students to look for commonalities and past trends to predict what future economic models will look like.

History. Teachers may ask students to study human migration patterns in history, using primary documents, to understand why humans elect to leave one geographical space and move to another. Having students engage in historical analysis of events in a cause–effect scenario allows students to form connections between events in history to understand how political and social movements affect where people decide to live. Studying these movements over a substantial time period becomes a study of patterns.

Mathematics. Students can engage in pattern recognition in all years of mathematics instruction, from looking at patterns associated with counting to using formulas/patterns, such as slope-intercept form, to determine a mathematical outcome.

Science. Students may look for patterns in nature focused on animal and plant classifications, much in the way a scientist would identify these features, to begin laying a foundation for disciplinary literacy in both computational thinking and science. Teachers may take students on a nature walk to document in a scientific log different plants, insects, and animals they find or observe to determine patterns that would place each in a certain category. Students might note that common patterns in flowers are the presence of leaves, a stem, petals or buds, and pollen. For mammals and reptiles, common patterns could be related to their outward appearance/features, habitat, and food sources. This and previous disciplinary examples highlight how a dual-disciplinary lens in computer science may be useful for targeting two disciplinary goals in literacy.

Abstraction

Pattern recognition alone does not help a reader fully understand a text. Similarly, pattern recognition alone does not lead to a complete solution to most problems. Thus, other computational thinking skills are also needed to deeply understand a text or problem. In the discipline of computer science, abstraction refers to the act of identifying the general principles and properties that are important and relevant to a problem (Cateté et al., 2018). Abstraction is the "process of removing physical, spatial, or temporal details or attributes in the study of objects of systems to focus attention on details of greater importance or relevance. It is a means to simplify, manage, and distill a complex system to its salient attributes" (Grover, 2020). In computer science, abstraction helps computer scientists determine principles that can be applied to the greater context to simplify a process or procedure. When computer scientists use abstractions to create algorithms, they abstract away the details and only include the most pertinent information for performing an operation. In a computer science classroom, students may be learning how to use abstraction to determine the key elements of a problem and strip away any extraneous details to determine the best way to generate a computer-based solution to the problem.

If drawing connections to other disciplines, such as ELA, abstraction is akin to asking students to determine the central theme or themes of a text. A theme that is abstracted from a story can be used to understand another situation or experience in one's life. Themes are abstract and need to be inferred from a larger story in which both highly relevant and less relevant details are included. When learning to determine the theme of a text, readers are taught that identifying the subject and summarizing the plot are useful. Students are taught to look past minor story details and to carefully analyze details of the characters, setting, and story action that will help them determine the overall message of a text. This message is often a type of life lesson that can be applied to many situations outside of the text in which it was originally found.

When carefully considered, we can see that the same type of skills are applied by both literary scholars and computer scientists. However, in each case they lead to outcomes that are specific to the individual disciplines. This example demonstrates how computer science disciplinary literacy, as a fundamental thinking process of abstraction, would help a student learn how to determine a theme or principle and can help students understand computational thinking to build foundational skills in computer science. This example also highlights the importance of discipline-specific vocabulary, a key area of disciplinary literacy, and how helping students to understand abstraction in a familiar discipline, such as ELA, may build understanding of the concept that may later be applied in an upper-level computer science classroom or classroom that utilizes more traditional computer science instruction. The following examples further expand on focusing on abstraction using a dual-disciplinary focus.

Economics. In many economics-focused lessons, students may use abstraction to eliminate unimportant variables to forecast an outcome. For example, a basic economics lesson might have students plan where certain industrial sites should be constructed based on population growth. Using abstraction, students can focus solely on population numbers to plan where industrial sites, and thus jobs, can be built, without considering other real-world factors such as human work preferences, the education level of people living in that area, and other variables that often affect where people choose to seek employment. However, abstraction allows students to clearly see connections between population growth and industry decisions surrounding business expansion.

Geography. Abstraction is often an important element of geographical study, and having students engage in abstraction in mapping is one way of engaging students in dual-disciplinary literacy. Teachers may have students create a map of the school building and the property on which it is located as an authentic learning activity. As is common in mapmaking, mapmakers must deliberately decide which features to focus on and include in a map, and which features should be abstracted to eliminate or lessen confusion in reading the map. Students making the map would need to decide which aspects of the school are not important in, or might complicate, navigating the school and its surrounding property. They eliminate any movable structures or features or more generally label playing fields and rooms that are used for multiple activities and sports, based on the season. In doing so, students are practicing abstraction in geographical study, but this skill is also a computational thinking skill.

Mathematics. Although mathematics is often connected to real-world learning in schools, abstraction is also necessary in mathematical study, and is a field of study for some mathematicians, as it allows primary or sole focus on the mathematical concept being studied. Particularly as students move into the upper grades where algebra and calculus are studied, students learn to work with operations and rules in math. In this type of study, real-world mathematical connections are less critical than the mathematical order, rules, and operations that must be followed. Mathematics is often a field where computational thinking is integrated. A disciplinary literacy as a fundamental computer science thinking process focus here may be useful for students to understand that mathematical abstraction is a type of computational thinking and also to consider the importance of the underlying operations necessary for mathematical study.

Science. Often in science, abstraction is necessary for students to learn important scientific processes that are a part of a larger area of study. For example, a science teacher may plan a genetics unit that first allows students to focus on Punnett squares to predict genotypes, which is an abstraction of one aspect of genetics but that is important for students to form a basic understanding of a complex area of scientific study. By highlighting that genotype predictions are an abstraction of understanding why living organisms inherit the traits that they do, teachers can promote a dual-disciplinary literacy focus on biology and computational thinking. This example highlights that abstraction, and other computational thinking skills, are often a part of different disciplines, but such skills can be explicitly taught in a discipline, such as science, to help students make connections. We argue that although disciplinary literacy has historically focused on the unique skills particular to each discipline (Shanahan & Shanahan, 2008), more recent curricular trends—such as the development of computer science and computational thinking standards in many U.S. states that rely heavily on the integration of computer science and computational thinking into existing content—require a slight reconsideration of disciplinary literacy so that computer science literacy might be considered outside of stand-alone computer science elective classes and isolated coding activities.

Decomposition

As with our discussion of the computational thinking skill of pattern recognition, abstraction alone does not lead to a complete solution to a problem. It must be used in combination with other skills, such as decomposition. In computer science, decomposition refers to breaking down data, processes, or problems into meaningful smaller, manageable parts (Cateté et al., 2018). Computer scientists must deconstruct a large problem into smaller functional subparts for ease of solving the problem (Grover, 2020). When students engage in decomposition in computer science classrooms, they may, for example, program a game and use decomposition to determine necessary codes for characters, settings, plot, and actions. Indeed, computer scientists generally decompose programming development into four levels (Grover, 2020). They first use it at the problem level to determine what the goal of program should be and its intended audience. They then use it at the algorithm level to turn an idea into a detailed plan or algorithm

(Grover, 2020). The next level, the program level, involves translating the algorithm into code using a specific programming language. Finally, at the program execution level, a computer scientist observes and reacts to how the code behaves when it is run on a machine and fixes bugs that are encountered. It is necessary for computer scientists to decompose a problem into a multilevel process to make it manageable.

Similarly, in literacy instruction, we often use story maps and graphic organizers to help students analyze the main ideas and plot of a story. Students must often decompose, or break apart, a story by paragraph, section, or chapter to comprehend the main ideas and to eventually determine the overall theme of a story. This literary and computational thinking skill will be useful if they choose a career as a computer scientist, editor, journalist, or literary author, but what if they choose a profession in a different field? In subsequent sections, we look beyond the language arts and computer science classroom and consider how this same skill is applied in other disciplines. The same skill that helps students break apart a story to determine its larger themes or code a game can also help prepare students to learn in other disciplines and ultimately in their future careers. Thus far, we have primarily provided disciplinary examples applicable to upper grade levels. In the following examples, we focus more heavily on examples relevant to elementary-grade learning to broaden the scope of how a dual-disciplinary literacy lens might be integrated into classroom learning.

Anthropology. A common unit of study in elementary-grade social studies is the study of cultures, both ancient and modern. Indeed, most elementary students will at some point in their early learning study ancient civilizations, such as the Maya civilization. Often in these units, students learn about a culture's traditions, history, and overall norms. Decomposition may be integrated into this type of study as students focus on "breaking down" the individual characteristics of a culture to form an overall understanding of its unique qualities that define the culture. Providing students with explicit instruction in how this breakdown follows the process of decomposition and in the vocabulary of decomposition itself forms direct connections between anthropology and computational thinking.

Mathematics. In elementary geometry, students learn how to find the area of a more complex shape, like an octagon, by decomposing it into smaller shapes, such as triangles, and then finding the areas of the individual triangles to calculate overall area. Again, teachers, particularly in the earlier grades, can deliberately use and highlight decomposition as important vocabulary that must be understood to engage in more advanced mathematical processes, which will support computational and mathematical thinking. This lesson can also incorporate abstraction as students think about why this particular mathematical order of operations is necessary to finding a solution.

Science. In studying the human body, students can decompose the different organs of a system, such as the digestive system, to study how this system works and its importance. Students can begin to form even basic medical understandings as they consider how each organ works individually to support the entire system and what might happen if an organ stopped working properly. Guiding students in understanding that decomposition allows for a more in-depth study of the human body provides direct connections to disciplinary study in biology and builds students' understanding of decomposition as a computational thinking skill.

Algorithms and Algorithmic Thinking

Algorithms are "precise step-by-step plans or procedures to meet an end goal or to solve a problem; algorithmic thinking is the skill involved in developing an algorithm" (Grover, 2020, p. 1). In computer science, algorithms are the formulas for building programs. Students engaged in disciplinary literacy in a computer science classroom would use algorithms to create programs and to solve defined computational problems in computing. Algorithms are the foundation of all computer programming, and students must apply the computational thinking skills of pattern recognition, abstraction, and decomposition to create algorithms that will lead to the program they intend to create or solve the problem they want to solve. Students must also understand components, such as programming language and hardware, to use algorithms appropriately and in the manner a computer scientist might.

At first glance, algorithms and algorithmic thinking may seem completely unrelated to literacy, but there is again a clear parallel to the kinds of skills that ELA teachers require of their students. Students are generating algorithms or thinking algorithmically, albeit often unknowingly, when they write a set of instructions, create a storyboard that will be used to construct a story, or construct a recipe or plan. They also can use algorithms to determine if a story they or a classmate has created is missing a critical literary element necessary for the plot to move forward and make sense. As students move into the upper grade levels, algorithms can be used, for example, to categorize literature into genres and subgenres.

Certainly, examples of algorithms abound in ELA. Yet, teachers often do not use the same terminology when referring to a student's expository or other formulaic writing and thinking or when considering the classification of literature and literary works. Considering disciplinary literacy in computer science as fundamental thinking processes highlights the potential of connecting computer science to other disciplines to better prepare students to learn and utilize highly relevant skills in today's world. The disciplinary vocabulary associated with computer science may be daunting or seem out of reach for students unless they are taught discipline-specific vocabulary and helped to see how skills they use in one discipline can be applied in a new way to meet the needs of another discipline. We considered the following examples for how algorithms and algorithmic thinking might be connected to other disciplines.

Civics. Algorithms are commonplace in today's technological world where large datasets are readily available to government and business agencies. For example, social media, online polling, and online shopping provide insight into people's habits and beliefs. Although in civics students might not learn or use algorithms, they could study the use of algorithms in political and social decisions and the consequences or outcomes of such use. Integrating such vocabulary provides insight into the purpose of algorithms and algorithmic thinking that connect civics and computational thinking in a fluid manner.

Mathematics. Perhaps the most common connections between algorithms and a discipline can be found in mathematics. Mathematics as a discipline as well as K–12 mathematics focuses on the use of algorithms and/or algorithmic thinking. Examples abound, from early grades where students learn simple addition and subtraction algorithms, to high school calculus where students engage in complex applications of algorithms. However, through our reconceptualization of disciplinary literacy in computer science, teachers can talk with students about how algorithms in math are a form of computational thinking that might translate to real-world scenarios

Science. Algorithms can be considered, in their most basic form, a series of steps that lead to a solution to a problem. In areas of science, such as physics, students can engage in experiments to understand how a determined set of steps leads to a particular outcome. And, if those steps are completed in the same sequence and under the same conditions, the outcome will be the same each time. In this way, algorithmic thinking and the use of algorithms can be readily incorporated into a physics classroom or into a lower-grade lesson that uses the basic principles of physics. Through this experimentation, students are learning what an algorithm is and how a physicist uses algorithms in experimentation within their study. This use of algorithms leads us to the next computational thinking skill, sequencing.

Sequencing

Sequencing is an important skill in most disciplines, but especially so in computer science. In computer science, algorithms are a set of steps to be carried out in sequence from the starting point to the end goal (Grover, 2020). The sequence of steps in an algorithm is of tremendous importance; without the correct sequence, an algorithm will not behave as planned and will not solve the problem it is intended to solve. In a computer science classroom, students often use this computational thinking skill to problem-solve or troubleshoot why a program is not performing as planned or written. Sequencing can be a difficult disciplinary literacy skill to master in computer science as it is easy to overlook what may seem like a minor, but critical, step in a sequence. For example, if programming a character in a digital game to eat an unopened bag of potato chips, each minute step that one needs to take to perform this action has to be programmed into a sequence. A student developing the program might write code that has the character open the bag of potato chips, pick up a chip, put the chip in his or her mouth, and chew. This sounds like the process for eating potato chips, right? Maybe, but don't you have to pick up the bag first to open it? Since the student didn't code for the character to pick up the bag of potato chips first, the rest of these sequence would not work properly.

Literacy and language arts teachers are no strangers to the concept of sequencing as it relates to a literary text. Teachers often teach sequencing as part of a battery of reading comprehension skills and ask students to retell a story by putting the story events in sequence. Similarly, teachers ask students to write many types of texts in which they must put steps or events in a correct sequence. Just as in the computer science example, students must remember to include all events in correct sequence, even the most minute details. Additionally, students can use sequencing skills to analyze where a problem might have developed in a work of literature or how that work differs from other works in a similar genre. The same skills used in language arts may be used in computer science, but we must teach students how these skills or thinking processes might look in computer science, making direct connections, for students to be able to apply them in the context of computer science. Sequencing may also be used in other disciplines.

History. Not only is sequencing used to study a general timeline in history, but historians also frequently use sequencing in the study of primary sources. For upper-grade students to engage in disciplinary sequencing practices in history, they might analyze historical artifacts to determine when they were written or produced to understand how the sequence of the artifacts shapes an understanding of or perspective on that event. In earlier grades, students might use sequencing to build a timeline narrative of a historical event using primary and secondary sources to scaffold their narrative.

Mathematics. The earliest math instruction entails counting and learning the sequence of numbers. As students move into upper grade levels, they learn to use a sequence of steps or operations to solve a problem. Taking a disciplinary literacy approach to sequencing in mathematics would have students first identify a problem and then determine a sequence of steps or a structured approach to solving that problem by carrying out those specific steps in the sequence to find an answer or resolution to the problem.

Science. Experimentation in and of itself is a series of actions taken in a specific sequence to produce a desired result or to test a sequence of steps. Consider the volcano eruption experiment that many elementary students engage in. This experiment requires a precise sequence of actions to produce a volcanic eruption. If, for example, the baking soda slurry was added first or in the middle of the experiment, no eruption or a faulty eruption might occur. It must be the last step in the sequence of steps for the ingredients to properly mix and produce the eruption.

Debugging

As considered in the volcano eruption example, what happens when the steps of an algorithm are not correctly sequenced? In computer science, the programmer must debug his or her code. Programmers must be able to construct a correct sequence of steps to make their code work as planned. Conversely, they must also be able to analyze all aspects of their code and determine what needs to be fixed when the code is not producing the desired result. This is referred to as debugging. In a computer science classroom, debugging is a major focus of disciplinary study as students in these settings are often engaged in figuring out why a program might not work or how it could work more efficiently.

Debugging code is akin to what we teach students to do when they revise and edit their writing. Students are taught to look for gaps in the plot of their story, omissions in a sequence of ideas or steps when writing about a process, mistakes in the grammar and punctuation, and so on. Teachers often assign students a peer editor to help them recognize parts of the writing that need revision. Similarly, computer scientists often do usability testing to reveal mistakes in their code or problems that the user faces when trying to proceed through a program. In each discipline, this same set of skills is applied in a different way, and different vocabulary and disciplinary norms and tools are used to describe and explain how the skills apply to the particular discipline.

Instead of highlighting individual disciplines as we have done in previous computational thinking skills sections, we highlight here that debugging is a part of all disciplines as experts or students who are studying content using disciplinary practices engage in forms of debugging. Really, debugging is a systematic process in which we determine where a problem occurred during study and how we can fix that problem. In our view, the process of debugging is as important as fixing the problem itself, and we encourage educators to consider how experts engage in debugging practices as we contemplate it from a disciplinary literacy standpoint in computer science. In the sciences, teams of engineers and scientists often collaborate to debug. Historians may go back to their primary sources and use organizational tools. Literary scholars or writers often rely on or work with editors to debug. Mathematicians frequently consider a variety of approaches to a problem to determine where discrepancies might emerge. Just as experts use their own debugging practices and approaches, it is important to consider how we might support students in debugging in the disciplines in a way that aligns with disciplinary study in computer science. Also, while we acknowledge that debugging in the disciplines described previously might not provide students with the technical skills to debug a computer program, helping them to think through a debugging process gives students a conceptual foundation that might support them when they must engage with computer science in the upper grades or professionally.

IMPLICATIONS FOR PRACTICE

As can be seen from our explanation of computational thinking skills, many of the same literacy skills used in language arts can be found in the discipline of computer science, and many other disciplines for that matter. However, here we point out how differently the same skills are applied in various disciplines. In computer science, the text that a student is using may be lines of code that he or she or another programmer has developed. In language arts, it is likely to be a literary text. For this reason, it is essential that we apply a disciplinary literacy approach to help students understand how these skills are used across domains. Computational thinking skills are only useful if they are taught through a disciplinary lens with an emphasis on how computer scientists apply these same skills to solve problems.

More importantly, we wish to point out how essential it is that these skills are not taught or used in isolation. The computational thinking skills enumerated in this chapter all play an important role in helping a computer scientist create a program to solve a problem. However, the application of a single skill will not lead to a viable solution. These skills must be used together because they work in concert to help computer scientists do the work of their discipline. We should not teach just computational thinking or just coding. Both are needed because it is only with both computational thinking and coding skills that students will be able to generate solutions.

REFERENCES

Berland, M., & Wilensky, U. (2015). Comparing virtual and physical robotics environments for supporting complex systems and computational thinking. *Journal of Science Education and Technology, 24*, 628–647.

Catete V., Lytle, N., Dong, Y., Boulden, D., Akram, B., Houchins, J., . . . Boyer, K. (2018). Infusing computational thinking into middle grade science classrooms: Lessons learned. In *Proceedings of the 13th Workshop in Primary and Secondary Computing Education* (Article 21, pp. 1–6). Association for Computing Machinery.

Code.org. (2018, August 27). *Girls and minorities break records in computer science as fastest growing group!* Medium. Retrieved from *https://medium.com/@codeorg/girls-and-minorities-break-records-in-computer-science-as-fastest-growing-groups-39d23425810e.*

Duke, N. K. (2000). 3.6 minutes per day: The scarcity of informational texts in first grade. *Reading Research Quarterly, 35*, 202–224.

Franklin, D., Coenraad, M., Palmer, J., Eatinger, D., Zipp, A., Anaya, M., . . . Weintrop, D. (2020, August). An analysis of Use–Modify–Create pedagogical approach's success in balancing structure and student agency. In *Proceedings of the 2020 ACM Conference on International Computing Education Research* (pp. 14–24). Association for Computing Machinery.

Grover, S. (2020). *Computer science in K–12: An A to Z handbook on teaching programming.* Edfinity.

Hutchison, A., Colwell, J., Gutierrez, K., Evmenova, A., Offutt, J., & Taylor, V. (2021). Designing a model of computer science professional development for elementary educators in inclusive settings. *Journal of Technology and Teacher Education, 29*(2), 165–193.

Lee, I., Martin, F., Denner, J., Coulter, B., Allan, W., Erickson, J., & Werner, L. (2011). Computational thinking for youth in practice. *ACM Inroads, 2*(1), 32–37.

Moje, E. (2008). Foregrounding the disciplines in secondary literacy teaching and learning: A call for change. *Journal of Adolescent & Adult Literacy, 52*(2), 96–107.

Moje, E. (2015). Doing and teaching disciplinary literacy with adolescent learners: A social and cultural enterprise. *Harvard Educational Review, 85*, 254–278.

Sentance, S., Waite, J., & Kallia, M. (2019). Teaching computer programming with PRIMM: A sociocultural perspective. *Computer Science Education, 29*(2–3), 136–176.

Shanahan, T., & Shanahan, C. (2008). Teaching disciplinary literacy to adolescents: Rethinking content-area literacy. *Harvard Educational Review, 78*(1), 40–61.

Shute, V., Sun, C., & Asbell-Clarke, J. (2017). Demystifying computational thinking. *Educational Research Review, 22,* 142–158.

Walker, C., & Gleaves, A. (2018). *Looking after literacy: A whole child approach to effective literacy interventions.* SAGE.

Wille, S., Century, J., & Pike, M. (2017). Exploratory research to expand opportunities in computer science for students with learning differences. *Computing in Science & Engineering, 19*(3), 40–50. Retrieved from *https://ieeexplore.ieee.org/document/7914581.*

OPPORTUNITIES AND CHALLENGES IN DISCIPLINARY LITERACIES

Centering Minoritized Voices in Disciplinary Literacy Instruction

Alexis Patterson Williams
Danny C. Martinez

In our own teaching of undergraduate and teacher education students interested in education as a career, we welcome a diverse group of students in our classes. A common experience we both share when we enter our classrooms for the first time are students expressing their excitement over having teachers who look like us: a professor who is a Black woman, and a professor who is Chicano. In particular, this has been our experience with students from our respective racial and ethnic backgrounds. We have witnessed students' excitement increase when we express ourselves in ways reflective of our racialized communities.

Whenever Danny engages in translanguaging practices where English and Spanish are used simultaneously, Latinx students in his classroom report how rarely they have been granted the opportunity to hear such practices in university settings, nor have they felt encouraged to do so themselves. He consciously chooses to use his translanguaging practices to make clear that the home and community linguistic practices that Latinx students might have been told were not "academic" enough are, in fact, appropriate for learning. Similarly, Alexis shares that she is intentional about using Black language when teaching all of her classes. She often couches the technical language of her field within the register of her home language, refusing to privilege academic English. In each course, when the topic of language in the classroom emerges, she highlights that this act of maintaining her home language is intentional, as Black language is often (falsely) associated with a lack of intelligence. As Danny shares, students often express appreciation through head nods, finger snaps, and other paralinguistic cues for seeing *and hearing* someone like them, particularly when university faculty rarely represent these communities. And, from our previous experiences as teachers in K–12 education, we know that this is the case with these students as well.

We share these experiences to highlight the ways in which we have come to model engagement in our disciplinary domains (science and English language arts [ELA]), and how our communicative practices can reflect our whole selves as Black and Chicano people. We enter this conversation about disciplinary literacies explicit about our commitment to providing students with access to the specialized literacy practices of respective disciplines while simultaneously working toward making disciplinary scholars and practitioners accountable for the repertoires of practice (Gutiérrez & Rogoff, 2003) and communication (Rymes, 2010) of communities of color that have been ignored, erased, and deemed deficient within many calls for disciplinary literacy instruction (Hinchman & O'Brien, 2019).

HISTORICAL CONTEXT FOR DISCIPLINARY LITERACIES

Rather than accept schooling and its structural commitments to disciplinary literacies that do not sustain the cultural, linguistic, and literacy practices of minoritized students, we propose that disciplinary literacy practices work toward expanding what counts as literacy and language for learning within the disciplines. Currently, notions of disciplinary literacy and larger academic literacy conversations negate the historical legacies of colonialism and subjugation (de los Ríos et al., 2019) that made the teaching of reading to enslaved Africans illegal and punishable by death (Baugh, 1999), that separated Indigenous children from their families to eradicate cultural and literate traditions (Lomawaima, 1995; McCarty, 2013), that deemed the Spanish language and literacy practices of Mexican children and their families as inferior (Menchaca, 1997), that treated the accented linguistic practices of Asian children as problematic for learning settings (Reyes & Lo, 2009). Over time, U.S. schools have continued to evaluate all children's knowledge via the literacy practices associated with white[1] middle-class

[1]We capitalize the "B" in "Black" when discussing Black people, and lowercase the "w" in "white" when referring to white people given the historical contexts of power, racism, and cultural significance in the American context. Capitalizing the "B" in Black acknowledges the shared cultural experiences of Black people (Laws, 2020); recognizes the significance of the collective struggles and achievements; and resists the historical marginalization and devaluation of Black people. Capitalizing the "W" in white reinforces notions of white supremacy. Lowercasing the "w" rejects the assumptions that being white is the dominant social and cultural norm (Johnson et al., 2017; Matias, 2016; Daniszewski, 2020).

norms (Lippi-Green, 2012). The consequences of these expectations have been measured in narratives associated with the so-called achievement gap whereby Black, Latinx, and Indigenous children lag behind their white and Asian counterparts on standardized assessments. However, Ladson-Billings (2006) reminds us of the educational debt owed to children for their participation in educational institutions that have been remiss with regard to their educational needs despite their historical participation in labor benefiting whites and their education.

In more contemporary times, Baker-Bell (2020) documents the origins of what we call "academic English" in U.S. schools, a term closely linked to academic and disciplinary literacy. While civil rights activists in the 1960s and 1970s were calling for an acceptance of the cultural and linguistic practices of racialized Black, Latinx, Indigenous, and Asian American communities, and for schools to leverage these resources rather than disparage them, scholars and practitioners invented the concept of *academic language* in schools. This move systematized whiteness and white ways with words as the medium of expressing knowledge in schools. Therefore, the consequences for racialized children in schools were laminated by expectations whereby expressing knowledge and competencies in a discipline was disconnected from their everyday lived experiences (Lee, 2008; García-Sánchez & Orellana, 2019).

Problems and Challenges

While we identify *problems* with disciplinary literacy practices that mediate instruction, these are different from the *challenges* that we must confront even when we make visible structural and ideological constraints. One must acknowledge that even when we leverage and level the literacies of all students in classrooms, disciplinary literacy practices will still be challenging for learners given the specialized language of the disciplines (lexical density, syntax, register). Across each discipline, there exist nuanced differences (Lee & Spratley, 2010; Moje, 2015; Shanahan & Shanahan, 2008). However, if we are seeking to engage in these challenges or tensions, it may be couched in an understanding that teaching the specialized literacies of the discipline does not negate the fruitful learning experiences that can happen on a learner's way to making important cultural connections to disciplinary knowledge. For example, Lee (2008) and others who have drawn on her cultural modeling tradition have not "forefronted" a need for learners to use the literacies of a discipline in order to engage in the practices of a discipline. In Lee's work, she starts with Black youths' tacit knowledge about a concept and builds from that rich knowledge, providing texture to their understanding and knowledge that expands students' literacy practices. There is no expectation for a learner to give up any part of their whole being.

Emergence of Disciplinary Literacies

While we are attendant to disciplinary literacies in this chapter, we also understand that they are a genre of academic literacies that remain a central feature of socialization within schooling. Just as every speaker of English will often struggle with academic literacy demands (Martínez & Mejía, 2020), we can say that everyone struggles with disciplinary literacies, practices that are more proximal to white ways of speaking and align with the hierarchical and oppressive nature of academic language and concomitant language ideologies. For minoritized communities, academic language and socialization toward disciplinary literacies have material consequences (Martínez & Mejía, 2020) when schools treat a student's performance on standardized exams as an indication of their academic achievement. In this case, academic and disciplinary literacies become a prerequisite for performing knowledge in schools, dismissing cultural and linguistic ways of knowing and showing an understanding of a disciplinary concept.

Given this history, it is important to also identify why scholars called specifically for the teaching of disciplinary literacies. For decades prior to the introduction of national standards in the United States, literacy scholars had difficulty convincing teachers who were not English language arts (ELA) instructors of their responsibility to teach literacy within their domains of instruction (Moje et al., 2017). It was believed that literacy instruction, the practice of socializing students so they become critical readers, writers, thinkers, listeners, and speakers, was the responsibility of the ELA teacher (Smagorinsky, 2015). Teaching students the necessary "skills" to engage the literacy practices associated with science, math, and social studies courses were assumed to be traits transferred from the skills acquired in ELA classrooms to other disciplines. Prior to the adoption of national standards, literacy scholars were making convincing arguments and calls for literacy instruction beyond the ELA classroom; however, little traction was gained via policy for practitioners. Early literacy scholars were convinced that teaching content only, separate from literacy practices associated with a discipline, would not prepare students to learn the skills required in respective disciplines (Shanahan & Shanahan, 2008) or to engage in the cultural practices agreed upon within these disciplines (Lee & Spratley, 2010; Moje, 2015). We are now at a point where disciplinary literacy instruction is a central concern of all teachers across the disciplines.

In this chapter, we consider the narratives involved in promoting the teaching of disciplinary literacy. We will highlight critiques of these calls as they continue to frame the practices associated with school, and disciplines specifically, as more cognitively demanding than those associated with children from stigmatized and minoritized communities, and finally, we propose a "noticing for equity" framework to further nuance our stance that we move away from reductive calls for disciplinary literacies and toward a repertoire approach to the development and use of language in classrooms. We will argue that making visible the standard/academic language ideologies prevalent in calls for disciplinary literacy require us to consider the harm of reductive/subtractive approaches, and that it is necessary to rethink notions of belonging/proficiency in the specific disciplinary domains considered and embrace a more pluralistic/culturally sustaining approach to language use within the disciplines.

As former secondary teachers of science and ELA, we come to this chapter having considered the varying ways literacy mediates disciplinary learning in our respective disciplines. As teacher educators, we are tasked with making clear the literacy practices through which students are being socialized in their respective disciplinary domains (Lee & Spratley, 2010). In this work, we wrestle with the tensions involved in prescribing for new teachers the practices that will inadvertently position and privilege the specialized literacy practices of respective disciplines while treating home and community literacy and communicative practices as inferior. Next, we consider scholarly contributions to notions of disciplinary literacy and how those have shaped the ways in which teachers are expected to facilitate literacy development in classrooms.

Academic language and literacy conversations have dominated narratives aimed at "remediating" and identifying students who lag behind their peers. In the United States, this narrative frames students of color as needing to attain academic literacy skills across content areas in order to be successful in schools. To consider the role of academic literacies among minoritized and stigmatized students in U.S. schools, it is important to consider the critiques of academic literacies/language rampant in many educational disciplines.

THE PROBLEMATIC NATURE OF DISCIPLINARY LITERACY

The process of developing disciplinary literacy is not a neutral act (Halliday & Martin, 1993; Gee, 2004). It is well documented across all disciplines that the acquisition of disciplinary literacy has had negative and at times harmful impacts on students. In science, Halliday and Martin (1993) argue that students feel "put off" and alienated by the "language of science." Gee (2004) highlights that academic success across disciplines, and in science specifically, requires learners to be willing and able to cope with academic language. He describes learners as having to put aside their lifeworld language, that is, their ordinary, everyday, nonspecialist vernacular to engage with the specialist language of science. In English education, Lee (2008) highlights how literary discussions in ELA classrooms rarely tap into the rich discursive practices of Black and other racialized learners whose participation structures and discourse practices do not align with schooling expectations.

Although there are benefits to using the language of a discipline, there are also sacrifices. Indeed, the acquisition of academic language is "tied to the learner's willingness and trust to leave (for a time and place) the life-world and participate in another identity, one that, for anyone, represents a certain loss. For some people, it represents a more significant loss. . . . " (Gee, 2004, p. 18). Science's academic language is more associated with middle-class values and interests; thus, engagement with science's academic language may require students who are not from this background to more greatly "disassociate" from their lifeworld (Gee, 2004; Brown, 2019). Baker-Bell (2020) also argues that disciplinary language in English mirrors the language practices of white, middle-class speakers.

Mainstream systems of education present and teach from a highly Eurocentric and Westernized perspective, leaving many students from marginalized groups feeling disconnected, unable to identify with, or develop an affinity-identity (Gray, 2014) for learning within the formal school system. Indeed, Brown (2011) argues that language and identity are inextricable. That students make linguistic choices in order to enact a particular identity. Asking students to exchange their lifeworld language for the specialist language of a discipline even for a moment is requiring students to give up a part of themselves and put parts of their identity on hold. Gee (2004) asks us to consider why a child would be willing to accept these losses or make that switch in identity? We wonder, what right do we have to make such a request of our children? Are we aware of the impact of such pedagogical decisions?

OPPORTUNITIES TO CENTER MINORITIZED VOICES

Here, we challenge educators and researchers to recognize the hierarchical nature of the academic language of disciplines and to shift to an instructional approach to disciplinary literacy that values and brings historically marginalized languages to the center of classroom learning. For many teachers, making this pedagogical shift will require unlearning racist perspectives about Black language and all stigmatized languages if they genuinely seek to value the languages represented in their classrooms equally. Indeed, Baker-Bell (2020) argues that "before ELA teachers can implement an Anti-Racist Black Language Pedagogy in their classroom, they have to interrogate their own views of Black Language and the ways in which they perpetuate anti-black linguistic racism in their classrooms" (p. 11). We believe that confronting anti-Blackness in disciplinary literacy research and practice can work to address the stigmas that other racialized groups face when their languages are not treated as resources for learning (Combahee River Collective, 1983).

Although we believe that teachers generally intend to create inclusive and equitable learning environments, intentions and beliefs do not always align with our actions. As residents in an inherently racist society, we are "smog breathers"—that is, the cultural images and stereotypes that affirm white people as superior and minoritized groups as inferior act as a kind of environment that surrounds us, like smog in the air (Tatum, 1997). It is no one's intention to breathe in the smog of racism and oppression, but we take it in because it is the only air that is available. As teachers, Goodwin (1994) describes how ways of seeing and thinking are transmitted from experts to novices. Taken together, the language ideologies that put academic language on a pedestal are "waiting to acquire us" (McDermott, personal communication, August 11, 2014) when we enter teacher training programs, if we are not actively working to disrupt those narratives.

There then develops a need to actively engage in a process of detoxification from the smog of raciolinguistic hierarchies and oppressive views we have breathed in, if teachers are going to center the linguistic practices of all students alongside academic language and disciplinary literacy. Enacting disciplinary literacy instruction that is additive, not subtractive (Valenzuela, 2005), requires a commitment to careful critical self-reflection and a commitment to linguistic plurality (Patterson Williams, 2020). Teacher commitment is imperative and encourages teachers to move from beliefs about equity and inclusion to intentional action focused on decentering academic language and disciplinary literacy as the pinnacle of content learning. As noted earlier, teachers desire to create safe and equitable learning environments for their students. However, good intentions are not enough to disrupt the raciolinguistic hierarchies within traditional classrooms. Teachers must make a commitment to creating equitable language practices in their classroom. Souto-Manning and Winn (2019) argue that commitment ensures teachers reflect and act on the pursuit of transformative and just learning environments.

Patterson Williams and Gray (2021) challenge teachers to make a commitment to developing their self-awareness. This commitment encourages teachers to "use strategies and tools to ground students' content knowledge in critical awareness of structures and institutions that create and maintain the racial, gendered, and economic hierarchies that characterize society" (Patterson Williams & Gray, 2021, p. 107). Its two major practices are critical reflection and the development of a critical consciousness by interrogating their beliefs and values. When teachers set the standard of academic language as the appropriate form of language in their classroom, they engage in oppressive views that marginalize and harm culturally and linguistically diverse youth (Patterson Williams, 2021; Baker-Bell, 2020;

Paris & Alim, 2014). Instead, teachers committed to linguistic plurality not only interrogate themselves, but also seek to understand themselves in relation to their students and the school community, including learning from and with communities about the deep histories and funds of knowledge that are central to resisting stereotypes and welcoming students' repertoires of language and knowledge. Interrogation is integral to deconstructing white supremist mindsets that privilege academic English in classroom discussion and in measures of academic success.

The process of critical self-reflection can be likened to Mason's (2002, 2011, 2021) discussion of the "discipline of noticing." *Teacher noticing* is what a teacher attends to within a classroom context and consists of three main components: attending to classroom interactions, interpreting or sense-making about what is observed, and deciding on how to respond to what is observed (Jacobs et al., 2010; van Es & Sherin, 2008). The discipline of noticing while consisting of the same components as teacher noticing differs, as the focus of the educator's attention shifts from outward to inward reflections of self and one's practice within the classroom context (Mason, 2021). For teachers committed to noticing for equity, that is, attending to equity themes and issues that arise and need redress (Patterson Williams et al., 2020), the self-reflection that occurs during the discipline of noticing is pivotal to strengthening a commitment to centering minoritized voices in the classroom.

Indeed, disciplined noticing is refined over time as teachers gain expertise in a particular aspect of their practice. For our purposes, we are interested in gaining expertise in noticing for issues of equity, particularly issues of linguistic equity. The cultivation of expertise is dependent on the development of an inner witness, or the intentional self-observation necessary to sustain disciplined attempts to notice (Mason, 2011). As Mason (2002) explains, "The mark of an expert is that they are sensitized to notice things which novices overlook. They have finer discernment because they have a refined sensitivity to professional situations and a rich collection of responses on which to draw" (p. 1). The inner witness is akin to a lens or magnifying glass that highlights relevant information and interactions according to the perspective the teacher has an interest in.

Mason (2002) highlights that the role of the inner witness is to take one's disciplined noticing from the place of retrospection to "spection," or noticing in the moment. The inner witness sharpens the ability to notice through reflection on action that leads to a change in future action (Mason, 2021). More specifically, the process includes teachers reflecting on a past situation, analyzing it, possibly locating resources or generating ideas for how to address a similar situation in the future. This imagined response is called "proflection" and provides teachers with the space to imagine creative alternative responses and outcomes for future occurrences (Mason, 2021). These imagined possibilities then become options for teachers to add to their repertoire of knowledge and tap into during future situations when a similar issue of equity arises. Teachers are able to notice a similar moment of (in)equity and act in more equitable ways. This thus becomes the pinnacle of disciplined noticing—to "support and enhance sensitivity to notice, and to make it possible to act upon that noticing" not in reflection but as the situation unfolds (Mason, 2002, p. 87).

Given the power of the inner witness to shift values of equity into actionable next steps, it is imperative that teachers have opportunities for disciplined noticing or critical reflection. These opportunities for reflection can come in the form of conversations with a trusted mentor, activities that call for critical reflection during professional development, or templates for individual reflection of past learning activities. These reflective tasks need to be supplemented by resources that support critical analysis of systems and institutions, frameworks that provide theoretical explanations for various phenomena, historical documents that provide a broader context, and culturally sustaining learning activities that can be integrated into future practice. Opportunities for mediated critical reflection strengthen the inner witness for noticing for equity within the classroom.

LISTENING TO OUR INNER WITNESS IN DISCIPLINARY LITERACY INSTRUCTION

Teachers attending to their inner witness, and noticing for equity in their practice (Patterson et al., 2020), should make a shift toward "looking closely and listening carefully" to minoritized students in their classrooms (Martínez & Mejía, 2020). When teachers engage in the discipline of noticing, they are able to sharpen their ability to notice issues of equity in the moment through *proflection*, the ability to imagine how future actions will be different. The process of reflection and proflection allows for opportunities of transformational learning experiences when teachers return to the classroom. Attending to our inner witness when it comes to promoting a pluralinguistic learning environment requires us to resist essentialist assumptions about minoritized students' cultural and linguistic practices, and proflect toward learning activities that build on and activate students' full communicative repertoires (Rymes, 2010). This practice can lead to moments where both teachers and students expand their repertoire of practices (Gutiérrez & Rogoff, 2003; Zentella, 1997). It is also within this proflection, with teachers looking toward future activity, where students' literacy practices can be promoted in ways that map onto disciplinary modes of reasoning (García-Sánchez & Orellana, 2019; Lee, 2008). While the work of mapping these features requires teachers and researchers to look closer at the literacy practices deployed within a learning context and to listen deeply for communication features that can be leveraged and leveled

(Zisselsberger, 2016) for learning, it is in these moments that we develop robust learning opportunities to add disciplinary literacy practices to an already expansive repertoire of literacy practices.

Raciolinguistic Ideologies of Literacy

While we have made the case that literacy is steeped in whiteness and colonial projects, the ideologies that help circulate these notions continue to mediate learning settings. We draw from Flores and Rosa's (2015) theorizing of raciolinguistic ideologies to remind ourselves that we must actively attend not only to the practices of the speaker (or writer as we attend to literacies), we must also notice the actions and practices of the speaker, or the "white speaking and listening subject," who actively evaluates minoritized language speakers through perspectives guided by monolingual ideologies. A raciolinguistic perspective, extended to understandings of disciplinary literacy instruction, must therefore attend to how we approach minoritized students in our classrooms when we seek to add disciplinary or "specialized" language practices to their already expansive literacy practices. Through active attention to their inner witness, teachers can work toward dismissing the white gaze that can mediate instruction, and work toward noticing for equity in the moment, or in the future.

CONCLUSION: TAKING IT TO THE CLASSROOM

As researchers and teacher educators who have critical orientations, we understand these perspectives; however, we are concerned about how academic literacy ideologies marginalize and have marginalizing effects on students who come to school with a range of literacy practices that may or may not include those deemed to be academic. We do believe that teachers can work to reimagine how disciplinary literacy instruction might be transformative for all students when we work to imagine future disciplines that benefit from the diversity of literacy practices that make up our pluralinguistic societies. We know this is possible by the range of empirical research that forefronts the rich resources of minoritized communities as a starting point in the execution of discipline-specific tasks (de los Ríos et al., 2019; Martínez & Martinez, 2019; Nasir & Hand, 2008).

In this chapter, we have made the case for reimagining academic and disciplinary literacies to be treated as expansive in order to create learning contexts where marginalized students belong in ways that spark learning opportunities that include the whole child. We move away from ideas of creating a "balance" between academic and home/community literacies since we acknowledge the supremacy of English, which will always dominate such asset-based projects (Flores & Rosa, 2015). Instead, we seek to concretize through examples of current instructional strategies what creating spaces of communicative belonging can look like for children whose literacy and language practices do not mirror those privileged in schools.

One mainstay approach to socializing students into academic literacies and those of the discipline is steeped in notions of remediation. Traditional remediation practices place blame on the learner for not acquiring knowledge, with little attention to the learning environment or the lack of meaningful cultural tools and artifacts to support a learner. Prime examples of this were the proliferation of test preparation courses that soon filled the schedules of students not performing well on standardized assessments. We concur with Gutiérrez et al. (2009) who advocate for a remediation approach to disciplinary literacy practices. They argue, building on Cole and Griffin (1983), that traditional remediation efforts treat learners as problems needing change. For example, in U.S. schooling reform efforts, students not meeting grade-level benchmarks are provided instruction attempting to "return to the basics," where skills are taught in reductive and decontextualized ways. A remediation approach does not treat the learner as the problem. Rather, Gutiérrez et al. (2009) contend that remediation efforts must purposefully reorganize the learning environment. This often entails making changes that provide learners with the robust tools to facilitate learning, including meaningful cultural and linguistic tools.

Several scholars have engaged in research in the spirit of remediating where students from minoritized communities are viewed as entering spaces of learning with rich language and literacy resources. In science education, Brown (2019) asks teachers to reconsider what counts as the "right answer" in science and encourages them to "recalibrate" their hearing and pedagogical approach—that is, moving away from looking for the "right answer" communicated using the "right" language (e.g., scientific terminology). Instead, teachers should be prepared to hear students' explanations in their own vernacular or home language. This requires teachers to untangle knowledge of science concepts from scientific terminology. This instructional approach is Brown's disaggregate instruction pedagogy and has four instructional phases: First, teachers pre-assess students' prior knowledge, listening for the robust funds of knowledge that learners bring to the classroom. Second, teachers provide content instruction in everyday language that is followed by explicit language instruction of the technical vocabulary. During this third phase, teachers connect scientific terminology to the everyday language initially used to describe phenomena. Finally, teachers provide opportunities (or scaffolds) for students to engage with and practice using the language of the discipline.

Additional scholars in science and mathematics education have highlighted the importance of embracing the language of minoritized students during content instruction. In science education, Larkin (2020) argues that "the first step toward sustaining culture is just getting out of the way, and resisting the urge to prevent students from using familiar patterns of communication and engagement, and then leveraging those student resources for deep learning." Teachers have the power to create space for students to make sense of phenomena using their everyday language. Ortiz and Ruwe (2021) offer a similar argument with regard to mathematics education. They argue that teachers must learn about and become familiar with Black English, so when students use it in math classrooms, their teachers can hear and acknowledge the mathematically complex and rigorous ideas being communicated. Both Larkin (2020) and Ortiz and Ruwe (2021) suggest that teachers incorporate culturally relevant realia and meaningful content topics in the curricula for students to make meaning around that spark of passion, for teachers to deeply connect with their students' reality and awaken sociopolitical critique and sense making. Madkins and Nasir (2019) provide an example of how the use of dominoes created a learning environment where Black youths' identity was supported, their authentic language practice was embraced, while also calling for "mathematical and strategic acumen."

In English education, scholars in collaboration with practitioners have leveraged and mapped cultural and linguistic practices onto subject-specific domains of instruction, building on the cultural modeling tradition of Carol Lee (2008). These include having Latinx children of immigrants leverage their roles as cultural and language brokers to summarize and paraphrase texts (Orellana, 2009; Martínez et al., 2008), promoting the use of Spanglish as a tool for learning in the ELA classroom (Martínez, 2010), developing curricular practices that draw on Latinx youths' songwriting practices that originate in the Mexican *corrido* genre (de los Ríos et al., 2019), and encouraging a "language of solidarity stance" across racialized communities in the ELA classroom (Martinez, 2017). Scholars have also developed curricular practices that raise the prestige of Black-language practices while teaching in the ELA classroom by mapping discourse practices such as "playing the dozens" and "signifying" onto features of literary analysis deemed part of the ELA curriculum. Additionally, scholars have developed critical language pedagogy (Baker-Bell, 2020) seeking to eradicate anti-Blackness that from its very inception the ELA has promoted.

These approaches make visible the literacy practices of particular communities and highlight how they benefit learning in ways that privilege the practices of minoritized communities while simultaneously adding robust practices to expand the literacy practices of learners. Thus, the work of teachers is to unpack bias that inhibits their ability to embrace multilingual discourse practices within the classroom and develop curricula and instructional approaches that sustain the cultural and linguistic identities of the diverse students they serve.

REFERENCES

Baker-Bell, A. (2020). Dismantling anti-Black linguistic racism in English language arts classrooms: Toward an anti-racist Black language pedagogy. *Theory Into Practice, 59*(1), 8–21.

Baugh, J. (1999). *Out of the mouths of slaves: African American language and educational malpractice.* University of Texas Press.

Brown, B. A. (2011). Isn't that just good teaching?: Disaggregate instruction and the language identity dilemma. *Journal of Science Teacher Education, 22*(8), 679–704.

Brown, B. A. (2019). *Science in the city: Culturally relevant STEM education.* Harvard Education Press.

Cole, M., & Griffin, P. (1983). A socio-historical approach to re-mediation. *Quarterly Newsletter of the Laboratory of Comparative Human Cognition, 5*(4), 69–74.

Combahee River Collective. (1983). The Combahee River Collective statement. In B. Smith (Ed.), *Home girls: A Black feminist anthology* (Vol. 1, pp. 264–274). Rutgers University Press.

Daniszewski, J. (2020, July 20). Why we will lowercase white. *The Associated Press. https://blog.ap.org/announcements/why-we-will-lowercase-white#:~:text=But%20capitalizing%20the%20term%20white,that%20white%20is%20the%20default.*

de los Ríos, C. V., Martinez, D. C., Musser, A. D., Canady, A., Camangian, P., & Quijada, P. D. (2019). Upending colonial practices: Toward repairing harm in English education. *Theory Into Practice, 58*(4), 359–367.

Flores, N., & Rosa, J. (2015). Undoing appropriateness: Raciolinguistic ideologies and language diversity in education. *Harvard Educational Review, 85*, 149–171.

García-Sánchez, I. M., & Orellana, M. F. (2019). *Language and cultural practices in communities and schools: Bridging learning for students from non-dominant groups.* Routledge.

Gee, J. P. (2004). Language in the science classroom: Academic social languages as the heart of school-based literacy. In R. K. Yerrick & W.-M. Roth (Eds.), *Establishing scientific classroom discourse communities* (pp. 28–52). Routledge.

Goodwin, C. (1994). Professional vision. *American Anthropologist, 96*(3), 606–633.

Gray, S. (2014). *Is science for all?: The relationship between middle and high school science students' perceptions of race and their science affinity-identities.* PhD dissertation, Stanford University, Stanford, CA.

Gutiérrez, K. D., Morales, P. Z., & Martinez, D. C. (2009). Re-mediating literacy: Culture, difference, and learning for students from nondominant communities. *Review of Research in Education, 33*(1), 212–245.

Gutiérrez, K., & Rogoff, B. (2003). Cultural ways of learning: Individual traits or repertories of practice. *Educational Researcher, 32*(5), 19–25.

Halliday, M. A. K., & Martin, J. R. (1993). *Writing science: Literacy and discursive power.* Taylor & Francis.

Hinchman, K. A., & O'Brien, D. G. (2019). Disciplinary literacy: From infusion to hybridity. *Journal of Literacy Research, 51*(4), 525–536.

Jacobs, V. R., Lamb, L. L. C., & Philipp, R. A. (2010). Professional noticing of children's mathematical thinking. *Journal of Research in Mathematics Education, 41*(2), 169–202.

Johnson, L. L., Jackson, J., Stovall, D. O., & Baszile, D. T. (2017). "Loving Blackness to death": (Re) imagining ELA classrooms in a time of racial chaos. *The English Journal, 106*(4), 60–66.

Ladson-Billings, G. (2006). From the achievement gap to the education debt: Understanding achievement in US schools. *Educational Researcher, 35*(7), 3–12.

Larkin, D. B. (2020). *Teaching science in diverse classrooms: Real science for real students.* Routledge.

Laws, M. (2020, June 16). Why we capitalize `Black' (and not `white'). *Columbia Journalism Review. https://www.cjr.org/analysis/capital-b-black-styleguide.php.*

Lee, C. D. (2008). The centrality of culture to the scientific study of learning and development: How an ecological framework in education research facilitates civic responsibility. *Educational Researcher, 37*(5), 267.

Lee, C. D., & Spratley, A. (2010). *Reading in the disciplines: The challenges of adolescent literacy* (Final Report from Carnegie Corporation of New York's Council on Advancing Adolescent Literacy). Carnegie Corporation of New York.

Lippi-Green, R. (2012). *English with an accent: Language, ideology, and discrimination in the United States.* Routledge.

Lomawaima, K. T. (1995). *They called it prairie light: The story of Chilocco Indian school.* University of Nebraska Press.

Madkins, T., & Nasir, N. (2019). Building on students' cultural practices in STEM. In I. M. García-Sánchez & M. F. Orellana (Eds.), *Language and cultural practices in communities and schools: Bridging learning for students from non-dominant groups* (pp. 59–75). Routledge.

Martínez, R. A. (2010). "Spanglish" as literacy tool: Toward an understanding of the potential role of Spanish-English code-switching in the development of academic literacy. *Research in the Teaching of English, 45*(2), 124–149.

Martinez, D. C. (2017). Emerging critical meta-awareness among Black and Latina/o youth during corrective feedback practices in urban English Language Arts classrooms. *Urban Education, 52*(5), 637–666.

Martínez, R. A., & Martinez, D. C. (2019). Chicanx and Latinx students' linguistic repertoires: Moving beyond essentialist and prescriptivist perspectives. In J. McSwan & C. Faltis (Eds.), *Codeswitching in the classroom: Critical perspectives on teaching, learning, policy, and ideology* (pp. 225–246). Routledge.

Martínez, R. A., & Mejía, A. F. (2020). Looking closely and listening carefully:

A sociocultural approach to understanding the complexity of Latina/o/x students' everyday language. *Theory Into Practice, 59*(1), 53–63.

Martínez, R. A., Orellana, M. F., Pacheco, M., & Carbone, P. (2008). Found in translation: Connecting translating experiences to academic writing. *Language Arts, 85*(6), 421–431.

Mason, J. (2002). *Researching your own practice: The discipline of noticing.* Routledge Falmer.

Mason, J. (2011). Noticing: Roots and branches. In M. G. Sherin, V. R. Jacobs, & R. A. Philipp (Eds.), *Mathematics teacher noticing: Seeing through teachers' eyes.* Routledge.

Mason, J. (2021). Learning about noticing, by, and through, noticing. *ZDM–Mathematics Education, 53*(1), 231–243.

Matias, C. E. (2016). White skin, Black friend: A Fanonian application to theorize racial fetish in teacher education. *Educational Philosophy and Theory, 48*(3), 221–236.

McCarty, T. L. (2013). Indigenous literacies: Continuum or divide? In M. R. Hawkins (Ed.), *Framing languages and literacies* (pp. 179–201). Routledge.

Menchaca, M. (1997). Early racist discourses: The roots of deficit thinking. In R. R. Valencia (Ed.), *The evolution of deficit thinking: Educational thought and practice.* Falmer Press.

Moje, E. B. (2015). Doing and teaching disciplinary literacy with adolescent learners: A social and cultural enterprise. *Harvard Educational Review, 85*(2), 254–278.

Moje, E. B., Giroux, C., & Muehling, N. (2017). Navigating cultures and identities to learn literacies for life: Rethinking adolescent literacy teaching in a post-core world. In K. A. Hinchman & D. A. Appleman (Eds.), *Adolescent literacies: A handbook of practice-based research* (pp. 3–20). Guilford Press.

Nasir, N. I. S., & Hand, V. (2008). From the court to the classroom: Opportunities for engagement, learning, and identity in basketball and classroom mathematics. *Journal of the Learning Sciences, 17(*2), 143–179.

Orellana, M. F. (2009). *Translating childhoods: Immigrant youth, language, and culture.* Rutgers University Press.

Ortiz, N. A., & Ruwe, D. (2021). Black English and mathematics education: A critical look at culturally sustaining pedagogy. *Teachers College Record, 123*(10).

Paris, D., & Alim, H. S. (2014). What are we seeking to sustain through culturally sustaining pedagogy?: A loving critique forward. *Harvard Educational Review, 84*(1), 85–100.

Patterson, A. D., Athanases, S., Higgs, J., & Martinez, D. C. (2020). Developing an inner witness to notice for equity in the fleeting moments of talk for content learning. *Equity and Excellence in Education, 53*(4), 504–517.

Patterson Williams, A. (2020). Sustaining disciplinary literacy in science: A transformative, just model for teaching the language of science. *Journal of Adolescent and Adult Literacy, 64*(3), 333–336.

Patterson Williams, A., & Gray, S. (2021). Promoting equity and justice in science classrooms via the (W)holistic Science Pedagogy. In M. Winn & L. T. Winn (Eds.), *Transforming teaching and learning through restorative justice* (pp. 105–118). Harvard Education Press.

Reyes, A., & Lo, A. (Eds.). (2009). *Beyond yellow English: Toward a linguistic anthropology of Asian Pacific America.* Oxford University Press.

Rymes, B. (2010). Classroom discourse analysis: A focus on communicative repertoires. In N. H. Hornberger & S. L. McKay (Eds.), *Sociolinguistics and language education* (pp. 528–546). Multilingual Matters.

Shanahan, T., & Shanahan, C. (2008). Teaching disciplinary literacy to adolescents: Rethinking content-area literacy. *Harvard Educational Review, 78*(1), 40–59.

Smagorinsky, P. (2015). Disciplinary literacy in English language arts. *Journal of Adolescent and Adult Literacy, 59*(2), 141–146.

Souto-Manning, M., & Winn, L. T. (2019). Toward shared commitments for teacher education: Transformative justice as an ethical imperative. *Theory Into Practice, 58*(4), 308–317.

Tatum, B. D. (1997). *Why are all the black kids sitting together in the cafeteria?: And other conversations about race.* Basic Books.

Valenzuela, A. (2005). *Subtractive schooling: US-Mexican youth and the politics of caring.* SUNY Press.

Van Es, E. A., & Sherin, M. G. (2008). Mathematics teachers' "learning to notice" in the context of a video club. *Teaching and Teacher Education, 24*(2), 244–276.

Zentella, A. C. (1997). Latino youth at home, in their communities, and in school: The language link. *Education and Urban Society, 30*(1), 122–130.

Zisselsberger, M. (2016). Toward a humanizing pedagogy: Leveling the cultural and linguistic capital in a fifth-grade writing classroom. *Bilingual Research Journal, 39*(2), 121–137.

Who Defines Disciplinary Literacy, and at What Grade Levels Should It Be Taught?

Rachael E. Gabriel
Shannon Kelley

The challenge of disciplinary literacy rests at the intersection of two concepts: complexity and specialization. Though there is some debate about its precise definition and purpose (Wenz & Gabriel, 2017; Dunkerly-Bean & Bean, 2016), a broad historical view might position disciplinary literacy as an attempt to bridge scholarship on the specific nature of text structures at postsecondary and professional levels (e.g., understanding the specialized nature of texts in the academic disciplines), with scholarship on the psychology and pedagogy of reading and writing from a primary or developmental perspective, in which scholars are concerned with how students can learn to read and write texts of increasing complexity. Therefore, the idea that specialized literacies are required to fully engage in the work of a given area of study can be understood as one that has trickled down from postsecondary settings and into the intermediate grades where it is used to explain some of the difficulties of text complexity and specificity after students have "learned to read" in the primary grades.

As study and/or participation in an academic discipline becomes more specialized and less general, students and educators must engage with texts produced by and used within a discipline, rather than those written about topics related to that discipline. Texts used by specific groups of people for specific purposes come to reflect the audiences, uses, conventions, and formats of text.

There are several fields of study concerned with the development of specialized literacies—that is, the skills, strategies, and awarenesses required to effectively read, write, and communicate about specialized or stylized texts. These include literary, linguistic, and sociological approaches to genre studies, which are most often focused on the nature of language and text use among adults engaged in the work of various academic disciplines. For example, the field of *English for specific purposes* is concerned with the teaching of English as a second or other language to those who plan to apply their language skills in particular domains, for example, business, medicine, and education. *Literary genre studies* is concerned with the analysis of structure and function of elements and patterns of use that appear in literature, film, and other cultural artifacts. *Systemic functional linguistics* is an approach to the study of language use that assumes text structures are reflective of the nature of the contexts in which they were produced (Halliday, 1992). Therefore, understanding context, and the ways it is reflected in the structures of text, may support understanding and creating such texts (Martin, 2014).

On the other hand, the idea that disciplinary literacy must be learned and/or developed over time through instruction in specific skills and strategies, and the acquisition of specific knowledge or awarenesses, might be viewed as representative of an extension of the process of learning to read that begins in the primary grades. Therefore, its place might be assumed to rest somewhere after fourth grade when literacy skills are understood to have "consolidated" (Chall, 1983) and can then be applied in purposeful ways (Shanahan, 2021). There are, however, several open questions about the nature of disciplinary literacy that depend, in part, on how it is defined, and have implications for when it should be taught. Each will be described in detail in the section that follows. They include:

1. Is the specialization of text and discourse that is evident in discipline-specific texts and literacy practices always more complex than generic or unspecialized text?
2. Are specialized literate practices reciprocal or cumulative, such that learning developed in the study of one might transfer to, rather than threaten or minimize, another?
3. Are disciplinary differences identifiable and stable, or are sensitivity and flexibility the goals of disciplinary literacy instruction?

The answers to these questions would either direct the teaching of discipline-specific literacies toward the latter half of the PreK–16 continuum, when disciplinary literacy knowledge is often used as an explanation for lower adolescent literacy rates than would be expected based on rates measured at fourth grade (cf. National Assessment of Educational Progress). Or, answers might distribute the teaching of disciplinary literacy all along the PreK–16 continuum, with even the youngest learners engaging in discipline-specific practices, and reading or writing specific text types for specific purposes and audiences.

CHALLENGES IN DISCIPLINARY LITERACY

Is Specific Always Complex, or Just Different?

Consider a textbook written about one particular subject in comparison to the texts used in the everyday work of individuals engaged in using that subject matter to do things in the world. More specifically, consider a page of a physics textbook compared with the schematics an architect draws and reviews as he or she engages in structural design processes. One is written to students about how structures are designed; one offers a representation of structural design that is used in communicating, revising, and producing design processes among designers. One is informational, the other, functional. One is written out in sentences and paragraphs using the generic conventions, text structures, and features associated with made-for-school texts. One uses the format, features, conventions, and symbols of the field of architecture, and specifically those associated with this kind of construction and, indeed, this architectural firm's cultural and communicative norms.

Is the text that is more specific to the work of architectural design necessarily more complex than the one written in a more general way to teach students about architectural design? And, perhaps more importantly, should students be able to read the textbook with understanding before they are exposed to or invited to engage with the texts architects use in their work? Might such exposure or engagement contribute to the development of more general literacy skills, or might it distract or even detract from general literacy development? These hypothetical questions can be answered by studying the ways students use text across different grade levels and settings.

For example, kindergarteners are often taught to observe seedlings as they grow, and to draw and label diagrams of them in a science notebook. This is not similar to a botany textbook found in a high school or college setting, but it is similar to the text a botanist might keep in his or her greenhouse when doing observations. It's a discipline-specific way of recording and sharing information, with attention to some of the details and conventions used by botanists and others concerned with the growth of seedlings, but it does not require many of the literacy skills students develop across the elementary grades. Though it is simple in terms of readability, as calculated by logarithms that include word familiarity, length, and sentence structure, it has the potential to be conceptually accurate and discipline-specific. The concept may be difficult, but the text relatively accessible, or vice versa.

In a recent study, Scott et al. (2021) analyzed the responses of a panel of scientists and educators reviewing writing samples from high school students who had only been learning English for a few months. The students had created graphic representations of weather changes with brief written explanations of each image, and short labels or keys where needed. Though the written English components of their science writing were brief, the graphs and their captions followed the conventions of scientific writing, captured scientific information in ways that were conceptually accurate and familiar to those who engage regularly in the work of environmental sciences. This work suggests that students who do not yet have full command of English for academic purposes can communicate in discipline-specific ways while maintaining conceptual accuracy and complexity, especially when the discipline includes multiple forms of representation beyond written language.

Therefore, although it may be too complex a task to write a personal narrative for English class in a new language, it may not be too complex to communicate complex ideas following the conventions of science, mathematics, social studies, art, business, or other disciplines in which the length and complexity of written English are but two of many ways to communicate concepts and ideas.

If conceptual accuracy and complexity can be preserved in formats that do not require traditional print-based literacy skills, then disciplinary literacy can and should be taught regardless of whether print-based literacy skills have fully developed. This is a way that disciplinary literacy can be used to increase equity and opportunity among students who may otherwise have been denied access to specialized or advanced study. If the need for reading intervention or remediation requires time that might otherwise be spent developing expertise in another area, those with reading difficulties routinely miss out on opportunities to develop disciplinary literacy. Likewise, if teachers of various disciplines avoid creating, critiquing, and sharing discipline-specific texts because of their own lack of familiarity with such texts, or their assumptions about students' capacity or need to engage with such texts, students will routinely miss out on opportunities to develop disciplinary literacy. If, instead, all instruction included explicit attention to the representation of ideas in the most relevant forms and formats, disciplinary literacy would develop independently of general literacy and may, in fact, contribute to it.

Is Disciplinary Literacy Cumulative, Reciprocal, or Sequential?

One of the most seminal articles related to disciplinary literacy instruction in K–12 settings presented disciplinary literacy as the tip of a triangle above intermediate and basic literacy (see Shanahan & Shanahan, 2008). Though the image was meant to illustrate increasing specialization of literacy skills, it has been used to suggest that disciplinary literacy quite literally relies on the strength of intermediate literacy, which relies on or requires the full development of basic literacy. This makes disciplinary literacy seem like it is the end goal of literacy development, rather than something that could develop in parallel with basic and general literacy, or that might even bear some reciprocal relationship to basic or general literacy. The order of development matters because it determines the grades in which disciplinary literacy could or should be taught.

Many disciplinary literacy studies of the early 2000s focused on studying the reading skills and habits of mind of experts in various fields to learn about differences in their reading processes (cf. Shanahan et al., 2011). This trend similarly positions disciplinary literacy as the outcome of expertise, rather than a mechanism for developing knowledge in a given area. Studies focused on comparing the reading of experts and novices similarly reinforce a sequential trajectory for development in which basic and intermediate literacies precede the development of specialized literacies, which are associated with the development of expertise. This perspective would allow disciplinary literacy to be defined by experts in a given discipline, identified by researchers, and taught by professors and instructors at the postsecondary and secondary level. It presupposes that instructors at these levels have the disciplinary knowledge or experience to engage in disciplinary literacy themselves. On the other hand, if disciplinary literacy is defined by instructors at any level, based on observation or analysis rather than personal experience or membership within a discipline, it could be taught in every grade, in developmentally appropriate ways long before a learner is an expert.

Expert studies aimed at characterizing the literate practices of a discipline are often conducted using academic experts at universities rather than discipline-specific practitioners or professionals. However, a broader view of what constitutes a discipline, beyond academic categorization, can be used to broaden views of what counts as disciplinary literacy, when it can be taught, and whom it might benefit. These issues are discussed in the section that follows. However, this more expansive understanding depends on a parallel or reciprocal pattern of development that would invite the teaching of disciplinary literacy from the earliest grades on. If taught in these grades, decisions about the content of disciplinary literacy cannot be left to experts alone, but must also be informed by educators and others responsible for planning instruction in secondary and primary school.

Rather than viewing disciplinary literacy as something only academic experts would display or be able to demonstrate, Moje (2015) suggests that disciplinary literacy varies not only within specific subdisciplines within an academic discipline (e.g., civil engineers in an engineering department), but also within the small subcommunities that engage in work within that specialty area. Each and every lab or group of professionals who routinely engage in communication to certain audiences about certain phenomena will develop some of their own conventions, habits, formats, and shared knowledge that will influence the texts they produce and their habits and strategies for processing texts as they are read. If these community-specific processes and practices can be considered the domain of disciplinary literacy instruction, then instructors need not be experts to demonstrate or understand them; they need only be keen observers to understand how certain text features and literacy practices have evolved and what these demonstrate or how they serve the community that produced them. This opens the possibility for PreK–16 educators to consider communities that routinely engage with the content they are teaching, and analyze the ways texts are used in terms of purpose, audience, and format.

For example, in the study described above, the science teacher working with students learning English for the first time did not need to be an expert on weather science. Rather, the teacher needed to consider how those who engage with weather data tend to represent it when working with such information and communicating with others. To do this, educators do not have to interview the chairs of academic departments or other experts found within the academy. Rather, they must look toward those who are routinely engaged in communities that use this area of knowledge or this set of content for some purpose. That means learning about weather is not just learning to "write like a scientist" or, more specifically, "write like an environmental scientist." It could also mean you are learning to "read like a" fisherman, air traffic controller, meteorologist, or other professional who routinely creates and uses representations of weather-related information in his or her work.

The proliferation of potential communities that could inform specialized literate practices, compared to the relatively static, historic categories of academic disciplines, raises challenges for answering the question of who defines disciplinary literacy, and indeed what counts as disciplinary literacy. Should educators be equally interested teaching students to read and write like a fisherman and an environmental policymaker? Does learning to read and write within any of these communities add up to being more fully literate, or does investing in one take away from another?

There are two ways to understand what is learned within disciplinary literacy depending on whether literacies are viewed as relatively static—that is, unchanging and widely shared—or dynamic in nature (Wenz & Gabriel, 2017). A more static perspective is influenced by the expert studies, and the idea of content-area reading in middle and high school. This static perspective views each discipline or content area as unique in its literate practices, and regards these practices as relatively stable and consistent across the discipline. Therefore, learning one set of practices does not necessarily prepare you to learn any other—except in the ways that learning any language prepares you to learn additional languages by developing some underlying linguistic competence (Cummins, 1981). In this way, disciplinary literacy competence could accumulate over time as students are exposed to literacies in different disciplines.

A dynamic perspective suggests that no discipline, subdiscipline, or community is static in its literate practices, and that the ability to flexibly respond to changes in language and text use across communities is more useful than learning one or more static approaches. This dynamic perspective would say that disciplinary literacy learning is reciprocal in nature, meaning that engaging with the literacy practices of one community directly contributes to and benefits from learning in any other. This would suggest it is as fruitful to investigate and engage with the literate practices of a fisherman (practitioner) who creates and consumes multiple representations of weather-related information, as the practices of a meteorologist (professional) or scientist (academic). Each is part of a community that uses these texts to do things in the world, and their literacies are not only distinct in some ways, but also likely to shift and change over time as their tasks and tools change. This means that the goal of disciplinary literacy instruction is not to know how historians or scientists read and write, but to flexibly identify and respond to the ways different communities use talk and text to represent their ideas.

This could mean that teachers are free to select disciplinary literacy perspectives that match the interests and background knowledge of their students, rather than always inviting students to be "like a scientist" or "like a mathematician," an idea that may be too abstract or otherwise uninteresting to them. It could also mean that the literacies students develop outside of academic settings might not only sometimes appear in school, but could also be viewed as potentially productive by having a reciprocal relationship with the school-based or academic literacies students engage with in class. Finally, it leaves room for the possibility that there is no benefit to reading "like a scientist" or another sort of professional. The real goal is to be able to read with flexibility and in response to specific purposes, formats, and audiences (Dostal & Gabriel, 2015).

Are "Disciplines" a Useful Category for Study?

There is general agreement that disciplines are better dividers of departments within a college than of bodies of knowledge or communities of practice. However, to whatever extent that U.S. high schools are modeled after the historic structures of the academy with departments representing four core academic areas (science, math, history, and English), the texts, assessments, curriculum, and expectations of high school still align with the idea of disciplinary learning. Interdisciplinary learning, or learning focused on specific subdisciplines, is often reserved for electives or upper-level courses. This is also true at the college level where general courses are taught early (e.g., Biology 101) and more specific courses that engage with specialized knowledge unique to a given community appear in upper-level courses, seminars, and experiential learning opportunities like working in a lab or on a research project. While the academy may still depend on the notion of disciplines, however, the world outside is better characterized by communities of literate practices that are created whenever people work together on a given set of tasks over time.

For example, the cast and crew of a musical might engage with a range of text types as they each carry out their work contributing to the production. There are set designs, scripts, scores, notes, signs, schedules, and so on, and these are used differently by different people in the community (written by some, memorized by others, played by some, conducted by others). Thus, each person might have a different orientation to or use of a text that is shared. What is important to note about this and many other examples is that the work of each individual in such a scenario is necessarily interdisciplinary. That is, people are engaging with texts originally created by and for music, art, theater, business, literature, management, among other pursuits. Within the community, they will develop a shorthand, certain conventions of representation and assumptions about shared background that will inform the texts created and shared over time.

Outsiders to this community will not be able to learn about its literate practices by reading a study about the dramatic literacies as demonstrated by a famous director or an expert dramaturg. They will have to observe, analyze, and even participate in that community to develop the literacies used or recognized as central to its shared work. The next time they engage in work related to the production of a musical, they would bring their knowledge and experience, but may need to adjust their habits to match the conventions, audiences, and purposes of a new community. In such cases, the community itself defines the literacy. The discipline is no longer the category of interest, but the understanding that there are many literacies or cohesive sets of literate practices relative to cohesive sets of text types, audiences, and purposes for reading and writing is preserved.

The same might apply for pursuits that are not as obviously interdisciplinary in nature. For example, doctors do not only read and write medical information in medical formats. They also write to patients, grant-making agencies, professional organizations, students, and insurance companies. They also read inventories, public health bulletins, and billing documents. When working with other doctors, they engage with medical texts, but also the output and displays of various technologies, the text of the human body itself, and information about the world and environment all around them. Since King (2015) has claimed that everything worth doing is already interdisciplinary, it is worth wondering what, if anything, division by discipline adds to the study of literacy development as it relates to proficient reading and writing across academic courses and communities.

OPPORTUNITIES IN DISCIPLINARY LITERACY

Research

In this section, we describe three targets for research that would guide agendas that create increased opportunities for learning in and across disciplines. First, there is a need to investigate whether and how discipline-specific literacies, that is, the ability to engage with representations of meaning that are specific to a given area of study, accumulate or develop reciprocity with one another. If they do, then effort spent on one might be assumed to transfer to others, and students could more readily specialize by investing in the development of a discipline of interest without being required to focus their efforts equally across the academic disciplines as many students are at the middle and high school levels. This specialization would not limit students to one area of study, because skills and strategies developed in one would support the more rapid development of equivalent skills and strategies that are fine-tuned to other disciplinary pursuits.

Second, there is a need to research whether and how the development of disciplinary literacy in any given area can support the development of general literacy skills, especially for students with reading difficulties, or populations that have historically received reading instruction not well matched to their inherent strengths. Rather than limiting students' exposure to the disciplines because of low general literacy proficiency, it is possible that developing and building on the development of discipline-specific literacies create more efficient pathways for generic literacy learning as well.

Finally, the ability to fully describe and assess disciplinary literacy development would support efforts to initiate and improve disciplinary-literacy-specific curricula and disciplinary-literacy-oriented instruction. Though such efforts can sometimes essentialize and reduce learning targets, they may also create opportunities for educators to measure and track their progress toward greater integration and improved implementation of disciplinary literacy instruction. This would additionally allow researchers to develop and implement varied approaches to disciplinary literacy instruction and teacher development for disciplinary literacy instruction.

Practice

Teachers engaged in teaching disciplinary literacy have the opportunity to engage and extend students opportunities for literacy learning in exciting ways. However, they may not always have a clear map for exactly how to do it: what to teach, what to emphasize, or what to expect. Resources that claim a finite version of what it means to "read like a historian" may not ring true or even apply to the tasks associated with your curriculum, let alone those engaged by people who use history in their work. The most fruitful opportunities for practice lie in inquiry into the texts and tasks that make up the discipline, subdiscipline, and/or community of practice that you view as most closely connected to the content you aim to teach. Catalog the texts you find involved in work related to the content you teach. Observe, consider, analyze, try out, take on, and copy those text, tasks, purposes, and contexts for reading and writing.

For example, if you aim to engage students with a specific mathematical concept, familiarizing them with its application in the world is not only important for building background, but also for inferring what is most interesting and important to attend to in the texts used to convey information about this concept. Exponents merely represent items to learn and symbols to memorize unless students can name something in their lives that grows and can be measured exponentially, unless they can visualize or recall the experience of feeling or witnessing the trajectory represented by an arc drawn on a graph. Somewhere between turning all of school into an exercise in experiential, project-based learning, and merely inserting students' names into the rote word problems they are required to solve, is a middle ground where we might find some invitations.

As educators, we are summoned to consider the processes, rather than only the information, that we can teach students through engagement and practice with phenomena of interest in our content areas. This requires becoming familiar with these processes, how texts facilitate and reflect them, and how we all can learn about a community's way of being and doing by studying the texts they use as artifacts as well as process maps for participation. In some cases, just looking at texts unique to a process, task, maker, or audience can tell you a lot about what went into them and how they are used. For example, a restaurant menu is broken down into sections that list food items which are similar in some way, and is generally organized in the order in which you might eat the dishes: appetizers/starters, entrees, desserts, and then beverages.

Depending on the type of restaurant, the item names might be expressed in more than one language, with pictures, or with descriptions, which tells us something about the nature of the restaurant and the degree to which it expects its patrons to know about whatever food items they are ordering. Restaurant menus with lengthy descriptions often serve food they believe is unique and entice you to choose based on that description. Restaurants serving well-known dishes use their familiar names and may not need to add descriptive details to communicate what you will get if you order them. Looking at a menu with students is a good way to address informational text standards related to text structure and text features. Likewise, having them create their own menus from school lunches and/or a shared meal experience can reinforce their understandings of how information may be organized, and what information is important to share. Students specifically studying culinary arts can even be assessed based on the specificity, vocabulary, and accuracy of the descriptions they use when writing menus because their ability to communicate about food to the public is central to their ability to offer such options to those they serve.

If you go behind the counter in a restaurant, the very same content is expressed very differently: in personal shorthand on the pads of waiters, and in a strategic format on the automatically generated tickets printed out from the computer systems that manage all orders. The tickets are organized by which part of the kitchen prepares each part of the order, and highlights important details in red or with asterisks to call attention to factors like allergies, substitutions, or changes to the typical makeup of the dish. This is because, unlike home cooking, a working kitchen depends on routines for efficiency, the division of labor, and the timing of processes to create many different dishes for many different consumers in one place, at one time. Anyone who has ever burned the bun before the burger is even done cooking knows how important relative timing can be to a good burger, and burgers are a relatively simple example of the many items a professional kitchen might create. The more complex the processes, the more stylized the conventions for communicating about them might be. Thus, learning to work in a new kitchen or under a new menu is as much about reading the text of the item you are grilling in real time to notice when it is charred, but not burned, as it is about quickly reading and immediately responding to a ticket that has just been printed out, or an order called to you as you work.

It is quite common for interviews with doctors and lawyers to highlight the importance of music lessons and sports in their early development. And, we would venture to say that there are many ways to develop the dexterity, discipline, and teamwork we so often associate with traditional afterschool activities. Workplaces, homes, community spaces, garages, and gardens offer the opportunity to read, respond, react, collaborate, decide, communicate, record, and share. They are facilitated by literate acts like making meaning from a set of symbols, recording information in a way that others can quickly understand, and the like. Therefore, you do not have to teach your biology students to think like a surgeon when reading about the anatomy of a squid. Thinking like a fishmonger, chef, or fisherman is not only just as reasonable; it's a good reminder that the thinking that accompanies anatomy and physiology is as much about visualizing and manipulating in three dimensions as it is about memorizing in two dimensions. Thinking of how people who use their knowledge of anatomy to do things in the world actually make use of such knowledge suggests ways to engage students in making use of it, too, and to thus teach them a process and application for item-level knowledge. This act of considering who utilizes a given set of content to accomplish certain tasks in everyday life, and then contemplating the range of potential applications and patterns across this range that highlight the processes central to related work, is a blueprint for classroom disciplinary literacy instruction because it allows teachers to access targets for instruction and activity that they would not otherwise have gathered from teachers' guides or expert interviews.

For their part, students are invited to grapple with texts that are central to the work of those who use your content in the world, rather than limiting students to reading about this work in texts written for school, and invite flexibility and curiosity about different ways of representing, interpreting, and sharing information. They need not be *like an expert* or professional; they can participate in the work or activity of such experts and professionals as themselves. In other words, they can *do* the discipline: take on its tasks, processes, texts, and talk as participants rather than as observers (Wenz & Gabriel, 2017).

When the texts and tasks are beyond the skill or understanding of your students, accept approximations and encourage students to represent their understandings in different ways. This will not only provide pathways to disciplinary literacy but also contribute to developing the flexibility and sensitivity needed to identify, respond, and adapt to different ways of using language and text as they move through their school day, across levels and grades, and beyond.

Most importantly, consider the possibility that teachers do not have to wait for expertise to develop to teach disciplinary literacy. Nor do they have to wait for experts to tell them what counts as disciplinary literacy. It is possible to aim for wide exposure to a variety of literacies throughout schooling as the goal of a liberal arts education in which multiple subjects are taught. Whether these accumulate or have a linear or exponential relationship, they will transform into flexibility about, sensitivity to, and awareness of language use in its many forms that will set up students to be powerfully literate in a changing world.

REFERENCES

Chall, J. S. (1983). *Stages of reading development.* McGraw-Hill.

Cummins, J. (1981). The role of primary language development in promoting educational success for language minority students. In California State Department of Education (Ed.), *Schooling and language minority students: A theoretical rationale* (pp. 3–49). California State University.

Dostal H., & Gabriel, R. (2015). Designing writing instruction that matters. *Voices from the Middle, 23*(2), 14–20.

Dunkerly-Bean, J., & Bean, T. W. (2016). Missing the savoir for the connaissance: Disciplinary and content area literacy as regimes of truth. *Journal of Literacy Research, 48*(4), 448–475.

Halliday, M. A. K. (1992). Systemic grammar and the concept of a "science of language." *Waiguoyu* (*Journal of Foreign Languages*), *2* (78), 1–9.

King, R. (2015). College reading in the age of disciplinary literacies: Change theory and mindfulness in moving the field forward. Paper presented at Symposium of the Literacy Research Association, Tampa, FL.

Martin, J. R. (2014). Evolving systemic functional linguistics: Beyond the clause. *Functional Linguist, 1,* 3.

Moje, E. (2015). Doing and teaching disciplinary literacy with adolescent learners: A social and cultural enterprise. *Harvard Educational Review, 85,* 254–278.

Scott, J., Dostal, H., Gabriel, R., & Graham, S. (2021). The science writing of deaf developing bilinguals. *Journal of Adolescent and Adult Literacy, 65*(2), 149–161.

Shanahan, C., Shanahan, T., & Misischia, C. (2011). Analysis of expert readers in three disciplines: History, mathematics, and chemistry. *Journal of Literacy Research, 43*(4), 393–429.

Shanahan, T. (2021). Disciplinary literacy goes to elementary school? *Reading Rockets.* Retrieved from *www.readingrockets.org/blogs/shanahan-literacy/disciplinary-literacy-goes-elementary-school.*

Shanahan, T., & Shanahan, C. (2008). Teaching disciplinary literacy to adolescents: Rethinking content-area literacy. *Harvard Educational Review, 78*(1), 40–59.

Wenz, C., & Gabriel, R. (2017). Three directions for disciplinary literacy. *Educational Leadership, 74*(5).

Cultivating Disciplinary Literacy Spaces for Youth Connection and Agency

Phillip Wilder
Michael Manderino

As Way et al. (2018) argue, there is currently a "crisis of connection" where people are increasingly disconnected from themselves and others, resulting in alienation, isolation, and decreased empathy. Now, exacerbated by the ongoing global pandemic and political protests concerning systemic racial oppression and violence, increased rates of depression, anxiety, loneliness, and social isolation reflect this increased personal disconnection. This crisis of connection manifests within marginalized communities through higher rates of addictions, mass violence, incarceration, hate crimes, domestic violence, and drastic income, educational, housing, and health care inequalities (p. 1).

Youth, and especially marginalized youth, are at risk for greater disconnection. With 39% of American teens experiencing persistent sadness or hopelessness in 2019 (up from 26% in 2009) according to the National Institute of Mental Health (2019), when we consider how youth continue to be affected by its economic impact on families, and the associated discontinuity of learning, discontinuity of health care, loss of security and safety, the current pandemic has exacerbated youth disconnection. As a result of essential quarantine and social distancing interventions to curb the spread of COVID-19, a February 2021 large-scale survey identified youth as having the highest rates (61%) of substantial symptoms of anxiety and depression, even surpassing the rates among older adults (Weissbourd et al., 2021). Thirty-six percent of all respondents reported feeling lonely "frequently" or "almost all the time or all the time" in the prior month; 61% of youth ages 18–25 and 51% of mothers with young children reported these chronic degrees of loneliness (p. 1). Forty-three percent of youth reported increased loneliness and were more likely than any other age demographic to lack basic forms of human attention and emotional sustenance, while over half of all youth surveyed stated no one in the prior 3 weeks had taken the time to ask how they were doing in a way that the youth felt expressed concern for their well-being (pp. 1–2). Research has linked loneliness with early mortality and a wide swath of grave physical and emotional problems (p. 1). Far more than feelings of isolation, loneliness can be defined as "the subjective feeling you're lacking the social connections you need which can feel like being stranded, abandoned, or cut off from the people with whom you belong" (Murthy, 2020, p. 8). As the current U.S. Surgeon General explains, loneliness can appear across relationships whether they be *intimate* (emotional longing for a close partner), *relational* (social longing for quality friendships and social connection), or *collective* (hunger for a community of people who share your purposes and interests) (p. 8). Given the traditional foci of school, to primarily attend to academic skills, coupled with the need to foster a greater sense of belonging (Murphy & Zirkel, 2015; Bottiani et al., 2017) for students, we ask the following question: How might school disciplinary literacy address the loneliness and disconnection among youth?

We use this chapter to argue that an expansive and culturally situated view of disciplinary literacy is necessary to avoid replicating reductive approaches that reproduce narrowed conceptions of disciplines, which obscure at best and silence at worst the disciplinary expertise, literacies, and lives of youth. These reductive approaches ultimately disconnect youth from their selves and their communities. We argue that an interrogation of both the conception of expertise and the purpose of disciplinary literacy can cultivate spaces of disciplinary literacy participation for youth to produce, critique, and leverage disciplinary knowledge for personal and community connection and reconciliation. Current conceptualizations and instantiated disciplinary practices in classrooms are useful only for developing habits of thinking that reproduce disciplines—and privileged access to knowledge creation. However, if the goal is to honor student agency leading to personal and community reconciliation, then we need to reimagine the purposes of disciplinary literacy and their concomitant practices. Otherwise, we waste the opportunity of disciplinary literacy at the occurrence of further disconnection of youth and communities.

Historically, school disciplinary curricula have a deep and troubling pattern of perpetuating a disconnect between the literacies and identities of youth and the sanctioned literacy practices valued by schooling (e.g., Haddix, 2009; Heath, 1983; Moll et al., 1992; Kirkland, 2013; Tatum, 2009). When school disciplines narrowly define literacy and sort and label youth accordingly, classrooms become spaces where youth identities are constricted, damaging youth self-concept, self-esteem, and self-efficacy. The messages youth ingest—about their literacies, knowledge, and identities—maintain subordination, inflict trauma, and reinforce an internal belief of being insufficient (hooks, 2003, p. 94). Instead, literacy within disciplinary classrooms can represent a tool of conscious reconciliation supporting identity work and ways of being (Alvermann, 2009; Morrell, 2015; Krishnamurti, 1969; Yagelski, 2011).

According to Way et al. (2018), the solution for bridging the crisis in connection, grounded in social and health science research detailing the dire consequences of loss of connection, lies in our human ability to cultivate connection and reconciliation through love. Far from the misguided and false assumptions we are taught about love being a fleeting feeling (hooks, 2018, p. 17), the solution—to pandemic isolation, addiction, mass incarceration, systemic racial oppression, domestic abuse, and housing inequalities—ultimately lies in "a love that includes the self and is rooted in justice and a sense of a common humanity" (p. 5). Ending domination in whatever form it appears (racism, sexism, homophobia, classism, etc.) must involve loving kindness for individual and communal liberation (hooks, 2017). During the current crisis of connection as youth bear the harsh impact of isolation and systems of oppression, classrooms can provide agentive spaces where youth are engaged in unlearning cultural conditioning and using literacy practices to address the societal and communal challenges that disconnect us from self, others, and a common humanity. Thus, the disciplinary literacy vision we present here is rooted in education that supports healing and wholeness, empowerment and liberation, transcendence and connection, ultimately leading to youths' reclamation of themselves and their just place in our world (hooks, 2003; Palmer, 2017).

A NEW APPROACH WITH FAMILIAR CHALLENGES

Disciplinary literacy as a construct may be relatively new with its focus on teaching the *specific* literacy practices *within* school disciplines (Moje, 2008; Shanahan & Shanahan, 2008), as opposed to a content-area literacy approach that focuses on teaching *generalized* literacy skills *across* disciplines (Herber, 1970), yet, in dominant instantiations, neither adequately addresses the increased disconnection of youth. With a content-area literacy approach, generalizable strategies were researched and developed to support student comprehension of complex texts in science, math, social studies, and English language arts (ELA). Examples included strategies to support comprehension and summary writing: generating interactions between schemata and texts (GIST; Cunningham, 1982), activation of prior knowledge such as Know–Want to Know–Learn (KWL; Ogle, 1986), or vocabulary acquisition through a Frayer model (Frayer et al., 1969), with the assumption these strategies scaffold *generalized* reading and writing processes used with any text in any school discipline. While content-area strategies can support the comprehension of texts valued in the discipline, they have been limited in their ability to support disciplinary ways of reading, writing, knowing, and thinking. For example, a strategy to deepen comprehension of a historical primary source does not deepen understanding of how to use that text to come to a historical argument or critique an extant historical interpretation. Whether foregrounding generalized strategies for accessing texts in disciplines or centering the literate practices within a discipline, student engagement still rests on a familiar challenge that must be addressed within school disciplines: an authentic and student-valued *purpose* for literacy within disciplines. Given the increased disconnection of students from self and loving communities, they need the field to take up a rigorous investigation of literate purpose within disciplines—purposes that support students in cultivating a powerful sense of self and connection within communities.

To support the challenges of learning in a discipline through textual engagement, disciplinary literacy has been primarily advocated as a way to address the larger literacy demands of text-based learning in a discipline (Moje, 2008; Shanahan & Shanahan, 2008). A disciplinary literacy approach to learning in science, history, literature, and other areas has meant using the habits of thinking, ways of knowing, habits of practice, and engagement with texts that are valued by the discipline (McConachie & Petrosky, 2009). Disciplinary literacy, then, has shifted the long-held stance of "every content teacher is a teacher of reading" (O'Brien et al., 1995) to one acknowledging the discipline-specific ways of learning through texts. For example, disciplinary literacy in science might focus on using observations and texts to construct an evidence-based argument through a claim–evidence–reasoning model, whereas inquiry in history might focus on corroborating primary and secondary sources to construct a causal historical argument. Disciplinary literacy is not just a new name from content-area literacy, but an approach to leveraging the epistemological, textual, linguistic, and discursive hallmarks of disciplinary inquiry to support student learning.

If we acknowledge that disciplinary literacy can foreground different things to different people, disciplinary classrooms remain contested sites in terms of what counts as knowledge or covered content. While much of initial disciplinary literacy research explored how readers approach disciplinary texts and produced findings about historical reading (Leinhardt, 1989, 1993; Leinhardt et al., 1994; Wineburg, 1991), scientific reading (Hand et al., 2004; Lemke, 1990; Lee & Fradd, 1998; Palincsar & Magnusson, 2001), the reading of literature (Lee, 2001; Lee & Spratley, 2006; Rainey, 2017), and reading within mathematics (Bass, 2006; Lemke, 2003), subsequent research explored epistemological processes of the disciplines (Akkus et al., 2007; Bain, 2006), linguistic processes (Fang & Schleppegrell, 2008; Fang et al., 2010; Schleppegrell & Achugar, 2003), and cultural modeling (Lee, 1995, 2001). With this view of disciplinary classrooms as contested sites, there is opportunity to bring greater intentionality to the purpose of textual experiences within disciplines (Tatum, 2020).

Recently, classroom examples of disciplinary literacy approaches have served as exemplars for researchers and practitioners alike. One such example comes from a large federally funded project, Project READI (Reading, Evidence, and Argumentation in Disciplinary Instruction), examining reading to learn through interventions designed to support evidence-based argumentation in the disciplines (Goldman et al., 2019). Through the use of design-based research, the project unearthed the vast complexity of designing instruction that supports evidence-based argumentation—a cornerstone of most disciplinary practice. However, the vast number of findings from the study suggested that there is no clear or singular approach to disciplinary literacy instruction that coincides with existent disciplinary literacies scholarship calling for a synergistic approach to the four primary orientations to disciplinary literacies (cognitivist, sociocultural, linguistic, and critical) (Fang, 2012; Wilder & Msseemmaa, 2019). We see particular opportunity for disciplinary literacies to be understood as social and cultural practices supporting youth metadiscursive awareness across texts (Moje, 2015) leading to critical and contemplative consciousness (Wilder & Msseemmaa, 2019).

CHALLENGES TO CURRENT INSTANTIATIONS OF DISCIPLINARY LITERACY

In a field fraught with philosophical disagreements, the search for what works becomes a pragmatic one, leading to narrowed lenses on complex phenomena or a conceptual drift in which the implementation of instructional practices often does not resemble the original vision of the espoused literacy teaching approach. In the case of disciplinary literacy, with the earliest research using a narrowed lens on expertise: interviewing and observing experts (i.e., university professors) to guide what it looks like to successfully engage with disciplinary texts, much disciplinary literacy instruction in the classroom continues to rely on an expert–novice paradigm teaching youth to read or write like disciplinary experts. Expert–novice binaries can create two problems for application to secondary classrooms. First is the transferability of "expert" practices to the practices cultivated in the secondary classroom. For example, the practices of a theoretical physicist may be so radically different than what is happening in a high school physics class. The disconnect between expert and novice is too wide. Second, the space between expert and novice is often where teacher experiences may be grounded. Secondary teachers have not engaged in expert practices like bench scientists or historians but rather have deeply studied the content knowledge often produced by experts. Apprenticing expert practices without considerations of task, context, and lived experiences can further disconnect students and teachers from the subject matter. Methodological traditions focused on cognitive and linguistic processing have identified common expert disciplinary practices approximated for middle and secondary classrooms. However, as Project READI (Goldman et al., 2016) found, implementing these varied practices can often be seen as a set of steps or activities, rather than guiding heuristics as they were originally intended. The results are frequently classroom practices based on trying to mimic expert behaviors. This unintended consequence has produced a wide swath of instructional approaches often misaligned with the goals of engaging deeply within disciplinary inquiry and practices.

As Paul Prior (2013) argues, all individuals engage in disciplinary practice and are thus disciplinarians. As individuals act with and in the world, they develop tools that keep them safe (potable water), foster communication (communication norms), keep them connected (storytelling), and develop standards for recording the past and the present (content curation). We interrogate the notions of expertise because a narrow definition of expertise as defined as academic work in the discipline has shaped what we think of as "legitimate" disciplinary practices. Much of this narrowing has come from the methodological approaches to the investigation of disciplinary literacy. Initial studies that are often used to define/describe disciplinary practices have used expert–novice think-aloud studies.

A methodological and theoretical result of privileging expertise as narrowly defining disciplinary practices has been to exacerbate the disconnection between school and life as mediated by disciplinarity. Early studies of disciplinary literacy leveraged expert–novice dichotomies through the use of think-aloud protocols (Ericsson & Simon, 1998) to elucidate differences in cognition between university scholars and high school or university students (e.g., Wineburg, 1991). While these studies ground heuristics that guide disciplinary meaning-making, they homogenize cognitive practices based on a small dataset assuming the cultural practices with texts, as well as the texts, and the discourse around texts don't vary significantly within contexts. While heuristics for disciplinary thinking are useful tools, they do not encapsulate universal habits of thinking. Moreover, as Manderino and Castek (2016) point out, habits of thinking do not account for the practices that are concomitant with disciplinary thinking. Disciplinary thinking alone disconnects youth from participation in knowledge construction.

The focus on what a narrow band of experts say they do when they read disciplinary texts can lead to further disconnections of the disciplines. For example, descriptions of thinking or practice that claim to be uniquely historical, scientific, or literary in nature belie the fact that history is a critical aspect of scientific inquiry or that historical argument is often bolstered by evidence from literature produced at the time period being interrogated. When these become the dominant practices valued in a discipline, the result is a further narrowed experience for students in secondary school disciplines with the goal of teaching students how to replicate the self-reported practices of privileged members based on a few think-aloud studies.

Not only are major disciplines disconnected from each other in their instantiations in secondary school subjects, but they are also disconnected within the disciplines themselves. If science, history, or literature is treated as a monolith, then the distinctions between subfields become obscured. For example, the ways in which a physicist approaches his or her inquiry is quite different than the practices of a biologist, let alone physicists or biologists in different professional areas in varied local cultural contexts and while exploring different scientific inquiries. Similarly, in social studies classrooms, reading "like a historian" heuristics might illuminate ways of knowledge construction in a history classroom for youth, but how do these translate into a sociology course or a government course? And what disciplinarians and their expert thinking comprise these latter two subfields? This is not to say there are no similarities across subfields, but to lump all subfields into a singular conception of disciplinary practices further disconnects the purposes of disciplinary inquiries.

Disciplinary practices as defined by the self-reports of experts also disconnect the disciplines from their enactment in community practice. By centering expertise as what university researchers report, it narrows and silences the disciplinary practices found in practice within other communities. Communities use disciplinary and interdisciplinary practices to shape life (Dewey, 1986). Public works departments rely on science as well as communication practices to alert community members to work in areas that need to be avoided. The consequences of not using scientific practices could lead to significant financial waste to citizens, inefficient use of precious natural resources, misuse of community spaces, or even community members falling ill or worse dying. The point here is that several cross sections of society use and rely on disciplinary literacies and yet they have rarely been the subject of study (Phillips & Leander, 2010) to understand and inform disciplinary literacy or disciplinary literacy pedagogy. The result is a disconnection between lived enactment of disciplines and those often abstracted or gate-kept by educational institutions.

By solely describing disciplinary literacy as a practice reserved in academic spaces, then epistemic understanding of those disciplines continually reproduces itself in Whiteness. If the accepted norm for disciplinary practice is defined as what occurs in academic spaces, then the lens of disciplinary literacy is shaped by the very Whiteness and privilege that dominate academic institutions. The result is an erasure of disciplinary practices that are community grown, refined, and shared for the purposes of community well-being. The dislocation of what "counts" as disciplinary literacy and how it is actually taken up in communities further disconnects students from their own lived experiences.

When disciplines are instantiated to mirror academic conceptions of disciplinary practice rather than as tools to support and guide youths' civic and community participation, then school is disconnected from authentic ways of understanding and interacting within the world. Schooling becomes a means to a credential and institutions of higher learning, instead of a means to empower youth to address critical issues and inequalities. The crisis of connection is amplified through school practices. And while one may argue hyperbole, you don't have to look far to see assessment practices, which have predated any disciplinary literacy approach, that serve only as a check of discrete knowledge that has been banked or curricular structures that have not changed in a century.

REPRODUCTIVE DISCIPLINES AND THE DISCONNECTION OF YOUTH

Schooling has historically reproduced dominant ways of using language and literacy that have reproduced power inequalities both within and outside of school (Anyon, 1981; Apple, 1977; Bowles & Gintis, 1976; Jackson, 1968; Nieto, 2002). When schools privilege monolingualism, mono-modality, and print-based literacy practices that serve the economic, political, and social needs of White, mainstream, middle-class individuals, inevitably, marginalization—of literacies and identities—disconnects youth from self and loving community (hooks, 2003, p. 94). Disconnection from self and community is not by accident, but culturally conditioned and maintained through discourses and social structures to preserve subordination, while resulting in the infliction of both external and internalized violence on a person (hooks, 2003; Krishnamurti, 1969). While the trauma resulting from this systemic violence is profound, life-altering, and transgenerational and cannot be excluded from a full understanding of the traumatic experiences of youth, disciplinary literacies can reject reproductive school disciplines and the internalized remnants of cultural conditioning that disconnect youth from loving community and self.

Disciplines as Disconnectors of Youth from Community

Situated in communities, literacy practices function based on shared values and dispositions of community members helping to explain how youth come to school with varied linguistic practices (e.g., Heath, 1983; Kirkland, 2009; Moll et al., 1992). Despite these varied linguistic and literacy practices, schooling attempts to mold youth according to societal design through sanctioned disciplinary knowledge and through a hidden curriculum of normative and dispositional meanings to students (Apple, 1977, p. 15). According to Jackson (1968), daily social interactions convey the "hidden curriculum" of schools empowering or marginalizing students by valuing or devaluing the capital students bring to classrooms. Apple (1977) argues the hidden curriculum is not accidental because "curriculum has its roots in the soil of social control" (p. 5) and "schools seem to, by and large, do what they are supposed to do . . . providing dispositions and propensities 'functional' in later life in a complex and stratified social and economic order" (p. 2). As an embodiment of larger processes of cultural politics, texts within classrooms play a major role in defining whose culture and whose knowledge are taught (Apple, 1992, p. 4).

For Wandera (2020), this sanctioning of literacies within secondary classrooms serves a colonial agenda intending to silence the local knowledge systems of marginalized youth. As Wandera (2020) posits, not only does a blindness to the meaning-making practices of ethnolinguistically diverse youth result in systemic inequalities within classrooms, it also serves a colonial agenda through a multipronged attack on the lives, languages, and epistemic traditions of these marginalized youth, their worldviews and cultures (p. 645). Since literacy is localized (Heath, 1983; Kirkland, 2013), any attempt to understand the situated use of literacy practices for meaning making, being, and liberation must be rooted within the soil of local epistemic traditions. In his study of the meaning-making activities of fifth- and ninth-grade youth in Kenyan language arts classes, Wandera sought to understand this colonial agenda (and the ensuing linguicide and epistemicide) by observing how ethnolinguistically diverse youth resourced explicit, exploratory, collaborative, oral commentary and texts as "diverse communicative resources" during classroom writing experiences (p. 646). By exploring the centrality of youths' collaborative oral and written participation in classroom literacy events, Wadera reports how these youth employed complex translingual practices through varied communicative resources from shared linguistic and community repertoires to write, communicate, participate, and make meaning within the disciplinary literacy activities (p. 658).

Reproductive disciplines demand assimilation and sustain coloniality by attempting to sever youth from the rich diversity of meaning-making practices and funds of knowledge within their lives and within their communities. Youth soon find "being a *successful* student requires identity work—adopting and affiliating with multiple new ways of talking, listening, acting, feeling, responding, interacting, and valuing, as well as writing and reading" (Gee, 2000, p. 225, italics added), with reproductive disciplines silencing youth by determining the possible identities youth can select and enact. Siloed disciplines in secondary schools, which privilege certain texts as "historical texts" or of certain textual practices as "reading in science," not only block youth from demonstrating, deepening, and leveraging their community meaning-making practices, but also disconnect youth from their communities and themselves.

As Kirkland (2013) argues concerning the silencing of young black men in secondary English, "literacy comprised the social memory of the group and its historical lineage. It also represented cultural ideologies, their particular and situated understandings of self and community—the stories of belief, imagination, and family" (p. 145). As social memory and knowledgeable brokers of their cultures and worldviews (Jezewski, 1990; Orellana, 2009) who hold rich out-of-class literacy practices (Kinloch, 2009; Ladson-Billings, 1998; Wilder & Msseemmaa, 2019), youth agentively resist marginalizing narratives (Irizarry & Raible, 2014) that coincide with sanctioned literacies, deficit-oriented identities, decreased educational access, shaming, and a double consciousness (Du Bois, 2015). Marginalized youth are taught to look at their literacy practices "through the eyes of others . . . measuring one's soul by the tape of a world that looks on in amused contempt and pity" (p. 3). Regardless of the promise of disciplinary literacy, any narrowing of disciplinary literacy curriculum can impose this double consciousness on marginalized youth by mandating whose disciplinary practices and identities hold value and represent expertise in classrooms, thereby positioning youth in opposition to the colonizing agenda that aggressively seeks to decenter and silence local knowledge systems (Grosfoguel, 2015; Mazrui & Wagaw, 1989; Smith, 2012). Opportunities for agentive disciplinary literacy practice—which leverage youth literacies and local knowledge—are wasted as reproductive practices perpetuate disconnection from literacies, languages, epistemologies, and self.

Disciplines as Disconnectors of Youth from Self

Just as language and the hidden ideologies of texts establish one's positioning within social structures of power, they also bureaucratize the minds of youth through cultural conditioning (Freire, 1968/1972, p. 69), carrying with them traumatic remnants of systemic, transgenerational oppression. Weedon (1987) asserts that the "meaning of the existing structure of social institutions, as much as the structures themselves and the subject positions which they offer their subjects, is a site of political struggle waged mainly, though not exclusively, in *language*" (p. 38, italics added). While language represents symbolic power and signifies cultural capital and authority (Bourdieu, 1991), it also illuminates the "inner speech" or monologue within one's consciousness (Vygotsky, 2012, p. 239). Inner speech is not an internal manifestation of talking but a "function in itself" and a psychological interface between external culturally sanctioned symbolic systems of meaning and internalized private "language" and imagery (p. 239). Here is where language and cultural conditioning become internalized meaning and construct identities. Since the relation of thought to word is "not a thing but a process, a continual movement back and forth from thought to word and from word to thought" (p. 231), thought and speech "turn out to be the key to the nature of human consciousness" (p. 271) with each word a representation of human consciousness (p. 271). Given how the words of others influence an individual's thoughts, language becomes an empowering or disempowering tool for expanding or limiting the consciousness of youth. For example, misogynistic terminology and gendered discourses populate dominant, hetero-normative narratives about how women *should* source personal and economic security from men in relationships at the expense of authenticity, personal power, and autonomy. Ladson-Billings (1998) outlines how racial narratives are consistently woven throughout every social institution of society and privilege those who align with the dominant racial, gendered, economically dominant norms of discourse representing the standard by which all other linguistic practices are measured. Language, and its textual lineages of exclusion, privilege, and domination, become the vehicle by which reproductive school disciplines attempt to culturally condition youth into acceptance of disempowering internal narratives, inauthentic even subservient identities, and disconnective practices.

With this bureaucratization of the mind, one often develops limited awareness of how language and these ingested narratives saturate thoughts, words, and deeds while inflicting violence on a person (Hanh, 2006, 2012; Krishnamurti, 1969). At a fundamental level, the cultural conditioned beliefs about self disconnect a person from the capacity to know what they feel, need, and how to act in honor of self. A narrow conception of disciplinary literacies privileges print-based practices aligned with the dominant majority while communicating not only that other rich meaning-making practices are inferior, but also that youth who utilize these practices are also less valued, less aligned with "academic" ways of being literate in disciplines, and must abandon these practices for dominant, print-based literacies. This view of disciplinary literacies disempowers youth and shames their literate identities, promoting less connection with self within secondary school classrooms.

Multivoiced Youth Literacies and Sense of Self

Literacy research has viewed identities as socially constructed through the negotiations of everyday interactions (Bloome et al., 2005; Erickson, 2004; Gee et al., 2001; Moje & Luke, 2009). Norton (2013) conceptualizes identity as multiple, a site of struggle, and fluctuating across time and space while asserting the mutable nature of identity. As complex social identity and language practices shift according to one's positioning in different social structures (e.g,. Miller & Kubota, 2013), the identities of youth do, too. Or, as Moje and Luke (2009) explain, a "person is called into an identity by the recognitions or assignments of others, and the meanings the person makes of the identities available to him or her serve to constitute a sense of self or subjectivity" (p. 419). For example, youth navigate multiple discourses within and across the day, yet this is rarely made explicit through school tasks and courses. Within this view, youth identities are dynamic, negotiated, and contextualized—used to agentively maneuver through contested spaces and reflective of a youth's sense of self.

These situated and negotiated identities construct a narrative of the self (Ochs & Capps, 1996). As youth experience and negotiate meaning, they develop a *sense of self* or a "reflective awareness of being in the world, including one's past and future . . . coming to know ourselves as we use narrative to apprehend experiences and navigate relationships with others" (p. 21). The stories youth tell of their experiences "bring experiences to conscious awareness," making meaning of interactions with others, of their place in the world, how they attend to and feel about events, and ultimately their sense of self (p. 21). These stories mediate experiences, represent "subjective involvement in the world," and challenge one to recognize "lives are the pasts we tell ourselves" (p. 21). Any narration of experience presents a fragmented intimation with any narrative having the potential to generate a multiplicity of partial selves (p. 22). Thus, disciplinary literacies can support how youth interrogate who ultimately benefits from these narrations of experience and to what extent they connect youth with their authentic self.

Just as language and literacy have been used as cudgels of cultural conditioning and disempowerment (Apple, 1977, 1983, 1992), disconnection from self and community becomes a consequence of narrowed notions of disciplinary literacies where youth are taught to ignore their literacies and need for authentic meaning-making in exchange for academic success. By limiting or ignoring opportunities for youth to utilize their literacies and knowledge, dominant forms of disciplinary literacies can disempower youth and exacerbate a sense of disconnection from self. As Gabor Maté describes disconnection:

> When I talk about being connected to ourselves, I'm talking about actually knowing what we feel and experience in a given moment, and being able to interpret that appropriately. Without that capacity, we're lost. We were born with that capacity—you've never met an infant who's not connected with its gut feelings. By the time you talk to adults, you find many people who even if they have their gut feelings, they ignore them. Something happens between infancy and adulthood that disconnects us. What that is, is our need for acceptance by our environment. (quoted in Benazzo & Benazzo, 2021)

Acceptance in secondary school environments that view disciplinary literacies in limited ways often requires youth to ignore their literacies, knowledge, and identities in exchange for the semblance of acceptance and academic rewards. With trauma long associated only with individuals who suffered the worst abuse and neglect, psychiatrist Mark Epstein (2014) asserts that trauma, with its varied levels of pain, is an indivisible part of human existence, taking many forms and sparing no one (p. 1). In situations with unbearable emotions, the self's only choice, according to psychotherapists, is to wall itself off from the threat, removing itself from what it assumes it cannot regulate (p. 73). This dissociation, whether conscious or unconscious, through the coping with addictions or not, is meant to distance one from feeling hard emotions and alienates one from aspects of self inconsistent with their experience of "me" at any given moment (pp. 73–74). While this dissociation offers immediate protection from traumatic emotions, it disconnects a person further from feeling and recognizing and honoring their needs. As Maté (2008) concludes, "when you shut down emotion, you're also affecting the immune system and nervous system with the repression of emotion, a survival strategy, becoming a source of physiological illness later on" (p. 357). Unchecked, the language and cultural conditioning of reproductive disciplines run the risk of intensifying youths' feelings of isolation and disconnection while failing to disrupt practices and policies that attempt to subjugate youth.

To be clear, youth are not victims and resilience is not the goal as this absolves schools, school leaders, policymakers, and community members from taking responsibility for the policies and practices that exacerbate youth isolation and disconnection in disciplinary classrooms. Instead, reconciliatory policies and practices are needed to widen notions of disciplinary practice, connect disciplinary spaces with local epistemic traditions, practices, knowledge, and discourses while reconciling the traumatic experiences of youth and supporting youth agency and connection with self and within communities.

Foregrounding Youth Consciousness and Agency in Disciplinary Classrooms

While the previous sections have called current conceptualizations of disciplinary literacy into question and outlined how, regardless of intentions, marginalizing disciplinary literacy can disconnect youth from self through a double consciousness, we shift the focus to possible trajectories of disciplinary literacy to support how youth connect to their sense of self and cultivate community. In Way et al. (2018), Noguera argues that the crisis of connection has a twin, the empathy gap, that is characterized by a growing inability to respond with compassion to the suffering of others and that obstructs the search for creative solutions to human problems (p. 152). Creative, preventative actions to a host of problems caused by disconnection in our world are often ineffective when a large swath of the population (and those in power) exhibit limited empathy for the suffering of others. Thus, the opportunities we present here are grounded in a desire to grow empathy, but also in a belief that education is about healing and wholeness, empowerment and liberation, transcendence and connection, ultimately leading to youth finding and reclaiming themselves and their place in the world (hooks, 2003; Palmer, 2017). As educators, service toward these ends in disciplinary classrooms are a form of political resistance (hooks, 2003, p. 91) where our "committed acts of caring let all students know the purpose of education is not to dominate or prepare them to be dominators, but rather to create the conditions for freedom" (hooks, 2003, p. 92). Disciplinary literacy then—with a widened recognition of youth, their identities, and local epistemic traditions, practices, and knowledge—can become an act of love and service demonstrating our resolute commitment to youth and to their liberation (Freire, 1968/1972) from systemic oppression and the bureaucratization of their minds and toward increased agency where youth know where they stand, identify what they feel and need, and use their voice to reauthor lives with greater authenticity, personal power, and sense of self. Beginning with the local affords the possibility to connect the abstract with what is most consequential in the lives of youth. Local, authentic practices belie the reifying of abstract practices that exacerbate disconnection for youth.

Centering Consciousness in Disciplinary Classrooms

Understanding how power is wielded and withheld to reproduce inequalities has been a dominant principle of critical theories (Freire, 1968/1972, 1985; Giroux, 2011; hooks, 1994; Janks, 2009; Shor, 1992) with any application of critical theory in disciplinary classrooms inseverable from issues of democracy and reconciliation. A youth's critical consciousness becomes "a way towards something apart from itself" (Freire, 1968/1972, p. 69), of rejecting everyday bureaucratization of the mind (Freire, 1985, p. 18). Yet, critical pedagogy often foregrounds the understanding of systemic oppression and backgrounds the inner terrain of youth where remnants of degradation, devaluation, and shaming traumatize and obscure a youth's sense of self (Wilder & Msseemmaa, 2019). While Freire emphasizes critical consciousness as a means of transforming systems of societal oppression, contemplative theorists (Hanh, 2006, 2012; Krishnamurti, 1969) emphasized consciousness of self, which brings awareness to one's culturally conditioned views of the relationship between self and people and objects. In *Freedom from the Known* (1969), Indian philosopher Jiddu Krishnamurti argues that recognizing the "roots of violence in society but also in oneself one can begin to move beyond it" (p. 50). By giving attention to how one reacts to cultural conditioning, one gains the freedom to doubt and question dependence, conformity, and acceptance of what does not serve one's humanity (p. 28).

Our proposed approach to disciplinary literacy engages youth in using local, community situated literacies to read and respond to the "lived world one is living inside of, and which is making him" (Freire, 1985, p. 18) while also producing a "revolution in the mind freeing one to doubt and question everything they have been told to believe about self" (Krishnamurti, 1969, p. 68). While critical consciousness can support unlearning of cultural conditioning, consciousness of self can support youth agency and deep personal connection to self. Agency, ultimately, is the ability to respond to your own needs and to the needs of your community, which requires both a consciousness of how language and systems work to disempower as well as establish a deep connection to what one feels and the need to live with integrity. To support youths' reconciliation and connection within disciplinary classrooms and within self requires a reimagining of expertise, knowledge, and purpose for youth participation in disciplinary practice.

DESIGNING DISCIPLINARY PRACTICE: DISCIPLINES AS AVENUES FOR YOUTH AGENCY

Disciplinary literacy can be reimagined as the tools to develop youth agency so they may more fully participate actively in their communities and close the empathy gap (Noguera, 2018, p. 152). To connect school as a site for communal connection means broadening expertise, practice, and participation. There are several examples of classroom approaches to humanizing school experiences (Arrastia, 2018; Dorney, 2018; Reichert & Nelson, 2018; Rhoades, 2018; Way & Nelson, 2018) that inspire us to connect disciplinary literacy with situated disciplinary activities that are relevant and authentic to the lives of youth. Disciplinary literacy can reconnect youth with their communities and each other by repositioning expertise.

First, we need to upend notions of expertise itself. Expertise should be bidirectional between teachers and students (Castek & Manderino, 2020). One way to rethink expertise is to look first to communal practices that are representative of disciplinarity (Prior, 2013). Rather than initially view disciplines as a set of ways of thinking or practices, we might regard them as situated communities of practice. Disciplines are neither monolithic nor homogenous in the ways they are used by individuals and groups. All activity is situated by people and contexts. Expertise is distributed across communities of practice, rather than reserved for a select few.

Work by Lee (1995) highlights the ways that community and Indigenous knowledge can be used to connect with discipline-specific practices such as literary analysis. Cultural modeling (Lee, 1995) is an approach to connecting the linguistic practices of youth to ways authors use language to communicate meaning in a work of literature. By deliberately connecting the language in use with the language in literature, youth are positioned as experts through language use rather than marginalized because of the language in use. Approaches like cultural modeling that leverage connections between community and lived experiences to generate content knowledge within a discipline (Lee, 1995) provide sites of connection for students to see their full selves in their own school-based inquiry.

Another promising practice that forges connections between the lived experiences of youth and the disciplines is through youth participatory action research (YPAR) as an inquiry approach (Mirra et al., 2015). By positioning youth as problem framers, posers, and solvers, expertise is a construct that is gained through practice. Students learn the tools to engage in rigorous inquiry and work alongside experts to develop solutions to community problems. YPAR as an approach leverages authentic learning while positioning the students as meaning-makers and problem solvers. Through the YPAR process, students learn not only the disciplinary tools to critique and enact change but also the content knowledge that is brought to bear through the inquiry process. Youth become the authors of their learning, connected to community experts in a quest to solve problems impacting their lives and communities.

Lastly, we argue for a multidisciplinary approach to learning, as opposed to siloed and abstract exercises couched as approximations of disciplinary practice. When students have opportunities to draw on repertoires across disciplines, they can begin to see the interconnectedness of the communities they inhabit. While disciplinary literacy scholarship has identified some key learning and literacy practices, there are also opportunities for understanding multidisciplinary practice. Rather than focus on narrowly defined skills, a multidisciplinary approach can leverage multiple forms of student knowledge. Because of the complex nature of inquiry, rather than the teacher as an expert, expertise is distributed. The distribution of expertise provides sites of connection that are lost when teachers are positioned as experts and students as novices. Bidirectional expertise (Manderino & Castek, 2020) in classroom contexts can not only support student agency in their inquiry but also foster an intellectual relationship (Stromholt & Bell, 2018) between teachers and students.

Rather than a focus on the disciplines themselves, a focus on centering youth in their funds of knowledge (Moll et al., 1992), lived experiences, situated expertise, and sense of self can lead to greater connections for youth. Disciplinary practices become tools for agency and liberation rather than habits of thinking that need to be approximated or replicated for the sake of "doing the discipline." When inquiry is anchored around local issues and questions, then localized knowledge and the bearers of that knowledge become integral to the inquiry. Personal investment in solving issues is foregrounded rather than abstracted ways of knowing and doing. Disciplinary literacy has the potential to become a tool for connecting youth with their selves and their communities.

DESIGNING DISCIPLINARY OPPORTUNITIES FOR YOUTH TO CONNECT TO SELF AND COMMUNITY

United Nations Security Council Resolution 2250 (United Nations, 2015) called on youth to be included in decision making at all levels in local, regional, national, and international efforts to counter violence, marginalization, and discrimination with peaceful resolutions that empower youth and address their emotional, physical, economic, and health vulnerabilities. Marginalized youth are increasingly demanding more equitable educational and economic opportunities and solutions with youth increasingly centered in efforts to address their multifaceted challenges. Education—for reconciliation and liberation—relies on both critical and contemplative consciousness with accompanying practices of self-study, nonviolent communication, and loving action to recognize and reject deleterious narratives of self and community. When disciplinary classrooms are designed as inclusive spaces for youth agency through a broadened view of expertise, practice, and participation in disciplinary activities, youth can cultivate greater loving kindness and self-compassion, which support the compassionate interrogation of local disciplinary problems with local meaning-making tools. When spaces are created through which youth can see their communal connections, they are then able to recognize their interconnectedness within the community. Youth can reauthor their role in these communities, emphasizing greater empowerment for self and others. By engaging in localized inquiry and leveraging their development of expertise, youth become a more integral part of the community, rather than being seen as adjacent or subjects of community concerns or successes. Only then can connection—to self and community—manifest personal and collective authenticity, reconciliation, and liberation.

Reauthoring Self in Disciplinary Classrooms

Relying on research on literacy as identity work, as ways of being (Gee et al., 2001; Yagelski, 2011), inherently dialogic (Bakhtin, 1981) and reflective of local knowledge systems (Krupnik & Vakhtin, 1997), we call for disciplinary classrooms to support how youth reauthor self through the unlearning of deleterious stories that accompany cultural conditioning and marginalizing experiences. This *reauthoring of self* is intricately connected to critical consciousness of how power is wielded and withheld to oppress and involves consciousness of how disempowerment can disconnect one from a sense of self and a recognition of inherent worth and agency. Reauthoring of self—for reconciliation and liberation—-can recover the voices of marginalized youth to dismantle external and internal systemic structures of domination and manifest more compassionate connection to self and community.

Through dialogic interactions (Bakhtin, 1981), youths' reauthoring of self has been characterized as counter-storytelling (Delgado, 1989; Solorzano & Yosso, 2001), writing the self (Morrell, 2015; Yagelski, 2011), and constructing the dialogical self (Fecho, 2011). Wagaman et al. (2018) conclude that "counter-storytelling" has led to increased self-definition of LGBTQ youth while recognizing the breadth of their experiences and complexity of intersecting identities. In research exploring how Black queer youth challenged heteronormative ways of being, Johnson (2017) argues, "[D]iscourse around authentic writing must address how writers might interrogate racialized, gendered, and othered worlds" (p. 17). Writing the self has focused on "helping us to understand and transform ourselves individually and together" (Yagelski, 2011, p. 21), with youth rewriting resulting in "care for the self" or a "repositioning of self with self" (Morrell, 2015, p. 167).

Drawing on the work of Hermans and Kempen (1993), who view the self as constructed of a range of highly contextualized and dynamic cultural identities, Fecho (2011) offers the case of Andy, a gay youth, to demonstrate how Andy's "cultural identities—high school wrestler, new driver, student with low self-improvement, reluctant reader, inquirer into gay lifestyles—remained in dialogue as he continued to construct a simultaneously unified and diverse self" (p. 96). The construction of his multivoiced self depended on where he was, how he had constructed himself to date, and to what extent he remained in dialogue with his various contexts and diverse identities (p. 96). Within his ELA classroom, Andy began to tell new stories about himself as a learner and see teachers and students as "sources of dialogue" instead of authoritative voices, as demonstrated by Andy's co-opting of a *Macbeth* essay assignment to unpack a recent argument he'd had with his family over gay marriage. Andy's reauthoring of self occurred as he "actively constructed who he was by knowingly engaging in dialogue between his many selves and the contexts he entered" (p. 97). As Fecho concludes, when the "wobble" (what we've termed disconnection) in youths' lives speaks too loudly to ignore, and they seek understanding, dialogue with others as well as disciplinary texts and multivoiced identities provide opportunities for constructing a more integrated dialogical self.

Literacy within disciplines can support a *literacy of being* where youth discursively and collectively use local literacy practices for *unlearning* cultural conditioning and for *becoming* a freer and more authentic version of self deeply connected within a loving community. To address the increased disconnection and loneliness of youth in the present moment, disciplinary literacy must cultivate dialogical, disciplinary spaces for youth to reconcile and honor the pain of having identities imposed and lost, of feeling the disconnection from self. But these dialogical, disciplinary spaces must also exist for youth to honor new cultural identities and to celebrate their reauthoring and integrity of self. We see promise in disciplinary pedagogies that (1) extend from our own personal work of unlearning and becoming; (2) foreground models of human unlearning and becoming; (3) model and cultivate space for introspection and dialogue with self (Wilder, 2019); (4) offer texts as opportunities to dialogue with multivoiced identities and self (Schreuder & Wilder, 2020); (5) ground pedagogy in responsive and liberatory practices intending to do no harm to youth; (6) infuse nonviolent communication to support empathetic communication with self and others. Collectively, we see these pedagogical directions creating disciplinary classroom communities of connection where a literacy of being, grounded in unlearning and becoming, manifests youth reconciliation and agency. Through increased consciousness of how language and systems of domination culturally condition and traumatize the mind and body, youth awaken into a literacy of being that draws their gaze inward, so they might unlearn the deleterious narratives of their oppressors. This literacy of being also relies on the wisdom of emotions and the construction of the dialogical self to illuminate their needs and guide them into greater integrity of self.

In *Teaching Community*, bell hooks (2003) warn in seeking to transform society one of the most intense struggles is the effort to maintain an integrity of being, stating, "All of the work we do, no matter how brilliant or revolutionary in thought or action, loses power and meaning if we lack integrity of being" (p. 164). By foregrounding a literacy of being in school disciplines and cultivating this internal locus of control within us and alongside students, classrooms can support how youth deepen authentic connection with self since to be "guided by love is to live in community with all life"—exactly what a culture of domination seeks to prevent (p. 163).

REFERENCES

Akkus, R., Gunel, M., & Hand, B. (2007). Comparing an inquiry-based approach known as the science writing heuristic to traditional science teaching practices: Are there differences? *International Journal of Science Education, 29*(14), 1745–1765.

Alvermann, D. E. (2009). Sociocultural constructions of adolescence and young people's literacies. In L. Christenbury, R. Bomer, & P. Smagorinsky (Eds.), *Handbook of adolescent literacy research* (pp. 14–28). Guilford Press.

Anyon, J. (1981). Social class and school knowledge. *Curriculum Inquiry, 11*(1), 3–42.

Apple, M. W. (1977). What do schools teach? *Curriculum Inquiry, 6*(4), 341–358.

Apple, M. W. (1983). Curriculum in the year 2000: Tensions and possibilities. *Phi Delta Kappan, 64*(5), 321–326.

Apple, M. W. (1992). The text and cultural politics. *Educational Researcher, 21*(7), 4–11, 19.

Arrastia, L. (2018). Love pedagogy. In N. Way, A. Ali, C. Gilligan, & P. Noguera (Eds.), *The crisis of connection* (pp. 231–249). NYU Press.

Bain, R. (2006). Rounding up unusual suspects: Facing the authority hidden in the history classroom. *Teachers College Record, 108*(10), 2080–2114.

Bakhtin, M. (1981). Forms of time and of the chronotope in the novel. *The Dialogic Imagination: Four Essays, 1*, 84–259.

Bass, H. (2006). *What is the role of oral and written language in knowledge generation in mathematics?: Toward the improvement of secondary school teaching and learning. Integrating language, literacy, and subject matter.* University of Michigan Press.

Benazzo, M., & Benazzo, Z. (Producers and Directors). (2021). *The Wisdom of Trauma* [Video file]. Retrieved from *https://drgabormate.com/the-wisdom-of-trauma.*

Bloome, D., Carter, S. P., Christian, B.M., Otto, S., & Shuart-Faris, N. (2005). *Discourse analysis and the study of classroom language and literacy events: A microethnographic perspective.* Erlbaum.

Bottiani, J. H., Bradshaw, C. P., & Mendelson, T. (2017). A multilevel examination of racial disparities in high school discipline: Black and white adolescents' perceived equity, school belonging, and adjustment problems. *Journal of Educational Psychology, 109*(4), 532.

Bourdieu, P. (1991). *Language and symbolic power.* Harvard University Press.

Bowles. S., & Gintis, H. (1976). *Schooling in capitalist America: Educational reform and the contradictions of economic life.* Basic Books.

Castek, J., & Manderino, M. (2020). Digital literacies for disciplinary learning: Interactions that build conceptual knowledge, practices, and habits of thinking. In M. Kuhn (Ed.), *Developing conceptual knowledge through oral and written language* (pp. 121–141). Guilford Press.

Cunningham, J. W. (1982). Generating interactions between schemata and text. In J. Niles & L. Harris (Eds.), *New inquiries in reading research and instruction: Thirty-first yearbook of the National Reading Conference* (pp. 42–47). National Reading Conference.

Delgado, R. (1989). Storytelling for oppositionists and others: A plea for narrative. *Michigan Law Review*, *87*(8), 2411–2441.

Dewey, J. (1986, September). Experience and education. In *The educational forum* (Vol. 50, No. 3, pp. 241–252). Taylor & Francis Group.

Dorney, J. (2018). Splitting the world open: Connection and disconnection among women teaching girls. In N. Way, A. Ali, C. Gilligan, & P. Noguera (Eds.), *The crisis of connection* (pp. 322–344). NYU Press.

Du Bois, W. E. B. (2015). *The souls of black folk*. Yale University Press.

Epstein, M. (2014). *The trauma of everyday life*. Penguin Books.

Erickson, F. (2004). *Talk and social theory: Ecologies of speaking and listening in everyday life*. Polity.

Ericsson, K. A., & Simon, H. A. (1998). How to study thinking in everyday life: Contrasting think-aloud protocols with descriptions and explanations of thinking. *Mind, Culture, and Activity*, *5*(3), 178–186.

Fang, Z. (2012). Approaches to developing content area literacies: A synthesis and a critique. *Journal of Adolescent & Adult Literacy*, *56*(2), 103–108.

Fang, Z., & Schleppegrell, M. J. (2010). Disciplinary literacies across content areas: Supporting secondary reading through functional language analysis. *Journal of Adolescent & Adult Literacy*, *53*(7), 587–597.

Fang, Z., Schleppegrell, M., Lukin, A., Huang, J., & Normandia, B. (2008). *Reading in secondary content areas: A language-based pedagogy*. University of Michigan Press.

Fecho, B. (2011). *Teaching for the students: Habits of heart, mind, and practice in the engaged classroom*. Teachers College Press.

Frayer, D. A., Fredrick, W. C., & Klausmeier, H. J. (1969). *A schema for testing the level of concept mastery: Report from the project on situational variables and efficiency of concept learning*. Wisconsin Research and Development Center for Cognitive Learning.

Freire, P. (1968/1972). *Pedagogy of the oppressed* (M. B. Ramos, Trans.) Herder.

Freire, P. (1985). *The politics of education: Culture, power, and liberation*. Greenwood.

Gee, J. P. (2000). Teenagers in new times: A new literacy studies perspective. *Journal of Adolescent & Adult Literacy*, *43*(5), 412–420.

Gee, J. P., Allen, A. R., & Clinton, K. (2001). Language, class, and identity: Teenagers fashioning themselves through language. *Linguistics and Education*, *12*(2), 175–194.

Giroux, H. A. (1983). *Theory and resistance in education: A pedagogy for the opposition*. South Bergin and Garvey.

Goldman, S. R., Britt, M. A., Brown, W., Cribb, G., George, M., Greenleaf, C., . . . Project READI. (2016). Disciplinary literacies and learning to read for understanding: A conceptual framework for disciplinary literacy. *Educational Psychologist*, *51*(2), 219–246.

Grosfoguel, R. (2015). Epistemic racism/sexism, Westernized universities and the four genocides/epistemicides of the long sixteenth century. In M. Araujo & S. R. Maeso (Eds.), *Eurocentrism, racism and knowledge* (pp. 23–46). Palgrave Macmillan.

Haddix, M. (2009). Black boys can write: Challenging dominant framings of African American adolescent males in literacy research. *Journal of Adolescent & Adult Literacy*, *53*(4), 341–343.

Hand, B., Wallace, C. W., & Yang, E. M. (2004). Using a science writing heuristic to enhance learning outcomes from laboratory activities in seventh-grade science: quantitative and qualitative aspects. *International Journal of Science Education*, *26*(2), 131–149.

Hanh, T. N. (2006). *True love: A practice for awakening the heart*. Shambhala.

Hanh, T. N. (2012). *You are here: Discovering the magic of the present moment*. Shambhala.

Heath, S. B. (1983). *Ways with words: Language, life and work in communities and classrooms*. Cambridge University Press.

Herber, H. L. (1970). Reading in content areas: A district develops its own personnel. *Journal of Reading*, *13*(8), 587–592.

Hermans, H. J., & Kempen, H. J. (1993). *The dialogical self: Meaning as movement*. Academic Press.

hooks, b. (1994). *Teaching to transgress*. Routledge.

hooks, b. (2003). *Teaching community: A pedagogy of hope*. Psychology Press.

hooks, b. (2017). *Building a community of love: bell hooks and Thich Nhat Hanh*. Retrieved August 4, 2021, from *www.lionsroar.com/bell-hooks-and-thich-nhat-hanh-on-building-a-community-of-love*.

hooks, b. (2018). *All about love: New visions*. William Morrow.

Irizarry, J. G., & Raible, J. (2014). A hidden part of me: Latino/a students, silencing, and the epidermalization of inferiority. *Equity & Excellence in Education*, *47*(4), 430–444.

Jackson, P. W. (1968). *Life in classrooms*. Holt, Rinehart & Winston.

Janks, H. (2009). *Literacy and power*. Routledge.

Jezewski, M. A. (1990). Culture brokering in migrant farm worker health care. *Western Journal of Nursing Research*, *12*(4), 497–513.

Johnson, L. P. (2017). Writing the self: Black queer youth challenge heteronormative ways of being in an after-school writing club. *Research in the Teaching of English*, 13–33.

Kinloch, V. (2009). Power, politics, and pedagogies: Re-imagining students' right to their own language through democratic engagement. In J. Scott, D. Straker, & L. Katz (Eds.), *Affirming students' right to their own language: Bridging language policies and pedagogical practices* (pp. 85–98). Routledge.

Kirkland, D. E. (2009). The skin we ink: Tattoos, literacy, and a new English education. *English Education*, *41*(4), 375–395.

Kirkland, D. E. (2013). *A search past silence: The literacy of young Black men.* Teachers College Press.

Krishnamurti, J. (1969). *Freedom from the known.* HarperCollins.

Krupnik, I., & Vakhtin, N. (1997). Indigenous knowledge in modern culture: Siberian Yupik ecological legacy in transition. *Arctic Anthropology, 34*(1), 236–252.

Ladson-Billings, G. (1998). Just what is critical race theory and what's it doing in a nice field like education? *International Journal of Qualitative Studies in Education, 11*(1), 7–24.

Lee, C. D. (1995). A culturally based cognitive apprenticeship: Teaching African American high school students skills in literary interpretation. *Reading Research Quarterly, 30*(4), 608–630.

Lee, C. D. (2001). Is October Brown Chinese?: A cultural modeling activity system for under-achieving students. *American Educational Research Journal, 38*(1), 97–141.

Lee, C. D., & Spratley, A. (2006). *Reading in the disciplines and the challenges of adolescent literacy.* Carnegie Corporation.

Lee, O., & Fradd, S. H. (1998). Science for all, including students from non-English-language backgrounds. *Educational Researcher, 27*(4), 12–21.

Leinhardt, G. (1989). Math lessons: A contrast of novice and expert competence. *Journal for Research in Mathematics Education, 20*(1), 52–75.

Leinhardt, G. (1993). Weaving instructional explanations in history. *British Journal of Educational Psychology, 63*, 46–74.

Leinhardt, G., Stainton, C., & Virji, S. M. (1994). A sense of history. *Educational Psychologist, 29*(2), 79–88.

Lemke, J. L. (1990). *Talking science: Language, learning, and values.* Ablex.

Lemke, J. L. (2003). Mathematics in the middle: Measure, picture, gesture, sign, and word. In M. Anderson, A. Saenz-Ludlow, S. Zellweger, & V. V. Cifarelli (Eds.), *Educational perspective on mathematics as semiosis: From thinking to interpreting to knowing* (pp. 215–234). Legas.

Manderino, M., & Castek, J. (2016). Digital literacies for disciplinary learning: A call to action. *Journal of Adolescent & Adult Literacy, 60*(1), 79–81.

Manderino, M., & Castek, J. (2020). Digital literacies for disciplinary learning: Pedagogies and literacies practices youth deserve. In E. Ortlieb, S. Grote-Garcia, & J. Cassidy (Eds.), *What's hot in literacy 2020* (pp. 3–15). IGI Global.

Maté, G. (2008). *In the realm of hungry ghosts: Close encounters with addiction.* Random House Digital.

Mazrui, A. A., & Wagaw, T. (1985). Towards decolonizing modernity: Education and culture conflict in Eastern Africa. In *The educational process and historiography in Africa* (pp. 35–62). UNESCO.

McConachie, S. M., & Petrosky, A. R. (2009). *Content matters: A disciplinary literacy approach to improving student learning.* Wiley.

Miller, E. R., & Kubota, R. (2013). Second language identity construction. In J. Herschensohn & M. Young-Scholten (Eds.), *The Cambridge handbook of second language acquisition* (pp. 230–250). Cambridge University Press.

Mirra, N., Garcia, A., & Morrell, E. (2015). *Doing youth participatory action research: Transforming inquiry with researchers, educators, and students.* Routledge.

Moje, E. B. (2008). Foregrounding the disciplines in secondary literacy teaching and learning: A call for change. *Journal of Adolescent & Adult Literacy, 52*(2), 96–107.

Moje, E. B. (2015). Doing and teaching disciplinary literacy with adolescent learners: A social and cultural enterprise. *Harvard Educational Review, 85*(2), 254–278.

Moje, E. B., & Luke, A. (2009). Literacy and identity: Examining the metaphors in history and contemporary research. *Reading Research Quarterly, 44*(4), 415–437.

Moll, L. C., Amanti, C., Neff, D., & Gonzalez, N. (1992). Funds of knowledge for teaching: Using a qualitative approach to connect homes and classrooms. *Theory Into Practice, 31*(2), 132–141.

Morrell, E. (2015). *Critical literacy and urban youth: Pedagogies of access, dissent, and liberation.* Routledge.

Murphy, M. C., & Zirkel, S. (2015). Race and belonging in school: How anticipated and experienced belonging affect choice, persistence, and performance. *Teachers College Record, 117*(12), 1–40.

Murthy, V. H. (2020). *Together.* HarperCollins.

National Institute of Mental Health. (2019, February). *Major depression.* Retrieved February 7, 2021, from *www.nimh.nih.gov/health/statistics/major-depression.shtml.*

Nieto, S. (2002). *Affirming diversity: The sociopolitical context of multicultural education.* Pearson Education.

Noguera, P. (2018). In pursuit of cur common humanity. In N. Way, A. Ali, C. Gilligan, & P. Noguera (Eds.), *The crisis of connection* (pp. 151–172). NYU Press.

Norton, B. (2013). *Identity and language learning: Extending the conversation* (2nd ed.). Multilingual Matters.

O'Brien, D. G., Stewart, R. A., & Moje, E. B. (1995). Why content literacy is difficult to infuse into the secondary school: Complexities of curriculum, pedagogy, and school culture. *Reading Research Quarterly, 30*(3),442–463.

Ochs, E., & Capps, L. (1996). Narrating the self. *Annual Review of Anthropology, 25*(1), 19–43.

Ogle, D. M. (1986). KWL: A teaching model that develops active reading of expository text. *The Reading Teacher, 39*(6), 564–570.

Orellana, M. F. (2009). *Translating childhoods: Immigrant youth, language, and culture.* Rutgers University Press.

Palincsar, A. S., & Magnusson, S. J. (2001). The interplay of first-hand and second-hand investigations to model and support the development of scientific knowledge and reasoning. In S. M. Carver & D. Klahr (Eds.), *Cognition and instruction: Twenty-five years of progress* (pp. 151–193). Erlbaum.

Palmer, P. J. (2017). *The courage to teach: Exploring the inner landscape of a teacher's life.* Wiley.

Phillips, N. C., & Leander, K. M. (2010, June). Modality and scale at AirMed. In

Proceedings of the 9th International Conference of the Learning Sciences (Vol. 2, pp. 161–163).

Prior, P. (2013). *Writing/disciplinarity: A sociohistoric account of literate activity in the academy*. Routledge.

Rainey, E. C. (2017). Disciplinary literacy in English language arts: Exploring the social and problem-based nature of literary reading and reasoning. *Reading Research Quarterly, 52*(1), 53–71.

Reichert, M. C., & Nelson, J. D. (2018). 14. I want to learn from you. In N. Way, A. Ali, C. Gilligan, & P. Noguera (Eds.), *The crisis of connection* (pp. 344–360). NYU Press.

Rhoades, V. (2018). 12. The courage to care. In N. Way, A. Ali, C. Gilligan, & P. Noguera (Eds.), *The crisis of connection* (pp. 299–321). NYU Press.

Schleppegrell, M., & Achugar, M. (2003). Learning language and learning history: A functional linguistics approach. *TESOL Journal, 12*(2), 21–27.

Schreuder, M., & Wilder, P. (2020). "I'm stronger than I thought": Mindful practices while reading *Things Fall Apart. English Journal, 109*(3), 37–43.

Shanahan, T., & Shanahan, C. (2008). Teaching disciplinary literacy to adolescents: Rethinking content-area literacy. *Harvard Educational Review, 78*(1), 40–59.

Shor, I. (1992). *Culture wars: School and society in the conservative restoration*. University of Chicago Press.

Smith, L. T. (2012). *Decolonizing methodologies: Research and indigenous peoples* (2nd ed.). Zed.

Solorzano, D. G., & Yosso, T. J. (2001). Critical race and LatCrit theory and method: Counter-storytelling. *International Journal of Qualitative Studies in Education, 14*(4), 471–495.

Stromholt, S., & Bell, P. (2018). Designing for expansive science learning and identification across settings. *Cultural Studies of Science Education, 13*(4), 1015–1047.

Tatum, A. W. (2009). Adolescents and texts: Texts, troubled teens, and troubling times. *The English Journal, 98*(4), 117–119.

Tatum, A. W. (Ed.). (2020). The fumbles and foibles of the race toward equity: Selecting texts with greater aims. *Journal of Adolescent & Adult Literacy, 63*(4), 473–478.

United Nations. (2015, December 9). Security Council, unanimously adopting resolution 2250 (2015), urges member states to increase representation of youth in decision making at all levels. Author. Retrieved from *https://press.un.org/en/2015/sc12149.doc.htm*.

Vygotsky, L. S. (2012). *Thought and language*. MIT Press.

Wagaman, M. A., Obejero, R. C., & Gregory, J. S. (2018). Countering the norm, (re)authoring our lives: The promise counterstorytelling holds as a research methodology with LGBTQ youth and beyond. *International Journal of Qualitative Methods, 17*(1).

Wandera, D. B. (2020). Resisting epistemic blackout: Illustrating Afrocentric methodology in a Kenyan classroom. *Reading Research Quarterly, 55*(4), 643–662.

Way, N., Ali, A., Gilligan, C., & Noguera, P. (Eds.). (2018). *The crisis of connection: Roots, consequences, and solutions*. NYU Press.

Way, N., & Nelson, J. D. (2018). 11. The listening project. In N. Way, A. Ali, C. Gilligan, & P. Noguera (Eds.), *The crisis of connection* (pp. 274–298). NYU Press.

Weedon, C. (1987). *Feminist practice and poststructuralist theory*. Basil Blackwell.

Weissbourd, R., Batanova, M., Lovison, V., & Torres, E. (2021). *Loneliness in America: How the pandemic has deepened an epidemic of loneliness and what we can do about it*. Retrieved August 4, 2021, from *https://static1.squarespace.com/static/5b7c56e255b02c683659fe43/t/6021776bdd04957c4557c212/1612805995893/Loneliness+in+America+2021_02_08_FINAL.pdf*.

Wilder, P. (2019). Conversations with myself: Literacy as conscious tool of healing. *English Journal, 108*(3), 60–66.

Wilder, P., & Msseemmaa, D. (2019). Centering disciplinary literacies on student consciousness: A Tanzanian case study. *Journal of Adolescent & Adult Literacy, 62*(5), 479–484.

Wineburg, S. S. (1991). Historical problem solving: A study of the cognitive processes used in the evaluation of documentary and pictorial evidence. *Journal of Educational Psychology, 83*(1), 73.

Wineburg, S. (1998). Reading Abraham Lincoln: An expert/expert study in the interpretation of historical texts. *Cognitive Science*, *22*(3), 319–346.

Yagelski, R. (2011). *Writing as a way of being: Writing instruction, nonduality, and the crisis of sustainability*. Hampton Press.

Transcending Disciplinary Literacy in a Digital World

Ian O'Byrne

As we consider the impact of disciplinary literacy on classroom instruction, we must account for the impact of new and digital literacy practices that are ubiquitous in society. The internet has become one of the major defining technologies for literacy and learning in the 21st century (Leu et al., 2011). Literacy, as a sociocultural practice (Street, 1993), is rapidly shifting from print to pixel as we continue to value different ways of meaning-making influenced by the emergence of multiple digital technologies (Cazden et al., 1996; Lankshear & Knobel, 2003). The future is already here as the average user spends almost 7 hours online each day (Twenge, Martin, & Spitzberg, 2019).

The challenge is that this future is not evenly distributed (Gibson, 1984) as we recognize that not all individuals have the same access to this vital resource (van Deursen & van Dijk, 2011). Education needs to focus on equity, inclusion, and agency as we prepare learners without relinquishing our own agency. Educators must adopt a flexible disposition and an appreciation for the complexities, advantages, and limitations inherent in online spaces. They must constantly consider changes to these spaces to permit new concepts, processes, and approaches of information delivery to continue developing in society. Educators and students work collaboratively together to continually define (and redefine) what it means to be able to read, write, and communicate effectively using digital texts.

Living in a connected world where the Web affords unprecedented learning opportunities has made information plentiful and put experts, figuratively speaking, at our fingertips. New, ubiquitous mobile technologies have made the promise of improved access a realistic, achievable goal. As such, our Web-enabled landscape has prompted a new vision for education, demonstrating the value of learning anywhere, anytime, and with equal access as a fundamental human right (Resta & Laferrière, 2015). Never in the history of civilization have we seen such a potentially transformative literacy technology adopted by so many in so many different places in such a short period of time (Leu et al., 2009).

The internet and digital social spaces are quickly becoming the primary environment where individuals read, write, collaborate, communicate, and socialize. This leaves the current generation of educators, researchers, and policymakers with the critical responsibility to help facilitate a cultural transition during this period of profound change, ensuring a successful and positive move from print to digital resources and the hybrid spaces in between (Livingstone & Blum-Ross, 2020). Additionally, it forces us to address print-to-digital shifts in a manner that guarantees equity for all learners across the globe. One paradox in our examination of these opportunities to authentically embed digital literacies in educational settings is that the one constant is change. What is also interesting, given the contents of this book, are considerations of literacy practices as they connect to the content areas, and the ways in which we prepare individuals for future disciplines are also constantly changing. As we consider the shifts in digital literacy and disciplinary literacy, we must also recognize that these practices and the tools we use to enable them are always changing as well (O'Byrne, 2018).

The challenge is that the one constant in these interactions is change. Adding further complexity to this issue is that the internet is becoming largely unintelligible. That is to say, the average user has little to no understanding of the data that are collected, archived, stored, and shared on a second-by-second basis as we use these tools. Furthermore, the algorithms that dictate many of these interactions are understood and controlled by a handful of individuals working for businesses. Even with these complexities, we are tasked with providing youth with the knowledge, skills, and disposition necessary for future contexts and disciplines (O'Byrne, 2014).

In this chapter, I will make the case for the tensions that exist as we consider disciplinary literacy in a digital world. These tensions will suggest that a certain amount of ambiguity or flexibility is necessary as we consider the intersections between disciplinary literacy and digital literacy. I will first outline my thinking about disciplinary literacy and digital literacy. In this framing, I will identify the commonalities and challenges as we examine these fields. I will then use this framing of the two areas to identify the mindsets necessary to better understand the intersection between disciplinary and digital literacies and how we might envision better possible outcomes. Finally, I will close the chapter by indicating the current challenges and opportunities that exist as we envision disciplinary literacy in a digital world.

WHAT IS DISCIPLINARY LITERACY?

As we begin this investigation, we will first identify and define our terms, the first of which is disciplinary literacy. As shown in this text, disciplinary literacy as a topic is a fluid and ever-changing construct. For the purposes of this chapter, we'll frame disciplinary literacy as focusing on the teaching of discipline-specific knowledge and the means to enact practices unique to the discipline (Moje, 2008; Shanahan & Shanahan, 2008). We must consider what is unique about the discipline in terms of reading, writing, speaking, and listening (Moje et al., 2010). Disciplinary literacy "involves the use of reading, investigating, analyzing, critiquing, writing, and reasoning required to learn and form complex knowledge in the discipline" (McConachie, 2010, p. 16). As educators bring these practices, abilities, and dispositions into the classroom, they might not just have to understand, but also reframe what *counts* in this examination of literacy.

To deeply engage with and learn content in a discipline, learners must not only know the content but also be aware of and engage in the "habits of thinking" valued by that discipline (Di Domenico et al., 2018; Lemley et al., 2019). To develop knowledge specific to the discipline, teachers need to teach the cognitive strategies necessary to comprehend discipline-specific texts contextualized in the discipline (Moje, 2008). The tools of knowledge construction and critique should be uncovered, taught, and practiced in the classroom (Moje et al., 2010) by placing emphasis on the knowledge and abilities possessed by those who "create, communicate, and use knowledge within the discipline" (Shanahan & Shanahan, 2012, p. 8). Education needs to focus on developing understanding while adopting the practices and protocols specific to each discipline, while also engaging in the discourse systems and learning dispositions specific to those areas (Goldman et al., 2016).

WHAT IS DIGITAL LITERACY?

As the internet becomes the dominant text in our society, digital social spaces become the public square where citizens communicate, socialize, and connect with one another. While today's students have been born into a digital world, they still have much to learn about reading in a digital context (Flynt & Brozo, 2010; Karchmer-Klein & Shinas, 2012; Redmond, 2015). We consider the online and offline literacy practices that our students will need as future events warrant. To prepare for this change, we must expand the definition of "text" to include visual, digital, and other multimodal formats (Serafini, 2012). We must recognize that text is not only ambiguous in nature (Belshaw, 2012) but also deictic, in the sense that what it means to be literate tomorrow will be defined by even newer technologies that have yet to appear and even newer discourses and social practices that will be created to meet future needs (Leu et al., 2017).

Lanham (1995) originally described digital literacy as the ability to understand and assimilate information delivered through new digital mediums of expression, sounds, and images. Gilster expanded this by focusing on communication in defining digital literacy as "the ability to understand and use information in multiple formats from a wide variety of sources when it is presented via computers" (Gilster, 1997, p. 1). Gilster's concept of digital literacy might be articulated as a set of practices, skills, and dispositions, but his understanding of digital literacy is not about technology-driven skill sets. Glister frames digital literacy through the lens of information, ideas, and mindsets.

REQUIRED MINDSETS

To transcend traditional notions of the intersection between disciplinary literacy and digital literacy, we need to adopt the following mindsets in our research, teaching, and service with others in our communities. To understand these shifts, we employ theoretical perspectives from new literacies, digital literacies, Web literacies, multiliteracies, and others. Within each of these perspectives, there are connections, but there are also elements that make them different. We must understand that even with these differences across perspectives, a fundamental need exists to understand the use of technology as literacy. There are several frames we can use to better understand this intersection to change pedagogy and prepare students for the world in which they will interact.

A Sociocultural Stance on Literacy

Important to our discussion of connections between disciplinary literacy and digital literacy, we must indicate that this shift from literacy to literacies is rooted in sociocultural theory, which views literacies as social practices (Yuan et al., 2019). To fully understand information and communicate with others, we need to understand the different ways of using digital tools within the varied social practices in which we use them (Bennett & Maton, 2010; Gee, 2015). Likewise, sociocultural theory suggests a dual process of shaping and being shaped, which posits that humans play an active role in using and transforming the tools of communication (Daniels, 2015; Smith, 2019). Digital literacy becomes an act of participation in a sociocultural activity, not a transmission of discrete cultural knowledge or skills (Polly et al., 2017). Digital literacy is more of a focus on individual and collective meaning-making as learners access, analyze, and create information in a multimodal, networked environment (Hobbs & Coiro, 2016).

A Broadened View of Text

There is a need to work with students to examine and redefine what is meant by reading, writing, and text. Teachers and students might act as collaborators as they learn among the complexities, advantages, and limitations inherent in the digital space. Educators have the opportunity to rethink literacy and learning; the decisions made to address change must be cognizant of all the factors at work (Manderino, 2011). Reframing what texts are or can be is the only way to guarantee the development of unique understandings about playfulness and cognition alike. It also provides the necessary vagueness to discuss and plan around as-yet undeveloped literacies and technologies (Hannafin et al., 1994). This requires a continual reexamination of text and the knowledge, skills, and dispositions utilized as we engage and connect (Thomas et al., 2020). Considering this shift, we need to evaluate opportunities to move learners from consumers to producers of digital content (O'Byrne, 2014).

The Role of Digital Skills in Digital Literacies

We must also be clear about what is literacy and what is a skill. Digital skills involve automatic actions that result in encoding and decoding digital information with speed, efficiency, and fluency and usually occur without awareness of the components or control involved (Wylie et al., 2018). Digital skills refer to a broad set of knowledge, work habits, dispositions, and strategies that encompass a wide-ranging and amorphous body of knowledge. Digital skills may include fairly granular tasks such as copying and pasting digital content or scaling up to considerations of critical thinking or synthesis across texts. Digital skills are important in just the same manner that reading skills impact literacy processes (Afflerbach et al., 2008). Digital literacy, on the other hand, refers to the ability to read, write, and participate in online spaces. This includes the awareness, attitude, and ability to use digital texts and tools to locate, organize, manage, evaluate, synthesize, and create digital content. Instruction must focus on the specific skills necessary as Web-literate citizens prepare for and negotiate digital spaces.

A Comfort with Vagueness

As shown with disciplinary literacy, considerations of digital spaces and the required literacy practices are also fluid and ever-changing. As the internet and other communication technologies transform ideas of literacy, learning, and pedagogy, it is important to adapt and react as future evolutions warrant. "While the pace of technological change may seem dizzying, the underlying practices of sociability, learning, play, and self-expression are undergoing a slower evolution, growing out of resilient social and cultural structures that youth inhabit in diverse ways in their everyday lives" (Ito et al., 2009, p. 4). Thus, within this examination of the field and consideration of the implications on praxis, we should allow for some ambiguity (Belshaw, 2012) as we cannot ensure exactly what the future and these new modalities will permit. We also are preparing learners for careers and disciplines that may not currently exist. We must understand the deictic perspective on technology and literacy (Leu, 2000) of these practices, as new technologies afford new digital spaces for literacy learning, which "will continuously be new, multiple and rapidly disseminated" (Coiro et al., 2008, p. 5). In short, we need to permit some ambiguity or "wiggle room" in our assumptions and definitions of these shifts as we move from print to pixel.

Change Is the Only Constant

Supporting the work of scholars focused on how digital technologies are shaping everyday literacies, the new literacies of the internet have been shown to be distinctive enough to require their own theoretical framework grounded in their social practices (Coiro et al., 2014). This is an attempt to theorize for the new literacies that will define our future, even when all literacy practices are defined by even newer technologies, discourses, and social practices that currently do not exist (Leu et al., 2017). A dual-level theory of New Literacies addresses these challenges by embracing the different contexts, technologies, and contingencies that exist in this rapidly evolving or changing landscape. This frames new literacies on two levels: lowercase (new literacies) and uppercase (New Literacies). Lowercase theories explore a specific area of a new literacy or technology and are better able to keep up with the rapidly changing nature of literacy in a rapidly changing, digital world. The insights gained from studying the lowercase new literacies also generate important insights for the remainder of the field, even though we might not share a particular focus, technology, or context. The second level of theory, an uppercase New Literacies, uses a symbiotic relationship to advance the field from these multiple perspectives (Leu et al., 2017). The dual-level theory supports the scholarship of the many new literacies studies but focuses on the literacies needed in formal school and work settings (Coiro, 2021).

Transdisciplinarity in Education

The concept of *transdisciplinarity* is in flux and with a plurality of definitions (Jao & Radakovic, 2017). A common way to define transdisciplinarity is by outlining a progression from multidisciplinarity, through interdisciplinarity, to transdisciplinarity (Pohl, 2010). Multidisciplinarity hints at using multiple disciplines in a way that there are clear boundaries between them and without the goal of unifying the disciplines (Alvargonzález, 2011; Kalla, 2005). Interdisciplinarity is a step beyond multidisciplinarity and brings together different approaches to address a common issue (Bammer, 2013). Pohl (2010) indicates (as cited in Jao & Radakovic, 2017) that as we move toward transdisciplinarity, we find research and praxis with the following features:

1. Focus on socially relevant issues and the common good
2. Transcending of disciplinary paradigms
3. Search for the unity of knowledge beyond disciplines
4. Interrogation and the anti-disciplinary transformation of knowledge

I recognize the tension that exists as we posit a frame of transdisciplinarity as we consider recognition of the new and novel parts of literacy practices in and out of specific disciplines. A transdisciplinary focus in our examination of praxis as it relates to the intersection of disciplinary and digital literacy allows us to seek pedagogy and assessment practices that are authentic and allow for transcending traditional paradigms of these spaces. This raises the question about whether we need to erase the boundaries between disciplines, or do we need to—in a sense—harden them so that students learn where they start and end and are therefore better prepared to use them in hybrid ways? A transdisciplinary lens, and the fluidity highlighted in current and future digital contexts, suggest that we should ignore a strong disciplinary literacy focus. To address these commonalities and concerns, I will close this chapter by focusing on information and the information resources used in our classrooms. There is a great deal we can learn from disciplinary literacy as we help our students use digital contexts to prepare for careers that do not currently exist.

INFORMATION, IDEAS, AND MINDSETS

As we have so far discussed in this chapter, our considerations of disciplinary literacy and digital literacy are both very fluid. That is to say, the one constant in these fields, and in the intersection between them, is change. Any examination of this work that informs practice or research needs to allow for a certain amount of ambiguity as we prepare for the unknown. We are not lost in this exercise as we consider praxis and its impact on learners. We generally understand the knowledge, skills, practices, and dispositions learners will need for future contexts (O'Byrne & Radakovic, 2017). We also can use the concept of information (i.e., what is conveyed or represented by a particular arrangement or sequence of things in pedagogy) as a point of inflection to make sense of the challenges and opportunities for classroom practice. To help us situate this discussion, we'll use an adaption of Gilster's model of information (1997) created by Markless and Streatfield (2007). This model discusses three interlinked elements that describe a focus on information and information resources in our classrooms:

- Connecting with information (orientation, exploring, focusing, locating)
- Interacting with information (thinking critically, evaluating)
- Making use of information (transforming, communicating, applying)

Connecting with Information

As learners interact with and read online and offline content and text they need to consider a wide variety of texts and contexts. This includes reading blogs, wikis, and social networks for personal and academic pursuits. Learners should read across multiple modes of information that include text, images, video, audio, and other graphical representations. It is important that learners synthesize across these varied modes and formats as they interact with charts, graphs, infographics, maps, and multimodal content. As digital technologies become more ubiquitous, it is important to recognize that the term *public* can mean different things for different purposes and practices. We live in a networked world where learning traverses online and offline, in- and out-of-school contexts, face-to-face, and virtual communication environments. As digital technologies become even more ubiquitous, there are multiple versions of public, or publics, as individuals identify, connect, communicate, and engage with others (boyd, 2008). These "networked publics" enable a specific type of community that signifies participation and engagement among a collective in digital spaces in which individuals are not just grouped together, but "transformed by networked media, its properties, and its potential" (boyd, 2010, p. 42)

To become competent in a number of academic content areas requires more than just applying the same old skills and comprehension strategies to new kinds of texts. It also requires skills and knowledge and reasoning processes that are specific to particular disciplines (Goldman, 2012). Digital texts and resources have the opportunity to enrich disciplinary thinking and collaboration. Learners can review information to gain clarity on their own preferences, content-area knowledge, and comprehension level (Calderon & Slakk, 2018). Learners can utilize and review the affordances of various texts and tools to understand their role in disciplinary practice (Moje, 2015; Ross et al., 2017). Literacy practices are enriched as the learner considers the data, information, and aesthetics as he or she considers audience, purpose, and design when sharing work process and product (Pacheco & Smith, 2015). Learners can consider how these elements impact how they think, feel, and comprehend the media and information they consume (Duke & Pearson, 2009; Ashley et al., 2017).

As detailed in the earlier section on disciplinary literacy, there is a need to understand not just the texts and themes in a discipline, but also the tools, work, and discourse systems. The interactions, needs, and concerns of these collectives are shaped and modified by the spaces and tools they use to congregate (O'Byrne, 2019). As citizens of networked publics, learners need to understand the challenges of participating and socializing in digital spaces. Before we can teach students to harness its power and become good citizens of the Web, we need to understand the intricacies of how it works and how it can be manipulated to mislead and even harm users. There is a need to revise and redefine existing power structures while advocating for ethics and empathy in digital and hybrid spaces. Research and practice need to better understand and problematize these complexities as we prepare learners to participate in complex disciplinary discourses using diverse digital tools.

Interacting with Information

As learners search and sift through online texts they are selecting, reviewing, commenting on, archiving, and sharing materials that are credible or relevant to the purpose of their inquiry. As learners gradually learn more about a topic as they read more content, they become better experts on the topic and the process involved as they build their own credibility on a subject. Digital literacies, which include technological, visual, and media literacies, can be used to support and further students' competencies in reading and writing for authentic purposes in the disciplines (Moore & Redmond, 2014). The internet is an amazing tool for teaching and learning. Disciplinary literacies that rely solely on print resources are no longer sufficient to fully convey complex and multilayered meanings. While today's learners are often proficient in using information and communication technologies (ICTs), they are not able to effectively choose, evaluate, and judge the multitude of media texts to which they are exposed (Redmond, 2015). Students need opportunities to explore nonlinear text, consider the validity or reliability of sources, ignore extraneous information, and make inferences from this mix of information (Karchmer-Klein & Shinas, 2012; Taylor & Kilpin, 2013).

Text, context, and the learner have to be viewed as integral pieces in a larger process as identity and background shape and influence the meaning-making of text (Rosenblatt, 1978). We have the opportunity to critique current educational and social systems that may be antiquated or serve to diminish the role of some members of the discipline and larger community (Lemke, 2001). We can research the everyday "learning lives" of our youth while preparing them for their futures (Kumpulainen & Sefton-Green, 2014). Citizens in digital global spaces can examine problems and take responsibility for challenges beyond our local contexts. These skills, practices, and dispositions go beyond a focus on disciplines as individuals in digitally connected communities can identify opportunities to serve as citizens to educate, empower, and advocate for others (O'Byrne, 2019). Engagement as a digitally connected citizen requires a redefinition of the purposes of our existence and the ways our service and agency are put to use in the world.

Teacher preparation and readiness to provide instruction as detailed in this chapter will involve an investigation of teachers' pedagogy and commitment in developing and implementing a technology-rich literacy curriculum (Redmond, 2012). Teacher development options need to be made available, and teachers need to be receptive to Web-based professional development in addition to traditional professional development methods (Barab et al., 2003). Time needs to be spent helping students integrate new and traditional literacies into their daily practices, while also considering how they connect with disciplinary instruction (Colwell & Enderson, 2016). Research needs to study authentic, digitally native literacy practices and connect this to the work required in the disciplines (Nagle, 2018; Larson & Marsh, 2014). Lastly, student assessments, public policy, and teacher evaluation metrics need to better support teachers' capacity to prepare students to communicate and use online information (Greenhow et al., 2009).

Making Use of Information

As they interact with information, learners have the opportunity to construct or create digital content. There are many parallels between online content construction and the writing process as learners plan, generate, organize, compose, and revise digital work products. This may include editing a wiki, building a website, producing a video, or creating an animated GIF. Literacy practices are shaped by cultural and social practices of the individual reading, writing, speaking, or listening (Moje et al., 2010). Learners are encoding and decoding meaning as they write, compose, and create with digital texts and tools. Rather than a wholly new core curriculum, digital literacy adds to disciplinary literacy by providing opportunities for communication, problem solving, and collaboration (Ashley et al., 2012). Learners have the opportunity to interact online with others in their discipline and enact the literacy practices as they ethically share, communicate, or repurpose information through the appropriate use of available digital technologies (Beetham & Oliver, 2010). These literacy practices inform and enact the ethics that guide citizens as they interact and connect with others for a variety of academic and personal purposes.

Educators add a vital digital dimension to the classroom as they practice literacy skills and embed collaborative professional learning experiences that will be in increasing demand in the future of work (Greenhill, 2010). Teachers can provide opportunities for learning that are socially embedded, interest-driven, and focused on developing educational, economic, or political opportunities (Ito et al., 2013). Disciplinary literacy has the opportunity to restore agency to the reader (Wineburg & Reisman, 2015). Education, literacy, and more specifically disciplinary literacy are not only about preparing learners to emulate and utilize the discourses and practices found in their disciplines. Keep in mind that many of the students in our classrooms are preparing for careers that do not exist yet. We are not solely preparing students to enter the workforce and engage with others, we are preparing them for the work required as they adhere to the rules and responsibilities required of a citizen (Kivunja, 2015; Wagner & Dintersmith, 2015). As we make space for digital literacy in our classrooms, we provide opportunities for learners to engage in a discussion with an active, authentic audience that may, or may not, seek the best interests of our learners (Curwood et al., 2013; Price-Dennis et al., 2015).

The integration of digital literacy in disciplinary literacy instruction provides opportunities for students and educators to collaboratively explore and make connections with the discipline, the community, and the world (Flynt & Brozo, 2010; Saine, 2013). The learning of specific ways of participating differs in differently situated practices (Hedegaard, 2014). In this sense, learning occurs when an individual has mastered and is able to demonstrate the specific practices in a particular community (Barab & Duffy, 2000). From a disciplinary literacy standpoint, the individual has mastered how to approach a text in a particular discipline and the proper way to communicate, through speech (Bakhtin, 1986) and writing, in a particular community. Disciplines are considered communities of practice (Leavy, 2011) as well as organizations, groups, classrooms, and workplaces

(Wenger, 1998). Students need to learn how to be a part of various literacy practices and given the texts, tools, and practices they'll need to succeed in the disciplines and a variety of social worlds (Greenleaf et al., 2001).

CONCLUSION

Several tensions have been uncovered in this chapter as we explore the intersection between disciplinary literacy and digital literacy. These constructs are continuously changing and the ways in which we conceptualize research and classroom praxis need to be flexible as well. Educators need to also be receptive to these fluid considerations of praxis as we integrate new technological advances and not fear that text-based literacies will be replaced by new literacies (Bowen & Whithaus, 2013). More to the point, we need to consider whether we are digitizing traditional research methods and instructional models, or developing new digitally native frameworks. These tensions that arise are crucial to understanding and developing teaching practice and educational research. Because of the tensions expressed in this chapter, teachers need to be prepared to manage the wide range of technologies and multiple text types present in our information ecosystem (Jagger & Yore, 2012). Teachers are called to change the way they think about information and expand the forms of interaction used in instruction.

A major issue that impacts much of this work centers on the challenges of equity and access as we consider technological capacity in our schools. Many schools do not have access to consistent high-speed internet service and need to be fully connected to it and have sufficient hardware to allow for all students to equally access technology (Saine, 2013). It is imperative that school districts receive the support and training needed to attempt to implement technology instruction (Dolph, 2017). COVID-19 forced many teachers and students into emergency remote teaching, and we, in turn, developed a better understanding of the insufficient and unreliable technology and ill-prepared educators in our school systems (Frederick et al., 2020). We need to also acknowledge that technological literacy has largely been ignored in educational reform (Leu et al., 2011; Botzakis et al., 2014).

In the United States, the Common Core State Standards (CCSS) are designed to ensure that students are ready for higher education and 21st-century vocations. This includes a focus on equipping students with the proficiencies needed to "gather, comprehend, evaluate, synthesize, and report on information and ideas, to conduct original research in order to answer questions or solve problems and to analyze and create a high volume and extensive range of print and nonprint texts" in a technological world (National Governor's Association, 2010, p. 4). Ironically, the bulk of this focus is contained in Anchor Standards 6 through 9 of CCSS for writing, and only found in Anchor Standard 7 for reading (Leu et al., 2011). This is further exacerbated as we see curriculum and adjustments made to the CCSS by states and local districts. The gap in the construction of the state standards implies that there is little desire to support initiatives to develop digital literacy in students or teachers (Nasah et al., 2010; Hicks & Turner, 2013).

Put simply, teachers need to become proficient in using and teaching technological skills because they are as equally important as conventional literacy skills and help prepare learners for future contexts (Moore & Redmond, 2014). Students, parents, and school administrators also need to provide flexibility as educators adapt and adjust to new tools and pedagogies (Korkmaz & Toraman, 2020). In this overview, I provided some context, while also indicating consideration of the affordances of these texts, tools, and spaces as we contemplate opportunities for research and praxis. We will need to rely on the thoughtfulness, creativity, and humility of educators working with youth to better understand these digital spaces, and the practices necessary as we consider opportunities to understand this intersection to change pedagogy and prepare students for future worlds.

REFERENCES

Afflerbach, P., Pearson, P. D., & Paris, S. G. (2008). Clarifying differences between reading skills and reading strategies. *The Reading Teacher, 61*(5), 364–373.

Alvargonzález, D. (2011). Multidisciplinarity, interdisciplinarity, transdisciplinarity, and the sciences. *International Studies in the Philosophy of Science, 25*(4), 387–403.

Ashley, J., Jarman, F., Varga-Atkins, T., & Hassan, N. (2012). Learning literacies through collaborative enquiry; collaborative enquiry through learning literacies. *Journal of Information Literacy, 6*(1), 50–71.

Ashley, S., Maksl, A., & Craft, S. (2017). News media literacy and political engagement: What's the connection? *Journal of Media Literacy Education, 2*(4).

Bammer, G. (2013). *Disciplining interdisciplinarity: Integration and implementation sciences for researching complex real-world problems.* ANU Press.

Barab, S. A., & Duffy, T. (2000). From practice fields to communities of practice. *Theoretical Foundations of Learning Environments, 1*(1), 25–55.

Barab, S. A., MaKinster, J. G., & Scheckler, R. (2003). Designing system dualities: Characterizing a web-supported professional development community. *The Information Society, 19*(3), 237–256.

Beetham, H., & Oliver, M. (2010). The changing practices of knowledge and learning. In R. Sharpe, H. Beecham, & S. de Freitas (Eds.), *Rethinking learning for a digital age* (pp. 177–191). Routledge.

Belshaw, D. A. (2012). *What is "digital literacy"?: A pragmatic investigation.* PhD dissertation, Durham University, Durham, NC.

Bennett, S., & Maton, K. (2010). Beyond the "digital natives" debate: Towards a more nuanced understanding of students' technology experiences. *Journal of Computer Assisted Learning, 26*(5), 321–331.

Botzakis, S., Burns, L. D., & Hall, L. A. (2014). Literacy reform and Common Core State Standards: Recycling the autonomous model. *Language Arts, 91*(4), 223–235.

Bowen, T., & Whithaus, C. (Eds.). (2013). *Multimodal literacies and emerging genres*. University of Pittsburgh Press.

Boyd, d. (2008). Why youth (heart) social network sites: The role of networked publics in teenage social life. In D. Buckingham (Ed.), *Youth, identity, and digital media* (pp. 119–142). MIT Press.

Boyd, d. (2010). Social network sites as networked publics: Affordances, dynamics, and implications. In Z. Papacharissi (Ed.), *A networked self* (pp. 47–66). Routledge.

Calderon, M. E., & Slakk, S. (2018). *Teaching reading to English learners, grades 6–12: A framework for improving achievement in the content areas*. Corwin Press.

Cazden, C., Cope, B., Fairclough, N., Gee, J., Kalantzis, M., Kress, G., . . . Nakata, M. (1996). A pedagogy of multiliteracies: Designing social futures. *Harvard Educational Review, 66*(1), 60–92.

Coiro, J. (2021). Toward a multifaceted heuristic of digital reading to inform assessment, research, practice, and policy. *Reading Research Quarterly, 56*(1), 9–31.

Coiro, J., Knobel, M., Lankshear, C., & Leu, D. J. (Eds.). (2008). Central issues in new literacies and new literacies research. In *Handbook of research on new literacies* (pp. 1–21). Routledge.

Coiro, J., Knobel, M., Lankshear, C., & Leu, D. J. (2014). Central issues in new literacies and new literacies research. In *Handbook of research on new literacies* (pp. 1–22). Routledge.

Colwell, J., & Enderson, M. C. (2016). "When I hear literacy": Using pre-service teachers' perceptions of mathematical literacy to inform program changes in teacher education. *Teaching and Teacher Education, 53*, 63–74.

Curwood, J. S., Magnifico, A. M., & Lammers, J. C. (2013). Writing in the wild: Writers' motivation in fan-based affinity spaces. *Journal of Adolescent & Adult Literacy, 56*(8), 677–685.

Daniels, H. (2015). Mediation: An expansion of the socio-cultural gaze. *History of the Human Sciences, 28*(2), 34–50.

Di Domenico, P. M., Elish-Piper, L., Manderino, M., & L'Allier, S. K. (2018). Coaching to support disciplinary literacy instruction: Navigating complexity and challenges for sustained teacher change. *Literacy Research and Instruction, 57*(2), 81–99.

Dolph, D. (2017). Challenges and opportunities for school improvement: Recommendations for urban school principals. *Education and Urban Society, 49*(4), 363–387.

Duke, N. K., & Pearson, P. D. (2009). Effective practices for developing reading comprehension. *Journal of Education, 189*(1–2), 107–122.

Flynt, E. S., & Brozo, W. (2010). Visual literacy and the content classroom: A question of now, not when. *The Reading Teacher, 63*(6), 526–528.

Frederick, J. K., Raabe, G. R., Rogers, V. R., & Pizzica, J. (2020). Advocacy, collaboration, and intervention: A model of distance special education support services amid COVID-19. *Behavior Analysis in Practice*, *13*(4), 748–756.

Gee, J. P. (2015). Three paradigms in reading (really literacy) research and digital media. In R. J. Spiro, M. DeSchryver, M. S. Hagerman, P. M. Morsink, & P. Thompson (Eds.), *Reading at a crossroads?* (pp. 49–58). Routledge.

Gibson, W. (1984) *Neuromancer*. Ace.

Gilster, P. (1997). *Digital literacy*. Wiley.

Goldman, S. R. (2012). Adolescent literacy: Learning and understanding content. *The Future of Children*, *22*(2), 89–116.

Goldman, S. R., Britt, M. A., Brown, W., Cribb, G., George, M., Greenleaf, C., . . . Project READI. (2016). Disciplinary literacies and learning to read for understanding: A conceptual framework for disciplinary literacy. *Educational Psychologist*, *51*(2), 219–246.

Greenhill, V. (2010). *21st century knowledge and skills in educator preparation*. Partnership for 21st-Century Skills, AACTE.

Greenhow, C., Robelia, B., & Hughes, J. E. (2009). Learning, teaching, and scholarship in a digital age: Web 2.0 and classroom research: What path should we take now? *Educational Researcher*, *38*(4), 246–259.

Hannafin, M. J., Hall, C., Land, S., & Hill, J. (1994). Learning in open-ended environments: Assumptions, methods, and implications. *Educational Technology*, *34*(8), 48–55.

Hedegaard, M. (2014). The significance of demands and motives across practices in children's learning and development: An analysis of learning in home and school. *Learning, Culture and Social Interaction*, *3*(3), 188–194.

Hicks, T., & Turner, K. H. (2013). No longer a luxury: Digital literacy can't wait. *English Journal*, *102*(6), 58–65.

Hobbs, R., & Coiro, J. (2016). Everyone learns from everyone: Collaborative and interdisciplinary professional development in digital literacy. *Journal of Adolescent & Adult Literacy*, *59*(6), 623–629.

Ito, M., Gutiérrez, K., Livingstone, S., Penuel, B., Rhodes, J., Salen, K., . . . Watkins, S. C. (2013). *Connected learning: An agenda for research and design*. Digital Media and Learning Research Hub.

Ito, M., Horst, H. A., Bittanti, M., Herr Stephenson, B., Lange, P. G., Pascoe, C. J., & Robinson, L. (2009). *Living and learning with new media: Summary of findings from the digital youth project*. MIT Press.

Jagger, S. L., & Yore, L. D. (2012). Mind the gap: Looking for evidence-based practice of science literacy for all in science teaching journals. *Journal of Science Teacher Education*, *23*(6), 559–577.

Jao, L., & Radakovic, N. (Eds.). (2017). *Transdisciplinarity in mathematics education: Blurring disciplinary boundaries*. Springer.

Kalla, H. K. (2005). Integrated internal communications: A multidisciplinary perspective. *Corporate Communications: An International Journal*, *10*(4), 302–314.

Karchmer-Klein, R., & Shinas, V. H. (2012). Guiding principles for supporting new literacies in your classroom. *The Reading Teacher*, *65*(5), 288–293.

Kivunja, C. (2015). Teaching students to learn and to work well with 21st-century skills: Unpacking the career and life skills domain of the new learning paradigm. *International Journal of Higher Education*, *4*(1), 1–11.

Korkmaz, G., & Toraman, Ç. (2020). Are we ready for the post-Covid-19 educational practice?: An investigation into what educators think as to online learning. *International Journal of Technology in Education and Science*, *4*(4), 293–309.

Kumpulainen, K., & Sefton-Green, J. (2014). What is connected learning and how to research it? *International Journal of Learning and Media*, *4*(2), 7–18.

Lankshear, C., & Knobel, M. (2003). New technologies in early childhood literacy research: A review of research. *Journal of Early Childhood Literacy*, *3*(1), 59–82.

Lanham, R. A. (1995). Digital literacy. *Scientific American*, *273*(3), 198–199.

Larson, J., & Marsh, J. (2014). *Making literacy real: Theories and practices for learning and teaching*. SAGE.

Lemke, J. L. (2001). Articulating communities: Sociocultural perspectives on science education. *Journal of Research in Science Teaching*, *38*(3), 296–316.

Lemley, S. M., Hart, S. M., & King, J. R. (2019). Teacher inquiry develops elementary teachers' disciplinary literacy. *Literacy Research and Instruction*, *58*(1), 12–30.

Leu, D. J. (2000). Literacy and technology: Deictic consequences for literacy education in an information age. In M. L. Kamil, P. Mosenthal, P. D. Pearson, & R. Barr (Eds.), *Handbook of reading research* (Vol. 3, pp. 743–770). Erlbaum.

Leu, D. J., Gregory McVerry, J., Ian O'Byrne, W., Kiili, C., Zawilinski, L., Everett-Cacopardo, H., . . . Forzani, E. (2011). The new literacies of online reading comprehension: Expanding the literacy and learning curriculum. *Journal of Adolescent & Adult Literacy*, *55*(1), 5–14.

Leu, D. J., Kinzer, C. K., Coiro, J., Castek, J., & Henry, L. A. (2017). New literacies: A dual-level theory of the changing nature of literacy, instruction, and assessment. *Journal of Education*, *197*(2), 1–18.

Leu, D. J., O'Byrne, W. I., Zawilinski, L., McVerry, J. G., & Everett-Cacopardo, H. (2009). Comments on Greenhow, Robelia, and Hughes: Expanding the new literacies conversation. *Educational Researcher*, *38*(4), 264–269.

Livingstone, S., & Blum-Ross, A. (2020). *Parenting for a digital future: How hopes and fears about technology shape children's lives*. Oxford University Press.

Manderino, M. (2011). Disciplinary literacy in new literacies environments: Expanding the intersections of literate practice for adolescents. In P. J. Dunston, S. K. Fullerton, C. C. Bates, K. Headley, & P. M. Stecker (Eds.), *61st yearbook of the Literacy Research Association* (pp. 69–83). Literacy Research Association.

Markless, S., & Streatfield, D. (2007). Three decades of information literacy: Redefining the parameters. In S. Andretta (Ed.), *Change and challenge: Information literacy for the twenty-first century* (pp. 15–36). Auslib Press.

McConachie, S. (2010). Disciplinary literacy: A principle-based framework. In S. McConachie & A. Petrosky (Eds.), *Content matters: A disciplinary literacy approach to improving student learning* (pp. 15–31). Jossey-Bass.

Moje, E. B. (2008). Foregrounding the disciplines in secondary literacy teaching and learning: A call for change. *Journal of Adolescent & Adult Literacy*, *52*(2), 96–107.

Moje, E. B. (2015). Doing and teaching disciplinary literacy with adolescent learners: A social and cultural enterprise. *Harvard Educational Review, 85*(2), 254–278.

Moje, E. B., Stockdill, D., Kim, K., & Kim, H. J. (2010). The role of text in disciplinary learning. In M. L. Kamil, P. D. Pearson, E. B. Moje, & P. P. Afflerbach (Eds.), *Handbook of reading research* (Vol. IV, pp. 453–486). Routledge.

Moore, D. C., & Redmond, T. (2014). Media at the core: How media literacy strategies strengthen teaching with Common Core. *Voices from the Middle, 21*(4), 10–15.

Nagle, J. (2018). Twitter, cyber-violence, and the need for a critical social media literacy in teacher education: A review of the literature. *Teaching and Teacher Education, 76*, 86–94.

Nasah, A., DaCosta, B., Kinsell, C., & Seok, S. (2010). The digital literacy debate: An investigation of digital propensity and information and communication technology. *Educational Technology Research and Development, 58*(5), 531–555.

National Governor's Association. (2010). Common core state standards. *Washington, DC.*

O'Byrne, W. I. (2014). Empowering learners in the reader/writer nature of the digital informational space. *Journal of Adolescent & Adult Literacy, 58*(2), 102–104.

O'Byrne, W. I. (2018). Empowering students as critical readers and writers in online spaces. In E. Ortlieb, E. H. Cheek, Jr., & P. Semingson (Eds.), *Literacy research, practice and evaluation: Vol. 9. Best practices in teaching digital literacies* (pp. 233–250). Emerald.

O'Byrne, W. I. (2019). Educate, empower, advocate: Amplifying marginalized voices in a digital society. *Contemporary Issues in Technology and Teacher Education, 19*(4), 640–669. Society for Information Technology & Teacher Education. Retrieved September 14, 2021, from *www.learntechlib.org/primary/p/188279.*

O'Byrne, W. I., & Radakovic, N. (2017). Educating digital natives: Possible and prospective futures of students in learning ecologies. In S. T. Slota & M. F. Young (Eds.), *Exploding the castle: Rethinking how video games and game mechanics can shape the future of education* (pp. 179–200). Information Age.

Pacheco, M. B., & Smith, B. E. (2015). Across languages, modes, and identities: Bilingual adolescents' multimodal codemeshing in the literacy classroom. *Bilingual Research Journal, 38*(3), 292–312.

Pohl, C. (2010). From transdisciplinarity to transdisciplinary research. *Transdisciplinary Journal of Engineering & Science, 1.*

Polly, D., Allman, B., Casto, A., & Norwood, J. (2017). Sociocultural perspectives of learning. In R. E. West (Ed.), *Foundations of learning and instructional design technology* (pp. 187–215). Pressbooks.

Price-Dennis, D., Holmes, K. A., & Smith, E. (2015). Exploring digital literacy practices in an inclusive classroom. *The Reading Teacher, 69*(2), 195–205.

Redmond, T. (2012). The pedagogy of critical enjoyment: Teaching and reaching the hearts and minds of adolescent learners through media literacy education. *Journal of Media Literacy Education, 4*(2), 106–120.

Redmond, T. (2015). Media literacy is common sense: Bridging Common Core Standards with the media experiences of digital learners: Findings from a case study highlight the benefits of an integrated model of literacy, thereby illustrating the relevance and accessibility of media literacy education. *Middle School Journal*, *46*(3), 10–17.

Resta, P., & Laferrière, T. (2015). Digital equity and intercultural education. *Education and Information Technologies*, *20*(4), 743–756.

Rosenblatt, L. (1978) *The reader, the text, the poem: The transactional theory of the literary work*. Southern Illinois University Press.

Ross, B., Pechenkina, E., Aeschliman, C., & Chase, A. M. (2017). Print versus digital texts: understanding the experimental research and challenging the dichotomies. *Research in Learning Technology*, *25*, Article 1976.

Saine, P. (2013). Implementation and assessment of technology-based Common Core State Standards for English language arts: An exploratory study. *New England Reading Association Journal*, *49*(1), 100.

Serafini, F. (2012). Reading multimodal texts in the 21st century. *Research in the Schools*, *19*(1), 26–32.

Shanahan, T., & Shanahan, C. (2008). Teaching disciplinary literacy to adolescents: Rethinking content-area literacy. *Harvard Educational Review*, *78*(1), 40–59.

Shanahan, T., & Shanahan, C. (2012). What is disciplinary literacy and why does it matter? *Topics in Language Disorders*, *32*(1), 7–18.

Smith, R. I. (2019). Values in history and social studies. In P. Tomlinson & M. Quinton (Eds.), *Values across the curriculum* (pp. 77–86). Routledge.

Street, B. V. (Ed.). (1993). *Cross-cultural approaches to literacy* (No. 23). Cambridge University Press.

Taylor, R., & Kilpin, K. (2013). Secondary school literacy in the social sciences: An argument for disciplinary literacy. *New Zealand Journal of Educational Studies*, *48*(2), 130–142.

Thomas, A., Kuper, A., Chin-Yee, B., & Park, M. (2020). What is "shared" in shared decision-making?: Philosophical perspectives, epistemic justice, and implications for health professions education. *Journal of Evaluation in Clinical Practice*, *26*(2), 409–418.

Twenge, J. M., Martin, G. N., & Spitzberg, B. H. (2019). Trends in U.S, adolescents' media use, 1976–2016: The rise of digital media, the decline of TV, and the (near) demise of print. *Psychology of Popular Media Culture*, *8*(4), 329.

van Deursen, A., & van Dijk, J. (2011). Internet skills and the digital divide. *New Media & Society, 13*(6), 893–911.

Wagner, T., & Dintersmith, T. (2015). *Most likely to succeed: Preparing our kids for the innovation era*. Simon & Schuster.

Wineburg, S., & Reisman, A. (2015). Disciplinary literacy in history: A toolkit for digital citizenship. *Journal of Adolescent & Adult Literacy*, *58*(8), 636–639.

Wylie, J., Thomson, J., Leppänen, P. H., Ackerman, R., Kanniainen, L., & Prieler, T. (2018). Cognitive processes and digital reading. *Learning to Read in a Digital World*, *17*, 57–90.

Yuan, C., Wang, L., & Eagle, J. (2019). Empowering English language learners through digital literacies: Research, complexities, and implications. *Media and Communication*, *7*(2), 128–136.

PART IV

RESEARCH AND TEACHING TEACHERS IN DISCIPLINARY LITERACIES

Methodologies in Research on Disciplinary Literacy in English Language Arts

Jodi P. Lampi
Jodi Patrick Holschuh
Leslie S. Rush
Todd Reynolds

Disciplinary literacy, as a field of study, grew out of a recognition that advanced and specialized literacy instruction that moved beyond basic skills and used authentic disciplinary practices was needed as readers progressed through school, such as using increasingly complex discipline-specific reading, writing, and communication processes (Shanahan & Shanahan, 2008, 2012). Reynolds and Rush (2017) suggested that disciplinary literacy is centered within three areas: cognitive theories that move beyond research on content reading strategies (e.g., Moje, 2007; Shanahan & Shanahan, 2012); functional linguistics (e.g., Fang & Schleppegrell, 2010; Shanahan & Shanahan, 2008); and expert–novice studies (e.g., Bazerman, 1985; Pressley & Afflerbach, 1995; Shanahan, 2012; Wineburg, 1991). In addition, Moje discussed knowledge and identity construction as precursors to disciplinary literacy, with the potential to provide socially just instruction within the disciplines (Moje, 2007, 2008).

Research in disciplinary literacy has centered on these themes, using a variety of research methodologies to collect and analyze empirical data and to advance our understandings of reading, writing, and communicating within the disciplines. Common research methodologies across the disciplines include examining experts and novices, instructional situations, linguistics, and epistemologies. This chapter provides an overview of research methodologies used in disciplinary literacy and then delves deeper into the methodologies of a single discipline, English language arts (ELA).

RESEARCH METHODOLOGIES IN DISCIPLINARY LITERACY

Expert-Novice Studies

Expert–novice studies are a longstanding staple in research on disciplinary literacy, based on an assumption that literacy practices specific to individual disciplines can be explicated through the reading and sensemaking techniques used by experts in their respective fields (Moje, 2007; Shanahan et al., 2011). To understand the literacy practices and processes used by experts, empirical expert–novice studies typically use think-aloud protocols as data collection mechanisms, in which study participants read a text out loud and describe their understanding of that text as it develops (e.g., Hynd et al., 2004; Shanahan, 2012; Wineburg, 1991). How expert and novice participants are defined can vary across the studies. Expert participants are frequently university faculty members but can also be graduate students in those fields. Novice participants can range from high school students to college students. Data in these studies are typically analyzed qualitatively, through reading, rereading, and developing codes, categories, and themes. In studies that compare expert and novice think-alouds, experts are typically found to have more knowledge about and experience with disciplinary texts, where the novices had less knowledge and experience. Some of the studies in this category focus on data collected solely through experts, including Shanahan et al. (2011), where experts participated in think-alouds, focus group discussions, and recursive member checking to examine the reading in history, chemistry, and mathematics. Data were analyzed through grounded theory with a goal of understanding the disciplinary moves used by experts while reading. A similar and more recent expert-focused study was presented by Fang and Chapman (2020) in the discipline of mathematics, where they examined the reading practices of one mathematician with the goal of informing secondary education literacy instruction. As a whole, these studies provide insight into both the processes used by experts and novices and the differences in the ways they approach making sense of text.

Instructional Studies

Some research in disciplinary literacy aims to create instruction to help students successfully negotiate the literacy demands across disciplines (Shanahan & Shanahan, 2012). Thus, several studies have explored these reading and writing disciplinary distinctions by examining instructional situations. The methodologies for these studies have typically consisted of either classroom observation of what is currently occurring, or interventions aimed at improving instruction or student learning (Goldman et al., 2016).

For example, Learned (2018) used observations and ethnographic interviews to examine the instructional, disciplinary practices used to support secondary students labeled as struggling in a history classroom. She also examined classroom artifacts such as lesson plans, reading guides, and student work. Data were analyzed using comparative analysis, which included both axial and selective coding and member checking. The student work was analyzed to further understand the students both as history and literacy learners. Neto et al. (2018) used video recording and repeated reading and coding of data transcripts to examine the current discursive practices in science classrooms used by three teachers in Brazil.

To aid students in learning mathematics in the classroom, Brozo and Crain (2018) investigated the use of a discipline-specific writing strategy that was more closely aligned with mathematical content and processes than generic content-area strategies. In science, strategy intervention research on argumentation provided ways to develop explanations, models, and arguments with data or with science activities (Goldman et al., 2016). Similarly, Mantz (2016) used an "epistemic levels" framework to examine the ways students construct evidence in science. Using video recordings, fieldnotes, and student artifacts, Mantz employed grounded analysis for coding and to identify patterns. Use of observation and intervention in disciplinary literacy research can provide a glimpse into current classroom practices and a means to investigate promising classroom practices.

Linguistic Analysis

Another perspective on disciplinary literacy comes from research that engages in examination of how language is used within disciplines. Often based on the seminal work in systemic functional linguistics of Halliday and Matthiessen (2004), these studies tend to focus on analyzing language within disciplinary texts in mathematics, history, or science. For example, Coffin's (2006) examination of texts used in secondary school history classes formed the basis of her professional development interventions, which engaged high school students in examining and recreating linguistic structures in social studies texts.

Schleppegrell's work in mathematics (2007) and history (2004) also used linguistic analysis of disciplinary texts and subsequently designed instructional strategies to support students in deconstructing the language of their textbooks in those disciplines. For example, Schleppegrell et al. (2004) used case study methods to collect observations and to conduct qualitative inquiry processes in a middle school social studies classroom, particularly focused on English language learners. Fang (2006) presented a similar discussion with regard to science, with information about the key features of language used in school science texts, based on his analysis of those texts; Fang and Schleppegrell (2008) described their linguistic analysis of science texts, producing a clearer understanding of the prevalence of nominalization in science. Green (2019) examined over 200 secondary school textbooks, representing eight different disciplines, for linguistic complexity. These studies provide insight into the disciplinary discourse and language use in contextualized settings.

Epistemological Understandings

A substantial focus of disciplinary literacy research centers on epistemological understandings, namely the beliefs, knowledge processes, and social practices that are unique to the disciplines (Goldman et al., 2016; Moje, 2015; Shanahan & Shanahan, 2012; Wineburg, 1991). Additionally, this area of research has discussed the challenges of maintaining disciplinary ways of thinking while implementing national/state/disciplinary standards. For example, in a conceptual piece, Miller et al. (2018) discussed the need for and challenge of "epistemic agency," or whose ideas and contributions shape knowledge construction and who decides what knowledge "counts," in science classrooms while implementing the Next Generation Science Standards (NGSS). In case study research of science teachers, Ke and Schwarz (2021) found differences in instructional practice with regard to scientific modeling and presenting complex messages that was reflected in student work. Researchers examined these epistemological understandings primarily through qualitative studies (e.g., Rainey & Moje, 2012; Shanahan & Shanahan, 2008), although there have been some quantitative (e.g., Spires et al., 2018; Reisman, 2012), and mixed-method studies (e.g., Achugar & Carpenter, 2012). These studies offer insights into the ways of knowing within the disciplines.

Overall, the field of disciplinary literacy has been expanding to disciplines beyond history, mathematics, and the sciences, which were prevalent in the early research defining the field. One such area is the burgeoning research interest in disciplinary literacy in English language arts (ELA). Below, we delve into the research within this discipline.

METHODOLOGY: REVIEW OF RESEARCH ON DISCIPLINARY LITERACY IN ELA

To discuss the types and range of research methodologies used by scholars engaged in disciplinary literacy scholarship in the field of ELA, we targeted our research review in three areas. First, because the focus is on ELA, we looked through the last 10 years (2010–2020) of articles in two of the leading research journals in English education: *Research in the Teaching of English* and *English Education*. We selected all articles that focused on the processes of engaging with literary texts in some way, regardless of the use of the term *disciplinary literacy*. Second, we examined some of the foundational studies in ELA, especially those that were cited in recent articles about disciplinary literacy in ELA. Third, we conducted a broad search for any articles specifically referencing disciplinary literacy and ELA or literary texts. We reviewed the articles for research design, methodology, and approaches used by ELA scholars engaged in any form of work related to specific ELA processes or explicit disciplinary literacy practices. The findings that follow offer an exploration and explanation of some of the general trends in research used in disciplinary literacy.

We begin our discussion by examining the empirical methodologies used by researchers in ELA, followed by a discussion of the two main approaches for inquiry and an overview of the data collection and analysis techniques used in the discipline.

Research Methodology

Our review of research revealed a preference for qualitative approaches to investigate disciplinary literacy practices in ELA. Research questions center on observing, describing, and defining disciplinary nuances in ELA, which is consistent with a qualitative methodology. Qualitative methodology has been used in foundational studies in disciplinary literacy across various disciplines, such as Bazerman's (1985) study in physics and Wineburg's (1998) study in history; in earlier works in ELA (Earthman, 1992; Peskin, 1998); and in more recent works specific to disciplinary literacy in ELA (Rainey, 2016; Reynolds & Rush, 2017). Additionally, ELA scholars have utilized other methodological approaches including mixed methods (Burkett & Goldman, 2016; Levine, 2019); quasi-experimental design (Levine, 2014; McConn, 2016); and intervention studies (Imbrenda, 2018).

Within studies reviewed for this chapter, two major qualitative approaches for inquiry emerged: expert–novice studies and case studies. The sections below describe the ways they are used in ELA research and how findings offer insights into disciplinary practices.

Expert–Novice and Expert Studies

As in other disciplines, one of the most prevalent research designs in ELA is expert and expert–novice studies. In early ELA expert–novice studies, researchers often asked the expert and/or novice participants to read a literary text, or multiple literary texts, and have them perform a think-aloud procedure during or after the reading. A common tactic when using think-aloud protocols with experts and novices was the use of "cold" texts (text that isn't a common read for either participant group, although it may be a familiar author or structure) to allow for a more natural and pure observation of sensemaking processes in the moment. For example, Earthman (1992) asked eight graduate students and eight first-year college students to read two short stories and two poems over the course of sessions. She modeled a quick think-aloud procedure with an unrelated text, and then had the participants read and articulate what they were thinking while reading. By asking them to think while they read, she formed a picture of their initial meaning-making strategies before they were influenced by classroom factors. She approached the data by looking for three *a priori* theoretical elements guided by reader–text transactions. Similarly, Peskin's (1998) participants were eight doctoral candidates in English and eight college or high school novices. Think-alouds were modeled during a short period after which participants used think-alouds for two poems. Peskin also analyzed the protocols by approaching the data with an *a priori* framework to look for specific elements that were relevant to each of her research questions. Her applied framework resulted in an explanation, like many other scholars, on the differences in meaning-making approaches and processes between experts and novices. Warren (2011) asked eight college literature professors to read four lyric poems from a variety of literary eras to examine how experts read poems both in their area of expertise and outside of it. Warren used Peskin's (1998) transcribed protocols to explain how to do the think-aloud process and then asked the participants to read the texts. Warren (2011) applied a quantitative approach and conducted a logistic regression to determine the binary relationships among participants' areas of specialization and their familiarity with texts. Participants were observed interpreting poems that were close to or far from their areas of specialization, and in light of how familiar they may have been with the poems. Although these particular researchers did not identify or label their work specifically as disciplinary literacy, their findings had an impact on how we think about disciplinary literacy in ELA and their work is foundational for current disciplinary literacy research in ELA.

In research that focused on disciplinary literacy specific to ELA and built on previous research, researchers used similar think-aloud protocols, and their data analysis prioritized emergent over *a priori* coding. For example, Rainey (2016) asked 10 college-level literature instructors to read two short stories, stopping when they had a thought; she also interviewed them after they finished to reflect on what they did as they read. Rainey applied constant comparative analysis using open coding to code the data and develop themes, after which she used axial and selective coding to further observe the development of theoretical schemes or interpretive models. Additionally, Reynolds and Rush's (2017) participants, four literature professors and four college freshmen, read one short story and one poem, and shared the thoughts they had while they read the texts. Reynolds and Rush (2017) began their data analysis of transcribed interviews with *a priori* codes from previous foundational ELA studies, after which they conducted a form of open coding to account for their own understanding as educators in ELA. They ended their analysis by sharing developing categories and processes that could be used to describe expert processes of reading literary texts, which were compared to those of novices to make claims about disciplinary literacy in ELA.

These studies provide a better understanding of the ways experts and novices develop meaning while reading literary texts. Earthman (1992) and Peskin (1998) were able to confirm framework elements and/or theoretical practices appearing in experts' behavior, and Rainey (2016) was able to begin building a model to explain the experts' disciplinary practices. Reynolds and Rush (2017) compared experts and novices' practices, which allowed them to begin identifying disciplinary process-based moves that both populations demonstrated doing, ultimately enabling them to formulate a heuristic for student learning in ELA (Reynolds et al., 2020, 2021). Expert–novice studies allow scholars to extrapolate about the strategies and skills needed for novices to learn to join the discourse of the disciplinary communities, or in some cases, offer an explanation regarding how the depth of disciplinary knowledge influenced students' engagement with text and ability to interpret texts.

Case Studies

The second major approach to inquiry within the studies examined for this chapter was the case study. Researchers in ELA used case studies (Merriam, 1998; Stake, 1995; Yin, 2005) to explore, observe, and describe particular disciplinary elements in play in their natural settings, such as bounding the unit of analysis (the case) by entire classes (Glenn, 2014; Jacobs & Low, 2017; Park, 2013), by a small handful of participants (Bentley, 2013; Williamson, 2013), or by a specific classroom activity, such as small-group discussions (Soter et al., 2010). And, sometimes within these bounded cases, a case study was used to develop theory or understand the role of theory in a particular space (Dyches & Thomas, 2020).

For example, Newell et al. (2014) used case study analysis to explore how participants' epistemologies were socially constructed, which allowed for the exploration and identification of patterns of differing argumentative stances, as demonstrated by various teachers of writing across schools. In this study, the case study method allowed for the in-depth observation and analysis of the participants to see how the "teachers' epistemologies for teaching argumentation [were] made evident" (p. 100). Rich data from fieldnotes, recordings of writing instruction, writing samples, and surveys resulted in the development of instructional chains (view of the writing unit at the classroom activity level). Analyzing the instructional chains by individual cases allowed the researchers to make claims about how participants organized writing instruction around differing argumentative epistemologies, which they argued were socially constructed and made visible through language use within the classroom events.

Di Domenico et al. (2019) designed participant cases from combined insights from reflective notes, interviews, observations, and fieldnotes. This approach yielded insights into participants' disciplinary literacy instructional practices and interactions with literary coaches. Working across multiple data sources, the researchers were able to develop a set of codes that were used to describe how one teacher participant and literacy coach worked together; challenges and successes experienced; and changes in approach and implementation of disciplinary literacy instructional practices. Three coaching priorities were described and developed, making arguments about how disciplinary-specific literacy instruction can be incorporated into ELA teachers' classrooms.

Haddix and Price-Dennis (2013) used the case study to highlight and offer situated representations of preservice teachers problematizing situations they may encounter in their field placements, particularly as they engage with diverse student populations. Using participant observational fieldnotes, transcripts, artifacts, and interviews, data were analyzed across data sources to describe the educational experiences of each case. Because this study explored how ELA teacher educators can facilitate critical dialogue about issues related to race, ethnicity, language, and class, analyzing each case and confirming insights through various artifacts allowed for situated representations to be made about teachers' critical encounters with literature through a critical literacy and critical pedagogy lens.

Case studies such as those highlighted here provide researchers with the opportunity to delve deeply into participants' contexts and beliefs, through rich description and multiple forms of data. In ELA, case studies are often utilized to unpack how beliefs and conceptualizations may influence instruction in ELA classrooms, to explore the roles and outcomes of professional development with preservice teachers, to observe discourse patterns within particular contexts, or even to learn how a particular ELA theory is envisioned and implemented in classrooms. While there are many other uses and outcomes of the case study in ELA studies, the nuanced observations of individual cases allowed for a very close look at various ELA elements in play, and many of the analyses offer insights into particular disciplinary literacy processes.

The next two sections explore the data collection and data analysis techniques used in ELA disciplinary literacy studies.

Data Collection

We observed several common trends in data collection approaches, which include classroom observations, interviews, and classroom artifacts. These data collection tools allowed researchers to explore understandings, processes, and behaviors as related to disciplinary literacy in ELA spaces.

Classroom Observations

Several studies in ELA disciplinary literacy studies used classroom observation. One of the most powerful outcomes of observations is the ability to capture human behavior, thoughts, and even the negotiated reality within shared spaces, particularly between teachers and students. In the ELA studies we reviewed, we noticed observing classes provided researchers with understandings about how disciplinary literacy functioned, both in the ways the courses were taught, in how discussions were held, and in how theory manifested itself in classroom activities. These studies occurred primarily in secondary English classrooms (e.g., Sherry, 2014), preservice methods courses (e.g., Wolfe, 2010), and professional development sessions (e.g., Lillge, 2019). The researchers had differing levels of proximity with the classrooms being observed and the observations came in a variety of forms, from teaching the class (e.g., Dickson & Costigan, 2011), to attending the class for a set period of time (e.g., Hall, 2016; Vetter, 2010), to focusing on one student's experiences throughout a number of classes (e.g., Wilson & Boatright, 2011).

For example, Dyches and Thomas (2020) used classroom observations on a unit co-created and co-taught by Dyches and a secondary ELA teacher on *The Adventures of Huckleberry Finn*, focusing specifically on critical race theory (CRT) and critical Whiteness studies (CWS). As an active observer as participant, Dyches worked with the students in a variety of ways, including observing, interacting with students on reading literary texts, and examining and analyzing the work that they did as they read and thought about the text from a CRT/CWS lens. This analysis of the classroom observations provided deep insights into human behavior and reactions to CRT/CWS in that the researchers were able to observe how these theories helped students notice "manifestations" of CRT/CWS while reading and also the challenges that students continued to grapple with.

Hall (2016) conducted 60 observations in one eighth-grade classroom over the course of an academic year. She documented instructional activities and materials, and transcribed student and teacher talk during whole-class lessons and discussions. Additionally, she purposefully selected five focal students to examine more closely. Observations of these focal students afforded a glimpse into the action and talk of each student within the classroom space, and Hall was able to develop insights into students' statements as related to interacting with texts. ELA classroom observations provided a *means* for capturing insights into how students read and interact with literary text during instruction, how they negotiated or used discourse, how they utilized and/or conceptualized theory and the role it played in their interpretations, and other activities.

Classroom Artifacts

ELA disciplinary literacy scholars often collected classroom artifacts, largely work produced in and for classrooms. Some, like Dyches and Thomas (2020) and Hall (2016), included artifact study as part of their classroom observations. Others used classroom artifacts as the primary data source. For example, Wilder and Yagelski (2018) collected final papers to examine the writing moves made by first-year writing students as they developed an argument that enhanced their previous papers. They analyzed the essay artifacts for evidence of four cross-disciplinary analytic moves. Results suggested a need for the development of new instructional approaches to cover disciplinary analytic writing tasks to improve students' ability to engage in specific disciplinary elements.

Sarigianides (2019) conducted a 10-week study in a senior AP English class. She collected all of the work that the students produced during that unit, as well as teachers' plans and reflections. Sarigianides utilized observations and interviews to explore what happens when a Black Jamaican English teacher "instructed Black and Latino students in AP English about adolescence as a construct and guided them to apply this sociocultural lens of youth to texts in English class and to their lives" (p. 376). Using a performative lens, these artifacts became essential in documenting how students engaged and acted with this particular construct through performative and formative measures. Regardless of whether the researchers were observing the classes, teaching the classes, or only collecting artifacts, the artifacts produced in the classes provided data for how the students engaged in literary activity in a variety of settings. While the collection of classroom artifacts continues to be a common practice, a strong outcome of artifact analysis in ELA studies is the ability of researchers to form insights around the efficacy of teaching elements related to ELA, the role of theory as students engage with it, the discourse used for and within particular settings, and in some cases, the conceptualization and application of ELA elements (like argumentative tactics) in student work.

Interviews

Another data collection tool utilized by researchers in ELA was the use of interviews with participants; however, the types and structures of interviews were different. A Rainey and Storm (2021) study conducted 44 semi-structured, retrospective interviews after students read and used a think-aloud over two short stories, capturing students' thoughts about their own interpretations of their thinking while reading literary texts. These interviews were able to explore "students' purposes for reading literature, the ways they work with texts to accomplish these purposes, and the ways that they approached teaching students to read and reason with literature" (p. 7). Burkett and Goldman (2016) also conducted think-aloud procedures, as well as a prompted interview task, but they focused their questions, "targeting literal, inferential, and interpretative aspects of understanding" (p. 463), which allowed the researchers to probe for disciplinary aspects that might occur while engaging with texts.

Researchers also conducted interviews with teachers and students about their work or their experiences in a class. For example, Ives (2012) interviewed a teacher at the beginning and end of an observed unit, and also conducted semi-structured interviews with focal students from the class. While additional tools were also used, Ives was able to use interviews as a data collection tool to describe and make sense of discourse, and in this specific case, to examine "how sixth-grade student's literacy practices disrupt, or dialogize, the official curriculum" (p. 42) through students' interactions in the classroom. Glenn and Ginsberg (2016) examined a high school young adult literature class taught by one of the authors. They utilized interview protocols focused on the participants' perceptions of what was happening at specific moments during the class, the students' life histories and reading attitudes, and experiences related to the course. The final interview was structured as a synthesis of both the previous interviews and the course itself. Skerrett (2013) focused on one student and utilized three semi-structured interviews with that student, as well as interviews with the student's mother and teacher. The data from the interviews allowed the researcher to "analyz[e] using theories of identity, positioning, communities of practice, and multiliteracies," finding that "within and across these communities, the dimensions of apprenticeship, positioning, and recruitment of multiliterate and multilingual repertoires were essential to the youth's development of writing practices and identities" (p. 322). Even though the formats of the interviews were different, it was clear that the information gained through the voices of the participants in interviews led to valuable information about how those participants interacted with texts or understood literacy, or how theory was enacted within ELA classroom spaces, whether they were literary experts, teachers, students, or even parents.

Overall, there was a great deal of overlap with these data collection methods. Classroom observations generally included examination of artifacts and interviews. Many of the studies that prioritized interviews also included some aspects of observation or artifact study. These three areas, in addition to the general expert–novice studies, help researchers to understand and articulate disciplinary literacy in ELA practices. Whether it is through the instruction of students, the production of work by participants, or the interviews with participants, these methods of data collection appear to be some of the more prioritized methods of understanding what literacy practices happen in ELA.

Data Analysis

There are strong trends in research design and data collection methods applied to studies on disciplinary literacy in ELA across the literature (think-alouds, classroom observations, artifacts). However, there was no consistent pattern of analysis applied to the data in these studies. In fact, after combing multiple journal and scholarly sources, the bulk of our review resulted in the majority of research identifying "basic coding" as their data analysis approach. There are, however, some emerging trends of specific data analysis approaches being used across the literature on disciplinary literacy in ELA. In this case, it is appropriate to say "emerging" as while we combed multiple sources, we found a handful of studies within each of these categories.

Discourse Analysis

One emerging data analysis method being used by researchers is discourse analysis (Fairclough, 2013; Gee, 2017). For example, Neugebauer and Blair (2020) applied tools from critical discourse analysis to drive inductive, descriptive coding of their qualitative data. With discourse analysis in mind, they examined how the students "discursively constructed the concept of reading," which allowed them to analyze the relations between those constructions and the broader discourses suggested. Similarly, using a linguistic process, Myers and Eberfors (2010) applied discourse analysis on their qualitative data of students' posted messages based on a semiotic model of meaning, allowing them to find instances when participants made references in their posting to a cultural interpretation. Johnson (2012) also applied a critical discourse analysis in her critical ethnographic study. Seeking to embed the analysis of discoursal practices within the setting, she analyzed the language her participants used to understand how they were questioning discourses and how they were reproducing them. Overall, she explored the discourses and sociocultural practices that were implicit in the students' language. These researchers explained their approaches to discourse analysis, helping readers to fully understand how this analysis process impacted the construction of their findings. Sherry (2014) focused on discourse analysis, which allowed her to extrapolate on "meaning-making made public through discursive interactions" (p. 149), without making assumptions about conversational moves being understood "in particular ways" by all of her participants. Lillge (2019) also applied a discourse analysis to explore participants' discourse-in-use, drawing on theory and scholarship that view language and culture as intertwined. Many studies in ELA relied on discourse analysis to explain the connection between the practices of the participations and the communities to which they belong (Chun, 2012; DeStigter, 2015; Johnson, 2012; Vetter, 2010; Vetter et al., 2018; Williamson, 2013). Largely what we found was that discourse analysis was utilized by many researchers as an analysis approach to probe the ways in which participants belonging to specific communities of practices, namely ELA settings, engaged, explored, utilized, or discussed ELA elements through discourse, which got at disciplinary practices.

Content Analysis

Content analysis was another common approach to analyzing data (Krippendorff, 2013; Merriam, 1998). Park (2013) employed content analysis in her qualitative study, allowing her to pay attention to the content of the language and form of the text. Using the content of teacher writings, she explored ideas, questions, and issues presented to students to understand the meanings that participants made in the context of their writing. She found, through triangulated analysis of her preservice teachers' sources, that "disciplinary reading encompasses several different approaches and tasks" (p. 370). Like Park (2013), Woodard (2015) employed content analysis to look for recurring phrases and practices used by her teacher participants, after which she was able to create narratives of how participants engaged in language and literate practices. Comparing participant cases with each other, she found that "each teacher appropriated distinct practices in discipline-specific ways" and was able to document ways "in which teacher-writers' literate and instructional activities dialogically inform one another in similar and distinct ways" (p. 44). Earthman (1992) similarly examined readers' initial responses to a text using content analysis, exploring her data for three *a priori* elements (theoretical) in the documents. Relying on reader-response theories, she was able to use content analysis to look for these elements: "the ways readers fill gaps in the text, the ways readers respond to text's repertoire or connections to reality outside the text world, and reader's ability to response to multiple perspectives or to general multiple levels of association as part of their evocation of the work" (p. 357).

Content analysis was utilized by several researchers to explore the presence of theory or ELA elements in participants' work, and to also observe for processes as related to ELA elements within participants' practices and processes.

General Coding

Finally, and perhaps the most common, many researchers in ELA do not name a specific data analysis approach beyond the coding approach. Some of the general approaches to coding include constant comparative (Glenn, 2014; Jacobs & Low, 2017; Rainey, 2016; Rainey & Storm, 2021), *a priori* coding, open coding, general coding schemes, or coding by research question (Dyches & Thomas, 2020; Hamel, 2003; Ives, 2012; Sarigianides, 2019; Sweeney, 2018; Wolfe, 2010). While the findings of all these studies are clearly identified and explained, we are unsure what type of lens guided the coding decisions, which is often what an identified analysis approach helps to do.

The collection of data through various tools offers researchers a plethora of material to analyze. This review of the research in disciplinary literacy offers unique insights regarding ELA writ large, including the identification of practices and processes valued in ELA spaces. In the case of our review of journal articles, we find that while most ELA scholars may not explicitly call their research "disciplinary," the decisions they made regarding data collection tools and data analysis has offered clear and useful findings about the disciplinary nature of ELA.

DISCUSSION

Research on the study of the reading, writing, and communication practices contained within a discipline has been conducted long before the term *disciplinary literacy* was used to describe them (Hinchman & O'Brien, 2019; Moje, 2007; Shanahan & Shanahan, 2012). As such, in the extant literature about disciplinary literacy, there are many conceptual and epistemological pieces aiming to explain the ideas contained in disciplinary literacy and to delineate it from other ideas, such as content-area literacy. However, as discussed throughout the chapter, there is a growing body of empirical research as well. Despite the growth in empirical research, one major criticism of the scholarship on disciplinary literacy is that it has been theorized far more than it has been researched (Spires et al., 2018). One of the challenges in understanding the state of research within this area, nevertheless, is that there are publications in related fields that do not explicitly name their work as disciplinary literacy but could be and should be considered in this light. In this chapter, we reviewed articles that referred specifically to disciplinary literacy and those that did not explicitly use the term but discussed the discipline-specific concerns in ELA that could be defined as disciplinary literacy. Researchers in ELA rarely use the term *disciplinary literacy*, but they are certainly investigating reading, writing, and communicating. For example, our 10-year search of *Research in the Teaching of English* and *English Education* yielded only five articles specifically using the term in the context of ELA.

In our review, we found that there are methodological similarities between the research in ELA and in other disciplines. Although not surprising, we believe that there may be disciplinary considerations to research methods themselves. For example, think-alouds, a common research tool used across disciplines, are often used in disciplinary ways. The texts used in history are different than those used in ELA. In fact, what "counts" as text, such as fiction, primary documents, film, lectures, is disciplinary as well. The aim of the think-aloud differs, too. For example, research in ELA often centers on investigating identity via think-alouds, while in history it is often used to examine argumentation. Additionally, the situation and activity in which the think-aloud occurs can be disciplinary. For example, reading a piece of literature in ELA, conducting a lab in the sciences, solving a proof in mathematics are all different disciplinary processes. Researchers may benefit from intentionally taking into account discipline-specific considerations both in design and methods.

Currently, much of the scholarship on disciplinary literacy uses qualitative methods, which is a good fit given the nature of the questions asked by researchers (Hinchman & O'Brien, 2019). However, our review found that there is often a lack of description about the type of analysis used other than "coding." In fact, after combing multiple journal and scholarly sources, the bulk of our review indicated that most of the research used "basic coding" as their data analysis approach. In the current literature, there is rich description about how the data were collected, but a paucity of information on how they were analyzed, which has been cited as a challenge in the extant qualitative literature base (Smagorinsky, 2008). Additionally, a consistent pattern of data analysis has not been applied to the data in these studies. This lack of a consistent pattern of data analysis may be explained by researchers not specifically naming their analysis approach beyond the description of various coding schemes, such as constant comparative coding, inductive coding, *a priori* coding, and so on, being used and applied. This does not negate the strength of the studies' findings, but it has left many curious about the type of analysis that guided those coding decisions and ultimate list of findings. In addition to naming and describing methods of data analysis, a thorough description of methods to ensure the trustworthiness of analysis through triangulation of the data would further strengthen the research that we examined (see also Park, 2013). As discussed by several of the articles reviewed in this chapter (Haddix & Price-Dennis, 2013; Wilder & Yagelski, 2018), generalizability is not the goal; instead, it is to provide in-depth description of phenomena within a specific context. We concur with Smagorinsky (2008) that providing a more detailed and specific explanation of research methods and analysis that is clearly aligned with a theoretical rationale helps readers make sense of the findings.

As the scholarship on disciplinary literacy continues to develop, we may see more longitudinal work, for example, studies investigating the development of disciplinary literacy instruction on students' learning as they progress through school. Currently, student populations in ELA studies are typically preservice teachers. As research continues in the field, we may see an increase in scholarship focused on applying disciplinary literacy research in K–12 and postsecondary settings. We may also see an increase in the number of quantitative pieces to examine disciplinary literacy with a broader lens.

CONCLUSION

We concur with Spires et al.'s (2018) idea that "the singular disciplinary literacy should be replaced with multiple disciplinary literacies. Talking about disciplinary literacies in the plural spotlights the variance dependent on discourse communities" (p. 1406). The work within ELA demonstrates this variance. Exploring the research traditions and practices within ELA provides insights into the disciplinary nature and understandings of the field.

REFERENCES

Achugar, M., & Carpenter, B. (2012). Developing disciplinary literacy in a multilingual history classroom. *Linguistics and Education, 23*(3), 262–276.

Bazerman, C. (1985). Physicists reading physics. *Written Communications, 2*(1), 3–23.

Bentley, E. (2013). Supernovas and superheroes: Examining unfamiliar genres and teachers' pedagogical content knowledge. *English Education, 45*(3), 218–246.

Brozo, W. G., & Crain, S. (2018). Writing in math: A disciplinary literacy approach. *Journal of Educational Strategies, 91*(1), 7–13.

Burkett, C., & Goldman, S. R. (2016). "Getting the point" of literature: Relations between processing and interpretation. *Discourse Processes, 53*(5–6), 457–487.

Chun, C. W. (2012). The multimodalities of globalization: Teaching a YouTube video in an EAP classroom. *Research in the Teaching of English, 47*(2), 145–170.

Coffin, C. (2006). *Historical discourse: The language of time, cause and evaluation.* Continuum.

DeStigter, T. (2015). On the ascendance of argument: A critique of the assumptions of academe's dominant form. *Research in the Teaching of English, 50*(1), 11–34.

Di Domenico, P., Elish-Piper, L., Manderino, M., & L'Allier, S. K. (2018). Three coaching priorities for enhancing teacher practice in disciplinary literacy instruction in the English language arts. *Journal of Adolescent and Adult Literacy, 63*(1), 73–82.

Dickson, R., & Costigan, A. (2011). Emerging practice for new teachers: Creating possibilities for "aesthetic" readings. *English Education, 43*(2), 145–170.

Dyches, J., & Thomas, D. (2020). Unsettling the "white savior" narrative: Reading *Huck Finn* through a critical race theory/critical whiteness studies lens. *English Education, 53*(1), 35–53.

Earthman, E. A. (1992). Creating the virtual work: Readers' processes in understanding literary texts. *Research in the Teaching of English, 26*(4), 351–384.

Fairclough, N. (2013). *Critical discourse analysis: The critical study of language.* Routledge.

Fang, Z. (2006). The language demands of science reading in middle school. *International Journal of Science Education, 28*(5), 491–520.

Fang, Z., & Chapman, S. (2020). Disciplinary literacy in mathematics: One mathematician's reading practices. *Journal of Mathematical Behavior, 59*, Article 100799.

Fang, Z., & Schleppergrell, M. J. (2008). *Reading in secondary content areas: A language-based pedagogy.* University of Michigan Press

Fang, Z., & Schleppergrell, M. J. (2010). Disciplinary literacies across content areas: Supporting secondary reading through functional language analysis. *Journal of Adolescent and Adult Literacy, 53*(7), 587–597.

Gee, J. P. (2017). *Introducing discourse analysis from grammar to society.* Routledge.

Glenn, W. J. (2014). To witness and to testify: Preservice teachers examine literary aesthetics to better understand diverse literature. *English Education, 46*(2), 90–116.

Glenn, W. J., & Ginsberg, R. (2016). Resisting readers' identity (re)construction across English and young adult literature course contexts. *Research in the Teaching of English, 51*(1), 84–105.

Goldman, S. R., Britt, M. A., Brown, W., Cribb, G., George, M., Greenleaf, C., . . . Project READI. (2016). Disciplinary literacies and learning to read for understanding: A conceptual framework for disciplinary literacy. *Educational Psychologist, 51*(92), 219–246.

Green, C. (2019). A multilevel description of textbook linguistic complexity across disciplines: Leveraging NLP to support disciplinary literacy. *Linguistics and Education, 53*, 100748.

Haddix, M., & Price-Dennis, D. (2013). Urban fiction and multicultural literature as transformative tools for preparing English teachers for diverse classrooms. *English Education, 45*(3), 247–283.

Hall, L. A. (2016). "I don't really have anything good to say": Examining how one teacher worked to shape middle school students' talk about texts. *Research in the Teaching of English, 51*(1), 60–83.

Halliday, M. A. K., & Matthiessen, C. M. I. (2004). *An introduction to functional grammar.* Routledge.

Hamel, F. L. (2003). Teacher understanding of student understanding: Revising the gap between teacher conceptions and students' ways with literature. *Research in the Teaching of English, 38*(1), 49–84.

Hinchman, K., & O'Brien, D. (2019). Disciplinary literacy: From infusion to hybridity. *Journal of Literacy Research 51*(4), 525–536.

Hynd, C., Holschuh, J. P., & Hubbard, B. P. (2004). Thinking like a historian: College students' reading of multiple historical documents. *Journal of Literacy Research, 36*(1), 141–176.

Imbrenda, J. (2018). Developing academic literacy: Breakthroughs and barriers in a college-access intervention. *Research in the Teaching of English, 52*(3), 317–341.

Ives, D. (2012). Kristina's *Ghetto Family*: Tension and possibilities at the intersection of teacher and student literacy agendas. *Research in the Teaching of English, 47*(1), 39–63.

Jacobs, K. B., & Low, D. E. (2017). Critical questioning in and beyond the margins: Teacher preparation students' multimodal inquiries into literacy assessment. *English Education, 49*(3), 226–264.

Johnson, J. D. (2012). "A rainforest in front of a bulldozer": The literacy practices of teacher candidates committed to social justice. *English Education, 44*(2), 147–179.

Ke, L., & Schwarz, C. V. (2021). Supporting students' meaningful engagement in scientific modeling through epistemological messages: A case study of contrasting teaching approaches. *Journal of Research in Science Teaching, 58*(3), 335–365.

Krippendorff, K. (2013). *Content analysis: An introduction to its methodology* (3rd ed.). SAGE.

Learned, J. E. (2018). Doing history: A study of disciplinary literacy and readers labeled as struggling. *Journal of Literacy Research, 50*(2), 190–216.

Levine, S. (2014). Making interpretation visible with an affect-based strategy. *Reading Research Quarterly, 49*(3), 282–303.

Levine, S. (2019). A century of change in high school English assessments: An analysis of 110 New York state regent exams. *Research in the Teaching of English, 54*(1), 31–57.

Lillge, D. (2019). Uncovering conflict: Why teachers struggle to apply professional development learning about the teaching of writing. *Research in the Teaching of English, 53*(4), 340–362.

Mantz, E. (2016). Examining evidence construction as the transformation of the material world into community knowledge. *Journal of Research in Science Teaching, 53*(7), 1113–1140.

McConn, M. (2016). An evaluation of extensive and intensive teaching of literature: One teacher's experiment in the 11th grade. *Research in the Teaching of English, 51*(2), 162–182.

Merriam, S. B. (1998). *Qualitative research and case study applications in education.* Jossey-Bass.

Miller, E., Manz, E., Russ, R., Stroupe, D., & Berland, L. (2018). Addressing the epistemic elephant in the room: Epistemic agency and the Next Generation Science Standards. *Journal of Research in Science Teaching, 55*(7), 1053–1075.

Moje, E. (2007). Developing socially just subject-matter instruction: A review of the literature on disciplinary literacy teaching. *Review of Research in Education, 37*(1), 1–44.

Moje, E. B. (2008). Foregrounding the disciplines in secondary literacy teaching and learning: A call for change. *Journal of Adolescent and Adult Literacy, 52*(2), 96–107.

Moje, E. (2015). Doing and teaching disciplinary literacy with adolescent learners: A social and cultural enterprise. *Harvard Educational Review, 85*(2), 254–278.

Myers, J. M., & Eberfors, F. (2010). Globalizing English through intercultural critical literacy. *English Education, 42*(2), 148–170.

Neto, A., Ribeiro do Amaral, E., & Mortimer, E. (2018). Analyzing discursive interactions in science classrooms to characterize teaching strategies adopted by teachers in lessons on environmental themes. In K. Tang & K. Danielsson (Eds.), *Global developments in literacy research for science education* (pp. 149–166). Springer.

Neugebauer, S. R., & Blair, E. E. (2020). "I know how to read and all, but . . . ": Disciplinary reading constructions of middle school students of color. *Journal of Literacy Research, 52*(3), 316–340.

Newell, G. E., VanDerHeide, J., & Olsen, A. W. (2014). High school English language arts teachers' argumentative epistemologies for teaching writing. *Research in the Teaching of English, 49*(2), 95–119.

Park, J. Y. (2013). All the ways of reading literature: Preservice English teachers' perspectives on disciplinary literacy. *English Education, 45*(4), 361–384.

Peskin, J. (1998). Constructing meaning when reading poetry: An expert-novice study. *Cognition and Instruction, 16*(3), 235–263.

Pressley, M., & Afflerbach, P. (1995). *Verbal protocols in reading.* Erlbaum.

Rainey, E. C. (2016). Disciplinary literacy in English language arts: Exploring the social and problem-based nature of literary reading and reasoning. *Reading Research Quarterly, 52*(1), 53–71.

Rainey, E., & Moje, E. B. (2012). Building insider knowledge: Teaching students to read, write, and think within ELA and across the disciplines. *English Education, 45*(1), 71–90.

Rainey, E. C., & Storm, S. (2021). English teacher interpretive communities: An exploratory case study of teachers' literacy practices and pedagogical reasoning. *Literacy Research and Instruction, 60*(4), 1–20.

Reisman, A. (2012). Reading like a historian: A document-based history curriculum intervention in urban high school. *Cognition and Instruction, 30*(1), 86–112.

Reynolds, T., & Rush, L. S. (2017). Experts and novices reading literature: An analysis of disciplinary literacy in English language arts. *Literacy Research and Instruction*, *56*(3), 199–216.

Reynolds, T., Rush, L. S., Lampi, J. P., & Holschuh, J. P. (2020). English disciplinary literacy: Enhancing students' literary interpretive moves. *Journal of Adolescent and Adult Literacy, 64*(2), 201–209.

Reynolds, T., Rush, L. S., Lampi, J. P., & Holschuh, J. P. (2021). Moving beyond interpretive monism: A disciplinary heuristic to bridge literary theory and literacy theory. *Harvard Educational Review, 91*(3), 382–401.

Sarigianides, S. T. (2019). Performative youth: The literacy of possibilities of de-essentializing adolescence. *English Education*, *51*(4), 376–403.

Schleppegrell, M. (2007). The linguistic challenges of mathematics teaching and learning: A research review. *Reading & Writing Quarterly, 23*(2), 139–159.

Schleppegrell, M., Achugar, M., & Oteiza, T. (2004). The grammar of history: Enhancing content-based instruction through a functional focus on language. *TESOL Quarterly, 38*(1), 67–93.

Shanahan, C., Shanahan, T., & Misischia, C. (2011). Analysis of expert readers in three disciplines: History, mathematics, and chemistry. *Journal of Literacy Research*, *43*(4), 393–429.

Shanahan, T., & Shanahan, C. (2008). Teaching disciplinary literacy to adolescents: Rethinking content-area literacy. *Harvard Educational Review*, *78*(1), 40–59.

Shanahan, T., & Shanahan, C. (2012). What is disciplinary literacy and why does it matter? *Topics in Language Disorders, 32*(1), 7–18.

Sherry, M. B. (2014). Indirect challenges and provocative paraphrases: Using cultural conflict-talk practices to promote students' dialogic participation in whole-class discussions. *Research in the Teaching of English*, *49*(2), 141–167.

Skerrett, A. (2013). Building multiliterate and multilingual writing practices and identities. *English Education*, *45*(4), 322–360.

Smagorinsky, P. (2008). The method section as conceptual epicenter in constructing social science research reports. *Written Communication, 25*(3), 389–411.

Soter, A. O., Wilkinson, I. A. G., Conners, S. P., Murphy, P. K., & Shen V. F. (2010). Deconstructing "aesthetic response" in small-group discussions about literature: A possible solution to the "aesthetic response" dilemma. *English Education, 42*(2), 204–225.

Spires, H. A., Kerkhoff, S. N., Graham, A. C., Thompson, I., & Lee, J. K. (2018). Operationalizing and validating disciplinary literacy in secondary education. *Reading and Writing, 31*(6), 1401–1434.

Stake, R. E. (1995). *The art of case study research.* SAGE.

Sweeney, M. A. (2018). Audience awareness as a threshold concept of reading: An examination of student learning in biochemistry. *Research in the Teaching of English, 53*(1), 58–79.

Vetter, A. (2010). Positioning students as readers and writers through talk in a high school English classroom. *English Education*, *43*(1), 33–64.

Vetter, A., Schieble, M., & Meacham, M. (2018). Critical conversations in English education: Discursive strategies for examining how teacher and student identities shape classroom discourse. *English Education, 50*(3), 255–282.

Warren, J. E. (2011). "Generic" and "specific" expertise in English: An expert/expert study in poetry interpretation and academic argument. *Cognition and Instruction*, *29*(4), 349–374.

Wilder, L., & Yagelski, R. P. (2018). Describing cross-disciplinary analytic moves in first year college student writing. *Research in the Teaching of English*, *52*(4), 382–403.

Williamson, P. (2013). Enacting high leverage practices in English methods: The case of discussion. *English Education, 46*(1), 34–67.

Wilson, A. A., & Boatright, M. D. (2011). One adolescent's construction of native identity in school: "Speaking with dance and not in words or writing." *Research in the Teaching of English*, *45*(3), 252–277.

Wineburg, S. (1991). On the reading of historical texts: Notes on the breach between school and academy. *Educational Research Journal, 28*(3), 495–519.

Wineburg, S. (1998). Reading Abraham Lincoln: An expert/expert study in the interpretation of historical texts. *Cognitive Science, 22*(3), 319–346.

Wolfe, P. (2010). Preservice teachers planning for critical literary teaching. *English Education*, *42*(4), 368–390.

Woodard, R. (2015). The dialogic interplay of writing and teaching writing: Teacher-writers' talk and textual practices across contexts. *Research in the Teaching of English, 50*(1), 35–59.

Yin, R. K. (2009). *Case study research: Design and methods* (4th ed.). SAGE.

Collaborative Inquiry to Drive Development of Disciplinary Literacy Pedagogy

Purposeful Experiences across Teacher Development

Christina L. Dobbs
Jacy Ippolito
Megin Charner-Laird

Teachers are the most important factor in student growth and achievement (Chetty et al., 2014, Rivkin et al., 2005). Yet, the learning opportunities afforded to teachers, across the career, starting first in preparation programs and moving into professional practice, often fail to center the unique strengths and needs of teachers (Borko, 2004; Darling-Hammond et al., 2017). Nor do they attend to the ways those needs change over time (Feiman-Nemser, 2001). When it comes to disciplinary literacy, many teachers struggle to gain a foothold, often due to the fact that learning opportunities around this important stance are few and far between, disconnected, or simply mismatched in approach to teachers' developmental needs at various points in their career. In this chapter, we outline the ways in which disciplinary literacy professional learning must be articulated across a teacher's career, including a launch in preservice preparation, followed by iterative learning and growth opportunities.

At the secondary level, schools are designed to focus on content-area teaching and learning, with the grammar of schooling (Tyack & Tobin, 1994) still strong. Students move between subject-area teachers, looked to for content-area expertise. Yet, we know that a simple focus on content-area instruction can leave students disconnected from the subjects being taught. With clearer entry points or facility with the discursive norms of a subject area, students may be more engaged in understanding the ways that content-area teachers communicate and engage across different content areas (Fang & Coatoam, 2013). Disciplinary literacy aims to deepen students' connections to the various content areas, making the communication habits and norms of each discipline visible, through a process of apprenticeship and induction. Simultaneously, the best disciplinary literacy instruction helps students to question and be critical of disciplinary norms—to push boundaries and eventually reimagine and expand disciplinary communities.

Given the complexities involved in enacting disciplinary literacy, it is vital that teachers have in-depth learning experiences to learn about and ultimately deepen and hone their disciplinary literacy practice. Disciplinary literacy asks educators not to simply teach reading and writing alongside their content areas (Jacobs, 2008), but rather to think carefully, to draw attention to, and then to support students in noticing and developing the habits of communication specific to their discipline. Making visible what is often invisible or second-nature to disciplinary experts is a challenge—one that must be tackled across the career.

Complex instructional practices require nuanced professional learning opportunities. Developing disciplinary literacy instruction requires adaptive thinking and change (Heifetz et al., 2009). While technical approaches to disseminating information to teachers may work in certain learning situations, such as those often found in 1-day workshops, trainings with textbook publishers, or even introductions to new teaching technologies, disciplinary literacy professional learning requires a more complex design. Specifically, we argue that an inquiry-based approach, allowing for learning, experimentation, and iteration, best fits the adaptive work of developing disciplinary literacy practices (Dobbs et al., 2017). Moreover, this inquiry-based approach is often best framed as collaborative work if we are to see widespread changes beyond individual classrooms. Professional collaboration brings with it opportunities to learn from colleagues' expertise, to learn in ways that are tailored to shared instructional contexts, and to learn in ways that involve critical discourse and reflection (Borko, 2004; Elmore, 2004). Ultimately, collaborative inquiry creates the ideal learning space for teachers developing disciplinary literacy practices, both in preservice and inservice settings.

THEORETICAL FOUNDATIONS

Professional Learning That Supports Teachers at a Range of Points in Their Careers

Any discussion of how inservice and preservice teachers learn to implement disciplinary literacy instruction must take into account teacher learning and development to understand key differences between the two groups. Just as with any learning space, the individual developmental needs of participants must be considered if learning is to be effective (Feiman-Nemser, 2001) and especially if it is to lead to change. This is a key challenge of designing professional learning about disciplinary literacy, though unfortunately, professional learning spaces often do not attend to the particular contexts or developmental needs of teachers (Bill and Melinda Gates Foundation, 2014). In disciplinary literacy professional learning settings, teachers are working to make connections between a number of types of knowledge to build new knowledge and skills, including content knowledge, knowledge of pedagogy, and pedagogical content knowledge, just to name a few. We use two frameworks of teacher development here to help illustrate these differences between inservice and preservice teachers, as they help illuminate how professional learning might best support teachers at various stages.

It is, first, important to consider the approaches that most teachers experience in both preservice and inservice professional learning and the many flaws in those approaches. Approaches to teacher preparation that focus solely on theoretical content, almost exclusively on teaching moves, or balance far more toward university-based learning versus field-based learning exemplify some of the preservice approaches that often lack comprehensive learning opportunities, particularly opportunities for disciplinary literacy preparation (Aldeman et al., 2011). Similarly, inservice professional learning in the form of 1-day workshops, stand-and-deliver presentations, or prepackaged series have similar faults in meeting teachers' learning and development needs (Gates Foundation, 2014). Designers of disciplinary literacy professional learning must consider the shortcomings of these approaches when designing meaningful learning opportunities. A disciplinary literacy approach to professional learning—both preservice and inservice—provides a unique opportunity to build conceptual coherence by connecting theoretical knowledge to instructional practice, with a focus on iterating in practice.

Nearly 20% of teachers enter teaching through alternative certification pathways (McFarland et al., 2018) after pursuing other career opportunities. And it is becoming increasingly common for teachers to enter the career by studying their content areas in depth first, followed by teacher preparation at the graduate level, especially for secondary content teachers (Hussar, 2020). This means that large numbers of teachers do their content learning about the disciplines they will teach prior to their teaching experiences, even in traditional teacher preparation, when student teaching is typically the final step in a program. Though the multiple pathways into the profession can all support those learning to teach, they offer very different experiences of content knowledge development, according to an individual's chosen path.

In considering the disciplinary literacy learning needs of teachers across various stages of preparation and practice, we begin with Fuller's (1969) stage theory (revised in the 1970s; see Rutherford & Hall, 1990) that focuses on the concerns that are central to teachers at various stages of their careers (see Table 15.1 for a brief overview of the stages). Paired with Fuller's work, we draw on concepts from Feiman-Nemser's (2001) continuum of learning to teach, considering the ways that what she frames as the "central tasks" of preservice, induction, and inservice professional learning open up opportunities for deep, meaningful, ongoing learning about disciplinary literacy instructional practices (see Table 15.2 for a brief overview of Feiman-Nemser's framing of the central tasks of learning to teach across the career span).

In our own work, we have found Fuller's stage model useful for understanding how teachers center various aspects of their work at different points in their career. For instance, when it comes to disciplinary literacy, it is key to understand teachers' perspectives about content, pedagogy, and their students. This stage model gives us insight into how various bodies of knowledge might be built and what considerations might be necessary to serve teachers effectively in professional learning. It also helps us understand how the concerns of teachers at various stages might be leveraged to dive deeply and meaningfully into both disciplinary literacy as an area with great potential for improving instruction and as a space where collaborative and inquiry skills can be built and refined.

Similarly, Feiman-Nemser (2001) outlines the central tasks of teacher learning at the preservice, induction, and ongoing professional stages of the career. Paired with Fuller's stages of teacher development, which helps us to hone in on how teachers are thinking about themselves in relation to the core of their work, Feiman-Nemser's ideas help us to consider the ways that professional learning about disciplinary literacy might be framed, delivered, and focused to meet the learning needs of teachers at these various stages. Taken together, these two frameworks help to illuminate both what teachers need and how best to meet those needs, in terms of learning about disciplinary literacy instructional practices across the career, and we use them here to explore the needs of teachers learning about disciplinary literacy.

For many teachers, disciplinary knowledge is primarily built prior to their focus on instructional practice, during what Fuller would term

Stage 0. If teaching preparation for preservice teachers does not focus on how to turn disciplinary habits of mind into questions of pedagogy, then teachers may not have learning spaces where they can do that work and they may not have done so before they come to teacher preparation. Disciplinary literacy professional learning for preservice teachers must make space to examine and connect their own disciplinary learning to the instructional practice they are hoping to adopt in their classrooms.

Fuller's Stage 0 Notable Takeaways: *Teachers may have learned about disciplinary content prior to teacher training. Additional support in later professional learning spaces is key to connect this learning to practice and helping to refine instruction.*

Professional Learning Considerations in Early Teaching

When teachers move into Stage 1, the early teaching phase of Fuller's model (1969), likely as student teachers, they begin to be concerned with themselves and their own competence. These teachers' early concerns can be connected to identities as mathematicians or historians that teachers might have already developed, in order to bridge toward new developing identities in new professional roles. These teachers might enter disciplinary literacy professional learning spaces with concerns about becoming practitioners, and these questions could be focused usefully on disciplinary identities and transitioning those identities toward instruction.

Taken through the lens of the central tasks (Feiman-Nemser, 2001), preservice learning is a vital time to weave disciplinary literacy learning into teachers' preparation. Feiman-Nemser (2001) notes the ways that prior beliefs "serve as filters" (p. 1016) as prospective teachers learn, and her phase model begins with early teacher preparation. In helping preservice teachers develop new beliefs and visions about teaching—one of the central tasks of this phase—there is a distinct opportunity to weave in learning

TABLE 15.1. Fuller's (1969) Stages of Teacher Development

Stage	Chief concern	When?
Stage 0: Preteaching	No concern about teaching	Prior to having any sort of teaching experience
Stage 1: Early teaching	Concerns about self	During first teaching experiences
Stage 2: Teaching	Concerns about tasks	Still in early teaching but with some experience
Stage 3: Late teaching	Concerns about students	Later in teaching experience

TABLE 15.2. Central Tasks of Learning to Teach, According to Feiman-Nemser (2001)

Career stage	Central tasks
Preservice preparation	• Analyzing beliefs, forming new visions • Developing subject-matter knowledge for teaching • Developing understandings of learners and learning • Developing a beginning repertoire • Developing the tools to study teaching
Induction	• Gaining local knowledge of students, curriculum, and school context • Designing responsive curriculum and instruction • Enacting a beginning repertoire in purposeful ways • Creating a classroom learning community • Learning in and from practice
Early (and ongoing) professional development	• Deepening and extending subject-matter knowledge for teaching • Extending and refining one's repertoire • Strengthening dispositions and skills to study and improve teaching • Expanding responsibilities for leadership development

about disciplinary literacy. For instance, to bring their disciplinary "filters" to light, preservice preparation might guide candidates to consider the ways that they have learned about and then mastered the various literacies within their chosen disciplines—be it learning the structure and style of writing lab reports or the approach to writing argumentative essays. Not only will these connections between content expertise and discipline-specific literacies likely resonate for preservice teachers, who may see themselves as more grounded in content knowledge than pedagogy, but digging into conceptualizations of disciplinary literacy also ties directly to the development of pedagogical content knowledge and initial teaching moves, another crucial central task at this stage.

Fuller's Stage 1 Notable Takeaways: *Teachers in this phase are developing identities as teachers, and disciplinary literacy professional learning can support them in the early development of identities closely connected to their disciplinary focus.*

Framing Central Tasks: *Through reflecting on and honing their beliefs about teaching, connecting content-area knowledge to instruction, and developing early instructional practices that lean into disciplinary literacy habits of mind, preservice educators can begin a substantive disciplinary literacy learning journey.*

Professional Learning Considerations as Teachers Grow Their Repertoire

As teachers move into Stage 2 of Fuller's developmental model, professional learning should be targeted differently, to focus on the teachers' concerns about instructional tasks as a way to build disciplinary literacy skills and practices. These concerns about tasks might point toward different concerns for different teachers in professional learning about disciplinary literacy. Teachers could come to disciplinary literacy professional learning with very real contextually driven concerns about curricular constraints, standardized tests, or data available about students that could be fruitful avenues for inquiry work to improve instruction.

Feiman-Nemser's (2001) framing of the induction years of teaching layers onto Fuller's second stage of teaching, with a focus on the tasks of teaching, as teachers grow their repertoire. One of the central tasks of teacher learning, during the induction stage, is a focus on developing instruction that is responsive to the students in a particular classroom or class (Feiman-Nemser, 2011). Similarly, Feiman-Nemser points to the need for professional learning, during this phase, that supports teachers in enacting instructional practices "purposefully" (p. 1029). Disciplinary literacy professional learning during teachers' induction years is well poised to provide teachers with a framework for responsive teaching. Through apprenticing students to the literacies of a particular discipline, in ways that connect to students' own ways of speaking, reading, and writing, teachers can enact disciplinary literacy as a component of responsive teaching. Rather than simply expecting students to know how to communicate effectively as a mathematician or historian, disciplinary literacy instructional practices call on educators to peel away these often hidden literacies to make them visible to all students. This approach entails not only responding to students and matching teaching tasks to their needs but also a considered approach to instructional practices, in which teachers determine the right pedagogical approaches to induct different students into their disciplinary communities.

Fuller's Stage 2 Notable Takeaways: *Teachers in Stage 2 will have concerns connected directly to school contexts and questions about tasks that are most effective, and professional learning will need to make room for teachers to consider these specificities in designing communities that will have the potential to change practice in a particular space.*

Framing Central Tasks: *Disciplinary literacy asks teachers to apprentice students into disciplinary communities. Through supporting novice teachers with professional learning focused specifically on the central tasks of developing a responsive curriculum and enacting purposeful instructional practices, a disciplinary literacy professional learning approach* *during the induction years can continue to deepen educators' approach to teaching from this stance.*

Professional Learning Considerations in Later Teaching

Fuller's stage model posits that in Stage 3 of teacher development, they become focused on students in a range of ways, and they are able to hold multiple perspectives about lessons as they consider how these lessons might impact particular students. The work of this stage often involves beginning to disentangle why instructional tasks work well for some students and not others, or to understand what pulls students toward or away from particular disciplinary pathways in their own lives. These are rich avenues for exploration in professional learning, and we have found that all teachers benefit from collaborating around these sorts of questions as they themselves are moving along in their own development.

While Fuller's third stage focuses on "late teaching," Feiman-Nemser's (2001) next phase of professional learning focuses on "early professional development," taking place in the handful of years following induction (p. 1039). In this phase, Feiman-Nemser (2001) focuses on a deepening and extension of knowledge and practice. One central task of this phase is the deepening of content knowledge, while another is the refinement and extension of the teaching repertoire. These two tasks of professional learning during these years resonate with Fuller's assertion that teachers focus more on students during this stage of development. As teachers consider the particular needs, interests, backgrounds, and resources of their students, this knowledge, paired with ever-deepening pedagogical and content knowledge, provides the perfect canvas for enhanced learning about disciplinary literacy. As teachers during this phase continue to delve into their content areas, they can simultaneously consider the literacies of these discourse communities and develop and revise instructional practices to make those literacies ever more available to students. During this phase of professional learning, teachers are able to delve deeply into their own practice, creating the ideal opportunity for inquiry into disciplinary literacy instruction as a cornerstone of professional learning and change.

Fuller's Stage 3 Notable Takeaways: *Teachers in Stage 3 will continue to have concerns connected directly to school contexts, and they will develop questions about students that are sometimes connected to questions of access, differentiation, or assessment. Professional learning will need to support the cognitive density of these sorts of questions and support teachers as they make instructional changes in classrooms and sometimes find themselves making calls for broader structural changes, too, to serve more students effectively.*

Framing Central Tasks: *With a deepened and more nuanced understanding of both pedagogy and content area, teachers during this phase are poised to sharpen their expertise in disciplinary literacy, considering the nuanced ways that literacies are enacted within particular disciplines as well as the instructional practices that will welcome all students into those disciplinary communities.*

Looking to models of teacher development and teacher learning provides a theoretical framework for approaching disciplinary literacy professional learning in both preservice and inservice settings. Not only do the frames explored above help to discern the particular needs of teachers at various points in their professional learning and preparation, they also point to the ideal inroads for that learning, given that learning must be tailored differently, depending on a teacher's tenure within the profession, be it during the preservice or inservice phases. In what follows, we pair these theoretical frames with consideration of the modalities of learning best suited to the development of disciplinary literacy instructional practices. Given the complexity of these practices, teachers across the career require learning opportunities that are in-depth, context-specific, and, ideally, collaborative. Collaboration provides the opportunity for critical colleagueship (Lord, 1994) and for the interdependent development of new instructional practices (Borko, 2004; Darling-Hammond et al., 2017).

Collaboration and Inquiry as Keys to Meeting Teachers Where They Are

In our own work, we have utilized a range of professional learning structures to support disciplinary literacy implementation (Dobbs et al., 2017; Ippolito et al., 2019). In our most successful endeavors, we have brought together professional learning communities, teacher leadership, and inquiry cycles to create professional learning that results in lasting improvement and changes in beliefs for teacher participants (see Dobbs et al., 2017). Not only does the opportunity to learn with peers provide the psychological safety (Edmondson, 2003) needed to envision and try new practices, but collaborative learning also creates opportunities for the shared iteration and idea development that are vital to developing new, disciplinary literacy instructional practices. In considering this work with preservice and inservice teachers, we find a few key issues to be relevant in supporting teachers to build improvement-focused teams.

When considering preservice teachers, it is often the case that they are having their early field experiences in a range of different sites. Little (1990) discusses how teams that do meaningful work together are interdependent, fighting against the typical isolated culture of schools that has been described as an "egg-crate" with teachers working near to each other but alone (Tyack, 1974). With teachers so early in their development, who are concerned with themselves and their own competence (Fuller, 1969), it is important to develop a sense of independence, without reinforcing this isolated stance toward the work of teaching, and this can be done by emphasizing the value of collaboration skills in learning spaces. By encouraging a collaborative and experimental stance toward teaching early in a teacher's career, we have seen new teachers be successful in developing a teaching identity without learning to be isolated at the same time. Disciplinary literacy gives teachers a key focus that can drive innovation, and it provides a shared focus for learning, and specifically learning with others, that can still be flexible enough to incorporate a range of content areas, perspectives, and contexts.

When it comes to inservice teachers, there is often a great need to support them in moving from more superficial to productive collaboration (Vangrieken et al., 2015). Superficial collaboration relies more on the casual sharing of resources, as opposed to discourse focused on instructional improvement at the individual level or at scale (Little, 1990). Making space and devoting conscious focus and resources to productive collaboration can result in teachers who are more likely to support one another in addressing their concerns about tasks and students in a way that is connected to the day-to-day business of instruction in a particular discipline.

The work of collaborative, inquiry-driven professional learning must be framed by an understanding of teachers' development. Disciplinary literacy provides a unique means by which to make connections among disparate content areas while remaining specifically focused on actual instruction. At the same time, collaborative inquiry provides entry points for teachers at various points in their development. Keeping these considerations in mind, it is possible to create space for teachers to experiment, to rely on one another for support and ideas, and to discern what is helping their own students learn in a detailed way. We close this chapter with examples and ideas from our own professional learning work with teachers across preservice and inservice contexts to describe how we have attended to teacher learners at various points in their development.

SUPPORTING DISCIPLINARY LITERACY EDUCATOR IDENTITY DEVELOPMENT ACROSS SETTINGS

Preservice Candidates' Identity Development as Disciplinary Literacy Teachers

We design and teach our preservice courses with awareness that candidates span a range of Fuller's stages and that they sit squarely within Feiman-Nemser's preservice phase. Across our courses, candidates are just beginning to transition from seeing themselves as learners within schools to seeing themselves as agentic teachers. Candidates are placed in schools to complete multiple fieldwork experiences closely connected to their rigorous coursework. This design allows for many opportunities to accelerate candidate development across Fuller's and Feiman-Nemser's stages and phases, with candidates often putting immediately into practice new ideas and pedagogical content knowledge from coursework.

Given their stage of teacher identity development, and the relationship between coursework and fieldwork, we have found the RAND Reading Study Group's (RRSG) 2002 model of reading comprehension to be quite useful in framing the ways that candidates might enter into disciplinary literacy work (Ippolito et al., 2019). The RAND model focuses teacher attention alternately on the reader, text, activity, and sociocultural context that defines each reading event. In our courses, we spend time exploring:

- The wide array of texts that might be utilized in their future classrooms (e.g., looking beyond textbooks to explore a broad range of text; crafting text sets)
- The literary needs of the students they are currently working with, to more fully imagine their own future students (e.g., multilingual language learners; learners with language-based disabilities)
- The tasks that might most effectively induct students into disciplinary communication (e.g., designing interactive reading guides that highlight discipline-specific features of text)
- The language, culture, and histories that students bring to the classroom (e.g., considering ways disciplinary classrooms can center and nurture students' home languages and cultures; exploring the intersections of languages and cultures)

It is within this framework that we take time to help preservice candidates begin to see themselves not just as teachers, but as disciplinary literacy teachers. The framework provides a structure for our coursework, spurring candidates to collaboratively explore the often invisible habits of mind associated with their disciplines. By asking candidates to wrestle with problems of practice related to texts, tasks, students, and culture, we plant seeds for deeper and broader professional learning, collaboration, and inquiry work when the candidates begin teaching. This approach deliberately moves candidates' focus from themselves (Fuller, Stage 1) to the tasks of teaching (Fuller, Stage 2). Utilizing instruction that allows candidates to revise their conceptualizations of teaching to include a focus on making disciplinary literacies visible, and developing beginning disciplinary literacy instructional moves, are just a few of the ways that the needs outlined in Feiman-Nemser's (2001) preservice stage play out for our preservice candidates.

Course Activities That Support Candidate Development

Making use of the coursework/fieldwork connection, many of the activities provide scaffolded opportunities for collaboration and inquiry, which support later inservice ways of engaging in professional learning. For example, early in our courses, we often ask candidates to interview teachers in their host schools, to inquire about how seasoned teachers apprentice their students into their disciplines, a task often eye-opening for candidates. It paints a picture, for the candidates, of the teachers they may eventually become.

In another course, we do a "Talk to a Local Expert" assignment, framed as follows:

> Find a "local expert" in your discipline (e.g., mentor teacher, professor, professional friend) and ask them the following two questions:
>
> - What do you think is an essential "way of thinking and working" in your discipline?
> - What is one thing that you wish all students could do in order to be better prepared to read like a ___________ (e.g., writer, mathematician, actor)?

The resulting conversations from these quick interviews are rich, and prompt candidates to engage in initial thinking about their goals as disciplinary literacy teachers. For example, one future history teacher wrote in response to this assignment:

> "I had the chance to talk with my host teacher at my pre-practicum site. She said that students should be able to make connections to the [historical] material that they are learning about. Many students think that history is only about memorizing dates and names, but it is so much more. . . . For students to be able to read like a 'historian,' my host teacher said that students should be looking for themes and look at the bigger picture of history. It helped me think about how I will help my students make connections to history."

Another mathematics candidate wrote:

> "I found that mathematics is a totally different beast than most disciplines because it has so many discipline-specific words. [My math professor] said that the hardest part of mathematics is that you have to think about it as if you do not know where the problem could go."

Each of our candidates' developing understandings of the ways of working within the disciplines are enriched through the inquiry process of interviewing a professional and reflecting, but also through collaborative conversations. Candidates are encouraged, within groups, to look for similarities and differences in the priorities of disciplinary experts as they talk about how they apprentice new learners. Some commonalities arise, such as a focus on vocabulary or a broader focus on a growth mindset. Alternately, in conversation, some real differences emerge, such as a focus on precision in mathematics, or an ability to connect the past to the present in history. We often find that these collaborative conversations with mentor practitioners and classmates focus teacher candidates on the specific disciplinary habits of mind that they will soon teach. And in some ways, focusing on differences helps teachers find ways to build a stronger foundation driven by what is common, which can lead to a clearer focus for teachers on what is shared and what needs to be taught specifically as a difference.

Activities such as these also prompt deeper candidate consideration about their own developing teacher identities. Within our courses, we nudge them to expand their thinking beyond concerns about themselves as new teachers to focus increasingly on students' disciplinary literacy learning needs and the tasks that will help achieve those instructional goals.

Supporting Practicing Teachers' Identity Development as Disciplinary Literacy Teachers through Collaboration and Inquiry

Alongside our formal university teacher preparation work, we also have had a wide range of experience supporting the professional learning of currently practicing middle and high school teachers (Dobbs et al., 2017; Ippolito et al., 2019). Inservice teachers fall more squarely within Fuller's Stages 2–3, as well as Feiman-Nemser's "induction" and "continuing professional development" phases. Much like with our preservice candidates, we also rely on the RAND model of comprehension to frame our disciplinary literacy professional learning work with these educators (detailed in Ippolito et al., 2019).

However, unlike our university coursework with preservice candidates, our professional learning work with inservice teachers is founded on a much higher degree of teacher autonomy, collaboration, and inquiry than found in the university classroom. Given the developmental needs of inservice educators, we create learning opportunities specifically tailored to this phase of the career.

Across most of our disciplinary literacy professional learning work with practicing teachers, we use the RAND model as a relatively simple starting point for disciplinary and cross-disciplinary teams to explore and inquire into problems of practice. A key difference is that practicing teachers often already have a strong sense of their mission to support adolescents' acquisition of content knowledge. Therefore, with inservice professional learning, we use the RAND model as an avenue to deepen practice by organizing potential avenues of exploration and inquiry that teachers might want to consider.

To begin collaborative inquiry into disciplinary literacy practices, we urge teachers to organize themselves into smaller teams (e.g., ideally groups of four to eight educators) who have a professional relationship that brings them together regularly. Often, this means that departmental or disciplinary teams will form, with history, math, or science educators across grade levels coming together to explore questions of how to best support students' disciplinary literacy skills in their content domains. Our goal is always to support these teams in becoming true communities of practice (Wenger, 1999), each of which support and guide one another's professional learning over time and well beyond the life of a particular disciplinary literacy professional learning project. We focus on building collaborative capacity among teams, such that the collaborations outlive our involvement as consultants (for more, see Dobbs et al., 2017).

Our goal is to help an entire group of educators understand how disciplinary literacy, as a set of instructional practices, supports students. However, simultaneously, we focus on whole-group learning about best practices in team development, facilitation of adult learning, and collaborative inquiry. Unlike the sometimes hierarchical learning that happens within a university, we are quite aware in schools that the adult professionals working with us usually have well-formed identities as content-area teachers. Part of our work, then, is to help them begin to see themselves as teams who are capable of surfacing and addressing dilemmas of disciplinary literacy practice.

Another major difference between our preservice coursework and inservice professional learning work is the boundedness of the endeavors. Coursework is often defined by the semester or academic year, with clear project deadlines and end-of-term grades. Contrariwise, collaborative inquiry into disciplinary literacy in professional learning spaces can often extend over long stretches, guided more by teachers' appetite for inquiry and school- and district-level factors that support such professional learning.

Professional Learning Activities That Support Teacher Development

Central tasks within our university preparation work focus more squarely on introducing teacher candidates to the ways in which teachers connect their own disciplinary training to disciplinary literacy work. Meanwhile, our inservice professional learning central tasks center more on the rich enactment of collaborative inquiry cycles and the investigation of how specific literacy elements function within and across disciplines.

Inservice teachers are typically steeped in the content of their discipline, and they often appreciate professional learning that helps them peel back the layers of literacy elements that support or hinder their students' fluidity with disciplinary material. Through a variety of learning opportunities, including focused time with us as consultants, shared time with multiple teams, and, most often, regularly scheduled team times, the tools of collaborative inquiry facilitate the in-depth learning needed for teachers during this phase of the career.

The interweaving of multiple types of professional learning opportunities reflects Feiman-Nesmer's (2001) understanding that continuing professional development focuses on extending and deepening teachers' subject-matter knowledge, instructional repertoire, and leadership skills. Many different learning opportunities and modalities are needed to meet these needs. Therefore, in professional learning settings, while we always focus on collaborative inquiry into texts, tasks, students, and culture, there is also focus on foundational literacy elements (e.g., vocabulary, comprehension, writing). For many content-area teachers, small amounts of explicit learning about domains of literacy instruction such as vocabulary can be eye-opening. It often provides teams with rich new insights into why content-area reading, writing, and discussion tasks may have proved difficult for students in the past. Moreover, it often leads to the design of new disciplinary literacy strategies and to continued investigations of disciplinary literacy practices over time.

Participants in multiyear, collaborative inquiry, disciplinary literacy–focused professional learning initiatives have reported a great deal of learning for themselves and students. Notably, the experience is focused simultaneously on learning more about their students, their disciplines, disciplinary literacy, and the power of collaborative inquiry as a professional learning mechanism. One participant on a cross-disciplinary middle school team had this to say about her collaborative learning team:

> "It's given us an opportunity, as colleagues and across our disciplines, to really take a hard look and a long look and a thoughtful look at how we engage our students in the process of reading and writing. I think it's given us an opportunity to really think about how we want to both unify it, as well as just explore certain ways of approaching literacy and writing in our own disciplines."

Another participant on the same team shared the following about his learning in the project:

> "There's a lot of learning that we did during our [workshop days] that I thought was very valuable. . . . I've incorporated some of those lessons

and had some interesting results; unusual or different writing prompts for the students, and I was—what I've been getting back has been impressive; the use of focus words . . . I think it's a neat way to look at literacy."

As you can hear in these brief end-of-project reflections from disciplinary literacy middle school project teacher-participants, their learning spans both literacy domains, new instructional practices and strategies, as well as new learning about collaboration, collecting and analyzing student data in the form of surveys and interviews of students, and sharing instructional practices across classrooms and disciplines. Again, as illustrated here, the learning that happens with collaborative inquiry–focused professional learning projects is fundamentally adaptive work (Heifetz et al., 2009), in which the teacher participants continue to develop and grow. As Fuller or Feiman-Nesmer might put it, they are progressing along and toward a more advanced end of the continuum of teacher development and learning.

FINAL TAKEAWAYS FOR PROFESSIONAL LEARNING

Designing professional learning that supports teachers at various phases in their careers is a challenging endeavor about which there remains much to learn. But our own work over time has shown us that a few principles are important to supporting teachers in learning to teach disciplinary literacy in a supportive, responsive, and critical way:

- Keep teachers' trajectories of learning in mind. Do not assume they have integrated disciplinary training with teacher preparation, especially if those learnings were sequential, rather than concurrent.
- Strive to make connections between teachers' disciplinary knowledge and identities; the various demands of their stage and phase of development; their pedagogical, content, and pedagogical content knowledge; and their unique contexts of teaching with students.
- Encourage investigation and integration of various identities, as students, teachers, disciplinarians, and members of particular communities, to support an embodied way of teaching and learning with students about various disciplines.
- Focus on collaboration and inquiry as ways to expand and invent new practices for disciplinary literacy, instead of reinforcing the isolation of teaching. Teams and inquiry cycle work can drive this focus to develop collaborative habits among teachers along the continuum of development.
- Encourage teachers at each phase to be critical about the ways that

they learned about and were inducted into disciplines, and how they might be more inclusive and critical in their own teaching to widen and eventually remove gates for their students' further learning in various disciplines.

Taken together, these principles create a foundation for effective disciplinary literacy professional learning across the continuum of teacher identity development. With the guidance and input of experts on local contexts and attention to teachers' developmental stages and phases, these are crucial building blocks toward developing effective disciplinary literacy instructional practices.

REFERENCES

Aldeman, C., Carey, K., Dillon, E., Miller, B., & Silva, B. (2011). *A measured approach to improving teacher preparation* (Education Sector Policy Briefs). Education Sector.

Bill and Melinda Gates Foundation. (2014). *Teachers know best: Teachers' views on professional development*. Author.

Borko, H. (2004). Professional development and teacher learning: Mapping the terrain. *Educational Researcher, 33*(8), 3–15.

Chetty, R., Friedman, J. N., & Rockoff, J. E. (2014). Measuring the impacts of Teachers II: Teacher value-added and student outcomes in adulthood. *American Economic Review, 104*(9), 2633–2679.

Darling-Hammond, L., Hyler, M. E., & Gardner, M. (2017). *Effective teacher professional development*. Learning Policy Institute.

Dobbs, C. L., Ippolito, J., & Charner-Laird, M. (2017). *Investigating disciplinary literacy: A framework for collaborative professional learning*. Harvard Education Press.

Edmondson, A. C. (2003). Managing the risk of learning: Psychological safety in work teams. In M. A. West, D. Tjosvold, & K. G. Smith (Eds.), *International handbook of organizational teamwork and cooperative learning* (pp. 255–275). Wiley.

Elmore, R. F. (2004). Bridging the gap between standards and achievement. In R. F. Elmore (Ed.), *School reform from the inside out* (pp. 89–132). Harvard Education Press.

Fang, Z., & Coatoam, S. (2013). Disciplinary literacy: What you want to know about it. *Journal of Adolescent and Adult Literacy, 56*(8), 627–632.

Feiman-Nesmer, S. (2001). From preparation to practice: Designing a continuum to strengthen and sustain teaching. *Teachers College Record, 103*(6), 1013–1055.

Fuller, F. (1969). Concerns of teachers: A developmental conceptualization. *American Educational Research Journal, 6*(2), 206–226.

Heifetz, R., Grashow, A., & Linsky, M. (2009). *The practice of adaptive leadership:*

Tools and tactics for changing your organization and the world. Harvard Business Press.

Hussar, B., Zhang, J., Hein, S., Wang, K., Roberts, A., Cui, J., . . . Dilig, R. (2020). *The condition of education 2020* (NCES 2020-144). U.S. Department of Education, National Center for Education Statistics.

Ippolito, J., Dobbs, C. L., & Charner-Laird, M. (2019). *Disciplinary literacy inquiry and instruction.* Learning Sciences International.

Jacobs, V. (2008). Adolescent literacy: Putting the crisis in context. *Harvard Educational Review, 78*(1), 7–39.

Little, J. W. (1990). The persistence of privacy: Autonomy and initiative in teachers' professional relations. *Teachers College Record, 91*(4), 509–536.

Lord, B. (1994). Teachers' professional development: Critical colleagueship and the role of professional communities. In N. Cobb (Ed.), *The future of education: Perspectives on national standards in education* (pp. 175–204). College Entrance Examination Board.

McFarland, J., Hussar, B., Wang, X., Zhang, J., Wang, K., Rathbun, A., . . . Mann, F. B. (2018). *The condition of education 2020, Spotlight A* (NCES 2018-144). U.S. Department of Education, National Center for Education Statistics.

RAND Reading Study Group. (2002). *Reading for understanding: Toward an R&D program in reading comprehension.* RAND Corporation. Retrieved from *www.rand.org/pubs/monograph_reports/MR1465.html.*

Rivkin, S. G., Hanushek, E. A., & Kain, J. F. (2005). Teachers, schools, and academic achievement. *Econometrica, 73*(2), 417–458.

Rutherford, W. L., & Hall, G. (1990). *Concerns of teachers: Revisiting the original theory after twenty years.* Paper presented at the meeting of the American Educational Research Association, Boston, MA.

Tyack, D. B. (1974). *The one best system: A history of American urban education.* Harvard University Press.

Tyack, D., & Tobin, W. (1994). The "grammar" of schooling: Why has it been so hard to change? *American Educational Research Journal, 31*(3), 453–479.

Vangrieken, K., Dochy, F., Raes, E., & Kyndt, E. (2015). Teacher collaboration: A systematic review. *Educational Research Review, 15,* 17–40.

Wenger, E. (1999). *Communities of practice: Learning, meaning, and identity.* Cambridge University Press.

Index

Note. *f* or *t* following a page number indicates a figure or a table.

B

C

D

E

L

M

Q

R